BRITHI
YESTERYEAR IN AN U
VALLEY COMMUNITY

Brithdir school children about 1938

Royston Smith

ISBN 978-0-9570426-5-0

British Library Cataloguing in Publication Data: a catalogue record for this
book is available from the British Library.

Published by Gelligaer Publishing
on behalf of Gelligaer Historical Society

Printed by
BookPrintingUK.com

Front cover photograph: courtesy of Morgan, my grandson.
Back Cover: Brewer family. L-R Top to Bottom: Sylvanus (my grandfather), Edward,
Granville and Clifton -- Leon, Margaret Jane (nana) Lovaine (Lol) -- Elizabeth (Betty),
Eileen (mam), Blodwyn Jane (Jenny) and Barbara -- Geoff, Royston Smith and John
Previous page: Brithdir children assemble at the New Hall, Workmen's Institute about
1938. Among those identified are Dilwyn Rees, Tom James, David Williams, Emrys
Williams, Gwyneth Williams, Elwyn Richards, Granville Brewer, Teddy Woods, Naomi
Gardner, Cissy Gardner, Denis Parry, Tom Abraham, Dorothy Foward, Titch Cooper and
Margaret Eynon.   Courtesy Dilwyn Rees

FOREWORD

It is my honour to introduce this history of Brithdir, the village in which I was born in 1938, and which I have been proud to call home ever since.

Brithdir has a fascinating past: for centuries this sparsely populated upland area was remote and rural but, from the mid-nineteenth century, the landscape and way of life changed as the coal industry developed in the upper Rhymney Valley. Coal dominated life and work for several generations of Brithdir people, and many of today's older Brithdirites have strong memories of life and work in the coal mining community of Brithdir. But society and economics have changed, and today's younger people are more likely to see coal in a museum than in a fireplace. While in many ways a typical coal mining community, Brithdir has its own story to tell and, after a decade or so of thorough research, my nephew Roy has unravelled the strands of that tale, so ensuring that our community's past will not slip into oblivion.

This volume will appeal not only to those with *Brithdir* stamped through us like a stick of rock, but also to the general reader interested in life and work in a little South Wales mining community.

Geoff Brewer

DEDICATION
In memory of my grandmother Nana, and mother Eileen
Dedicated to my wife Jennifer for all her support.

AUTHOR

I have been asked many times *Why write about Brithdir?*
As my parents were serving in the British Army, my home for the first two years of my life was the garrison town of Shoeburyness, near Southend-on-Sea. However, my mother and I returned to Brithdir in 1946, and 1 Wellington Terrace, home of my grandmother, Margaret Jane Brewer, and her family, became my home.

My Brewer ancestors, leaving their native Devon before the 1871 census was taken, settled in Rhymney and my grandfather, Sylvanus, was born in Rhymney in 1892. He married Margaret Jane Edwards and they set up home in Pontlottyn where their first five children (including my mother, Eileen) were born. Having moved to Brithdir in 1930, the family was extended with the births of five more children. From 1946 onwards, I grew up within this family, and, as many of these uncles and aunts also settled in the village, I soon had cousins galore living nearby.

My first playground, the place where early friendships were forged, was *Brewer's Corner*, where Wellington Terrace met East View. When a little older, my horizons broadened to encompass Welfare Playground, Cefn Brithdir mountain and the banks of Rhymney river. Those of us who grew up in Brithdir in the fifties enjoyed complete freedom in a community where doors were never locked, neighbours were friends and saying you knew everyone was not a boast. Along with my playmates, I attended the village schools before completing my education in Bargoed and entering the world of work.

In 1966, I married Jennifer and moved to her hometown, Caerphilly, where we raised our three children, and, where we still reside. Even though I had moved from Brithdir, I played football for the village team, and later, as a member of the Constitutional Club, I was part of its skittle team and a member of the party on the bi-annual rugby trip to Scotland. Since my mother passed away in 2011, my trips to Brithdir are less frequent, but I travel to Brithdir for Remembrance Sunday each year. Although I have lived more years in Caerphilly than in Brithdir, my roots are firmly planted in Brithdir.

I spent my working life as a mechanical engineer. I became interested in family and local history and attended various university courses in Cardiff where, in 2002, I was awarded Elsie Pritchard Prize and, in 2004, attained the Certificate of Higher Education.

Margaret Jane Brewer, my grandmother, was a very special person: her love and guidance welded the Brewer family and helped me create so many happy memories of Brithdir. And that is why I chose to write the history of Brithdir.

ACKNOWLEDGEMENTS

I gratefully acknowledge the help and support of countless local residents, exiles and expats who gave of their time to share memories, photographs and memorabilia relating to life and work in Brithdir. Some who warned me at the outset that they had very little to offer proved to be great storehouses of information, recalling with clarity, incidents and individuals from their past in Brithdir. It has been a privilege not only to hear your stories and insights but also to share memories evoked by your many wonderful photographs and mementoes relating to our village.

While space does not allow me to list everyone who has helped tell the story of life and work in Brithdir over the decades, it would not be invidious to name some individuals. I am especially grateful to the late Morfydd Williams née Cresswell who, even in ill-health, welcomed our weekly chat, even ticking me off when I missed one occasion. Particular mention is also due to late Stan West, whose professionalism during many years as Brithdir's *Merthyr Express* correspondent, ensured a valuable legacy for the history of Brithdir. I am grateful to Professor Bernard Knight for sharing information on his ancestors who lived at Gwaelod y Brithdir, and I appreciate the valuable help from Ken Baker and Ray Lawrence who both gave advice freely, and generously shared details from their own research into coalfield communities.

 Thanks are due to archivists and librarians at National Library of Wales, Royal Commission on the Ancient and Historical Monuments of Wales (RCAHMW), The National Archives, Glamorgan Archives, Gwent Archives and South Wales Miners' Library, as well as librarians at Bargoed, Caerphilly, Cardiff, Newport, Pontypridd, Aberdare and Treorchy. I am indebted to Lois Pratt, Community Librarian at Sheerness Library, Kent, for help in locating Sheerness World War Two evacuees to Brithdir. And, to D. J. Salmon, Assistant Archivist North Yorkshire County Record Office, staff at Whitby Library and M. Oakley H.M. Coroner, Molten, North Yorkshire, my gratitude for their collective work sourcing a coroner's report.

Every effort has been made to seek permission to use images selected for this publication and credits are given accordingly. No copyright infringement is intended whatsoever.

As a member of Gelligaer Historical Society, I thank the Society and its members for encouragement and support without which this volume would not have been published.

Finally, and above all, special thanks to my wife Jennifer for her encouragement over a decade of research and writing.

BIBLIOGRAPHY

This local history is based on a wide range of written and non-written sources, some accessible in libraries or archive offices while others are in private hands. They are referenced within the text. There are many publications on the history of the coal industry, transport and life and work that are relevant to the history of Brithdir, some mentioned within the text.

The following published and unpublished works are of specific interest.

Published books

Buick, Greg, *Parish of Gelligaer – The farms and their families, Volume 2, Brithdir Hamlet* (Gelligaer Historical Society, 2011)

Gelligaer Historical Society, *Bargoed and Gilfach, a local history* (Gelligaer Historical Society, 2011)

Jones, Judith M., *Gelligaer and Merthyr Common* (Merton Priory Press, 2003)

Shore, Leslie M., *Peerless Powell Duffryn of the South Wales Coalfield* (Lightmoor Press, 2012)

Thomas, W. Gerwyn, *Welsh coal mines* (National Museum of Wales, 1979)

Articles

Smith, Philip Campbell, *Thomas Lewis DCM* - Gelligaer, Vol. 19 (2012) pp 59-61.

Smith, Royston, *Brithdir Yesteryears, George Inn Board School 1879-1905* and *Samuel Davies 1896-1915* - Gelligaer, Vol. 20 (2013) pp 34-55.

Smith, Royston, *In the footsteps of heroes* – Gelligaer, Vol 21 (2014) pp 74-85.

Smith, Royston, *Captain Edwin William Sidney Martin* - Gelligaer, Vol. 21 (2014) pp 105-110.

Smith, Royston, *Herbert Gwyn "Bert" Turner* - Gelligaer, Vol. 22 (2015) pp 32-38.

Smith, Royston, *Brithdir Schools 1914-1926* - Gelligaer, Vol. 23 (2016) pp 35-43.

Williams, Glyn, (reproduced by permission of his son Dr. E. D. G. Williams) *Army Service* – Gelligaer, Vol 21 (2014) pp 59-73.

Internet

Database of names on Brithdir war memorial:
www.gelligaerhistoricalsociety.co.uk/index.php/wwi-memorials

Welsh coal mines website: www.welshcoalmines.co.uk/

TABLE OF CONTENTS

CHAPTER 1 INTRODUCTION

This book is about Brithdir, the Rhymney Valley village in which I grew up in the mid-twentieth century. Although not living in Brithdir, I have visited regularly, calling on family and friends and socialising, seeing Brithdir in various guises as it changed from the thriving coal mining community I knew to the present post-coal industry village. One of several communities across Wales known as Brithdir, *my Brithdir* lies a mile or so north of Bargoed, on the west (Glamorgan) side of Rhymney river. Although it developed in the nineteenth century as a coal mining community, Brithdir has outlived that industry in the local area, and today, coal mining is an important memory.

Historically, Brithdir was in the county of Glamorgan and the parish of Gelligaer.

- *Bargoed and Gilfach a local history* Chapter 5 offers a brief overview of the history of government and politics in the county.
- Gelligaer, a large upland parish in north east Glamorgan, extended some 14 miles from Carn yr Helyg (north of Bute Town and A465 road) southwards to Ysbyty Ystrad Fawr, and some 4 miles between Rhymney river in east and Bargoed Taff to the west. The parish comprised five hamlets (Brithdir, Garthgynydd, Ysgwyddgwyn, Cefn and Hengoed). Brithdir, the village in which I grew up, lay in south of the long narrow hamlet of Brithdir, a hamlet that was about 2 miles at its widest east-west point between Rhymney river's west bank and Bargoed-Rhymney (Darran) river, and some 8 miles from its northern point, to Pontaberbargoed (near Bargoed railway station) in the south. From 1894 to 1908, the parish was within the area administered by Gelligaer and Rhigos Rural District Council (G&R RDC). Gelligaer Urban District Council (GUDC) came into being in 1908 and administered the area until local government reorganisation in 1974. After that, both sides of the valley lay within the same administration, Rhymney Valley District Council (RVDC) from 1974 to 1996, and since then Caerphilly County Borough Council (CCBC).

If the fact that my home village shared its name with the hamlet in which it was situated is not confusion enough, it should also be noted that the now-lost village of Penybank, just 3 miles north-west, in the Darran Valley, was, in the nineteenth century, known as Brithdir. And, to add a further complication, my Brithdir was originally called George Inn.

Brithdir has always been a special place to me, and I have spent much of my retirement years in researching its history. When I started my research, I thought it would be difficult to find anything of interest to write about the small mining community of Brithdir, but it has been a pleasant surprise to discover that Brithdir is so widely known. My researches have taken me on a roller coaster ride to all corners of the British Isles, including Ireland, and across the world to Australia, New Zealand, Canada, U.S.A., South America and South

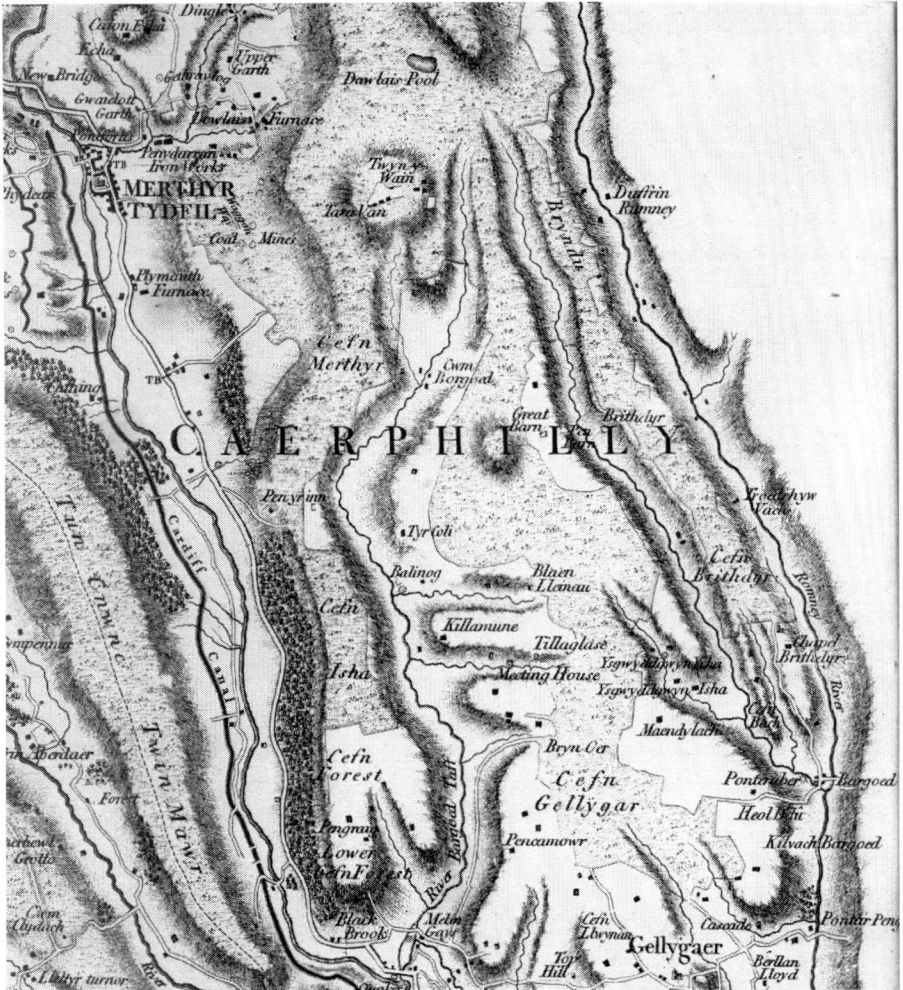

Extract from George Yates' map of Glamorgan (1799) (Republished jointly South Wales Record Society and Glamorgan Archives 1984)

Africa, all in the wake of Brithdir folk over the decades. Throughout the journey I have been amazed by the talented people associated with a community with never more than just over 300 dwellings. After ten years dedicated to research, it is time to write Brithdir's story. I hope that readers, those who have lived in Brithdir as well as others who have not had that privilege, will find something of interest in what follows.

The village of Brithdir owes much to the coal industry, levels and small pits as well as Powell Duffryn Steam Coal Company's pits in the New Tredegar basin, while the railway lines either side of Rhymney river not only helped move locally-mined coal to its market but also was (and, in the case of that on the west bank, still is) important for passenger traffic. But the people who lived in the community -- clergymen, school teachers, doctors, stationmasters and village bobbies, as well as countless individuals who devoted time and energy to running various activities and clubs -- all helped shape the character of the place and day-to-day life in it. Much of this is reflected in sources such as school logbooks, local newspapers (particularly *Merthyr Express*) and GUDC's minute books, as well as in the memories so many people have shared.

The area before the Victorian era

For a general description of the geological and geographical context, as well as prehistoric and medieval developments in the area, see B*argoed and Gilfach a local history* chapters 2 and 3.

George Inn / Brithdir in the Victorian era

Gelligaer parish tithe award and 1841 and 1851 census returns combine to provide an early Victorian snapshot of the area that later became Brithdir village. Then as shown on previous page the extract from Yates' Glamorgan county map of 1799, a sparsely populated rural area probably little changed since the sixteenth century, it was home to farmers who struggled to make a living on thin soils on the slopes rising from west bank of Rhymney river to Cefn Brithdir's open moorland. Although the pastoral beauty of the narrow valley bottom and steep slopes was still untouched by industry, at the start of the Victorian era, developments upstream (near Rhymney and Pontlottyn) meant that fish no longer swam in Rhymney's water.

Readers not familiar with the sources mentioned may be interested to know that they can be consulted locally in Bargoed Library:

- Dated 1842, Gelligaer parish tithe award (a large-scale map and accompanying schedule giving details of ownership, occupation, land use and acreage of every parcel of land), like those for most parishes across Wales and England, was produced in consequence of Tithe Commutation Act of 1836. This link to Cynefin's Wales-wide project cynefin.archiveswales.org.uk/en/tithe-maps/ (select Glamorgan county and Gelligaer [the second includes Brithdir] parish) allows comparison between tithe map and modern Ordnance Survey (OS) map.
- The UK's first modern census in 1801 was a count of the country's population. Similar counts followed in 1811, 1821 and 1831. Censuses of 1841 and later, with details of individuals, offer the opportunity to recreate the contemporary community. Those for 1841-1911 have been used but, unfortunately, some pages of 1861 census for Brithdir area are missing.

By the 1850s, the local area was changing: railways linked upper valley industry with Bristol Channel ports, Cardiff and Newport, and industrialisation rolled down the valley as new coal mines, both levels and deep mines, attracted incomers in search of employment. Bryn Tawel (later known as Ivy Row) was built on land of Brithdir Ganol and, during the later Victorian era, as evidenced by the deeds of properties in Brithdir village, the new coal mining community developed on the lower fields of Brithdir Ganol and Cefn y Brithdir, while farming life continued around it.

Brithdir since 1901

Before the end of the nineteenth century, the community, formerly called George Inn, was known as Brithdir (and Darran Valley's Brithdir had become Penybank). Brithdir was a thriving and lively coal mining community when the twentieth century started, but, as in communities across the country and beyond, that confidence was shattered when, in the second decade of the century, many of its young men left for war service. Sadly, as the village war memorial testifies, some never returned. There is further information on these local casualties on gelligaerhistoricalsociety.co.uk/index.php/brithdir-ww1.

Life was different after the war. The community united in the face of economic, social and political dislocation in the inter-war years as evidenced by the concerts and community events organised especially at the height of industrial conflict. After decades of inward migration, Brithdir saw outward migration as some individuals and families sought a better way of life elsewhere. Local people learned more about a world outside the upper Rhymney Valley through films, especially the *talkies*, and many homes had its own wireless with BBC news and entertainment.

By the end of the 1930s, local people, the second time in the lifetimes of many, were plunged into a major world conflict. Local people served in the war, and sadly again, some did not return. Post-war life did not return to the pre-war norm. In particular, women's lives changed not only because some, including munitions workers, had grown accustomed to the social and economic independence work outside the home gave them, but also because of the easier availability of labour-saving domestic devices. Events such as the royal wedding, Festival of Britain and coronation added same colour in a drab post-war society. However, as time passed, television and family cars, as well as increased emphasis on home comforts combined to improve the quality of life of many local families from the late 1950s onwards, although sometimes at the expense of the close community life.

Brithdir 2017

The Brithdir of 2017 is very different from that in which I grew up. Inevitably many people from the 1950s, the characters, the caring neighbours, the figures of authority and some mates, are no longer in Brithdir. The bond of coal is no more. Brithdir does not have the services --- shops, doctor's surgery, places of worship, police station and education – as in my youth. In the 1950s, children played in the streets and neighbours shared happiness and sadness. In 2017, the streetscape is dominated by cars, yellow lines and wheelie bins, while satellite dishes adorn the terraces, and children play indoors and often online. At the time of writing, *The George* (formerly the George Inn) and the Constitutional Club are both open and there is just one shop in the community. The chapels have gone and the Anglican church struggles to remain open. There is no school within the community and, a sign of the times, a modern care home for the elderly occupies the former site of one school.

SUMMARY OF INFORMATION RELATING TO LOCAL FARMS IN PARISH TITHE AWARD			
Land/Farm	According to tithe schedule		
	Acreage	Owner	Occupier
Mill and land, including public house	5 acres	Crawshay Bailey Esq.	William Lewis
Tir y ferch Gryno	83 acres	Marquess of Bute	
Gwaelod y Brithdir	122 acres	Crawshay Bailey Esq.	Thomas Williams
Brithdir Ganol [Brithdir Farm]	85 acres	George George	Thomas Llewellyn
Cefn y Brithdir	225 acres	George George	Thomas Rees
Tir Evan Thomas [Plas Milfre]	36 acres	John Jones	Richard Williams
Tyr y Capel	65 acres	Thomas Williams	Jenkin Thomas

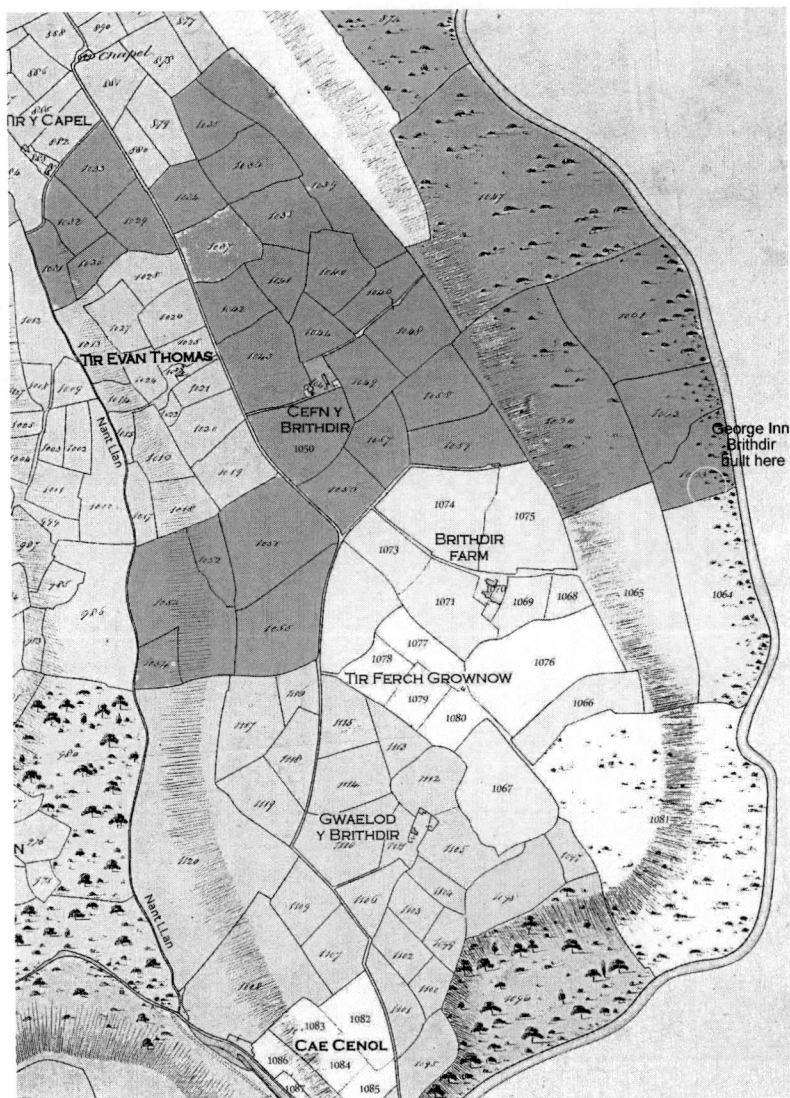

CHAPTER 2 FARMS AND FARMING FAMILIES

In *Parish of Gelligaer – The Farms and their Families 1540-1840, Volume 2, Brithdir Hamlet, 2011* Greg Buick traced the history of farms and farmers in the sparsely populated Brithdir hamlet, and this chapter moves the story forward from the start of Queen Victoria's reign for Gwaelod y Brithdir, Tir y ferch Gryno, Brithdir Ganol, Cefn y Brithdir, Tir Evan Thomas (Plas Milfre) and Tyr y Capel. As the story continues into the later nineteenth century and more recent times, life and work on the farms is influenced by the changes associated with industrialisation and urbanisation nearer the valley floor.

Gwaelod y Brithdir

In 1841, 40 year old Thomas Williams occupied Gwaelod y Brithdir, a 122-acre farm which (like the mill, 5 acres and public house occupied by William Lewis, to the south at Pontaberbargoed) was owned by Crawshay Bailey. Thomas Williams was still tenant at the time of the 1851 census when he was described as farmer of 50 acres. A report in *Merthyr Telegraph and General*

The original Gwaelod y Brithdir farmhouse, part of which probably dates from the seventeenth century. The house has now been modernised and extended (as indicated on the left).
Courtesy Eryl Wigley.

Advertiser for the Iron Districts of South Wales, April 3 1858, noted that, at Merthyr Police Court on March 29 1858, he was appointed *Overseer of the Poor* for Brithdir hamlet for the ensuing year. The 1861 census return for this farm is missing. He died before the 1871 census was taken, when his 71 year old widow, Jemima, was listed as the farmer, but presumably son, also Thomas, was responsible for the farm work. Son Thomas was still there in 1876 when he was named in *Monmouth Guardian and Bargoed and Caerphilly Observer*, July 1 1876, as judge of a sheep shearing competition at Pontllanfraith, an indication that a local farmer was at the forefront of the contemporary drive to improve farming skills.

The freehold property of Gwaelod y Brithdir was described as *situate at the Junction of the Rhymney River with the Bargoed Rhymney River, containing 155 Acres or thereabouts (less about 13 Acres of the surface, occupied by the Rhymney Railway Company), but including the Minerals thereunder* when it was advertised for sale in *Cardiff and Merthyr Guardian*, May 11 1872. Presumably Thomas Williams was the *yearly tenant* paying £60 a year for this pastoral farm with *a large quantity of timber and right of common*, and the mill and land was let to *another yearly tenant* (possibly Thomas Lewis) at £30 pa. Perhaps the purchaser was eager to make capital from the property as, in April 1873, *large quantity of SUPERIOR OAK, FIRS, BEECH, ASH, BIRCH, OAK*

STORES, and strong UNDERWOOD, suitable for Pitwood, growing on the Gwaelod y Brithdir Estate was offered for sale in several lots. Its proximity to Bargoed Station, with lines to both Cardiff and Newport, was noted in newspaper advertisements.

An early photo of an unknown subject at Gwaelod y Brithdir. Courtesy Dilwyn Rees.

It is not clear when Jemima Williams and son Thomas left Gwaelod y Brithdir, but, by the time the 1881 census was taken, they were in Tymawr (near the mill) and Thomas was described as a farm bailiff. There were two households in Gwaelod y Brithdir when the 1881 census was taken: one was headed by Katherine Lawes (niece to mining magnate, Sir George Elliot, see pages 285-286 for more on her family) and comprised seven of her eight children, while farm labourer, Benjamin Oakley, headed the other. Kelly's Directory of South Wales 1884 lists William Thomas as bailiff at Gwaelod y Brithdir and Dolphin Cole was farm bailiff when 1891 census was taken.

For many Brithdirites, Gwaelod y Brithdir is synonymous with the Price family. Rees Price, a native of Breconshire, took his family to Gwaelod y Brithdir before 1895, as a school log book entry of March 15 1895 noted his 6 year old son, David Price, *does not know his figures because he don't* [sic] *attend school regularly because he lives a great distance from the school in a farm house*. Rees Price farmed Gwaelod y Brithdir for many decades and was sitting tenant when the farm was offered for sale by auction in 1939. William (*Will*) and John (*Jack*) Price took over the farm on their father's demise in 1943. In 1956, by purchasing the 73 acres of Brithdir Ganol, they amalgamated the two farms. It is said Will and Jack Price were great diarists who, year on year, kept daily records about the weather and events affecting the village. However, at the time of writing, this documentation of local history has not surfaced.

When I was young, Will Price sold milk in the village. Stopping his horse, Dobbin, and milk cart at *Brewer's Corner*, Will dismounted. On hearing him knock on their doors, his customers gathered at the cart where Will ladled milk from the big churns into each customer's jug. Sometimes, my friends and I waited until Will was a safe distance away, then pretended to step up on the back of the cart. Dobbin, thinking it was his master, walked on to the next stop, with Will, hurling abuse at us, scampering after him.

But, things were changing in the 1950s, as reflected in this story, reported in *Daily Mirror*, September 5 1955:

Dobbin trots off on ghost milk round

Old Dobbin [as the reporter called him, to us he was Dobbin} *neighed with delight when she heard the early morning rattle of the milk churns on the farmyard cobblestones. The comforting bump bump heralded another exciting day on the milk round for the old mare. But for her master, cheery Will Price, sixty-five-year-old bachelor, it was a ghost round. There were no jugs or bowls to fill at the doorsteps of the cottages in Brithdir. There was no jingling of coins in the collecting bag. For the churns on the milk float pulled by Old Dobbin were empty. Will and Dobbin had set off every day for thirty years from Gwaelod y Brithdir, their hillside farm, to sell milk. Then Will had to give up the round. Dobbin, still a frisky*

This milk bottle, found on Cefn y Brithdir farm, is a reminder of days past when people in communities like Brithdir bought milk from local farms. Brithdir's milkman was Will Price, while Lewis of Plas Milfre supplied Tirphil. Later, deliveries were by local dairies, and today, most local people pick up their milk in one of the big supermarkets or at its petrol station.   Courtesy Margaret Coonick.

Welsh cob at the ripe age of thirty-six, felt it was the end of her world. Soon after the milk round ended Will harnessed her to the float for a trip to the village to collect stores. Dobbin refused to budge. Then Will hoisted the empty churns on the float – and Dobbin set off happily. So now when Will goes to the village three times a week, the float is always loaded with empty churns. He said yesterday: "For Dobbin's sake I go out of my way over the old milk round. Dobbin still stops at the same houses to wait for the titbits she loves and to give the children a ride. She is now happy again and so am I. I pop in again on some of my old customers who always had a cup of tea for me. It's not my milk in the tea anymore – but it tastes just as nice to a chap who had missed his pals."

The deaths of Will and Jack Price (recorded on this gravestone in Gwaelod y Brithdir Cemetery) ended the Price family's eighty year link with Gwaelod y Brithdir. Bryn Wigley, formerly farming in Cynon Valley, was next to farm Gwaelod y Brithdir, and members of his family are there today.

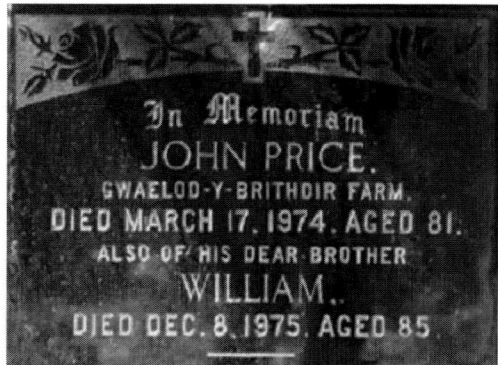

In Memoriam
JOHN PRICE.
GWAELOD-Y-BRITHDIR FARM.
DIED MARCH 17, 1974. AGED 81.
ALSO OF HIS DEAR BROTHER
WILLIAM..
DIED DEC. 8. 1975. AGED 85

1991 Photograph of *Cracker* as a colt.
Courtesy Eryl Wigley

Captured on canvas by Brithdir-born artist
Yvonne Garner.   Courtesy Bryn Mathews.

In the later twentieth century, the Wigley family and Gwaelod y Brithdir were becoming known in the horse world. *Cracker*, sire *Ebbw Victor* and dam *Tregare Lily of the Valley*, and with show name *Bryn Melys Cracker*, has won numerous prizes including the coveted *Red Rug* for Senior Stallion at 2003 Royal Welsh Show. Born at Gwaelod y Brithdir, he was sold as a three year old to Bryn Matthews of Rhymney, and became the main stallion at Brynbach Welsh Cob Stud.

General View of Aberbargoed and Collieries.

Aberbargoed with Bargoed Colliery c.1955,
the scene depicted in L.S. Lowry's famous painting,
as seen from the southernmost fields of Gwaelod y Brithdir.
Courtesy Brian Hedgecock.

Brithdir Ganol (also known as Brithdir Farm)

While, in sources, this farm appears variously as Brithdir Ganol and as Brithdir Farm, it is referred to as Brithdir Ganol in this book. Today, what remains of Brithdir Ganol's farmstead stands defiantly on the hilltop overlooking the south end of Brithdir village. Greg Buick suggests Brithdir Ganol dates back to at least 1540. The farmhouse, described as *an ancient mansion* in a 1693 Covenant (Glamorgan Archives DLH/7/8), was once a substantial building with some medieval features. Evidence within the derelict building's stonework suggests the original building was added to over the years with some of the earlier features being drastically altered. Falling into disrepair in the early twentieth century, it became known locally as *haunted house*.

Brithdir Ganol farmhouse (see overleaf), a two-and-a-half storeyed building entered through a storeyed porch, is rare among Glamorgan buildings in that it is securely dated by inscription. RCAHMW survey found the date 1604 cut into the main beam of a ceiling over an upper room. That upper room (possibly a parlour) had a lateral chimney on the north side, and was separated from a passage by a post and panel partition. All first floor chambers were heated. The hall's large gabled fireplace had a bake-oven built into its rear, and the attic above the hall housed a fine corn-drying kiln. The farmer took the corn up to the attic, spread it on sacking (supported by two parallel rollers fixed between timbers) which was raised to ceiling level. The corn was dried as heat from the oven in the hall chamber below passed through a perforated tile floor set on beams. The hall had direct access to a cross-passage within the cowhouse attached to the east gable. There were two stairs giving access between the floors. From the passage's north end, the main stairs, with solid timber treads, rose with straight flights to first floor and lofts as well as upper floors over a service room behind the parlour. There was also a mural stair that led from the passage to the first-floor room over the porch. Perhaps Dilwyn Rees and his uncle, Trevor Rees of Tir y ferch Gryno, were the last people to use it, when (probably mid/late 1940s) they found the remains of a horse's skeleton-head which Dilwyn took to Brithdir Boys' School to add to its museum. A stone-tiled five-tier barn with attached stables was added, opposite the house, in the late seventeenth century.

Belonging to George George (whose estate of 310 acres, the eleventh largest in Gelligaer parish at the time of the tithe survey, had been in his family for a century or so), this 85 acre farm was occupied by tenant farmer, 60 year old Thomas Llewellyn, in the early Victorian era. During the nineteenth century it changed hands several times as tenant farmers came and went. Jonah Meredith, a native of Breconshire, its tenant when the 1851 census was taken, worked the farm with wife Ann, son William and daughters Mary and Elizabeth. However, by 1861 the family had given up farming and moved to George Inn Hotel (see page 119).

It is unclear whether Jonah Meredith was directly succeeded as tenant of Brithdir Ganol by Richard Lewis, son of Samuel Lewis and a native of Fishguard who had arrived in Gelligaer parish before 1841. When, in December 1851, Richard Lewis married widow Jane Llewellyn, daughter of Christmas Davies, both bride and groom lived in Pontlottyn. Richard was a *bowler* (making the rounded part of spoons before casting). Probate information suggests Richard Lewis remained tenant to his death, June 30 1866.

Brithdir Ganol, with its storeyed entrance porch intact.   Courtesy Charles Williams.

An interesting feature at Brithdir Ganol - a detailed head carved into the exterior stone work over the porch doorway.
© Crown Copyright: RCAHMW

Plan of Brithdir Ganol Farmhouse © Crown Copyright: RCAHMW

Image of the Barn
© Crown Copyright: RCAHMW

Right: Example of timber post and panel type partition. Note also the wooden beam and joist ceiling.
© Crown Copyright: RCAHMW

This advertisement for auction sale appeared in *Merthyr Telegraph and General Advertiser of the Iron Districts of South Wales*, December 1 1866, and, when the 1871 census was taken, Jane was living in Union Street, Pontlottyn, with her widowed brother, James Davies.

Gelligaer born William Lewis was enumerated as Brithdir Ganol's farmer of 84 acres in 1871. On census night, his wife Mary was visiting her widowed mother, Jane Davies at Ty Gwyn farm, Bedwas. By 1881 William Lewis was farming 130 acres assisted by farm servant Roger Bevan from Brecon and 16 year old Elizabeth Bevan general servant, the latter was daughter of William and Alice Bevan of George Inn village (see pages 260-264).

BRITHDIR FARM, GELLIGAER.

One and a half mile from Tir Phil Station on the Rhymney Railway.

Mr. WILLIAM MORGAN

Has received instructions from Mrs. Jane Lewis, widow, who is giving up Farming,

TO SELL BY PUBLIC AUCTION,

At the above Farm, on TUESDAY, October 16th, 1866,

THE whole of the STOCK, Implements of Husbandry, Crops, and part of the Household Furniture,—comprising 9 cows in calf and 2 calves, of the pure Hereford breed; also 13 cow chains, 2 excellent cart mares, with their harness; 2 store pigs in good condition, 1 sow with a litter of six pigs.

The IMPLEMENTS consist of 1 cart, nearly new; 1 Irish car, 2 iron ploughs, 1 pair of iron harrows, Lantries, 1 chaff machine, and 1 hand chaff cutter; 50 fencing rails, 12 hurdles, a quantity of picks, shovels, spades, rakes, grubber, mattocks; a grindstone, in new framing; a number of reaping hooks, scythes, snathes, sieves, ladders, &c.; a good wheelbarrow, 2 bundles of iron wire, 1 new seed basket, &c.

The CROPS comprise 2 ricks of well-harvested hay, about 22 tons; 2 mows of oats, 2 mows of barley, 1 mow of clover, about 9 tons; 2 sacks of wheat; 40 sacks of good potatoes, 1 acre of good swedes, hay knives, shears, &c.

The FURNITURE and DAIRY UTENSILS consist of an excellent clock, a bedstead, 2 coffers, 4 tables, new steelyards, 3 cheese presses, 2 churns, a number of pails, casks, tubs, and other dairy utensils, and also a large quantity of miscellaneous goods.

Refreshments will be provided at Eleven, and the sale to commence at Twelve o'clock precisely.

Four month's credit will be given on approved bills, for £5 and upwards, or a discount of 6d. in the Pound for prompt cash.

☞ The Auctioneer has much pleasure in inviting the attention of his friends and the public to the above sale. The cows are young, in good condition, healthy, and of pure Hereford breed, whilst the Implements of Husbandry, Stock, &c., are such as he can confidently recommend to his friends. He also respectfully solicits punctual attendance, the day being short and the lots numerous.

Gwernyblithe, September 17th, 1866. [5750

Thomas Lewis (apparently not related to this William Lewis, but younger brother of William Lewis of Cefn y Brithdir – see below) may have moved to Brithdir Ganol following his marriage, at Bedwellty parish church on February 13 1883, to Annie Davies of Rhymney. The family was there when 1891 and 1901 censuses were taken.

Press announcements of the death of Thomas Lewis at Brithdir Ganol on Monday, November 26 1906, as well as obituaries and reports on the funeral, not only shed light on the Lewis family but also show their farming network extended beyond the immediate Brithdir area. *Tarian y Gweithiwr*, December 6 1906, described Thomas Lewis as one of the best-known farmers in the Rhymney Valley. The funeral, on December 1 (reported in detail in *Merthyr Express*, December 8, started with a short service at the farmhouse before the cortege, nine horse-drawn coaches, proceeded to Gelligaer Cemetery. The family mourners, travelling in carriages behind the hearse, were:

Carriage 1: Mrs. Lewis, widow; Miss M. Lewis, daughter; W. Thomas Lewis, son; James Lewis, son.

Carriage 2: L.D. Lewis, son; Eddie Lewis, son; Miss Jones, niece; James Davies, nephew.

Carriage 3: W. Lewis, brother; Mrs. Jones, sister, Cardiff; Mrs. Gethin Lewis and son, Cardiff.

Carriage 4: Mr. and Mrs. Theo Davies, Aberdare.

19

Carriage 5: Mr. and Mrs. James Lewis, brother, Plas Farm.
Carriage 6: Mr. Collier and Miss Davies, Rhymney. Mr. and Mrs. George Davies, Groes Farm, Abergavenny.
Carriage 7: Mr. and Mrs. Llewellyn and Mr. and Mrs. R. Owen, Treharris.
Carriage 8: Mr. M. Williams and Family, Brithdir.

Among the farming community paying their respects that day were some immediate neighbours including Mr. and Mrs. Rees Price, Gwaelod y Brithdir; Miss Greenacombe, Tir y ferch Gryno; Edwin Williams, Tyr y Capel; and Thomas Davies, Cefn y Brithdir; as well as some from the wider farming community such as Mr. and Mrs. John Mathews, Cartwright farm; Mr. and Miss Edwards, Gilfach-Fargoed farm; and David Phillips, Greenmeadow farm, Pengam.

His widow, Annie Lewis, continued to live at the farm. On her death, aged 77, in March 1932, she was also buried in Gelligaer.

As noted below, heavy losses sustained during the severe 1947 storm, forced Tom Price and his son Alan to leave Cefn y Brithdir and move into the then partially-ruined Brithdir Ganol farmstead for several years. Although the dwelling has been uninhabited since, the Prices of Gwaelod y Brithdir used some of the farm buildings in the 1950s and 60s.

A later view of Brithdir Ganol farmhouse with its porch in rubble. Courtesy Dilwyn Rees.

Cefn y Brithdir

The parish tithe award shows Cefn y Brithdir, a 224 acre farm near Capel Brithdir, was owned by George George, and had been in his family for a century or so. Greg Buick suggests Thomas Rees became tenant of Cefn y Brithdir in 1819 and still occupied the farm in 1841. According to 1851 census return, Thomas Price, a native of Breconshire was the tenant, farming 150 acres. It is not clear when he relinquished his tenancy but inscriptions on a family tombstone, in Hengoed Baptist Chapel burial ground, show William Lewis and his family were at Cefn y Brithdir by 1865. The panels of the tombstone tell part of the Lewis family's tragic story, one that, sadly, is not unlike that of many other contemporary families, as readers who have researched their own family histories may confirm:

To the memory of MARY LEWIS, wife of WILLIAM LEWIS of Cefn Brithdir, in this parish, who died September 21st 1865 in the 59th year of her age.

Also the above named WILLIAM LEWIS, who died April 23rd 1873, aged 84 years.

Others mentioned on separate panels around the tombstone are:

WILLIAM, son of William and Mary Lewis died Dec 5th 1833, aged 3 days

THOMAS, their son who died Mar 28th 1844, aged 14 months

THOMAS, their second son who died Dec 1st 1865, aged 17 years

MARGARET, daughter of William & Mary Lewis who died Oct 22nd 1865, aged 12 years.

And there was further loss, as *Cardiff and Merthyr* Guardian, December 22 1865, reporting that William Lewis buried 22 year old daughter, Hannah on December 19 1865, noted *she was the ninth death in this family in the short interval of eight months, from malignant typhoid fever.* A happier event took place on July 20 1867 when daughter Elizabeth married Lemuel Howard, surveyor of Pontypridd Highway Board. Sometime later William made his home with daughter Mary, and husband Thomas Rees, farmer of Tir Jack farm, where William died on April 23 1873.

Miles Williams, formerly of Aberdare, was farming 200 acres at Cefn y Brithdir when the 1871 census was taken. However his stay was probably short as Edmund Pritchard and wife Mary were living there when, as reported in *Y Tyst a'r Dydd*, May 28 1875, their sixteen month old daughter, Ann, died and was buried in Llanfabon churchyard.

By 1881, William Lewis (yet another local farmer with this name!) had moved to Cefn y Brithdir. This William Lewis, born at Bryn Rhe farm in Ysgwyddgwyn hamlet (Darran Valley) was son of James and Sarah Lewis. His household in 1881 comprised his brother Thomas (who helped him farm until, as noted above, he moved to Brithdir Ganol) and housekeeper, Mary Llewellyn, formerly general servant to his parents at Bryn Rhe. William married Annie Edwards of Penallta Isha on June 14 1887 at Hengoed Baptist chapel.

Much has been written about the contemporary tithe war in north east Wales, but less is known about such nonconformist activities in south east Wales. *Merthyr Express*, October 1 1892, reported on legal proceedings instituted against William Lewis, an ardent Welsh Liberal nonconformist, for £10. 6s. 4d due to Rector of Gelligaer for outstanding tithes from 1890. A warrant was issued and two cows (equivalent to the value of the sum due) were seized for sale by auction. Unsold, the cows were returned to William Lewis who not only paid all dues but also established an amicable relationship with the Rector.

Merthyr Express followed with a report on a public meeting, filled with William Lewis's supporters, at Brithdir schoolroom on the following Tuesday evening. William Lewis, who had acted on his nonconformist principles, remarked *that in refusing to pay tithes he had no objection to the Church of England as a church; but as regards the compulsory aspect of tithes, he preferred attending to the precepts of his bible than the unjust laws of the clergy.* The meeting supporting the abolition of tithes, unanimously agreed on an anti-tithe movement across the parish.

William Lewis was probably less successful as a contractor, making losses as sub-contractor in building a school in Brithdir, and five houses in Warne Street, Fleur de Lys. According to report in *Merthyr Express*, June 12 1909, he appeared in Merthyr Bankruptcy Court. He left the farm for the village: enumerated in Cefn Bryn in 1901 and East View in 1911 censuses.

Thomas Davies was farm bailiff at Cefn y Brithdir when the 1901 and 1911 censuses were taken. Like his predecessors at the farm, he quickly established a good relationship with Brithdir villagers, as reports in *Merthyr Express* show.

On June 30 1902, the newspaper reported that the coronation day celebratory school sports took place on the field known locally as *Spion Kop* and, on July 23 1910, St. Paul's Gymnastic Club fund raising event was held on the same field.

Photographs (*Merthyr Express*, June 19 1937) of William Lewis (aged 84) and wife Annie (aged 77), of 5 East View, on their Golden Wedding, 1937.

Less than two years after the end of World War II, in common with the country in general, Cefn y Brithdir faced one of the harshest winters experienced in the British Isles and perhaps the snowiest winter since 1814. As winter continued at its most savage in March 1947, severe blizzards, with snow drifts often in excess of ten feet, meant cruel losses to agriculture. Tom Price, then tenant farmer, lost his cattle, frozen to death in snow-bound fields, a loss that meant he and son Alan left the farm for the partially-ruined Brithdir Ganol farmhouse.

By the turn of the century, industrialisation had rolled down the valley, not only creating employment and new communities like Brithdir, but also having a dramatic impact on the local landscape as the former rural beauty gave way to ugly spoil tips. Much of Cefn y Brithdir was engulfed by the waste from Elliot Colliery and the tip (shown right) was known locally as *Spion Kop*.

The great black mountain that was *Spion Kop*, marching endlessly across Cefn y

22

Cefn y Brithdir farm some 1400 feet above sea level surrounded by a landscape of colliery waste, circa 1970.　　　　　　　　Courtesy Margaret Coonick

Brithdir, was a dangerous attraction for local youngsters. Bill Jones was tenant farmer in the early 1950s when, after attending chapel one Sunday, friend Billy Bennett and I walked over the mountain and coal tip. Negotiating our way across the waste tip, we slipped on the steel chute meant for the waste. It sent us both tumbling down *Spion Kop*. We survived the fall, but how could we go home with our Sunday best in such a state? Mrs. Jones kindly prepared a tub of hot water and, while Billy and I washed the muck off, she cleaned our clothes and removed the evidence.

Frank Symons of Graig Farm, Mynyddislwyn, took over the tenancy of Cefn y Brithdir in 1955 and remained active up to his ninetieth year. His daughter, Margaret, and her husband, John Coonick, have run the farm for the past thirty years and they are still in residence at the time of writing.

Tir y ferch Gryno

Tir y ferch Gryno was the most southerly farm in Bute possession in Brithdir hamlet in 1841. Bute lands in Gelligaer parish were part of a vast estate in South Wales and beyond that had come into being piecemeal over a long period and by a variety of means. There is further information about the Bute estate in John Davies's *Cardiff and the Marquesses of Bute* (first published 1981).

Tir y ferch Gryno c.1930: Back row L-R: Bryn Rees, Olwen Rees, Dr. O'Shea, Gwladys Rees, Dr. Carmichael, and Gilbert Rees (killed during World War II). Seated are Arthur Gwilym Rees, centre, with wife, Margaret and brother, David Rees (headmaster in Cardiff, holding the dog). In front are Joan Rees, Elwyn Rees and Edith Rees. *Nora* the dog, completes the group.

Left: The Rees sisters, L-R: Olwen, Joan and Gwladys of Tir y ferch Gryno with, in front, friends Alice Davies and Minnie Bowlson.

Below: Trevor Alun Rees born 1902 and raised on the farm, was the last member of Rees family to live at and work the land of Tir y ferch Gryno.

Dilwyn and Trevor Rees take a breather from turning the hay.

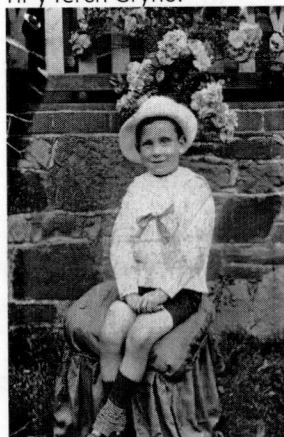

Top Photo courtesy Elizabeth Spillane née O'Shea, Australia, others courtesy Dilwyn Rees.

Rees Family of Tir y ferch Gryno

While the fields of Tir y ferch Gryno were detailed on the tithe survey, there was no homestead, and the William Lewis named as occupier of the 84 acre holding was probably the miller living in Pontaberbargoed Mill House. The earliest evidence of the existence of a farmhouse is on first edition OS map, and census returns from 1881 onwards show it was inhabited by its farmers, Thomas family in later nineteenth century, followed by the Rees family.

William Thomas, a native of Llanwonno, was the 69 year old farmer (with 60 acres) at the time of the 1881 census. When the 1891 census was taken, Mary, his widow, headed the household and youngest son David was the farmer. A report in *Merthyr Express*, June 18 1898, noted that during the coal strike of that year, David Thomas gifted three quarts of milk each morning for the children in Brithdir schools. When war was declared on the Boer in 1899, he volunteered for service and sadly died there (see on page 183). His sister, Jane, described as cook in the 1901 census return was described as head of the household when the 1911 census was taken.

Many readers will remember the Rees family of Tir y ferch Gryno. Older residents knew Joan and Olwen as *Miss Rees*, both teachers at Brithdir Schools. Both are mentioned in school log book entries and that of February 27 1930 in Girls' School, noted *Miss Rees absent on account of her father's death.*

Plas Milfre:

Plas Milfre owner Howard Jones fits a new sign to the gate in 2006.

Originally known as Tir Evan Thomas (Evan Thomas's land), its farming families were closely associated with the inhabitants of Brithdir. In 1841, Richard Williams (whose identity is unclear) occupied this 35 acre farm beside Nant Llan just to the south of Tyr y Capel, and a close neighbour to Cefn y Brithdir farm. Anecdotal evidence has it that the ever-changing acreage of local farms, so confusing for today's researching historian, was because farmers met socially to play cards, and fields often changed hands on the turn of a card. If that is true, this is the only farm untouched (whether by non-participation or good fortune) by the *card school*, as sources studied to date consistently show a 35 acre farm.

Ebenezer Phillips was its farmer when the 1851 census was taken and during the four decades or so while the Phillips family farmed it, it appears as Plas y Milvia in sources.

Twentieth century occupants wondered why the farmhouse had three chimneys and only two hearths. However, renovation work on the farmhouse in the 1980s uncovered not only a third hearth blocked from view but also six bread-ovens hidden behind a false wall. As it was unlikely that members of the

The identities of the people and the contents of the baskets on the cart shown in this plate-glass image dating from about 1865, reproduced courtesy Billy Bennett, are uncertain. Perhaps the people are members of the Phillips household and the baskets filled with bread.

household could eat the produce of so many ovens, was it a commercial venture employing some family baking skills to augment the household income?

When the 1891 census was taken, James Lewis, younger brother of William, of Cefn y Brithdir, and Thomas, of Brithdir Ganol, was the farmer at Plas Milfre (as it become known). Farming there until his death, he was forced to diversify as, in April 1909, GUDC contracted him to scavenge (remove household rubbish) from Brithdir, and in 1910 he was also contracted to haul limestone to Brithdir from Tynant Quarries in Taffs Well. Taking over the farm on his father's demise in 1910, Elvet Lewis and his family remained at Plas Milfre for many years. One of life's characters, *old Elvet* would sell anything to make a penny and I remember well the home-made cider he sold at 6d. a glass. With the ridge road running alongside, the farm was a convenient watering hole for travellers including those *en route* to Waun Fair.

More recently, Plas Milfre has been farmed by the Jones family. Howard Jones retired from farming following the foot-and-mouth epidemic in 2001 but continued to live at the farm until his death. To the time of writing, his son has kept horses on the farm.

Tyr y Capel

The Williams family, a well-known local farming family, has been at Tyr y Capel for at least 175 years, during which time they had strong links with the Brithdir community.

Thomas Williams was listed in the tithe schedule as owner of this farm which, according to both tithe schedule and 1841 census return, was occupied by Jenkin Thomas, whose identity is unclear. Owner Thomas Williams, who had inherited the farm in 1834, was not enumerated in Tyr y Capel in 1841, but was he the 20 year old, of independent means, enumerated in the Gwaelod y Brithdir household headed by another Thomas Williams? By the time the 1851 census was taken, not only was he farming at what was called *Chapel Farm* in the census return, but he was a family man, with wife, Ann, and two infant sons. He continued to farm it until his death in the 1890s. His 82 year old widow, Ann, was described as the farmer in the 1901 census return when four sons, Charles, Lewis, Edmund and Edwin, worked on the farm. Presumably widow Ann died before the 1911 census was taken when sons Lewis and Edmund were listed as the farmers. It is not clear when son Charles, took over the farm, but he was succeeded by his son Thomas Charles and, at the time of writing, Thomas Charles's son, also named Charles, is the farmer.

The following details about the changes made to the farmhouse come from the present occupants, Charles Williams and his wife Irene. The original farmhouse was entered via the cow-house through a doorway to one side of a large stone hearth. Thomas Williams added a small wing to the original longhouse in 1836 and a further extension was added by Charles in 1899. Although the cow-house end of the earlier longhouse has been demolished, a winding stone stairway survives on the opposite side of the large stone hearth, originally open to the roof. The fireplace is now blocked and the stone stairs has been turned into a feature in the room.

This oil painting, by George Frederick Harris (one of three paintings sold in 1920 to pay for his family to emigrate to Australia), (reproduced courtesy Charles Williams), shows Derby winner *George Frederick*, reputed to have trained on the old road running alongside the farm. Owned and bred by William Sheward Cartwright of Ely Farm, Cardiff, and trained by Tom Leader, this horse won the prestigious race in 1874 with Harry Custance, a famous mid-Victorian jockey, in the saddle.

Life and work on the farms

Successive census returns shed light on the local farming fraternity. When the 1841 and 1851 censuses were taken the local farms were the only households in the area, and family members and live-in servants worked the land, tended the animals and carried out household and farmyard (dairying and poultry-keeping) duties. The bar chart shows that, at the start of the Victorian era, more than half the land on these farms (61.81%) was grazing pasture for livestock; just 18.61% was

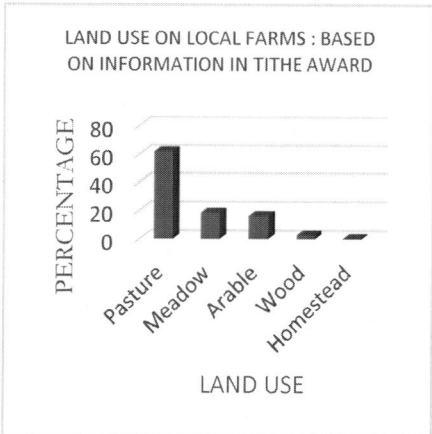

LAND USE ON LOCAL FARMS : BASED ON INFORMATION IN TITHE AWARD

PERCENTAGE: 80, 60, 40, 20, 0

Pasture, Meadow, Arable, Wood, Homestead

LAND USE

given over to hay meadows; arable fields accounted for only 16.22%; wood for 2.82% and the various homesteads together were 0.54% of the total area of enclosed parcels of land. The meadow and arable fields, often no more than parcels of some two or three acres, were generally on the higher areas, on fairly flat land near the homesteads. The steep slope, rising from the west bank of Rhymney river, including that on which the community later developed, was pasture land.

Although, during the nineteenth century, pastoral and arable farming adapted and changed to meet some of the needs of the new industrial society in Wales and England, farming remained a labour-intensive activity until well into the twentieth century. Both male and female workers, whether family members or paid employees (living-in or in nearby cottages) worked long daylight hours. Men did the farm work on the fields while women were generally responsible for household and farmyard tasks. It was not unusual for women, and, as the new community developed, colliers eager to earn a little extra between shifts, to help out in the fields during busy times, lambing and, especially, harvesting.

Generations of local farmers, especially in pre-railway days, aiming to be as self-sufficient as soil, gradient, climate and contemporary farming practices allowed, relied on the produce of their land together with trade at Waun Fair or occasionally a market at Abergavenny. Local geography made arable farming difficult, but the grain-drying kiln at Brithdir Ganol, as well as the tools and implements listed in the 1866 notice of sale (included in the farm account above), show that grains (oats, barley and wheat according to the sale notice) were grown in the area. Some may have been cut green. The same notice shows that a few acres were also devoted to potatoes (already harvested before the sale) and swedes (for human and animal consumption), while hay, harvested on the meadows, provided fodder for farm livestock when, during the long winter months, they could not survive by grazing on the pastures and common (at the time all these farms enjoyed common rights).

It is not clear whether any other local farmers grew grain, but this notice of sale of livestock and crops at nearby Cefn y Brithdir, taken from *Merthyr Telegraph and General Advertiser for the Iron Districts of South Wales*, October 12 1867, includes similar livestock -- cattle, sheep, pigs and working horses -- as well as hay. (However, why, the following week, did the same paper carry a notice dated October 16 and in the name of W. Lewis, Cefn y Brithdir, that the sale *WILL NOT TAKE PLACE*?)

The diet of members of farming households probably consisted largely of bread baked in farmhouse ovens, dairy produce (milk, butter and cheese),

28

vegetables (including potatoes and swedes), fruit and herbs grown in kitchen gardens and orchards and, perhaps eggs, as well as bacon from pigs fattened for slaughter, and mutton. Prior to the 1870s, their education probably extended little beyond what they learned on the family farm and in their place of worship. The progress of local education is noted in the chapter on education, as is the fact that two of the Rees daughters of Tir y ferch Gryno served as teachers in village schools. Their homes, like most dwellings erected in the village, were, until the later twentieth century, heated by fireplaces (burning wood or coal) in upstairs and downstairs rooms.

Since the mid Victorian era, local farming families saw many changes as neighbouring farmers came and went, and production and markets fluctuated, but it is likely that the impact of the industrial revolution with, in particular, the growth of the small community on lower fields of Brithdir Ganol and Cefn y Brithdir farms (as described in the next chapter), was one of the greatest.

Tommy son of Dilwyn Rees stands in front of a hay-laden truck from *Tirferchgryno farm*

29

CHAPTER 3 THE VILLAGE

Whilst the previous chapter about the farms and farming families hinted at the ways in which industrialisation and urbanisation changed this part of the Rhymney Valley, this chapter will deal with how and when the village developed. It is followed by a chapter on the local coal industry which was to shape the lives of the people who lived in the new community.

George Inn or Brithdir

At first, both railway station and community were known as George Inn, a name probably taken from that of the local landowner, George George. According to correspondence (now in The National Archives) between Postmaster's Office, Cardiff, Rhymney Railway Traffic Department Clearing House and Board of Trade, the name officially changed from George Inn to Brithdir (the original name of George George's estate) on October 1 1891.

A report about the Golden Wedding anniversary of Mr. and Mrs. William Lewis (then of East View, and formerly of Cefn y Brithdir) in *Merthyr Express*, June 19 1937, noted *he* [William Lewis] *was responsible for the name change*. However, a letter to columnist *Cosmos*, published in *South Wales Daily News*, October 1 1891, had thanked Cornelius Lundie (general manager and engineer) and directors of Rhymney Railway Company (RR) for changing the name of George Inn Station to Brithdir Station. In response to a petition from George Inn inhabitants some months earlier, Cornelius Lundie had promised to do all he could to secure change. William Lewis was probably one of the petitioners and possibly the person who penned the letter. Cornelius Lundie and RR directors had listened to public opinion.

Early Victorian era

In 1841, David George, of Heol Evan Gwyn, Pontlottyn, was census enumerator of the still-rural area between rivers Rhymney and Bargoed Rhymney. He started his journey in the south, at Mill House, Pontaberbargoed, before proceeding along ancient tracks, visiting households on either side of Cefn Brithdir ridge, part of Merthyr and Gelligaer Common, as far north as Pen Waun Goch, near Pontlottyn. A more detailed examination of the people named in the 1841 census return shows that the majority of residents, like generations of their ancestors, were born in Gelligaer parish or in neighbouring parishes. The pattern was the same when the next census was taken in 1851, but, as shown in the previous chapter, Brithdir's farming families were different on all but Gwaelod y Brithdir.

Birth of George Inn village

The 1850s and 1860s was a time of change in and near the area: not only did RR line open in 1858 but small clusters of cottages, like those at George Inn, were erected to house the growing population as miners, some with families, moved in to work in the developing coal industry. The two houses called Ty

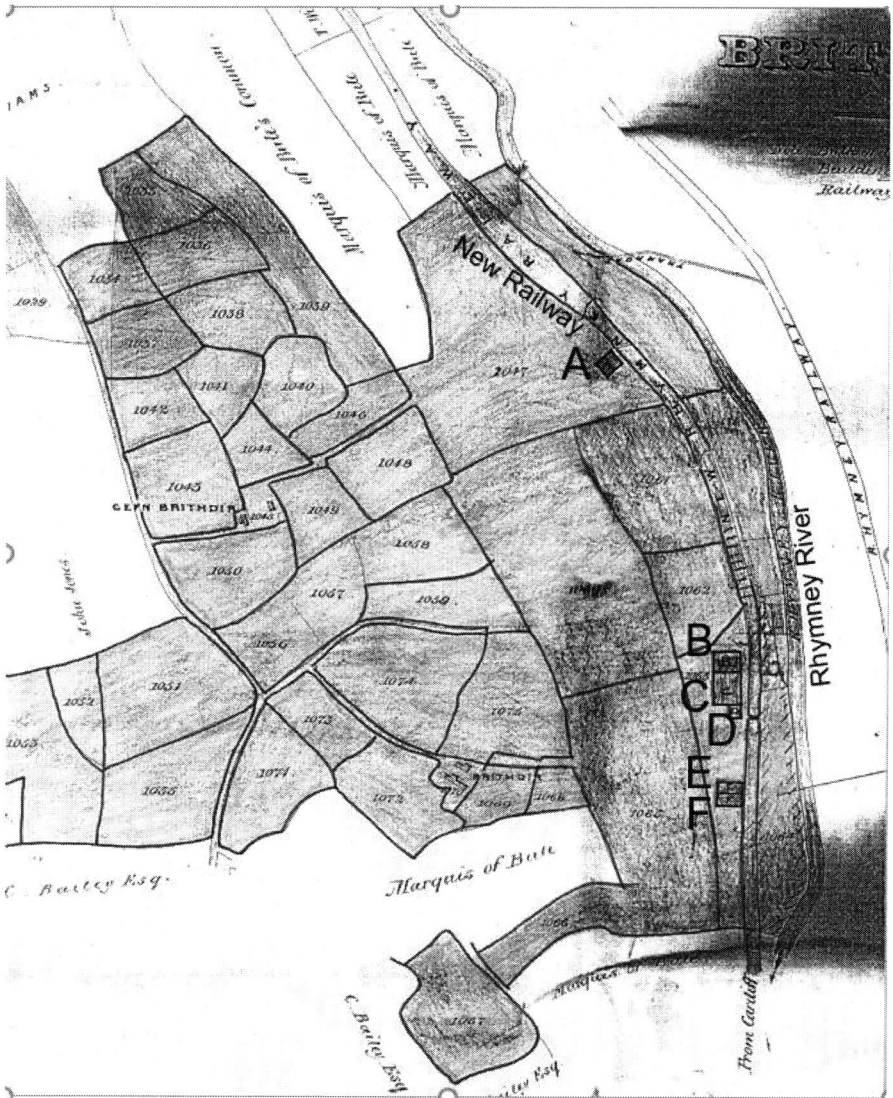

Coch were built on the lower field of Tir y ferch Gryno about 1860 and were homes to two families when the 1861 census was taken.

Brithdir Estate map of 1858 (courtesy Malcolm Winmill) shows George Inn village in its infancy. The first buildings and family homes were subsequently erected on the six parcels of land shown as blocks A, B, C, D, E and F.

- Plot A, separated by some distance from the other plots and leased by Francis Francis has not been identified at the time of writing.
- Edmund Morgan, a collier of Mynyddislwyn, leased Plot B upon which he erected what became Nos 29, 29a, 30 and 31 Station Terrace.
- A group, headed by Edward Nicholas, leased Plot C and built what was later Nos 19 to 28 Station Terrace.
- George Inn Hotel was erected on Plot D.

31

- William Bevan and John Morgan leased adjoining plots E and F respectively and each erected a cottage on their plot. The 1861 census enumerator called the cottages Bryn Tawel, and there is further information about the Bevan family and these cottages on pages 260-264.

George Inn village 1861

The area was changing by the time Daniel Lewis, a miller of Pontaberbargoed and census enumerator, made his return in 1861. Although some pages (including those relating to three Brithdir farms) are missing, it is clear from extant returns that the number of people living in George Inn's recently erected dwellings and earning a living from coal mining exceeded that on local farms and in agriculture.

In 1861, George Inn consisted of 15 dwellings (plus one uninhabited) housing 89 people (51 males and 38 females). Most of these people were born locally: just under one fifth in Glamorgan, and the majority in the neighbouring Monmouthshire parishes of Bedwellty and Mynyddislwyn. The majority of men worked in the coal industry, 17 were described as miners (including two 10 year olds and one aged 11), 12 others as colliers and 1 coal tipper. The 3 quarrymen were probably employed at a local stone quarry, maybe quarrying stone for local buildings. It is not clear where the 3 hauliers and 1 woodcutter worked and the 1 engine driver could have been working in the coal industry, or possibly on the railway. The majority of women, described as wives, were occupied with domestic duties and caring for their families. There was little paid employment available for females and just a few, unmarried females, had occupations. The 16 year old daughter at George Inn was a barmaid, a 20 year old daughter in another household was a farmer's servant, while her 15 year old sister was a housemaid, and a 22 year old niece in yet another household was a dressmaker. Just 8 children, aged between 5 and 11 years and from four different families, were described as scholars but it is not clear where or how frequently they received lessons. Other children of school age do not appear to be attending school at the time.

George Inn village 1871

The village's housing stock and its population expanded in the decade to 1871, not dramatically, but sufficient for RR to open George Inn railway station in census year. As colliery owners, unlike iron masters, did not usually build homes for their workforce, it is likely private speculators met the demand, building houses which they let or leased to colliers. William Bevan and John Morgan had each completed two adjoining cottages on their properties at Bryn Tawel (later known as Ivy Row) and five more dwellings were added to those near the George Inn Hotel. It is difficult to identify each of the dwellings with certainty in the 1871 census return, but 26 dwellings described as *Brithdir Terrace*, plus George Inn and a colliery manager's house close to Old Brithdir Pit, housed a population of 136 (73 males and 63 females). Every household was dependent on the developing local coal industry which is discussed in the next chapter.

The first edition OS map (right) published 1878, surveyed 1873-76, shows the rural setting of George Inn village, a small community near the railway station which was opened in 1871.

George Inn village 1881

According to the 1881 census return, Brithdir's population totalled 209 (120 males and 89 females) in 46 separate households, and the housing stock comprised Bute Terrace, Ty Coch, Bryn Tawel, Brithdir Terrace and George Inn Row, with Schoolroom and George Inn included in the latter.

The village was built in three phases; the first phase by individuals who had leased a plot of land and erected a family home and, in some cases, also two, three or more cottages to rent out. The second and third phases were the work of building companies. The following *Schedule of Properties forming portions of Cefn Brithdir Farm and Brithdir Ganol Farm*, courtesy Malcolm Winmill, gives a good indication of Brithdir's steady growth.

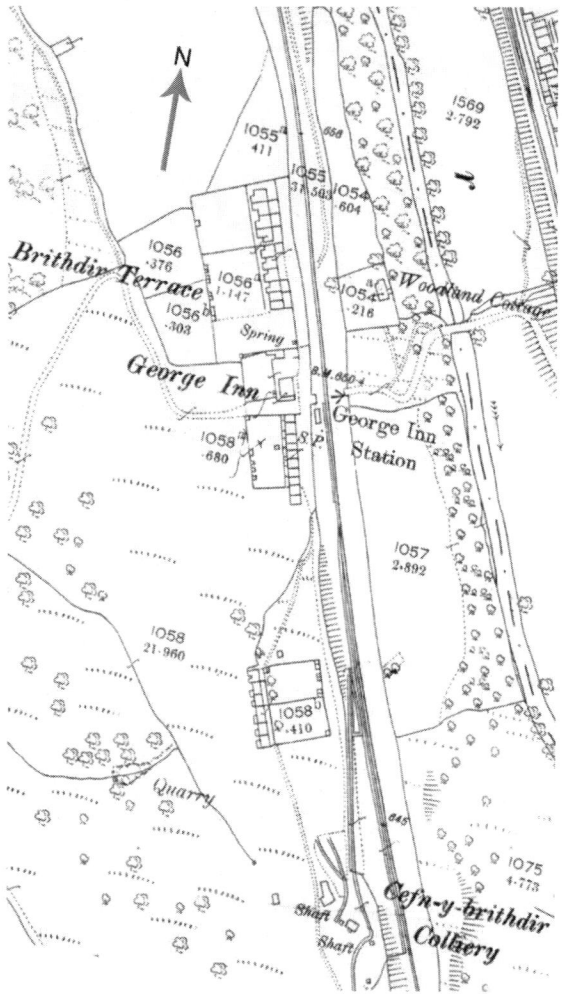

Date of Lease	Original Lessee	Premises	Start of Term
1858 January 18	Jonah Meredith	George Inn	14 May 1855
1856 September 9	Edward Nicholas et al.	19-28 Station Terrace	1 September 1856
1856 November 2	Edmund Morgan	29, 29a, 30, 31 Station Terrace	
1858 January 18	William Bevan	1 to 3 Ivy Row	1 November 1857
	John Morgan	4 to 6 Ivy Row	1 November 1857
1873 June 28	John Davies	Rosehill Cottages, 20, 21 Bristol Terr.	1 May 1858
1886 November 5	W. Lewis	Half Way House, Mountain Gate	1 May 1866
1867 April 5	William Lewis	13 to 18 Station Terrace	1 May 1867
1867 September 2	Mary Morgans	11 Station Terrace	
1870 September 1		12 Station Terrace	1 May 1870
1875 March 1	Enoch Moore	1 to 10 Station Terrace	1 May 1874
1879 October 18	Enoch Moore		1 May 1879
1892 December 31	W.A. Davies et al.	Penuel Chapel	
1891 September 16	Taliesin Isaac	17, 18, 19a Bristol Terrace	1 May 1891

1891 September 28	Brithdir Dwellings Supply Company Ltd	Beulah English Baptist Chapel	1 May 1890
		1 to 6 Bristol Terrace (a), 1 to 16 Bristol Terrace (b), 1 to 28 Charles Street, 1 to 28 Herbert Street, 1 to 28 James Street, 32, 32a, 33, 33a Station Terrace. Bridge House, Station Terrace	
		Land for Infants' School	
1894 April 2	Sam Williams	Springfield Villa, George Hill	1 May 1892
1894 March 1	David Davies	1 to 3 The Villas	
1895 May 23	William Jones	Brynglas, George Hill	1 May 1894
1896 February 12	Evan Jones	2 to 9 School Street	1 June 1895
1895 December 18	S.E. Lewis	10 and 11 School Street	
	Walter Price	12 School Street	
1896 March 31	James Price	1 School Street	
1896 September 10	Thomas Williams	Church Villa, Station Terrace	1 May 1896
1896 September 19	James Price	1 to 3 Railway Terrace	
1907 June 4	Edwin Bufton	Additional rent, re: above lease	
1898 March 12	Thomas Williams	Wesley House, George Hill	1 September 1896
1899 January 27	Job Harry	Llansoar House, 5 Russell Street.	1 November 1898
1901 December 31	William Speake	Radnor House and Rock House	
1903 September 15	William Lewis	Leargaidh (1 Cefn Bryn) Brythonville (3 Cefn Bryn)	1 May 1899
1901 December 31	William Lewis	Bronhaulwen (2 Cefn Bryn)	1 Nov 1899
1903 September 11	M. Williams	Salem House (6 Russell Street) Trefwig House (7 Russell Street).	1 May 1900
1903 September 11	William Davies	Rosemary Cottage	1 May 1902
1903 September 1	John Thomas	1 and 12 East View	1 November 1902
1903 September 1	Sam Williams	2 to 7, and 11 East View	
	R.T.E. Davies	8 East View	
	Jenkin Davies	9 East View	
	Joseph Williams	10 East View	
1906 December 31	Glamorgan CC	Brithdir School	
1904 August 15	James Price	Rose, Laurel and Primrose Cottages 1, 2 and 3 Russell Street	1 May 1903
1908 June 25	Edwin Bufton	Church Villa and Barton Villa	1 November 1905
1908 November 25	Cefn Brithdir Bldgs Co. Ltd.	1 to 20 Nelson Terrace	1 May 1906
1908 November 26		1 to 21 Wellington Terrace	
1909 March 18		1 to 16 Milton Terrace	
1909 July 5		1 to 16 Tennyson Terrace	
1909 November 17		1 to 13 Salisbury Terrace	
		1 to 11 Harcourt Terrace	
1912 March 20	Glamorgan CC	Brithdir School	1 November 1911
1923 November 15	G.R. Pennant et al.	Church Hall	24 June 1923

1891 census

1891 census return shows Brithdir's population totalled 293 (170 males and 123 females) in 51 separate households, with two uninhabited dwellings in the community. The housing stock had altered little in the decade since the 1881 census was taken, but, in 1891, 21 people including two families (one of 7 and the other 5 members) as well as nine single men, occupied railway contractor's huts near George Inn Hotel. Research to date has not made it clear what railway project occupied the male workforce in the huts.

1901 census

1901 census returns show Brithdir village's population totalled 1041 (565 males and 476 females) in 204 separate households, with eight uninhabited dwellings in the community. The new terraces, Charles Street, Herbert Street, James Street, School Street and Russell Street, providing an extra 100 homes, were named after landowner Charles Herbert James and his son, Charles Russell James. East View was added by 1903.

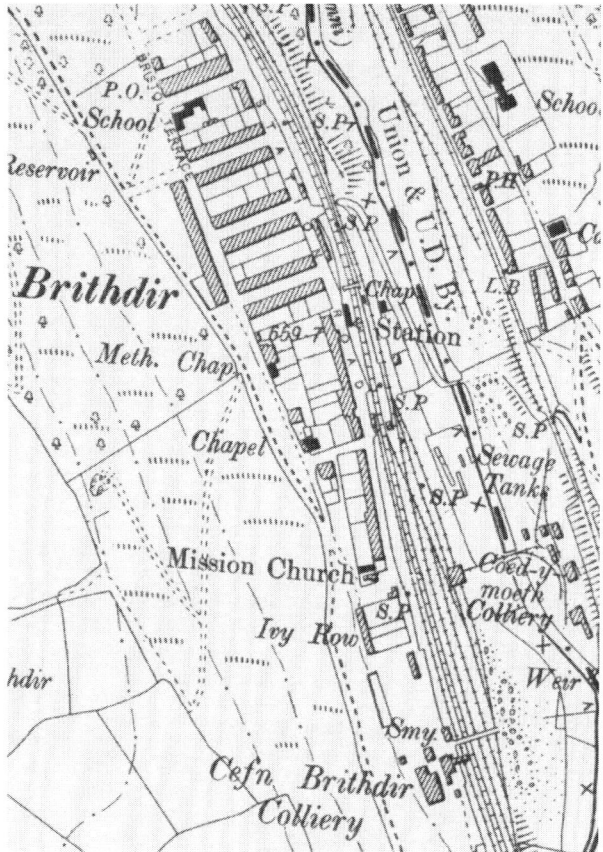

OS Map 1901 taken from 6 inch to mile

Early buildings

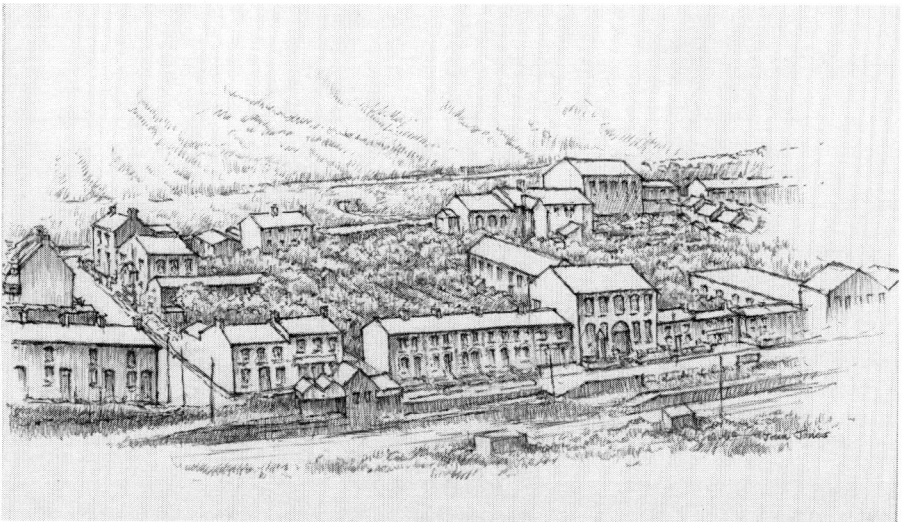

Some of the early buildings of George Inn are captured in this pencil sketch by artist John (*Jack*) Jones, formerly of Brithdir. Used with the keyed sketch opposite it will help those who are not familiar with the area.

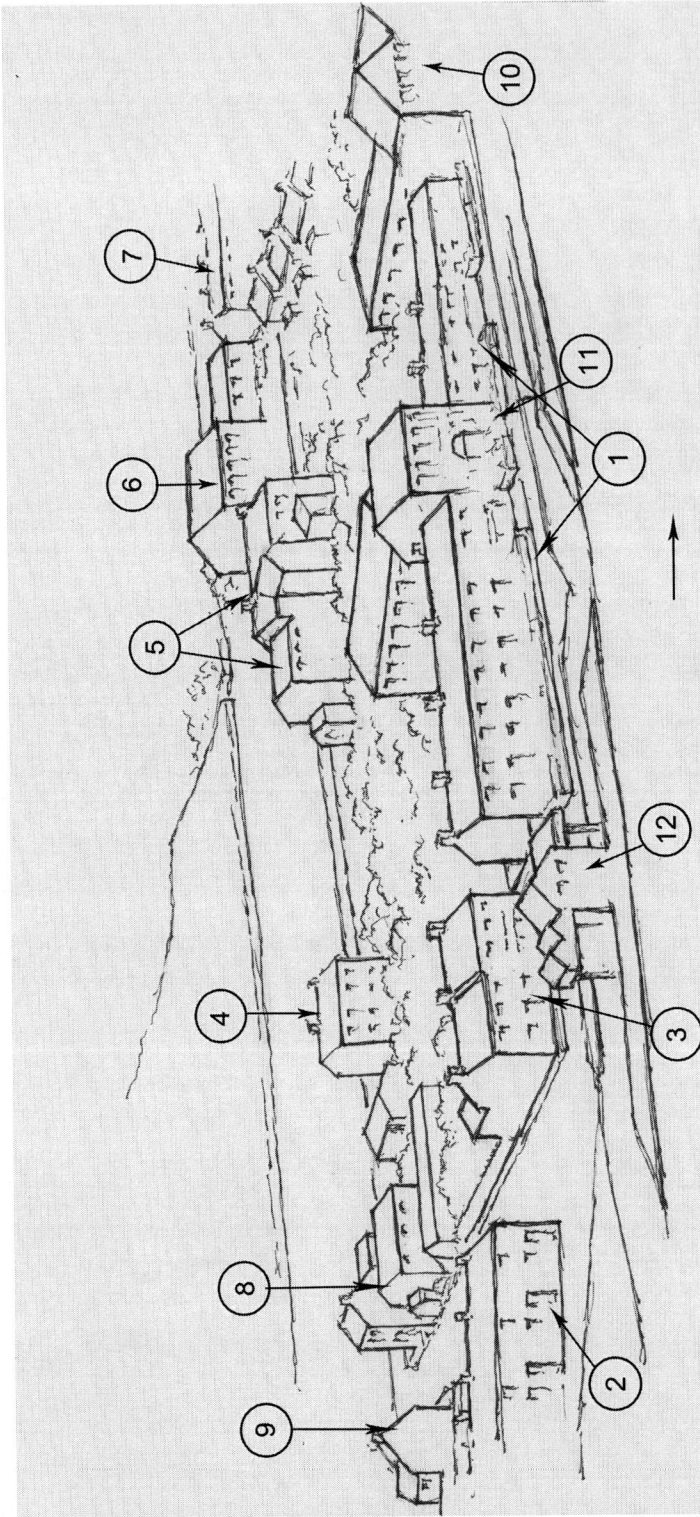

1. Nos 19 to 28 Station Terrace - Nos 25 and 26 were later knocked down to accommodate the building of the New Workmen's Institute and Library (No 11)   2. Nos 1 to 18 Station Terrace.   3. George Inn Hotel.   4. Rose Hill Cottages (20-21 Bristol Terrace.
5. Old Bristol Terrace (Nos 17-19) with Penuel Chapel annexed to No 19.   6. Beulah Baptist Chapel & Vestry.
7. Nos 1 to 16 Bristol Terrace.   8. In descending order, Wesley House, Wesleyan chapel and schoolroom
9. Bryn Glas and Springfield cottages.   10. Constitutional Club.   11. Workmen's Institute and Library (the long building behind is the New Hall) .   12. Site of the original George Inn railway station, later the parcel depot of Rhymney Railway.

Building Companies

Whilst some Brithdir dwellings were the work of local speculating builders, two limited companies, Brithdir Dwellings Supply Company Limited and Cefn Brithdir Building Supply Company, were responsible for most later residential buildings in and near Brithdir.

Registered November 18 1889, the former company was established to erect houses upon Charles Herbert James's freehold (he had purchased the Brithdir Estate in the late 1870s) at George Inn (Cefn y Brithdir Farm). The company built Charles, Herbert and James Streets, a total of 78 houses, and new Bristol Terrace with 22 dwellings. The main shareholders were members of the James family and Powell Duffryn Steam Coal Company (PD), and as soon as the houses were built they were leased to the latter company.

List of Persons holding shares in Brithdir Dwellings Supply Co. Ltd. February 18 1895

Shareholder	Address	Occupation	Shares
PD	18 Leadenhall Street, London	Colliery Proprietors	500
Gwilym Cristor James	Gwaelodygarth, Merthyr Tydfil	Solicitor	}
Charles Russell James	Merthyr Tydfil	Barrister at law	} 400
Edward Pritchard Martin	Dowlais	Manager of Steel Works	}
Charles Russell James	Merthyr Tydfil	Barrister at law	100
Edmund Mills Hann	Aberaman, Aberdare	Colliery Manager	100
Herbert Thomas	Ivor House, Redland, Bristol	Esquire	100
Blanche Jones	Greenhill Farm, Gelligaer	Wife of Thomas Jones	80
Gwilym Cristor James	Gwaelodygarth, Merthyr Tydfil	Solicitor	50
Edward Pritchard Martin	Dowlais	Manager of Steel Works	50
William Pritchard	Terrace House, Rhymney	Agent	40
Jonathan Williams	Bargoed	Colliery Proprietor	30
Charles Henry James	8 Courtland Terrace, Merthyr Tydfil	Engineer	20
Margaret Davies	44 High Street, Merthyr Tydfil	Wife of Francis Davies	20
Harriet Phillips	3 Courtland Terrace, Merthyr Tydfil	Wife of David Phillips	20
John Davies	41 Wellington Street, Merthyr Tydfil	Solicitor	20
William Smith	Rhymney	Colliery Manager	20
Emily Harrison	Rhymney	Widow	20
William Edwards	1 Cilsanws Lane, Cefn Coed	Contractor	20
Emma Nauce	5 Plasturton Place, Cardiff		20
Mary Williams	14 Rees Street, Merthyr	Spinster	10
Thomas Griffiths	London Provincial Bank, Merthyr Tydfil	Bank Manager	10
Gomer Llewellyn Thomas	Somerset Place, Merthyr Tydfil	Ironmonger	10
Thomas James Webster	Brynglas, Merthyr Tydfil	Surgeon	10
Thomas Thomas	130 High Street, Merthyr Tydfil	Ironmonger	10
Henry Lewis	2 Castle Street, Merthyr Tydfil	Auctioneer	10

In a letter of November 20 1889 to RR, Charles Herbert James expressed his concerns about PD's eagerness for about 100 new dwellings near George Inn before action was taken with regard to the awkward and dangerous level crossing nearby. He advised that instead of changing the existing level crossing, the archway under the railway, some 400 yards from George Inn, should be altered. He proposed the railway company should make the archway into a road way as far as their land extended, that PD should continue that to the extent of their sidings, and the parish should continue it to the bridge. This proposal would involve raising the bridge and that would be the work of the two parishes, Bedwellty and Gelligaer. The two parishes agreed on this and Charles Herbert James, as landowner, promised £50 towards the expenditure of Gelligaer. He finished by noting that if his proposition was carried out, the level

The archway was converted to a road.
Courtesy Keith Pyle

crossing would be abolished and the 100 additional houses built.

By July 1891 plans for the new houses were well under way and local newspapers, such as *South Wales Daily News*, July 6 1891, carried advertisements inviting contractors to tender for *laying on water* to the 100 houses. By May and June 1892, those same newspapers carried advertisements for painters and plasterers to apply on job. (And, while all this work was going on, a new school was under construction.) In one year, Brithdir developed from two groups of houses into a well-arranged, well drained and sewered, and well-built village with some public buildings. An advertisement in *South Wales Daily News*, January 5 1893, invited builders to send tenders by January 12 for the erection of two shops and houses at Brithdir for the building company.

Cefn Brithdir Building Supply Company had Frank Hodges and Gomer Thomas as directors and Isaac Edwards was secretary. *Bargoed Journal*, February 1 1906, declared *the demand for houses at Brithdir still continues, and we are told 150 houses will be commenced in the spring on the Tirphil side of Bristol Terrace.* As noted on page 96, headmaster Samuel Davies was concerned about the impact on school accommodation and his fears were proved correct as there were 134 children of school age among the families in the 97 houses in the new terraces of Harcourt, Salisbury, Tennyson, Milton, Nelson and Wellington.

The deeds of 13 Salisbury Terrace show that on November 17 1909, Gwilym Cristor James, Charles Russell James and Edward Pritchard Martin, trustees of Deri and Brithdir Estates (presumably trustees of will of C. H. James, the first two being his sons and the third named, his son-in-law) leased 1100 square yards to Cefn Brithdir Building Supply Company Limited upon which the company erected 11, 12 and 13 Salisbury Terrace. The company engaged contractors Williams and Sons of New Tredegar, later builders of in Wellington, Tennyson, Nelson and Milton Terraces. Known at first as *New Houses*, these dwellings were occupied by the time the 1911 census was taken. Locals affectionately called this group of terraces *The Buildings* or *The Buckets*, the latter because of their proximity to an aerial ropeway carrying buckets of waste from the colliery to the mountain-top spoil heap.

Brithdir's final terraces, affectionately known as *the Buckets*
Courtesy Martin Loader (Honda Wanderer Website)

1911 census

According to the 1911 census 1779 people (979 males and 800 females) lived in 349 separate households in Brithdir. (Note – the number of households exceeded the number of houses as some people, especially young married couples, *lived in rooms* in a house occupied by another household.) Most of them had come from rural Wales and south west England, sometimes via earlier industrial settlements within the upper Rhymney Valley (and elsewhere), and arrived in Brithdir for employment and a better future.

Later

The 1919 OS map overleaf shows that the village had filled its space. Registers of electors and later maps, as well as people's memories, show little further building apart from Workmen's Institute and a few dwellings. Before the end of the twentieth century, on ceasing to serve their original purpose, some properties such as schools and chapels were converted for alternative use. The former Infants' School is now a private dwelling, while Wesleyan Methodist chapel was demolished and a dwelling house constructed on the site.

When the 2011 census was taken, most people living in Brithdir had been born in Wales and lived in the terraced houses built before 1911. The coal industry had dominated the community for about a century and a half, but by 2011 the three largest employment sectors for local people were manufacturing, retail and construction.

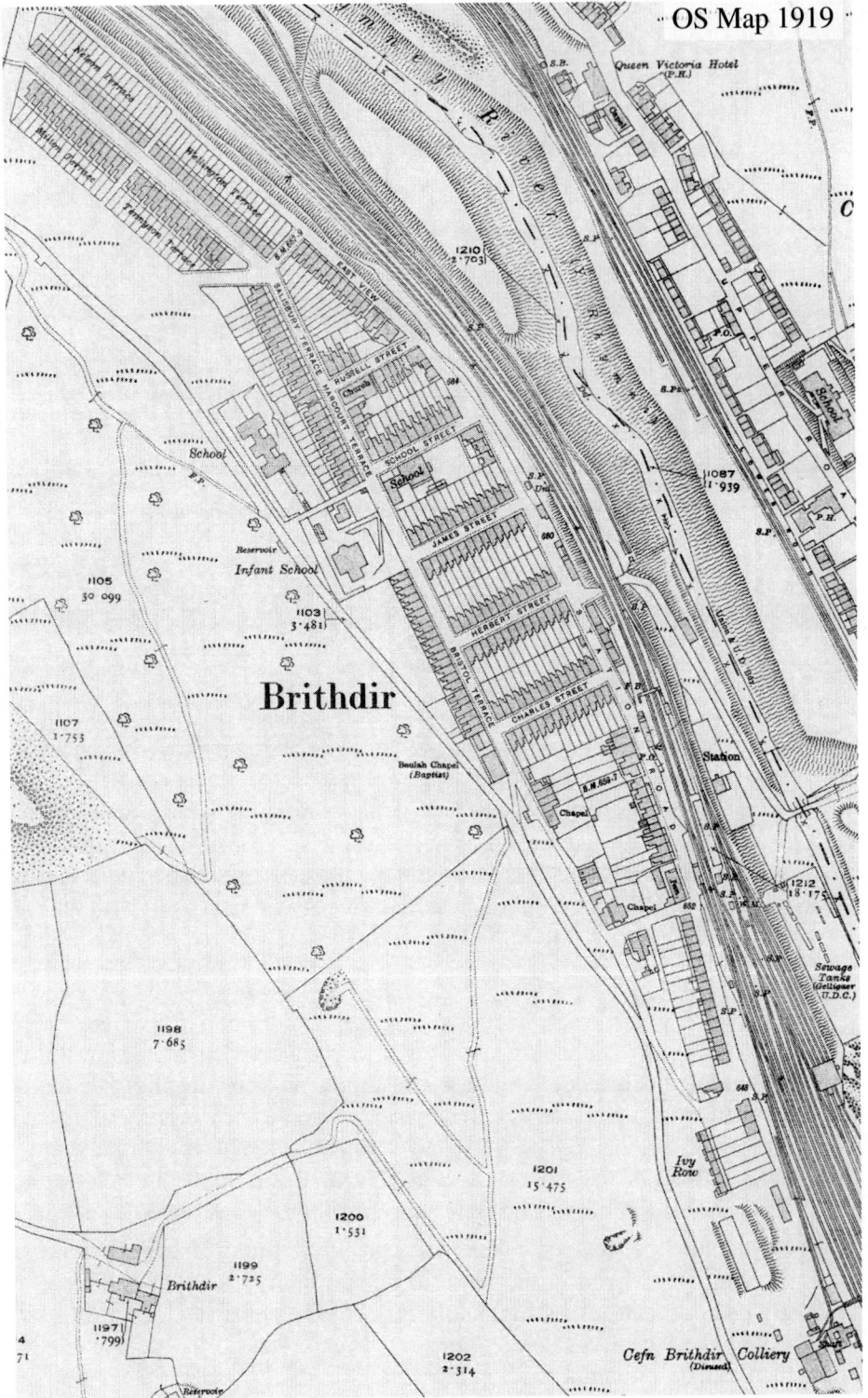

OS Map 1919

Brithdir

Station Terrace circa 1921, showing some of the earliest buildings in the village. The young man with the dog is one of the Rogers' boys (Fred or Billy) aged about 14. The man holding the long cue is standing outside the entrance to the Workmen's Club. Thomas John Cole was the licence holder of the Billiard Hall - Note the poster in the window advertising two silent movies *A Fool's Paradise* and *Sheik*. The end building (right) is Joseph Coles (fruiterers) shop, and it would seem Fry's Chocolate was just as popular then as today. The collier, with his blackened face, is likely on his way home from a shift at the George Pit, a reminder of the days before pit-head baths. Courtesy Alan Rogers.

Station Terrace
Brithdir

41

CHAPTER 4 THE COAL INDUSTRY

Although coal had been mined in South Wales since Roman times, the vast potential mineral wealth lying beneath the surface was not exploited before the mid-eighteenth century. At first, it was mined to power the iron industry along a heads of the valleys strip from Hirwaun in the west to Blaenavon in the east, but, by the mid-nineteenth century, the sale-coal industry's deep mines developed to fuel steam locomotives and steam ships, and an industrial and semi-urban society rolled southwards over the rural landscape. As the history of the coal industry in UK and in South Wales is well documented elsewhere, both in print and on websites such as www.welshcoalmines.co.uk, what follows is some information about issues and developments in and around the emerging community of Brithdir since the early nineteenth century.

The histories of the local coal industry and of George Inn/Brithdir community are intertwined: the industry developed, and, as noted in the previous chapter, census returns and OS maps show the community emerged and grew as people arrived in search of work. The local economy was based on coal; coal miners' wages paid for the roof over their heads as well as their food and clothes. Thus businesses grew, while organisations developed in response to social, cultural and spiritual needs. Life in the emerging coal community was frequently hard: men worked in difficult, dirty and dangerous conditions (in local pits as well as some more distant ones), while their womenfolk sometimes struggled to feed and clothe their families, maintaining the public face of the family as best they could. And, all too often, family life was adversely affected by strikes, lock outs, short time working and wage reductions, as well as accidents resulting in death or injury, the cruel ravages of diseases such as smallpox and diphtheria, and, sometimes, unfortunate and unsavoury repercussions when breadwinner(s) spent wages on alcohol. However, adversities helped strengthen community spirit and encourage mutual help and ambition.

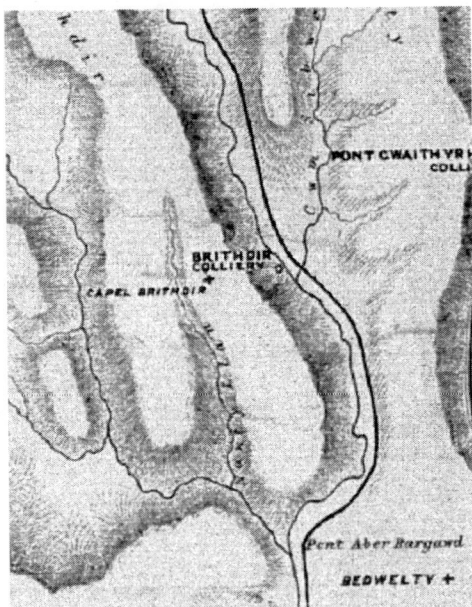

A section of map of Ironworks and Collieries in Monmouthshire by John Prujean, 1843, shows Brithdir Colliery in isolation.
Courtesy Gwent Archives

Brithdir Colliery

Brithdir Colliery, in production pre-1843, was the first colliery in the area. Situated on the west bank of Rhymney river, to the north of the land on which Brithdir village

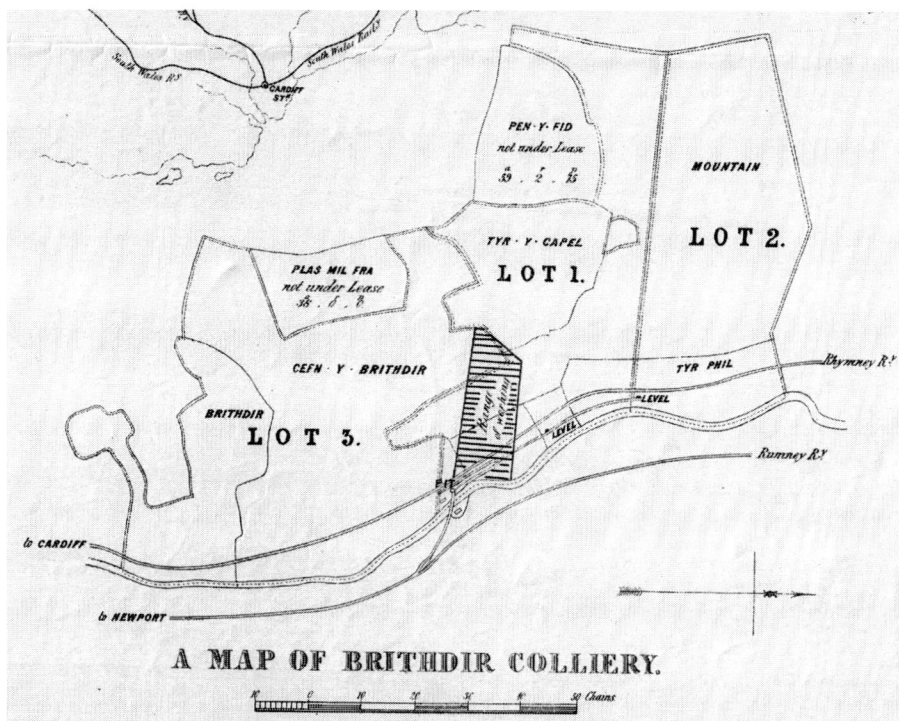

Map of Brithdir Colliery by Edmund Palmer, taken from *Sale Notice of Leasehold Collieries in the Rhymney valley*, 10 Sept 1857. Courtesy Glamorgan Archives

developed, it (and probably Craig Rhymney Pit) was served by a spur from Rumney Tramroad, and thus linked to the port of Newport. It opened on the Brithdir Vein by a pit twenty-eight yards deep and worked by a steam engine of 30-horse power. The identity of its earliest owner(s) is unclear but in the 1850s, it seems to have been in the hands of Dunraven United Collieries, a limited company formed by Thomas Joseph of Merthyr (who also owned Craig Rhymney Pit).

The site included twenty coke ovens (each seven tons), blacksmith, carpenter and locomotive engine shops, stable, tips, engine house as well as extensive sidings and railway, and a dwelling house for the manager. The identities of successive managers are unclear, but at the time of 1871 census, 37 year old Breconshire-born colliery manager, Edward P. Jones, headed a household that included his wife, a 20 year old son employed as a surveyor's clerk, and one male boarder, a coal miner, who like the manager's wife, hailed from Cardiganshire.

By 1848 Brithdir Colliery was in regular work and capable of supplying from 100 to 200 tons of coal per day. Its house coal made superior coke, highly desired in smithies and forges. The colliery closed before 1896.

George Pit (Cefn Brithdir Colliery)

The pit, known locally as *George Pit*, was officially called *Cefn Brithdir Colliery;* however, in some directories and, occasionally, in the press, it was referred to as *George Inn Pit*. According to his reminiscences (*Merthyr Express,*

43

A rare glass plate image of George Pit by keen amateur photographer William Samuel Cresswell (see page 331).

Courtesy Kay Williams

April 17 1920), postman David Edwards claimed it was one of only two collieries in the district in the 1890s. Its two shafts were started in 1873 by Rhymney Iron Company (RIC) and, working the Brithdir house-coal seam, coal was first raised in 1875. It is likely that many George Inn people worked in this local colliery, but accident reports show people from neighbouring communities also found employment there. In its earliest days, women worked on George Pit's surface screening plant. Their work involved pushing trams, and Nellie Dando of James Street recalls her mother recounting her experiences when working there.

From time to time, life in local communities was blighted by industrial action: miners disliked being idle, their womenfolk struggled to feed their families and local retailers faced cash flow problems. The following extracts from contemporary local newspapers provide the narrative of a seven week strike that affected miners at George Pit in 1879:

- *Cardiff Times*, July 5 1879: *The colliers employed at the Rhymney Iron Company's George Inn Pit brought their tools out today on strike against a reduction in wages.*

- *Western Mail*, July 16 1879: *At a meeting of thirty delegates representing the house coal colliers assembled at the Nelson Inn, Llancaiach, David Edmunds*

Miners at George Pit, Brithdir

Miners at George Pit.   Courtesy David Dodge

44

representing the men of Cefn Brithdir stated he had 230 against the reduction and now on strike; with no intention of yielding.

- *South Wales Daily News, August 12 1879: At the Cefn Brithdir Colliery the strike still exists, and the workmen, almost to a man, had succeeded in obtaining work elsewhere. A large number of them are employed by the contractors on the parish road now being made between Tirphil and Bargoed.*

George Pit in work, viewed over the roof-tops of early buildings
South Wales Coal Annual 1905, courtesy Glamorgan Archives

George Pit was not without its disasters as witnessed by this report in *Western Mail*, August 24 1888:

Hundreds of people flocked to the top of the pit on Wednesday 23rd when a dreadful disaster occurred in the pit, involving the loss of life of two workmen and endangered the safety of 200 men. David Davies (George Inn) and Benjamin Evans (Bargoed) both firemen, were engaged in examining an old level which had been stopped for years, when a rush of water burst through the heading with such force that both men were hurled away a considerable distance and killed. There were over 200 colliers in the pit at the time who with difficulty made their escape, it was stated that there was from 12 ft. to 13 ft. of water in the sump at the bottom of the shaft.

South Wales Echo, on August 24 added:

The pumping machinery was speedily set in motion, and an exploring party, consisting of Mr. William Smith (manager), Mr. Abraham (Rhymney Iron Company), Mr Evans (overman, and nephew of one of the deceased), Mr William Davies (overman of the Darran Colliery), and others were able to descend the pit. At that time at least nine men, including the two firemen, were known to be missing, but seven of these were found in a heading above the reach of the water, working away totally unconscious of what had taken place in other parts of the pit. These were sent to the surface, and then search was made for the missing firemen. The body of David Davies was quickly recovered, standing in an upright position and clinging to a post some forty yards from the spot at which the water had found egress. Beyond here, however, the exploring party could not penetrate, owing to the depth of water, and so nothing remained but to return to the bank, and

45

there wait till the pumps extracted sufficient water. This was not possible till about eleven o'clock on Thursday morning, when the body of Evans was found lying within a yard or two of the place where he was at work when the accident occurred. The body of David Davies was taken to his late residence at Brithdir Terrace, George Inn, and that of Benjamin Evans to Bargoed, where he carried out a small business as a bookseller and stationer.

Rhys J. Rhys, district coroner, held an inquest into the circumstances of the deaths at Old Mill Inn, Bargoed, on Monday, August 27, and the jury returned a verdict of *accidental death. South Wales Echo*, August 29 1888, reported that the funerals took place that afternoon, the body of Davies being taken by special train from George Inn to Rhymney for interment at Graig Chapel burial ground and that of Evans from Bargoed for burial in Tabor Welsh Congregational Chapel-yard, Maesycwmmer.

Not all Brithdir miners worked in the local pit, as shown by this report in *Cardiff Times*, July 9 1892.

FATAL ACCIDENT. — On Wednesday a man named Thomas Lewis, whilst employed as a collier in White Rose Level of the Powell Duffryn Company, was struck on the chest by a heavy stone from the top, which so materially affected him internally that shortly after arriving at his home at Brithdir he succumbed to the injuries sustained.

In 1898, South Wales miners went on strike against the Sliding Scale which regulated wages according to the selling price of coal. Further details appear on en.wikipedia.org/wiki/Welsh_coal_strike_of_1898 and in R. Page Arnot's *South Wales Miners 1898-1914*, (1967), pp 25-62. The dispute, to improve wages from 15s to 22s per week, started on April 9 and colliers, lacking resources or funds to sustain them, faced a bitter five month struggle. Headmaster Samuel Davies's entries in the local school log book shed light on the impact of the strike not only on the school but also within the community:

- April 22 1898: *The attendance this week is poor –which I attribute chiefly to the coal strike now taking place. The children are kept at home to gather coal from the rubbish tip and there is cause to believe that even now at the end of three weeks the pinch of hunger is being felt in some families. I received a note to that effect from one family this week.*

- May 9 1898: *Owing to the serious condition of the Great Coal Strike in this place and other places throughout South Wales, Soup Kitchens have been established. Scores of children are supplied with food daily at this school between 1 and 2 o'clock.*

- May 31 1898: *Several boys who are out on strike owing to the coal dispute have been admitted to school. I have done this thinking it would be better to do so, than to be mischief-making about the place.*

- June 10 1898: *The attendance this week has been pretty good - Free breakfasts have been given to the neediest of the children during the week at 08.30 every morning. The little ones seemed very thankful for our kindness.*

- July 29 1898: *The attendance this week is very poor. The prolongation of the strike, plus some children being obliged to help their parents to carry coal from the rubbish tips, while others are away picking wimberrys, are the chief causes.*

- August 29 1898: *Re-opening of the school after the Midsummer Holidays. The attendance of the children is poor. Much of it appears to be the effect [sic] of the Great Coal Strike which still continues – having already lasted about five-months.*

- September 1898: *The attendances were badly affected throughout the month with many children absent – owing to the want of shoes, boots and clothes – due to the Coal Strike.*

It is clear from the 1901 census return that most Brithdir families depended on the coal industry and so, as Samuel Davies's log entries illustrate, the 1898 action made a significant impact on the whole community. There were 315 colliery workers in Brithdir in 1901 and of those 229 were described as coal hewer, while others - mining engineer, fitter, blacksmith, plate-layer, haulier, ostler, tipper, crusher, banksman, brakeman, weigher and labourer --- were all colliery-employed. It is likely that such a lengthy dispute would have affected others, such as those working at the coke ovens and on the railway, as well as local shopkeepers.

Research to date has not uncovered any specific references to hardship in Brithdir, but it is likely that many families faced difficulties. As Samuel Davies noted, local strikers and their families risked picking coal, so essential for heating and cooking, illegally from the nearby waste heaps. Whether or not any local families resorted to the pawnbroker, or to other means of acquiring some money for essentials, is unclear, but it is likely that some Brithdir families empathised with the narrative of Rt. Hon. Sir Samuel Thomas Evans, then Liberal M.P. for Mid-Glamorgan, quoted by R. Page Arnot:

... Doleful tales are told about the manner in which the household goods have gone to the pawnbrokers. First the pictures and ornaments, then the furniture, even to the bedstead and the bedding; the plates and dishes and cups have gone one or two at a time for a few pence with which to buy bread; then they have been obliged to take away the very clothes...

Further industrial strife followed. *Evening Express*, Saturday, August 31 1901, reported *that all the workmen (some 600 men) engaged at the Rhymney Iron Company's pits (Darran, Gilfach and Cefn Brithdir) brought out their tools. The workmen had tendered a month's notice for a demand of 2s per yard for cutting bottom.* Just a stone's throw away, men working the same seam of coal at Coed y Moeth Colliery (see below), were already in receipt of the 2s per yard. The anticipated short struggle of a few weeks before a settlement would be reached, escalated and after 33 weeks, the strike in which 600 men and boys were engaged showed no sign of coming to a close. A report in *Cardiff Times*, May 3 1902, revealed:

Rents of the houses of strikers living in Gilfach had been raised, and the men were now charged 17s per ton for coal which they have hitherto had at a nominal figure. They, however, declared they will either win the fight or close the pits.

The two sides took a firm stand. RIC, not only benefiting from revenue from the coal trade, but also enjoying profits of an extensive business as grocers, drapers, brewers and general merchants, refused to grant the men's demand for 2s per yard. The miners were just as determined: a report in *Barry Dock News*, July 11 1902, shows they were intent on raising funds to support the strike:

A party of singers, composed of colliers on strike from the Gilfach, Darran and Cefn Brithdir, under the leadership of Mr. Evan Thomas [miner's agent], visited Barry Island on Monday last and gave a concert at Whitmore Bay, collections were made in aid of the strike fund. The concert party went on tour from Barry.

Cardiff Times, May 30 1903, reported on a fire, probably caused by a spark from a locomotive that could have wrought considerable damage to the idle colliery:

What might have proved a disastrous fire broke out on the screens of the Cefn Brithdir Colliery, owned by the Rhymney Iron Company, at Brithdir on Wednesday evening. The colliery, which is idle in consequence of the house coal strike, is close to the Rhymney Railway, and the fire originated from a spark from a passing engine. An employee of the company named Brown, who discovered the fire in its earliest stage, immediately summoned assistance, and the outbreak was speedily got under.

RIC Directors' report for year ending March 28 1903, confirmed that after 21 months the strike ended June 11 1903. Although it claimed a loss of 99,305 tons due to the strike at the three pits, RIC still showed a profit of £65,733. *Cardiff Times*, June 22 1903, reported that on Monday, June 15 about 50 men at each colliery (Gilfach, Darran and Cefn Brithdir) started preparing the working places for the entire returning workforce. The strikers had won this battle, but conditions in the collieries changed little, and *Evening Express*, August 12 1903, reported the three collieries were idle on August 12 owing to slackness of trade.

Although the *George* was not troubled by gas, it had its share of accidents, and the fatalities were mainly the result of a fall of roof or of a large bell-shaped stone falling from the roof, without warning, as in the following examples:

- Beneath a headline in *Western Mail*, June 30 1890, announcing *Fatal accident at George Inn Colliery* readers learned *On Friday morning one of the workmen named Philip Williams was killed at the George Inn Colliery. While at his work the poor fellow was crushed by a portion of the roof termed a "bell," which fell upon him. Deceased was an elderly man.*
- *Evening Express*, July 7 1906, reported *The fall of enormous stone from the roof of the Cefn Brithdir Pit this morning was responsible for the almost instantaneous death of Tom Lawrence aged 28, who resided at Rock Cottage, Church-street, Bargoed. It took fifteen men to heave the stone off the body. Poor Lawrence was the sole companion and only support of an aged father, and in local cricket circles was popularly dubbed "Banky,"*

by reason of his ability to rise to the occasion with bat and ball. The fatality was the first at the pit for several years.

The end of George Pit was reported in *Evening Express*, June 5 1909:

One day's notice to terminate contracts was served on Friday by the Rhymney Iron Company to all employees at the Cefn Brithdir Colliery, consequently all the men will bring out their tools to-day. It is understood that the available coal is exhausted, although it is stated that a considerable quantity is still left in a portion of the pit known as the Tirphil area. Some 200 men and boys are affected. Work will most likely be found for the majority of the workmen at this company's new pits at Pengam and Groesfaen.

Although production had ceased, pumping continued to 1910. It re-opened in 1916 to help with the war effort, but production was not started until 1919, only to close down again in January 1921. In 1920 there were 69 employed.

After closure the buildings were dismantled and the site neglected until, in 1933, work started to develop a children's playground there. The resulting ground sported a full set of rides - slide, jigger, swing-boat, roundabout, maypole, swings, see-saws and horse jiggers, as well as plenty of space for countless hours of football. As children, we did not know our playground was on the former colliery site, and until the 1970s the potential danger was not realised. Mike Bevan's placid pony *Brandy* was a village pet, ridden by many local youngsters. Elwyn Evans remembered how, in the 1970s, when leading *Brandy* across the playground, *Brandy* persistently refused to cross a particular

It is hard to believe the rural scene in this modern day photograph was once the site of Cefn Brithdir Colliery (George Pit). The football field is where the playground was situated.   Courtesy Morgan Smith (2016).

spot, repeatedly raising his front foot off the ground. Knowing the pony so well, Elwyn sensed *Brandy* was trying to warn that something was amiss. He contacted GUDC and investigators arrived who, on hammering a long steel bar into the earth, were shocked to find it drive easily into the sod by some three or four feet. On further examination, they discovered the capping of the old colliery shaft had deteriorated so much that immediate repair was essential. Thus, thanks to this loveable pony, a serious accident was averted.

Coed y Moeth Colliery, Cwmsyfiog

PD started sinking operations on this pit, on the east side of the valley, a mere stone's throw from George Pit, in the first week of January 1893. The pit, described in *South Wales Daily News*, January 7 1895, had two shafts worked by a set of separate engines. In 1896, it employed 241 men working underground and 44 on the surface, and by 1900, 378 men. A number of Brithdir residents were among Coed y Moeth Colliery's workforce.

Like Cefn Brithdir Colliery, Coed y Moeth Colliery suffered with *fall of roof* as illustrated by the following accidents:

- *South Wales Daily News*, May 28 1900, reported that, on May 25 1900, 12 year old David James Howard, of Bargoed, having only recently left school to work with his brother in the pit, died under a fall of roof at Coed y Moeth.
- *New Tredegar, Bargoed and Caerphilly Journal*, June 10 1905, reported that on June 3 1905, William Mills, 18 James Street, was badly wounded when a fall of stone from the roof struck his foot and leg.
- *Evening Express*, December 14 1906, reported that collier Arthur Williams of Charles Street, was killed by a fall of stone.

Merthyr Express, October 29 1904, reported on a sensation when, on October 24 1904, 14 year old Fred Richards, employed at Coed y Moeth Colliery, disappeared. Having left his stall, his light went out and, thinking he was heading for the bottom of the shaft, young Fred wandered into old workings, where, as he reported later, he lay down, hoping to be found the next morning.

Coed y Moeth Colliery
The washery buildings of Cefn Brithdir Colliery, can be seen top left, with the long row of Station Terrace cottages
South Wales Coal Annual 1905, courtesy Glamorgan Archives

50

This photograph, taken by A. Stevens in early 1900s, shows two working collieries, George Pit (far left on west side of Rhymney river) and Coed y Moeth Colliery (right foreground on the east side of Rhymney river).

courtesy Mike Bevan

When he failed to return home (New Row, Machen) on the workmen's train, his distraught widowed mother sought the help of neighbours. Arriving at the pit on Tuesday morning, they set out on a careful search. That band of workmen, including John Cox, Owen Davies, T. Evans, John Pane, W. Davies, T. Davies, W. Morgan and Robert Godfrey, found him, exhausted and covered with clay and mud, in the long-closed pit workings. He had been there for some 20 hours before being found and taken to the surface. Happy and excited, he went home to the great relief of his mother and seven siblings.

The mine, dogged with flooding problems throughout its short life, was abandoned in 1910. One of the shafts of this colliery was supposedly made *safe* by bricking a square wall around the opening, but many people remember lobbing stones over the wall and listening for the sound as they hit the shaft bottom.

William *Tunnel* Williams and sons

A native of Blaenavon, William Williams married Mary Richards at Govilon parish church in 1882, and the newly-weds settled in Blaenavon where six of their eight children were born. They arrived in Brithdir before the 1901 census was taken when they were living in 1 Herbert Street. Involved in contracting work on the third and final phase of house building in Brithdir, the deeds (now in possession of his great grandson Thomas Melvyn Williams) show he moved his family into 16 Milton Terrace. Later, William and Mary moved to 1 The Villas. When, aged 82, he died in Brithdir in November 1942, he was described in the local press as Brithdir's second *oldest male citizen*.

William and Mary Williams. Possibly taken to celebrate their Golden Wedding in 1932. Family photos and details courtesy Thomas Melvyn Williams and Maureen Ellis née Williams

William Williams had a sixty year career in the coal industry, starting work aged 8 (often carried to and from work on his father's back) and working until he was 68. He earned his nickname *Tunnel* from the many roadways and tunnels he dug underground in several local mines. It was reported in *Merthyr Express,* July 9 1932, that he worked in Elliot Colliery for 34 years, and he was one of the first contractors at Bargoed North Colliery, opening the seam from the shaft bottom, under the supervision of George Hann.

Son Arthur, born about 1894, a World War I casualty, is remembered on Brithdir war memorial. Son Israel, born about 1888, was well-known as overman at Elliot Colliery. I grew up knowing son Henry *Harry* Jacob as grandfather of boyhood friend, Mel, and as the well-respected councillor who represented Brithdir-Tirphil ward on GUDC for many years. It was while he was GUDCs Chairman, 1952-53, that the new wrought iron gates were installed at Bargoed Park's Wood Street entrance. Later, a bronze plaque, bearing his name and dedicated to his memory, was added to the gates, but unfortunately not in situ at the time of researching.

Son, Ivor Stanley (*Stan*), born 1903, the youngest of the eight children, became widely-known as local Mines Safety Inspector. In November 1929, aged just 26, Stan sat Home Office mining examination for second-class mine manager's certificate at City Hall, Cardiff. His family and the community were pleased to congratulate him when, early in 1930, they heard of his success. In February 1935 he topped the poll for workmen's Inspector of Mines for Pengam to Rhymney District (including Groesfaen, Elliot, Ogilvie, Bargoed and Britannia collieries). Not relevant to the coal industry per se, but interesting to note, is that Stan and his wife lived in Springfield on George Hill, a house so named because a mountain spring exited via a pipe in the garden wall, giving villagers water in time of drought or when the *moving mountain* above Tirphil and Troedrhiwfuwch damaged the water main supply.

Cyril Samuel Harris

Born in Lower Stanley, Elliots Town, Cyril Samuel Harris was son of coal miner Charles Edward Harris, and, like many of his contemporaries, he began his working life underground aged 12. As his army records have not survived, little is known of his years as Private in Machine Gun Corps during World War I. When the war ended he returned to the pit, still with his earnest desire to do his best not only in his work but also for the mining community and the village of Brithdir. He continued his links with New Tredegar Rescue Station, often leading from the front in rescue

53

operations. During his last twenty working years (after Stan Williams retired) he was workmen's Inspector of Mines. Having passed mine manager's examination, he was often stand-in for an absent manager, and earned the respect of management and workmen alike, especially as his concern for safety in mines was always paramount. Outside work, Cyril gave much time to local St. John Ambulance Brigade, and he helped raise funds for wheelchairs so that injured miners could enjoy events such as the annual Bargoed Show, and, as secretary, he worked tirelessly for Rhymney Valley Hospital Television Fund.

As can be seen in the report, *Western Daily Press,* October 31 1934, of an incident at Taff Merthyr Colliery; Cyril Harris and his team put themselves in danger to save others.

Photographs and details courtesy Cyril's daughter, Ceinwen Bevan, née Harris.

GASSED IN OLD MINE WORKING.

Mystery of Under-Manager's Death.

A verdict of "Death by misadventure" was returned at a Nelson (Glamorgan) inquest, yesterday, on Major J. R. Gibbons (49), of Trelewis, under-manager of the Taff Merthyr Colliery, whose body was found in an old working of the colliery after he had been missing for 15 hours.

Cyril Harris, captain of the new Tredegar rescue brigade, said that they had to put on gas helmets to recover the body.

Mr David Hughes, manager of the colliery, said Major Gibbon's lamp might have gone out, and in trying to find his way back to the bottom of the pit he must have lost his way.

It was stated that the cause of death was methane or marsh gas poisoning.

The coroner (Mr R. J. Rhy) said they could only guess what Major Gibbons was doing in the old workings. How he met his death would remain a mystery.

New Tredegar Rescue Brigade with C.M. Kitto superintendent, the suited gentleman far left. His team captain, Cyril Harris, is standing right of back row.

Courtesy Paul Waites collection.

Life of coal miner's family (prior to 1939)

Life was difficult for the families of Brithdir colliers at the best of times. During strikes it was worse. The men, cut adrift from their usual routine, may have occupied themselves by seeking other work to supplement the meagre strike pay, growing food for their family in the garden or allotment or trying to better themselves by reading newspapers and attending classes at the local Workmen's Institute. However in the homes a different story unfolded for their womenfolk. The daily grind of cooking, housecleaning, laundry and mending (patching and darning) became more difficult with a constant struggle to survive on the few shillings strike pay. While men were the bread winners, their womenfolk kept family and home together as best they could, and it was on their efforts that the family was judged in the eyes of society.

Spare a thought for a local family -- that of coal hewer Caleb Green, enumerated in 17 James Street in 1901. While it is not clear where he worked, it is likely that he and his family were affected during local strikes and by news of accidents to fellow miners. Born in Treorchy in the early 1860s, he had moved his family to Rhymney Valley in late 1880s, presumably in the expectation that his mining experience was

In Loving Memory
OF THE
MEN killed in the Disastrous EXPLOSION at BARGOED,
On Friday, October 29th, 1909.

NAMES OF MEN KILLED IN BLAST.

Dd. Edwards, married, Deri	James Weeks, Deri
Joe Vincent, Brithdir	John Morgan, Deri
John Tovey, Deri	David Jenkins, Bargoed
Henry Edwards, Deri	Chas. Vaughan, married, Deri
Dan M'Carthy, married, Deri	Daniel Cleary, married, Deri
Wm. Barker, married, Deri	Wm. Davies, married, Deri
Mor. Coombes, married, Deri	John Baregwenith, mar., Deri
Amb. Jones, married, Deri	John John, married, Deri
Ernest Roberts, Deri	Evan Prosser, Fochriw
Lewis Morgan, Bargoed	Wm. Brown, married, Deri
John Evans, Deri	

RESCUERS WHO DIED.

W. Bowen, married, Bargoed	Wm. Edwards, Groeswen Hse
G. Griffiths, married, Bargoed	Ex-councillor David Lewis,
D Morgan, mar., Fleur-de-lis.	married, Gilfach

Not gone from memory, not gone from love,
But gone to their Father's home above.

sufficient to secure steady employment there. With ten children, aged from 16 years down to just four months when the 1901 census was taken, his wife Sarah, probably helped by the older daughters, had to feed and clothe the large

The clean faces of this group suggest they were captured at the start of their shift at what appears to be White Rose Level, New Tredegar; photograph courtesy Mavis Mahoney. White Rose Level was opened in 1850, owned by Thomas Powell in the 1860s, and still mining coal and clay in 1896.

family and, especially in the winter, keep the house warm, and pray they kept safe from diseases such as smallpox and diphtheria. By the time the 1911 census was taken, the family, extended by the births of three more sons, had moved to 5 Salisbury Terrace, and Caleb Green was a haulier underground, while his sons of working age were colliers. The family, like most of their neighbours, lived with the ever present fear of pit accidents and death or severe injury. News of the sad fate of Joe Vincent, 18 year old collier of 6 Bute Terrace, amongst the 27 killed in the blast at Darran Pit on Friday, October 29 1909, would have highlighted the ever-present danger.

Coal mining memories

Named after George Elliot, PD's Elliot Colliery, one of Rhymney Valley's first modern *super pits,* was workplace of many Brithdir men. When I was young, after World War II, I remember colliers, then working for National Coal Board (NCB) walking along the back lane behind my grandmother's home in Wellington Terrace, going to work, or returning home in dust laden clothes and with their allocation of firewood tucked under one arm. This was the usual route for some Elliot Colliery miners, but others, particularly those living in Wellington, Tennyson, Milton and Nelson Terraces, went via the steps at the end of Nelson Terrace to the back lane, alongside the railway track and perimeter fence of Elliot Colliery, to the pit-head. It was an era of black faces and dust-filled lungs, when *black diamonds* were won by hard labour in dimly lit stalls and roadways deep below ground. It was heavy work in dusty, humid atmospheres and wet places, with the constant threat of roof collapse or explosion.

Pit head baths were officially opened at Elliot Colliery April 12 1947, and *Merthyr Express*, April 12 1947, reported they were to be first used by the day-shift on Monday, 14. What a difference that made, not only to the miners, but also to their womenfolk who had prepared the hot water for post-shift baths in front of kitchen fires. When, in 1967, Elliot Colliery closed, its workforce transferred to other collieries and some continued there until closures – Groesfaen (1968), Ogilvie (1975), Bargoed (1977) and Britannia (1983).

A sketch by John (*Jack*) Jones showing Elliot Colliery and Washery, and the back lane, the route the colliers used as they walked to and from work.

Post-1948 view of Elliot Colliery, photographed from the lower slopes of Cefn Brithdir.
Courtesy Paul Waites collection.

The snuff box - a relic of a time when the village was named George Inn - belonged to Josiah Jenkins. Born in Cwmsyfiog, Josiah was a young boy when the family moved to George Inn.
Courtesy grandson Ray Denham.

The Miners' Safety Lamp No 16 was used daily at Elliot Colliery by Tom Watkins
He had the opportunity to buy it when he retired and later it was passed to me.

Denis Rawle at the end of a shift at Taff Merthyr Colliery.
Courtesy Margaret Price, née Rawle.

Ron Edwards pictured at Bargoed Colliery pay office. He started as a 14 year old at Elliot Colliery, and later transferred to Bargoed Colliery.
Courtesy Geraldine Cook and permission of son Ronnie Edwards.

The Washery Boys 1949, back row L-R Tom Saunders, Johnny Morgan, Jack Williams*, Dennis Lancett, Elwyn Richards and Tom Perry*. Front row; Bill Shutte, Phil Davies* and Dai Griffiths*.

Hard work but happy days. L-R Back row: unknown, Dai Williams*, Harry Mundy, Tom Saunders, Vic Price, Elwyn Richards and John Morgan. Front row; Bill Lewis, Elwin Evans, Bill Thomas, Dai Griffiths*, Phil Davies*, loco driver Jack Harold*, and Alan Butler.

Those marked* are from Brithdir. Both photographs courtesy Henrietta Jones, names Phil Davies.

CHAPTER 5 TRANSPORT AND COMMUNICATIONS

Ridgetop tracks and farm lanes, as shown on the parish tithe map, had served the community for generations but as they proved grossly inadequate for the emerging industrial society, railways and new roads were built nearer the valley floor from the mid-nineteenth century onwards.

Railways

For about a century both goods and passengers enjoyed a rail service that some may envy at the present day. Terry McCarthy's map (*Gelligaer* Volume 21 Great War Edition 2014, page 148) shows the local railway lines and stations that not only linked the area to Newport and Cardiff but also, in their heyday, connected it to the national rail network and offered comparatively easy access to other British industrial and business regions as well as to seaside resorts and places of interest and recreation.

Rumney Tramroad (later known as *Old Rumney*), incorporated as a tram road May 20 1825, opened with horse traction in 1826 from Rhymney Ironwork's at Abertysswg, and ran on the Monmouthshire side of the river giving access to Newport, In 1836 it became the Rumney Railway (not to be confused with the later Rhymney Railway (RR)). It was purchased by Brecon and Merthyr Tydfil Junction Railway Company (B&MR) in 1863. As George Pit had opened in 1843, it is likely its coal was taken across the valley, possibly on the tramroad marked on Brithdir Estate plan of 1858, to this line.

RR line running on the west (Glamorganshire) side of the river and linking Rhymney to Cardiff, was cut through the land of local farms bordering the river. There is further information on RR in R. W. Kidner's *The Rhymney Railway* (Oxford, 1995). The line was formally opened to freight traffic on February 25 1858, and, according to the local press, the opening was a spectacular event. Two trains (one taking iron, 24 trucks laden with 150 tons of RIC's iron, and one with coal, 40 mineral wagons containing 240 tons coal from Thomas Joseph's colliery at Craig Rhymney), decorated with flags and evergreens, travelled from Rhymney to the terminus at East Bute Dock. The line was opened to passengers on March 31 1858.

Train *timetables* appeared in various local newspapers and those published in *Monmouthshire Merlin*, April 1858, show that initially there were two trains a day, weekdays and Sundays, but it soon increased to three on weekdays, as shown in *Cardiff and Merthyr Guardian, Glamorgan, Monmouth and Brecon Gazette*, May 8 1858. However, for over a decade George Inn residents did not have a station in their community, until, as reported in *Cardiff Times*, April 8 1871,

Public Notices.

RHYMNEY   RAILWAY.

GEORGE INN STATION.

On and after October 1st 1891, the NAME of ABOVE STATION WILL BE CHANGED to BRITHDIR.

CORS. LUNDIE, Manager.
Manager's Office, Cardiff, Sept. 10th, 1891.   5263

George Inn Station (called Brithdir Station from October 1 1891) opened.

A report in *Western Mail*, October 26 1893, noted builder Thomas Davies of Pontlottyn listed *the erection of the Brithdir Railway Station* as one of the contracts he blamed for his insolvency.

Brithdir Station (early 20th century). The sign in the apex reads Van Houten's Cocoa, while the other signs advertise Bovril and Bass beers.

For decades, the station was a traveller's first and last impression of the village, and the station master, an important figure in the local community, ensured the station was run efficiently to offer the full range of services for passengers and goods. He also, as witnessed by the memories of Allan Rogers, took pride in the cleanliness and attractiveness of the station, including frequently tending a station garden. The following information on local station masters is based on census returns, trade directories and reports in local newspapers.

William Greenhouse, a native of Llandrindod Wells, was living in Merchant Street, Pontlottyn when appointed first station master at George Inn Station. It is not clear when he left, but, by 1880, he was in charge at Pontlottyn Station. He was replaced by Thomas Probert (a widower) and, on his transfer to Deri, John Rees became George Inn's next stationmaster. When the 1881 census was taken, Thomas Probert and John Rees were near neighbours in George Inn village. The station name changed in 1891, and Lewis Edwards was both last station master of George Inn Station and first of Brithdir Station He witnessed the exchange of the *passengers fares information boards*, and readers may be interested to know that the George Inn Station board and the first Brithdir Station board (large boards, each about 6' by 4'), are now in The National Archives. It is not clear when Lewis Edwards left Brithdir, but Joseph Thomas, stationmaster in Deri, was transferred to Brithdir in 1909 before, just weeks later, a further transfer to Ystrad Mynach. As the account of the achievements of his son (Morgan Joseph Thomas MBE on page 335) shows, he returned to Brithdir later, and was probably stationmaster from about 1916 to 1923. In the meantime, Samuel Morgan and John Thomas were stationmasters: the former was chief clerk at Llanbradach before being promoted to fill the vacancy at Brithdir, and while at Brithdir he lived at 2 The Villas, but research to date has shed little light on the identity of the latter who was listed in a 1914 trade directory. The first post-amalgamation stationmaster was E. James Rees who remained in Brithdir until moving to take charge at Tirphil Station at the beginning of 1934. He was replaced by Thomas Williams, formerly station master at Pant, Dowlais, who was followed by A. Pritchard (research has not uncovered any information apart from his name). As mentioned on page 236, the first two to take charge of the station post-war had seen war service: James Lock followed Pritchard as stationmaster before, in 1949, W.R. Westhead (from Llanbradach) took charge as clerk not as stationmaster. In the 1950s, Ianto Evans of Bargoed was Brithdir's stationmaster, and Frank James was booking clerk.

The only person identified in this photograph of porters, c.1920, is David Maxey, left back row.
Courtesy Morfydd Olsen née Maxey

The stationmasters worked with a team of station staff, and local railway companies also employed a sizeable workforce to maintain the line and operate the trains. Both RR and B&MR railway lines were near Brithdir, and successive census returns captured some workers possibly employed by these companies, or perhaps on colliery company lines, as, for example in 1901 census returns, Ernest Arthur Moss described as *foreman platelayer on railway*, his brother John *platelayer on railway*, Septimus Price *foreman platelayer on railway* and his son Frederick *railway porter*, James Price *platelayer on railway*, James Lewis (son of Thomas Lewis, Brithdir Ganol) *booking clerk in railway station*, Frederick Lewis and William Wood *platelayers on railway*.

The following serve as examples of some railway employees captured in memories or on photographs.

Many Brithdir people remember Jack Harold and Ron Goodwin, well-known and popular loco-drivers in the 1950s. Growing up in an age less obsessed than the present with health and safety issues, my friends and I enjoyed the rides on the foot-plate with Jack Harold.

Phillip Lewis Willetts, (shown right courtesy Idwal Morgan Kavanagh) resident signalman, Brithdir South signal box, was well-known in Brithdir as one of the stalwarts on the

Workmen's Institute committee during its heyday.

Amongst the first with the Expeditionary Force in France, George Young (shown left), Lance Corporal in King's Shropshire Light Infantry, was killed in action October 23 1914 at the battle of the Aisne. Prior to enlisting for the army, he had been a porter at Brithdir railway station, and very popular within the community. In 1911, George, aged 15, and fellow railway porter 19 year old Charles Beck, both natives of Herefordshire were boarders in the household of William and Jane Moore, 22 Herbert Street.

Prior to joining Grenadier Guards in April 1914 James George Christmas Harding (shown right) was employed at Brithdir Station. Private Harding was killed by a shell on July 7 1917, and buried at Canada Farm Cemetery, Belgium. His name is remembered on the Tirphil war memorial and one to parishioners of St. Mary's and Christchurch in St. Mary's parish church, Abergavenny. He was son of Mrs. Beet, stepson of Sgt. Major Beet, of Somerset Inn, Abergavenny, and nephew of William Evans, Pleasant View, Tirphil. For more details about Harding and his family, see *Gelligaer* volume 23 pp 98-102.

In the large area of shunting sidings near the railway station, coal trucks were formed into trains ready for the railway company locos to transfer them to the docks. The following four photographs are of the little workhorses of the day:

No 14 on buffer-line adjacent to Workmen's Institute, with goods shed in distance behind signal. There were 7 roads in the sidings: road 1 for incoming goods for colliery, pit props and empty wagons; roads 2-6 for outgoing traffic and shunting purposes. A further road (7) was used by Cambrian Wagon Inspection and Repair workshop. Any faulty loaded coal wagon was identified with a red-stop label, and shunted into road 7. (Origin unknown.)

These two photographs, courtesy Ivor Lewis, are proudly displayed on his living room wall. His grandfather, Tom Barrett, is centre of the three men and left of the two men, c.1897.

NCB 7754 (purchased by NCB from BR — the locomotive is preserved on Llangollen Railway) at the weigh bridge on loop line behind main down-line platform. All coal trucks coming from Elliot Colliery went over it, to be weighed and labelled for destination.
The roadway in the background linked Brithdir and Cwmsyfiog.
©Ben Brooksbank-CCL

Railway Accident

On Tuesday, May 10 1904, a train accident occurred near Brithdir South signal-box, adjacent to George Pit. As reported by *Cardiff Times*, some wagons of a heavy train of coal from PD Colliery's sidings was on the main line when a down mineral train, also heavily laden, crashed into the trucks. The mineral train's engine overturned on impact, completely blocking up and down lines, and piling up rolling stock two or three wagons high. The contents of four wagons were discharged over the bank into Rhymney river. Driver W. Marks and his fireman on the down main line train, had a miraculous escape, as, anticipating the collision, they jumped off their engine about 50 yards from the point of impact. A dozen wagons were damaged, including four smashed into splinters. The engine was damaged, its funnel and dome cover hurled some distance and the main bearings broken. Traffic was blocked, and, throughout the day, passengers alighted on either side of the obstruction and walked about

Courtesy Elizabeth Jones

63

300 yards to join waiting trains to resume their journey. Mineral traffic north of this point was entirely suspended.

Well Done, Boys – headline in *Merthyr Express*, November 2 1928

Two Brithdir lads – Willie Price John and Raymond Webb – enjoying half-term holiday from school, went to River Field to check if it was likely to be fit for their football match on Saturday, little knowing that they were about to avert a possible railway tragedy. On hearing a rumbling noise up on the railway, they ran up the bank and found a large portion of the upper bank had slipped down on to the railway line (B&M section of GWR) completely blocking the rails. Without hesitation, they ran to tell the porter at Cwmsyfiog Station, who, in turn, phoned the signalman in the nearest box. As the Newport train was just coming into sight, the signalman was able to stop it in time. Rail traffic was held up for several hours while breakdown gangs worked to clear the track. Although passengers, including colliers returning from work, were delayed, they were grateful as the boys' prompt action probably prevented an accident, saving injuries, and perhaps lives. Both Willie and Raymond were very proud because, as reported in the press, someone *official* shook hands with them, and took their names and addresses. A few weeks later, the newspaper reported that the two boys were invited to divisional headquarters at Pontypool, where, on Saturday, December 1, they were each presented with a ten-shilling note, box of chocolates and a bound volume of *The King of Railway Locomotives*.

The U shaped field centre of photograph, (courtesy Keith Jones and credited to S.Rickard/J&J Collection), is River Field, lying (as its name suggests) close to the river, and also between the two railway lines – former B&MR line to Newport on right (east bank of river), and, on left (west bank of river), former RR Rhymney to Cardiff line with Bute Terrace cottages above.

On Thursday, February 21 1929, the two boys and about 60 fellow pupils of Brithdir Boys' School as well as headmaster Henry Judd and teachers Tommy Davies, E Evans and Frank West, were guests at GWR Works Swindon. Setting off at 8.30 a.m., they travelled by ordinary train to Newport where they boarded reserved corridor carriages. On arriving at the Works, the boys and their teachers enjoyed a guided tour, seeing carriages in various stages from the tree trunk to the luxurious saloons and new sleeping carriages with two storeys. They were especially interested in work in the engine shed, seeing processes from casting the small parts to the finished engines, but the highlight of the visit was the opportunity to

mount the footplate and examine *King Edward V11*, one of the large "King" class steam engines.

Although the inter-war era was a difficult period, teachers and parents made every effort to ensure that local children were offered opportunities to broaden their horizons, as illustrated by the following school educational visits reported in the local press. At 10 a.m. on July 18 1930, boys, accompanied by headmaster Henry Judd, teachers Tommy Davies and Frank West (then also *Merthyr Express* correspondent for the village) and some parents, left Brithdir, on what, to that date, was probably the longest train to have steamed out of that station. They visited London, seeing the sights and spending two hours at National Zoological Gardens. Entries in the school log refer to further visits in subsequent years: in July 1931, they visited Windsor Castle and took a river steamer to the site where Magna Carta was signed, and, in June 1932, 45 boys and 25 adults visited Liverpool docks and the liner *Duchess of Atholl*. When in July 1933, Frank West reported on the fifth annual school visit -- to Bristol Zoological Gardens – he noted *this school was the first in the valley to be granted an educational trip. They have visited Swindon and saw the making of engines; to London and saw some of the most important buildings in the world; Windsor, and on a big liner – the Duchess of Atholl.*

Rail users from Cwmsyfiog

As noted in chapter 7 school log book entries shed light on community issues including those relating to the importance of the bridge (presumably for passengers rather than vehicular traffic) crossing the river between Cwmsyfiog and Brithdir. The bridge was damaged in August 1884 and taken down in October 1890. The destruction of the bridge became a concern for parents and for Cwmsyfiog inhabitants in general, especially those who wanted to use Brithdir railway station, as recorded in *Merthyr Express*, July 2 1910:

> *Cwmsyfiog to Brithdir – Proposed bridge across the valley*
> *At the meeting of the Bedwellty District Council on Monday a deputation consisting of Mr. J. Morgan, and three other residents of Cwmsyfiog, submitted a resolution, passed at a public meeting recently held at Cwmsyfiog to ask the Council to consider the necessity of erecting a footbridge between Brithdir and Cwmsyfiog. Mr. J. Morgan said that the inhabitants at Cwmsyfiog suffered very much by reason of the absence of more direct access to Brithdir, the present road taking them to the extreme southern end of the village over a very lonely way. There had been several instances of persons being waylaid and numbers were afraid to pass that way at night. It was also a lengthy journey and the Brithdir railway station was being used by an increasing number of people. Numbers of children went daily to the secondary schools down the valley and had to return at evening time, and moreover the matter of saving time was one of growing importance.*

As a direct result of the meeting, Bedwellty UDC wrote to GUDC in August 1910 suggesting a proposed joint venture in the erection of a foot bridge between Cwmsyfiog and Brithdir. Plainly no action was taken as GUDC minutes show a similar request was made in December 1913.

Memories of Brithdir Railway Station in the 1950s

Thanks to Allan Rogers (shown here with his mother, Florence, and step-father, Frank James, booking clerk, Brithdir Station) and his wife June, for the following memories of working life at Brithdir Railway Station in the 1950s and a description of his role as number taker.

In the 1950s Brithdir station was manned by station master, Ianto Evans from Bargoed, Frank James, booking clerk, two porters, Dai Morgan and Roy Williams, number-taker, Lawrence Rogers (until 1954) and then Allan Rogers (1954 to 1956), and two resident signalmen, Phil Willetts and Trevor Thomas.

The station was very busy six days a week. The station office was a stone building on the up platform and comprised a waiting room with ladies' toilet,

booking and parcel offices. The gent's toilet was a separate building, just before the platform bridge. The down platform also had a waiting room. In the winter the waiting rooms always looked cosy with coal fires.

At night, the station was lit by gas lamps which gave it an atmospheric ambience (shown left courtesy Sheila Hutchinson-Berney Arms Past and Present) *and all signals were lit by oil lamps which were changed every Monday morning.*

In the 1950s, trains ran hourly (in each direction) until 6 p.m., then every two hours until 10 p.m.. In addition, the school train in the morning at 8.40 to Bargoed, Pengam and Hengoed (followed by the 9 o'clock) and at 2.40 in the afternoon (followed by 3 p.m.) train. The 2.40 on a Saturday was always busy with people and teenagers going to Bargoed for the first showing of films at any of the three cinemas.

At practically every station one could get full information about any sort of journey, complicated or otherwise, and purchase a travel ticket for any destination in the country.

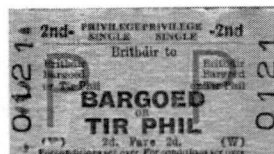

Courtesy Mike-womble22 ebay

The main goods train, called the D4, came up after the 1 o'clock train and brought either empty wagons for Elliot Colliery, or wagons loaded with pit props from St. Fagans. It went up to East View and back over the down line in order to be able to back into Road 1 of the colliery sidings where there were six-roads in total. A great deal of shunting followed on the other five roads before a train left with its load of coal trucks after the 3 p.m. train.

Once a month a special train of engine, single truck of coal and guards-van delivered a load of coal to the station, which the porters and I unloaded and stacked in the coal shed, next to the gent's toilet. The morning shift porter lit the fires which were fed by all from an ever-full coal bucket. If the coal was running low and a delivery was not due in time, the engine driver or fireman of the D4 would throw us a few lumps from the engine to keep us going.

Brithdir Station, looking north east, 1965.
Courtesy Ben Brooksbank

The main part of the number-taker's job was taking down all the wagon numbers full of coal from Elliot Colliery that came down the colliery line to pass over the weighbridge situated almost behind the down platform waiting room (see picture left) *and also taking the numbers of the wagons of coal that were in the broad sidings. Each wagon was labelled with its destination, and NCB was charged by British Rail for the tonnage, and most wagons were loaded by 1-ton weight. There were also those wagons destined for Newport Docks that went via the Cwmsyfiog line which meant going to another weighbridge to record their numbers. All the numbers were given to the booking clerk on a daily basis for charges detailed and sent to NCB for payment. My other duties included cleaning and changing the signal lamps, there was a shed at the bottom of the down platform for cleaning the lamps - there were 8 signals to maintain between Bute Terrace and the end of Nelson Terrace.*

The station garden was an important feature of many stations in more leisured times when there was sufficient manpower to tend them. Railway station staff took great pride in their waiting rooms and spent hours tending their little gardens on the station platforms, cultivating flowers and even vegetables while waiting for the down or the up train to arrive. In 1955, Ianto Evans, station master, and myself made a little garden on a piece of ground near the steps of the bridge on the up side platform which won second prize one year in the competition for the best railway station garden in the valleys.

Although competition from motor vehicles, lorries, buses and especially cars, threatened the railway in the twentieth century, the line of the former RR was not a victim of Beeching cuts in the 1960s. It continues to operate to the present, and Brithdir railway station still serves the local community with trains running hourly in both directions, north to Rhymney and south (via Cardiff) to Penarth.

Roads

Better road links nearer the collieries and communities alongside the river were also essential, and there were significant developments in the decades preceding the outbreak of war in 1914. Gelligaer District Highway Board's advertisement in *South Wales Daily News*, June 3 1879, invited tenders *for the CONSTRUCTION of a NEW ROAD from a point at the north end of Tirphil Village to a point on the fence wall at the north end of George Inn Village* and from there *to a point near Groesfaen Bridge.* By August, as noted in the chapter on coal, some local strikers were working on this part of the parish road. When the 1901 and 1911 censuses were taken, William Lewis (formerly farmer at Cefn y Brithdir, but in 1901 living in Cefn Bryn and in 1911 at East View) was described as a *road contractor* and may well have been involved in local road projects. George Coombs, a colliery stoker when the 1901 census was taken, was a *roadman* (in the employ of urban district council, presumably GUDC) a decade later.

Road transport became increasingly important as the twentieth century progressed. Since the 1920s, Brithdir has been served by council-operated and/or privately-run bus services, taking local people to work, shopping or on pleasure trips to neighbouring communities. The increase in private cars from the 1960s onwards affected passenger numbers and now the service balances on a fine line between what is affordable and what is considered necessary to the community. While bus services use the route through Brithdir via Coedcae to Tirphil, many vehicles, both cars and heavy goods vehicles travelling between Bargoed and Pontlottyn, bypass these communities and use A469 via Pleasant View or the road on the east side of the valley linking Aberbargoed to New Tredegar.

The growth in numbers of both domestic cars and commercial vehicles of all sizes has been phenomenal in recent decades, and Brithdir, in common with most other places originating in the pre-motor era, has found it difficult to adapt. In some cases, local car owners have built garages on gardens where earlier residents grew vegetables to feed their families, but many rely on on-street parking, a growing problem given the narrow streets, especially when households have two or more cars. Not only are the streets narrow, some of them are also steep, and that causes problems particularly during adverse weather conditions.

General Post Office

From its establishment in the second half of the seventeenth century to dissolution in 1969, General Post Office (GPO) was responsible for mail and, from the later nineteenth century, for telephones.

In October 1891, a wall letter box was erected at Brithdir Railway Station, and, about six months later, a post office opened at Station Terrace, the start of the 116 year history of Brithdir post office. Martin Luther Thomas was sub-postmaster until 1896 when coal miner, Walter Price, 1 School Street, became sub-postmaster and daughter, Margaret, was post office clerk. Walter Price, resigned charge of the post office in 1906, and Mrs. E. James, 1 Bristol Terrace, took his place. While a report on postal charges in the contemporary local press noted *it is rumoured that both telegraph and telephone will immediately be installed at the above address, and this, if true, will prove a great boon indeed to the inhabitants, who have at present to journey to Bargoed or New Tredegar to wire or phone messages*, there does not seem any evidence for such installation. Whether or not she was unduly negligent when, according to the local press, in 1908, a school girl stole a two-shilling piece from the money drawer whilst Mrs. James the postmistress, was in the kitchen, collier Charles Young of 1 Charles Street was sub-postmaster, with his wife Frances as sub-postmistress, by the time the 1911 census was taken.

According to GUDC minutes September 1919, *W.F. Hares, Post Office, Brithdir, submitted an application for a licence to sell confectionery, tobacco and stationery.* As the 1911 census return shows William Hares, carpenter, and his wife Margaret, general dealer, living in 11 Herbert Street, it is likely the post office moved there sometime between 1911 and 1919. An April 1923 entry in GUDC minutes refers to Mrs. Place *Old Post Office*, 9 Herbert Street. Maggie Place's was a front room shop where we, as youngsters, bought comics and fireworks in the 1950s. The entry in the council minutes goes a long way to explain why Maggie served behind a counter with a metal security grill -- likely a relic from the shop's post office days.

Mrs. Winifred Flo Harris was listed *post-office and stationer* in a 1926 trade directory, but both her address and the length of her service are uncertain. The next reference to the local post office in sources studied to date, M*erthyr Express,* May 9 1941, reveals *George Gwynne of Charles Street, having resigned the position of postmaster at Brithdir, the post office now moves to James Street where it will be in the charge of Edward and Mary Clarke.* The Clarke family ran the post office until they left for London about 1961. After that, John Kelk (who brought his family from Bargoed) followed by Mrs. Greenaway (from Aberbargoed, with her son and mother, Mrs. Baker) took charge of the James Street post office. While Bryn Edwards was in charge, he and the post office moved to 5 Bristol Terrace, where he was succeeded by Billy Gibbs. Finally, Nathan Williams and girlfriend Rachel ran the post office until, part of a round of sweeping cuts across the country, the small village post office at 5 Bristol Terrace was closed February 27 2008, This was not just the closing of a 116 year chapter, nor even the end of a convenient way of life, but the loss of a life line, impacting harshly on the community, especially its older and/or disabled residents.

It is not clear when Brithdir's public telephone box, sited at the end of Co-op House garden was put there, but I remember it in the 1950s. Since then, and especially from the 1960s, many families had a telephone installed in their homes, giving them quick and easy opportunities to keep in touch not only with family and friends locally, nationally and internationally, but also local businesses and the emergency services. By the time of writing, such terrestrial lines are less important as many people rely on increasingly-sophisticated mobile phones, not only for telephone calls, but also to make quick contacts via text messaging and emailing as well as online social media. If this book is still being read in ten years' time, such devices may themselves sound old-fashioned, such is the pace of technological progress affecting Brithdir as well as the rest of the world.

Television

For Brithdir people, like those in other communities across the country, the grainy, grey television images of the colourful coronation ceremony on that damp June day in 1953 probably did little to enthral them. However, a decade or so later, many families were proud to have a television set, first black and white, and before the end of the 1960s, maybe colour, taking pride of place in their homes. So much has changed since those early days, and today's non-stop and on-demand viewing on a range of devices, provides not only entertainment and education, but also 24/7 world-wide news, so placing Brithdir people at the heart of world events.

Left: Sandra Maggs aged 10 standing in Salisbury Terrace c.1955

Courtesy Ken Maggs

Below: Salisbury Terrace 2017 with lights and all the conveniences of modern living - cars, bins, TV satellite dishes.   Courtesy Denis Dunn

CHAPTER 6 CHURCHES AND CHAPELS

Introduction

There is evidence of human settlement on the open moorland since early times, but perhaps the earliest indication of spiritual life in the area is the Tegernacus Stone, an inscribed tombstone, dating from c. AD 600, formerly sited alongside a trackway on Cefn Brithdir, but, since 1923, housed in the National Museum Wales. Its Latin inscription reads *TEGERNACVS FILIVS MARTI HIC IACIT* (Tegernacus, son of Martius, lies here). Whilst in situ, the Tegernacus Stone attracted the interest of many scholars including Rev. John Jenkins, Hengoed Chapel, who, in 1817, recorded the Latin inscription.

For many centuries, local people living west of river Rhymney worshipped in Gelligaer parish church (St. Catwg's) or in the chapel of ease, Capel y Brithdir, high on the moorland above the village, while their neighbours to east of the river worshipped in St. Sannan's, Bedwellty parish church. After the sixteenth century Protestant Reformation, local Welsh-speaking people may not have understood the English services any more than the Latin Roman Catholic services they replaced, and it is not clear how many of them could read the Welsh bible (published 1588).

By the second half of the nineteenth century, nonconformity had taken hold across many communities in Wales and England, and incoming nonconformists built three chapels in the new Brithdir village. In a belated response to the changing demands of the new industrial society, the Anglicans divided the large Gelligaer parish. Brithdir lay within the new parish of Pontlottyn, created in 1870. A new parish, Bargoed with Deri and Brithdir, was created in 1904 and parish boundaries were redrawn in 1916 when Deri became part of the parish of Fochriw (a parish created in 1907 and where Deri remained until the 1970s). Since the 1970s, local Anglicans have been part of the parish of Bargoed and Deri with Brithdir.

Roman Catholic

For some 1,000 years prior to Henry VIII's Protestant Reformation, local people sought spiritual satisfaction from the Roman Catholic Church's Latin services conducted by the parish priest. There may have been some pro-Catholic sympathisers locally in the following three centuries. With an influx of Irish labourers in the later nineteenth century, the first post-Reformation Catholic Church in the Rhymney Valley was set up by Father Frederick Dent, at St. John's Rhymney (as noted in St. *Peter's Parish - A Brief History* www.pontypriddrcdeanery.org.uk). However, as the local Catholic congregation grew, it needed a place for worship further down the valley and, on February 2 1903, St. Peter's Roman Catholic Church was officially opened

71

on a site near Bute Terrace. The corrugated iron structure, paid for by Catholic miners giving up two days' pay, was erected on a site, granted free of charge, on the Bute estate, adjacent to Ty Coch. Registered for solemnising marriages on June 12 1908, it served local Catholics for over a decade, until they purchased a former nonconformist chapel in Bargoed's Usk Road. In October 1915 Father Frederick Dent suggested GUDC purchase the disused iron building for use as a smallpox hospital. GUDC officers rejected it as the surveyor's report of November 1915 revealed not only the poor condition of the building but also that its position, just 50 feet from inhabited dwellings, rendered it unsuitable for use as a smallpox hospital. It is not clear how the building was used until, in the early 1930s, it became British Legion headquarters.

Capel y Brithdir

Reputedly built by Goronwy ap Vlaidd in 1553, alongside the ridge road atop Cefn Brithdir, it is clearly marked, as *Brethder* on Speed's map of 1610.

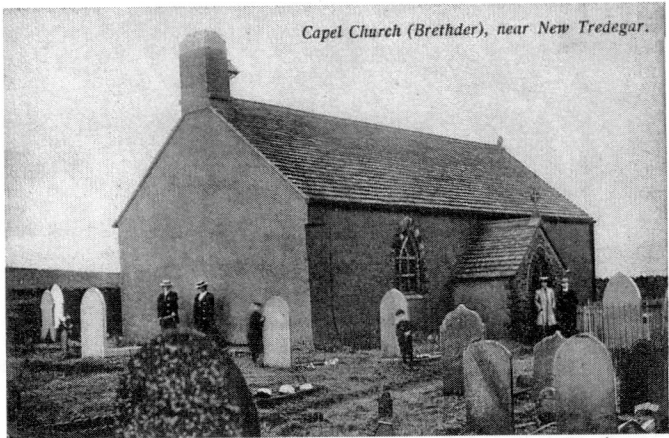

Capel Church (Brethder), near New Tredegar.

The small church was destroyed by fire in February 1952. Today the site is marked by a

An early postcard, published by Maurice Jones, New Tredegar.
Both photographs courtesy Charles and Irene Williams

raised stone plinth beneath a replica of the inscribed Celtic cross once embedded in the Capel wall (the original is in St. Gwladys Church). Around this, and within the old stone wall boundary, are the gravestones, etched with the names of many former local people. Few stones stand erect, and most are all but hidden by mountain grasses, moss and brambles.

Prior to industrialization, generations of Brithdir hamlet's sparse population -- farmers and craftsmen, together with their families and servants -- worshipped in this mountain top chapel of ease and buried their dead in its graveyard. *Gelligaer* XVI carries a transcript of a 1734-35 document (National Library of Wales LL/CC/G/758) that mentions a recent restoration as well as the parishioners' right to provide their seating. During the nineteenth century,

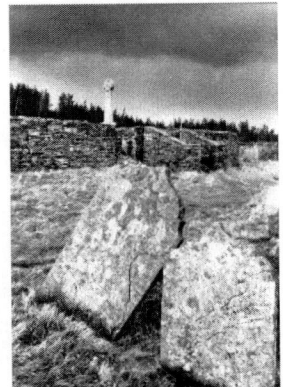

Capel y Brithdir - 2016

the congregation was enhanced by colliers, ironworkers and their families.

On June 5 1858 *Merthyr Telegraph* reported that the church bell had been stolen:

The good folks of Brithdir are in a state of unusual excitement. A few days ago it was discovered that the bell placed on the church or chapel of ease had been taken away, and up to the present date no clue can be obtained of the man or men who committed this sacrilegious wrong. We have not heard how the fact was found out; if only when the appointed individual began to pull the rope, in order to summon church-goers to their devotions, we can easily conceive that worthy's astonishment. The bell weighed upwards of a hundredweight.

It is not necessary to itemise the strenuous efforts of Rev. G.C.F. Harries to ensure that, while he was rector (1862-1879), the Anglican church met the long-neglected needs of people across the large parish of Gelligaer. Suffice it to say that, when he arrived in the parish the Capel was closed, but within a year, Capel y Brithdir was refitted and it reopened about 1863.

South Wales Daily News, November 3 1879, noted that, according to the report of Dr. Dyke, medical officer of Merthyr Rural Sanitary Authority, there was space for 150 new graves at Capel y Brithdir burial ground. Such was the rapid change in the area that, on December 5 1907, *Evening Express* reported the graveyard was full. However, according to *Register of Burials at Capel y Brithdir 1904-1971* (Glamorgan Archives P142CW/6), there were a further 83 burials between March 23 1908 and January 4 1971 as, although the graveyard was deemed full, burials were possible if there was room in a family plot. Thirteen of the 83 were Brithdir folk.

Bargoed Year Book, 1912, gives a graphic description of the *tall, lean personage* of Rev. Mr. Davies, who *tied a handkerchief round his head, making himself appear very quaint and picturesque and resembling very much an Oriental merchant traveller* as he rode from Mynyddislwyn to take services at Capel y Brithdir.

During the half century or so before the outbreak of World War I, previously little-known beauty spots and places of archaeological and historical interest like Capel y Brithdir attracted visitors from outside the immediate local area. *Aberdare Leader*, March 31 1906, reported the South Wales Teachers' Rambling Association included Capel y Brithdir in its 1906 season of excursions and, on Saturday, March 24, Samuel Davies, headmaster, J.D. Jones (Brithdir Council School) and Miss Rees of Troedrhiwfuwch, met the group of walkers at Brithdir Station and led them on the steep climb to Capel y Brithdir where they saw *several recently erected tombstones in the burial ground* – possibly marking the last burials before closure. At the Tegernacus Stone, Samuel Davies delivered an address, and presented each visitor with a photograph of the Stone. Local school log books reveal attempts to stimulate school children's interest in local heritage. On October 23 1919, the mistress of Brithdir Girls' School noted their first lesson in what she called *rural lore*:

A class of 60 senior girls accompanied by three teachers made an excursion to an old chapel on the hill top. Here Mr. Gill the local clergyman met them and gave an interesting lecture conveying the history of the ancient building.

A group outside Capel y Brithdir, circa 1950
Courtesy Joyce Jones

The impact of such lessons on pupils growing up amidst post-war traumas is unclear.

In spite of its inaccessibility, and the new St. Paul's church in the village, Capel y Brithdir was not abandoned: Kathleen Lewis (*In the steps of St. Gwladys*, 1959) noted there were a few morning services during the year, and occasional afternoon services, as well as services on Palm Sunday and Harvest Festivals, and *Merthyr Express*, July 5 1930, reported that, on Sunday, June 29 1930, *a large number of church members assembled there for an evening service – the first for 74 years; the service being conducted by the Rev. W. Hopkins.* However, there were no services between April 2 1939 and October 18 1942. The vicar, Dr. Lawrence Thomas, oversaw repairs and, on May 23 1943, Dr. John Morgan, Bishop of Llandaff, visited and preached what he described as a *Service of Reconciliation* in Capel y Brithdir. Less than a decade later it was destroyed by fire.

Brithdir Anglicans

Much of the information on the history of local Anglicans is based on reports in *New Tredegar, Bargoed and Caerphilly Journal* and *Merthyr Express* as well as memories of the late Morfydd Williams née Cresswell recorded over several weeks in 2007.

In the early twentieth century Brithdir Anglicans were served by a succession of curates-in-charge. In 1903, Rev. S.T. Boughton was curate-in-charge and, after he left for Newchapel, Stoke on Trent, Rev. R Morgan B.A. served 1904-1906. He was succeeded by Rev. John Swinnerton M.A., blind son of Vicar of Llandevaud, in Brithdir 1906-1908. Rev. William Phillips L.D., (shown second left in photograph, courtesy Paul James) lived at Barton Villa and was curate-in-charge from 1909 to 1915.

The first Anglican place of worship in the community was a wooden mission church at the south end of Station Terrace. Possibly once a navvies' hut, it was both unsafe and unhealthy but they worshipped there for over a decade prior to 1906.

Determined to have a more suitable place of worship, local Anglicans, through collections and fund raising events, raised £800 by autumn 1905. On Monday, October 30 1905, a procession of clergy and choristers marched from the mission church to the site of the new church where, using an inscribed silver trowel, the wife of Bishop of Llandaff, laid the foundation stone, inscribed *To the Glory of God. This memorial stone was laid by Mrs. Hughes, The Palace, Llandaff, October 30th 1905*. Costing £1,550, the new church, built in Gothic style with red brick pillars and forest stone dressings, and with a bell tower, was erected by William Speake of Brithdir, who, at the same time, also built two adjacent dwellings, Rock House and Radnor House. The church could seat a congregation of nearly 300, and the basement housed a hall (schoolroom) to accommodate fifty, as well as Musgrave's heating apparatus. St. Paul's Church, at the top of Russell Street (a street known to many older

St. Paul's Church (built 1906, demolished 1927)   courtesy Elizabeth Jones

Brithdir people as *Church Street*), was opened for worship in 1906, by Bishop Joshua Pritchard Hughes of Llandaff. The new church was very special to Brithdir: Lance Corporal John Thomas (who as noted on page 184 died in South Africa) was remembered on a memorial tablet inserted into the masonry of the new church. Inside furnishings were donated by local people as follows:

- Forest of Dean stone font from Mr. and Mrs. Llewellyn Lewis, George Inn Hotel
- Altar Cross from Miss M.E. George, Cwmsyfiog
- Pulpit from James Harry, Tredegar, formerly of Brithdir
- Altar Cloth from Mrs. Jones, Hengoed
- Altar Linen from Mary Howard, Brithdir
- Lectern from Mr. Stockqueler, Brithdir

• Hymn Board from Mr. H. Parry, Brithdir.

Sources studied to date suggest that Brithdir Anglicans did not have a curate-in-charge from 1915 to arrival of Rev. Dalis Davies in 1924. When he emigrated to Australia in 1927, there was another gap before Rev. William Hopkins B.A. of Caerau, Maesteg, arrived in 1929, and served to 1933. The period of these curacies was a difficult time as far as the fabric of the church in Brithdir was concerned. In 1927, cracks appeared in the walls and, on paying a visit of inspection on Friday, July 29, Bishop Hughes declared that *service must be discontinued at once.* On Sunday there was no church bell to call people to worship as there was no service. Within three months the building was demolished.

In 1929 the Ambulance Hall became the Anglicans' temporary place of worship. However, as ambulance classes were being held in the Workmen's Institute, it was available for more permanent use. Unemployed church members converted it into a church and, in May 1935, dedicated by the Bishop of Llandaff, the former Ambulance Hall became St. David's Church. Thus, by the time curate-in-charge, Rev. J.T. James arrived in 1936, Brithdir Anglicans were worshipping in St. David's.

In 1974, Brithdir Anglicans suffered another disaster when St. David's was destroyed by fire. When the alarm was raised, Morfydd Williams raced to the scene, arriving in time to witness the final collapse of the building and to hear its bell for the last time as it struck the ground. The bell was restored in 1997 and installed in St. Gwladys Church, Bargoed. As, in the mid 1970s, the cost of a new building was prohibitive, the wife of vicar Rev. John Oeppen suggested that an existing village property could be

Interior of second St. David's Church.
Courtesy Kay Williams

converted into a church, A former betting office and general store in Station Terrace was purchased. Some nine months later, it opened as the new St. David's Church, furnished largely using materials from the former Maesycwmmer Church.

Worshipping first within Brithdir's Anglican congregation, both Albert Jesse Gauntlett Chard and Thomas Douglas Harris, B. A. entered the church.

Born on December 16 1903, and baptised in Brithdir's Mission Church, June 21 1905, Albert Jesse Gauntlett Chard was the third of nine children born to Alfred James Chard and Louisa, née Gauntlett, of Charles Street. Family member, Marlene Shaw, née Chard, noted that, like his siblings, he bore his mother's maiden surname. It is likely that he received his early education in Brithdir. *Crockford's Clerical Directory* (1932) sheds light on his clerical training and career. He trained for the priesthood at Kelham Theological College (1923), a monastic institution near Newark, Nottinghamshire, and at St. Michael's Theological College, Llandaff (1925). In 1926, he was ordained deacon in the Church of England and the following year, priest. While he was curate of St. Catherine's, Cardiff (1926-28), reports in *Merthyr Express* show he attended St. Paul's Church, Brithdir, on at least two occasions. He read the lessons at the Harvest Festival service in October 1926 and, in July the

Rev. Chard
Courtesy Thomas Price

following year, he attended the annual flower service. As noted above, services at St. Paul's were discontinued from Friday, July 29 1927, so Rev. Chard, a product of the village, was present at the last service in the church prior to its demolition. While, from 1928 onwards, Rev. Chard served the church in various roles in England, it is likely that he did not have many opportunities to visit Brithdir and worship there.

The occasion on which this photograph (courtesy Sandra Evans) was taken is unclear. It shows a group outside the Vicarage, Bargoed. Seated next to the lady (possibly the vicar's wife) is Harry James, with Wilfred Bennett next and Rupert Bennett next to him on the end chair (right). In front of Harry sitting cross-legged is Albert Bennett (3rd from right) and Cyril Hewitt is standing directly behind Harry and Wilf.

Son of Thomas and Agnes Harris, 3 Harcourt Terrace, Thomas Douglas Harris (right courtesy Kay Dennis) was educated at Brithdir Infants' and Boys' Schools before entering Lewis School Pengam where he matriculated. Proceeding to University College of South Wales and Monmouthshire at Cardiff, he obtained B.A. in English and Music. He decided to take up the ministry and studied at St. Michael's Theological College, where in March 1948 he passed the first part of the general ordination examination and in May attained his finals

in Old and New Testament studies with Greek, Christian ethics, worship doctrine and church history. On December 18 1949, a number of Brithdir

Church Choir courtesy Alf Weatherly who is in the back row with Pat McDonald. Others identified are Ken Dando, John Hook, Ron Evans, John Rawle, Richard Williams, Brian Evans and Raymond Edwards

people, hiring a motor-coach, travelled to the Cathedral Church of St. Peter and St. Paul to attend the ceremony when he was ordained deacon by the Bishop of Llandaff. Rev. Douglas Harris began his ministry as curate in the parish of Llandough with Leckwith and Cogan and he served as curate in the parish of Bargoed with Brithdir 1953-1956. From 1956, he was rector in a Vale of Glamorgan parish.

Gwladys Griffiths (right courtesy Ceinwen Bevan) now of Australia shares this memory of the Whitsun March:

We stopped and sang outside the 'George' and the 'Club' where on one occasion one of the drinkers invited the vicar, who was the Rev. Douglas Harris, a Brithdir boy, to come and have a drink. The vicar accepted on condition they would meet at the church the next Sunday. Needless to say the vicar didn't have his drink.

Local Nonconformists

As census returns show that many nineteenth and early twentieth century Brithdir families originated in rural Wales or south west England, areas where nonconformity was strong, it is not surprising that Brithdir had nonconformist chapels. These chapels, Penuel Calvinistic Methodist, Wesleyan Methodist and Beulah Baptist, were not just places of worship; they were centres of cultural and social activities for people of all ages, including, as noted on pages 132 - 133, the popular and much anticipated annual outings. Although the Congregationalists did not have a place of worship in the village, they held Sunday School in the community and, from time to time, performed concerts and operettas in the local 'Stute.

Penuel Calvinistic Methodist Chapel

Penuel Calvinistic Methodist chapel, a little building on the end of Old Bristol Terrace, (shown opposite courtesy Morfydd Williams) was the first purpose-built chapel in the village of George Inn. It housed the new George Inn Board School from September 1 1879 (see page 84).

Ceinwen Bevan, née Harris, formerly of Brithdir, has fond memories of the chapel:

78

Before moving to Charles Street we lived in the cottage next door to the Penuel Chapel and I can remember as a child lying in bed and hearing the church choir singing their songs. They used to practice on the grass opposite the big gates (the gates were situated next to the chapel and gave entrance to the New Hall).

Wesleyan Methodist Chapel

It is not clear when local Wesleyan Methodists started to worship in the village, but anecdotal evidence refers to services being held in homes of adherents prior to 1894. On Thursday, August 9 1894, a large crowd, including

This pre-1915 photograph of Brithdir shows the original Wesleyan Methodist chapel, a former army hut, on the river side of railway line. The Baptist chapel was on the opposite side on Jarvis's Bank.   Courtesy Paul Waites collection

Brithdir Wesleyan chapel members and friends 1938
Some familiar faces are Phil Willetts (far left), Mr. James, Harry Williams (teacher), Lily Cox (check coat), and on Lily's left is Rose Price, four along from her is Sarah Bevan, then Gertrude Davies (Bryn Glas), Mary Ann Hayes, Miss Jenkins (Ivy Row), Jack Brawn and Florence Thomas.   Courtesy Bill Thomas

children absenting themselves from school, witnessed Miss A. Woodward, Tredegar, presumably daughter of Enoch Woodward, a Tredegar butcher who presided at the public meeting that evening, lay the foundation stone of the new Wesleyan Methodist chapel on George Hill. Mr. T. Edwards, of Tredegar was contracted builder of this chapel to accommodate about 200 worshippers, and it was officially opened on November 22 1894.

William Hughes, (left, courtesy Ronald Rogers) was one of several people who played an important role in Brithdir's Wesleyan Methodist Chapel as Trust Secretary, Sunday School Superintendent and general factotum. Recognising his 30 years of Sunday School work and 14 years as its Superintendent, *Brithdir Methodist Inaugural Magazine* 1936 noted *Perhaps the most important event of the year was the little unveiling ceremony of a photograph of William Hughes which took place on December 22 1935.*

Although the photograph above suggests the cause was strong in pre-World War II Brithdir, in common with many other places of worship, the number of members fell. Eventually, remaining members joined other local Methodist congregations, the building was sold and, in 1984, demolished. Eddie Griffiths (mentioned in Bevan family pages 260 - 264) built a house, Ty ar y Bryn, on the site in 1985.

Beulah Baptist Chapel

In May 1890, in consequence of a stoppage at Rhymney Iron Works, many members of Rhymney's English Baptist Church left that town. About eighteen of them arrived in Brithdir by autumn 1892 and Baptist school and services were held regularly at the Station Terrace home of Mr. and Mrs. Randall. The cause prospered in the community, and, in April 1893, they erected a corrugated building to seat 200 below the bridge near the railway station. Pastor R. Owen, Beulah, Rhymney, tended the flock until he left for Pwll, Llanelli, in 1896, and, while they were pastorless, Henry Brown, a deacon of the church, did much until, in 1901, Rev. Evan George of Argoed, accepted the call to Beulah. Such was the strength of the local Baptists that, on May 18 1903, Mrs Llewellyn, Hengoed; Miss King, Brithdir; Miss Phillips, Brynsyfi, New Tredegar (presumably one of the three daughters of Nehemiah Phillips); Miss Jones, Brynglas, Brithdir; Miss Evans, McLaren House, Abertysswg; and Mr. W. Price, New Tredegar, laid foundation stones for a new stone chapel at the southern end of Bristol Terrace. It would be interesting to know if any of the silver trowels presented to these people are still within the local community.

Built by D. Williams of New Tredegar at a cost of £749, the English Baptist Chapel, with seating for 400, was known as Beulah and was officially opened on August 31 1903. Beulah (left courtesy Mel Williams) was a big building with a raised stage overlooking the congregation pews and at its centre a beautiful large pipe organ.

As Rev. George developed eyesight problems which eventually rendered him totally blind, he resigned the pastorate in February 1906. He was succeeded in September 1907, by Rev. Harry West (right, and for more on the West family, see pages 347-356). After 16 years as minister of Beulah, Rev. West accepted a call from Mount Pleasant, Penydarren, Merthyr, and in May 1923, local Baptists and representatives of surrounding places of worship paid respects on his departure.

Beulah was damaged by fire and the chapel was eventually demolished. Arthur Harris who worked on the demolition of the building recounts *the whole roof of Welsh slate tiles was bought by an American who shipped them back to his homeland.*

Annual Procession of Witness

In general, the various congregations within the community worshipped and socialised (especially for musical events and outings) within their own premises, but they united for some events including the annual Procession of

Witness, popularly known as the *Whitsun Walk*, which was an important highlight in the life of the Christian community in Brithdir and elsewhere. Each Whit Monday, Sunday School scholars, usually dressed in new clothes, paraded the streets from Station Terrace to Milton Terrace and via Bristol Terrace before returning to their respective school rooms for tea and entertainment. Reports in *Merthyr Express* show that, while this was an annual event for the nonconformist Sunday Schools, Brithdir Anglicans did not regularly join them: in May 1931 it was noted that *for the first time for a number of years, the scholars from St. Paul's joined the procession.*

George Coombs, Charles Street (wearing bowler hat, on right of banner) at head of Beulah party outside their chapel on Bristol Terrace.

Courtesy Lily Williams, his granddaughter

Wesleyan Sunday school procession between Wellington and Tennyson Terraces with Nelson Terrace in the distance. The children spectators are on the corner of Tennyson Terrace.
Courtesy Ivor Harris

A Whitsun Walk from the post World War II era
Courtesy Alf Weatherly

Marriages

Brithdir's Anglicans went to the parish church, first St. Catwg's in Gelligaer, and later St. Gwladys Church in Bargoed, for marriage services, but the three village nonconformist chapels were registered for solemnising marriages: Beulah on February 21 1913; Wesleyan on April 20 1920 and Penuel on May 19 1949. *Merthyr Express*, June 11 1949, reported on the first marriage ceremony performed in Penuel Chapel on Monday, June 6 1949, when Lewis Ivor Lewis, 22 High Street, Troedrhiwfuwch married Non, youngest daughter of Mr. and Mrs. Isaac Jones, 8 Station Terrace.

Left: Ernest Edward Pritchard and his bride Mary John on Boxing Day 1935 in the garden of the John family home in Russell Street after their marriage at Beulah.   Courtesy Gillian Pritchard.

One time boy soprano Melville Davies of School Street (see page 293) and Dilys, daughter of Mr. and Mrs. Emlyn Jones, Moorland Road, Bargoed, were married at Penuel Chapel, September 1952

Courtesy Ceridwen Evans, née Davies.

Outside Wesleyan Chapel October 1952: L-R Tom Watkins (best man) Mrs. Hayes, Irene Brewer, William Hayes (groom), Eileen Smith née Brewer (bride), Granville Brewer, Elizabeth (Betty) John née Brewer, Margaret Brewer (bride's mother) and Royston Smith.
Courtesy Linda Winmill.

CHAPTER 7 EDUCATION

Introduction

For centuries before the late nineteenth century, most local children in this sparsely populated Welsh-speaking area received little education beyond what they learned within the home, workplace and their place of worship. Forster's Education Act (1870) created a national structure of locally-elected school boards to ensure an elementary education for all children. Gelligaer School Board, first elected 1871, faced a challenging task across a parish that was rapidly changing as industrialisation and the associated urbanisation rolled south from the heads of the valleys. Some local children were being educated at the time of the 1871 census when three children at Plas Milfre (aged 14, 10 and 8) and 12 year old Edwin Williams at Tyr y Capel were described as *scholars*, but it is not clear where they received lessons.

George Inn (later Brithdir) School 1879-1905

On the morning of September 1 1879, 19 year old Clara Tovey, set off from her lodgings in Pontlottyn for a short train journey south. From George Inn Station, Miss Tovey, appointed by Gelligaer School Board to take charge of the Board's new George Inn School, had a short walk to her temporary classroom, a room just 30 feet long and 23 feet wide, and rented from Penuel Calvinistic Methodists at £8 p.a..

The previous May, a sub-committee of Gelligaer School Board reported there was no local school and 49 local children of school age were not having the statutory elementary education. George Inn was linked by road to Tirphil, just a mile to the north, but the Board's school there was full, and, while there were vacant places in the Board's school in Bargoed, about a mile to the south, there was no suitable road for children to walk, just a railway link. Thus the sub-committee recommended the Board rent accommodation in George Inn until such time as purpose-built premises could be erected in the community.

The rented room was hardly sufficient for the teaching of an all age mixed class, and proved difficult and uncomfortable for both teachers and pupils. Admitting 34 children during the first week, Clara Tovey divided them into four divisions; 20 Infants, 9 Standard I (none of whom knew anything of arithmetic, and 7 unable to read or write), 3 Standard II and 2 Standard III.

Born in Llangattock where her father, Aaron Tovey, was Baptist minister, Clara was educated in the local school. She was about 13 years old when she started training as a pupil teacher, a common starting point for a career in the teaching profession prior to 1902 Education Act. She moved to Pontlottyn to take up a teaching position in the local girls' school. In 1879 she was appointed as mistress of the new George Inn School on a salary of £35 p.a.. Clara Tovey was the school's sole teacher until, in February 1880, Mary Jane Lewis was appointed pupil teacher.

Much of what follows is based on what Clara Tovey and her successors wrote in Brithdir school log books (Glamorgan Archives ECG7). School log books (diaries) are fascinating sources that shed light not only on day-to-day school life but also issues, including infectious diseases and industrial disputes, affecting the local community. From time to time, the master/mistress logged unexpected happenings and local and national events that impinged on school and community life.

Considering the inadequate accommodation and lack of equipment together with disruption as scholars came and went (so common in new industrial communities like this), the inaugural inspection report, copied into the log book in January 1881 by Rev. J. Parry Williams, school correspondent and Board member, was pleasing:

This little school has been well started. The first and third Standards, to which the Instruction was confined, were very satisfactory. The Infants were also, under the circumstances very fairly proficient. The Discipline is good.

Since government grants depended, in part, on pupil attainment and attendance at school, it is not surprising that average attendances in George Inn School were logged regularly, and incidences of anything likely to affect attendance and pupil progress were recorded carefully. Children's attendance at school was affected by their health (or lack of!) and, sadly, log book pages are littered with references to sickness and its inevitable impact on attendance and pupil attainment. Wintry conditions, as well as heavy rain and storms in almost any season, were noted as they often kept children away from school, or from returning to school in the afternoon if their clothes and footwear were very wet. The following extracts from Clara Tovey's entries illustrate the impact of both illness and inclement weather:

January 18 1880: *The school opened three times this week, the weather being too severe and the snow too deep for the children to come to school.*

In February 1881: *several children were prevented from attending school, with mumps being the chief complaint.*

December 8 1882: *Only eleven children managed to get to school due to the severity of the weather* [deep snow]*, they were sent home and the school closed for the day.*

September 18 1883: *Dr Dyke, Medical Officer of Health closed the school for one month due to Scarlet Fever being prevalent in the George Inn village.*

August 1 1884: *The attendance at school is now very low on account of measles being prevalent in the neighbourhood.*

October 16 1885: *Several scholars are absent, being ill with Scarlet Fever.*

School attendance and pupils' progress were affected by the constant population movements as families moved in and out of the new community in search of work. The entry logged April 28 1882 reads *Three children left the school for Australia.* The children were born in one of the small cottages near the school (later known as Station Terrace) and the story of the oldest child, Mary Jane Clee, appears on page 338.

For some children, particularly those living on outlying farms, the journey to and from school was long, arduous and sometimes dangerous. On October 28 1880 Clara Tovey had the heart-breaking task of logging *One of the scholars from the Infant Class met with his death on the engine road.* In common with many of her contemporaries in other schools, Clara Tovey recorded death and/or funeral of a pupil without identifying the child by name or disclosing the cause of death. On February 13 1885 she wrote *School was opened on Thursday afternoon at half-past one and closed at half-past three, for the purpose of the attending the funeral of one of the scholars.* And she sometimes made reference to local events such as the sad news recorded May 7 1880 - *a half-holiday was given on Thursday afternoon on account of the funeral of the station master's wife of this place.*

Clara Tovey's last entry in the school log was on November 23 1885 - *My duties as Head Mistress of this school terminate today. The school will now be left in charge of the Assistant Mistress* [Mary Jane Lewis, her first pupil teacher] *until the arrival of the newly appointed Head Mistress.* Clara Tovey was a dedicated teacher, who, in spite of early hardships, raised standards during her six year tenure. The annual inspection reports consistently praised the quality of the little school and her devotion to duty. The number of scholars on roll had risen to 92, and average attendance was 50-60.

Entries in the log book show that, even though pupil teacher Mary Jane Lewis had many absences because of sickness, she performed well at the yearly examinations, being awarded prizes on at least three separate occasions. When, having completed her apprenticeship, Mary Jane Lewis left the school on Monday, November 1 1884, her mentor, Clara Tovey, noted how lack of teaching staff made it difficult to work to the time table. However, she returned as assistant mistress on Monday, December 8 1884 at a salary of £30 p.a., and, on Clara Tovey's departure, she was left in charge until a new mistress was appointed.

That new mistress, Agnes Davies, took charge of *George Inn Board School Mixed and Infants Departments* on December 14 1885. Her teaching career, starting as pupil teacher in the early days of Gelligaer School Board before gaining Board of Education certificate in the early 1880s, culminated in Brithdir where, for nearly four decades (1885-1924), she influenced generations of local school children. Although her home was 45 Merchant Street, Pontlottyn, Agnes Davies built a strong link with Brithdir where she became widely known, highly respected, and well-liked by all who came into contact with her. She witnessed many changes in Brithdir, including the handover from Gelligaer School Board to the Local Education Authority

(LEA), Glamorgan County Council, following 1902 Education Act. Brithdir's first purpose-built school, the Mixed Department, opened while the Board was in being, but Glamorgan LEA was responsible for the other two.

Like Clara Tovey, Agnes Davies faced difficulties in George Inn School, including that of overcrowding, which did not go unnoticed by Her Majesty's Inspectorate. In his report of 1891, HMI William Lewis highlighted the unsuitability of the facilities:

> *The room is too crowded and is not adapted for teaching infants and older scholars together. The Mistress in consequence has great difficulties to overcome in conducting the school. It is understood that the Board is about to provide better premises.*

But, as this extract from the 1892 report shows, Gelligaer School Board seemed in no haste to improve the accommodation:

> *The school is still held in the same unsatisfactory room with insufficient desk accommodation, and it is to the credit of the mistress that the work in the elementary subjects continues to show a very fair average of quality. The Infants have been very successfully taught considering the circumstances.*

However, *Merthyr Express*, January 21 1893, reported on change:

> *Gelligaer School Board received a letter from the Education Department stating that H.M. Inspector of schools had written them stating that the school at Brithdir was in a dangerously overcrowded state. The Department recommended, the Infants should be excluded from the school now in use, or a temporary building procured as the health of the children was of the first importance. The mission room was obtained on loan from the Gelligaer Rector for the purpose of a classroom until the new building would be completed.*

Agnes Davies's log dated January 28 1893 reads:

> *The Rev. Jones, Rector of Gelligaer agreed to allow the Board the use of the Church Mission room at Brithdir to accommodate the Infants.*

The Infants moved to the Mission Church schoolroom, at the south end of Station Terrace, on Monday, January 30. Agnes Davies made her last entry in the Mixed and Infants log book on October 31 1893 before she was transferred to the Mission Church schoolroom to take charge of the Infants' Department on November 1 1893 when the new Mixed Department opened.

After some twelve years in charge of the infant pupils in temporary accommodation in the church, Agnes Davies surely felt great relief and satisfaction when, on January 13 1905, she opened the school log book to pen *School closed Monday owing to the opening of the New Infants School; officially opened by one of the Managers, Rev. Harri Edwards, Baptist Minister, Bargoed.* Having moved with her pupils to the new purpose-built premises, Agnes Davies continued in charge until her retirement in 1924.

INFANTS' SCHOOL, BRITHDIR

Brithdir Infants' School and the neighbouring headmaster's house, were built on a site opposite the Mixed School. *New Tredegar, Bargoed and Caerphilly Journal,* January 14 1905, reported they were designed by Cardiff architects, James and Morgan, and built by John Lewis of Caerphilly. The school was officially opened on January 9 1905 by Rev. Harri Edwards of Bargoed, one of the school managers. It would be interesting to know the present whereabouts of the magnificent inscribed gold key presented to the reverend gentleman by architect Mr Morgan.

Many of Agnes Davies's school experiences were typical of her time, as witnessed by the following notes based on her entries in the school log book:

January 10 1887: only 20 children present in school - *Nearly all the children of the Infants Class were in the Whooping Cough. The weather is also very cold and the roads are so slippery that it is dangerous for them to come.* The infants' class was closed for 5 weeks.

Scarlet Fever was prevalent in the district in May 1887 and schools were closed for some weeks.

Late March 1888: *three children had been taken ill with Typhoid Fever.*

May 4 1888: *Martha Edmunds, Third Year pupil teacher is seriously ill with Typhoid Fever.*

May 18 1888: a *half holiday was given Friday afternoon because nearly all the children stayed home in order to attend a funeral.* It is not clear whose funeral it was. An entry three weeks earlier noted the death of the brother of Annie Lewis, first year pupil teacher.

March 7 1890: *One boy from Standard V left this week to work at the Drift.* But, seven months later, Agnes Davies welcomed him back and placed him in Standard IV because she found *he had forgotten his Standard IV Arithmetic and Grammar.*

88

August 1890: a pupil died from *Rheumatic Fever.*

October 31 1890: *The Measles has broken out at Cwmsyfiog, and there are seven children from this school in it. It has also been the means of keeping several of their brothers and sisters away from school.*

June 1891: Board members, Rev. Aaron Davies, J.P. and Isaac Phillips authorised a two-day closure as the mistress and three of her teachers *were very ill with influenza.*

September 4 1891: *Resolved by the Board in order to commemorate the establishment on September 1 next, of Free Education, that the whole of the schools be closed on the day previous thereto namely August 31.*

January 19 1903: *School was closed Wednesday afternoon, that the teachers may attend the funeral of a little boy named Trevor Evans of this school who was buried at Gelligaer.* This boy was Lewis Trevor R. Evans (known as Trevor), the 4 year old son of Brithdir Police Constable William Evans and his wife Margaret of 20 Station Terrace.

June 12 1903: *One little girl named Winifred Coombs died from Diphtheria last Sunday and was buried on Thursday,* Winifred Coombs was 4 year old daughter of George and Elizabeth Coombs of Charles Street.

Agnes Davies retired in 1924 and *Merthyr Express*, January 31 1925, carried a report on a farewell social held the previous Tuesday at the Infants' School.

Brithdir Infants' in 1915. (Courtesy Jacqueline Amy Tiernan.)
Future opera star Zoe Cresswell (see page 287) is back row fifth from right.

Those present included Samuel Davies (master of Boys' School) and Muriel Davies (new mistress of Infants' School) with their respective staffs – Dan Jones, W. Williams, and Tommy Davies (each accompanied by his wife), Frank West, Olwen Davies, Olwen J. Rees, Olwen Evans, Winifred Jones, H. Fryer and Joan Rees. Former teaching colleagues presented Agnes Davies with a mahogany lounge chair inscribed *Presented by the Brithdir Schools' Staff to Miss Agnes Davies as a slight token of their esteem and appreciation of her valued services as headmistress for 39 years.*

It was not only former colleagues who showed appreciation of her work in Brithdir, as, on Wednesday, October 7 1925, a large cross-section of Brithdir society met in the Girls' School to honour Agnes Davies. The gifts, a beautiful barometer presented by William Lewis, one of Brithdir's oldest inhabitants, and a silver cake basket, presented by William Jenkins, were tokens marking the respect she had earned during nearly four decades in the community.

Agnes Davies seated with, L-R, Olwen Davies (daughter of Samuel Davies and sister to Muriel), unknown and Olwen Rees (Tir y ferch Gryno farm).
Courtesy Sian Hayworth

Pupils from Cwmsyfiog

From the start, children from Cwmsyfiog, the community on the opposite bank of Rhymney river, attended George Inn School. As Cwmsyfiog was in Bedwellty parish, the respective Boards would have discussed and agreed terms. Any issues with the bridge crossing the river affected their school attendance as illustrated by some log book entries. On August 1 1884 Clara Tovey wrote *the bridge, which crosses the river connecting the two parishes, is broken and has been for some time, thus preventing the scholars from the other parish from attending school.* Six years later, Agnes Davies revealed greater difficulties when, on October 17 1890, she logged *the Bridge which the children have to cross in coming from Cwmsyfiog has been taken down this week, and several children are absent in consequence.*

A new school in Cwmsyfiog opened in 1889 and, on January 25 1889 Agnes Davies noted *some of the smaller children leaving to go to this new school.* However, in spite of the lengthy journey to the next crossing point (at Pontaberbargoed), older children continued to attend George Inn School. On December 8 1892 Agnes Davies wrote: *19 boys and 11 girls left the school, 13 of the boys and the 11 girls have left because they live at Cwmsyfiog. The Board members have ordered me to send all the children from the other side out.*

Brithdir Board School

From 1893 the Mixed and Infants' Departments operated independently. Agnes Davies took charge of Infants' Department in the Mission Church schoolroom while David W. Jones was master of Mixed Department, housed in new purpose-built premises. The first reference to the latter as Brithdir Board School seems to be by William Lewis HMI in report of May 1893. Reports in *South Wales Daily News*, December 9 1891 and November 2 and 15 1893, show the new building was the work of architect John Williams of Merthyr Tydfil and builder Thomas Davies of Pontlottyn. The new school was officially opened on Wednesday, November 1 1893 with David Jones, former headmaster of Gelligaer Village Board School, as headmaster.

Just seven months after taking control, David Jones, concerned about irregular attendance of the pupil teachers under his charge, logged *I hardly know what to do. I think it best to resign for I can never teach and obtain good results in this school with my present staff.* After three years' service he was transferred to another school and Samuel Davies was appointed in his stead.

Samuel Davies

When Samuel Davies commenced duties as headmaster of Brithdir Mixed School on November 2 1896, he started what was to be a three decade link with education in the local community. During his thirty years in Brithdir, he took a keen interest in all aspects of the welfare of school, its staff, and scholars, as well as of the community, as witnessed by the content and tone of his entries in the school log book and by reports in the local press. He faced difficulties, some of a personal nature, but was determined to rise to the challenges presented during years of industrial disputes and international war, and do his utmost to improve the quality of life through education.

After a few years schooling at Pentwyn (Fochriw) church school, 10 year old Samuel Davies started work in a coal mine but, following the 1870 legislation, he left the mine and returned to school. Sometime later, he was among the third batch of Gelligaer School Board's pupil teachers before, some six years later, gaining recognition as an uncertificated teacher (UT). He served three years as UT at Garnfach, Nantyglo, under Aberystruth School Board, and gained a Queen's Scholarship in July 1877. On completing two years training at Bangor Normal College, Samuel Davies became a certificated teacher (CT) and was appointed master in charge of Alltwalis Board School, near Carmarthen. After that, he spent two years at Georgetown, Tredegar, before being appointed by Gelligaer School Board to take charge at Pantywaun Mixed School, a post he held for three years before securing the post in Brithdir. He was in charge of Brithdir Mixed Department for nineteen years and, in 1915, became first headmaster of the new Brithdir Boys' Department, where he remained until his retirement in 1926.

His first entry, on November 3 1896, reported illness: *Frederick J Williams, 2nd Year pupil teacher was obliged to leave school today on account of illness.* On November 25 he wrote: *Several of the children are away from school today with Cold, Catarrh, Tonsillitis, and Scarlatina.* Samuel Davies then made this sombre entry *One of the scholars named Fred Gwynne died this afternoon from Typhoid.* There are many entries relating to illness as well as attempts to bring epidemics under control by lengthy school closures. An outbreak of measles prompted the Medical Officer of Health, on October 4 1897, to close the school for three weeks. On January 31 1898, the headmaster logged:

Many children are absent through illness. Epidemic Catarrh is very prevalent in the neighbourhood. On average about 50 children are absent this week. The neighbouring school at Cwmsyfiog is closed on account of the epidemic.

Epidemics were a great fear in Victorian communities, at home and in school, and words like *measles, scarlet fever, diphtheria* and *whooping cough* crop up regularly in school log books.

Merthyr Express, December 1 1906, reported thus on a measles epidemic: *this scourge still continues in the district of Cwmsyfiog and it has been deemed necessary to keep the schools closed for a further period of three-weeks making six-weeks in all. The scourge has made a sad havoc among the infantile population there being no less than twenty interments last week at Bedwellty Cemetery.*

The following show Samuel Davies was not immune to illness, or personal tragedy:

- May 5 and 6 1898: *I was unable to attend these days on account of serious illness in the family.*
- May 10 1898: *Received a telegram today informing me of the death of my little boy. - I put everything straight and in working order before departing.*
- April 7 1902: *I received notification from the Medical Officer today not to attend school during the week owing to Scarlet Fever at my house.*

Truancy was another problem.

March 18 1898: *there are two boys attending this school who are totally the worst kind of truants. I have tried every means in my power to make them attend regularly but all in vain. They ought without hesitation to be sent away to the Truant School.*

South Wales and Monmouthshire Truant and Industrial School opened 1894, in Quakers' Yard. Samuel Davies's predecessor, David Jones, had cause to punish four boys for playing truant in December 1893. In September 1899, Samuel Davies reported: *Four of the boys are truanting; they have been fined on several occasions.* It would seem being fined was no deterrent and had little affect on the offenders as his entry for November 17 shows:

I sent away the names of six children and their attendance for the last three-months to the Clerk of the School Board. These children are incorrigible truants.

In the log for January 27 1899 the master wrote:

the two boys (worst offenders) are truanting for the last month or so. I have reported them to the Board who I hope will deal with them severely; and will thus be a warning to some of the other very bad attendees.

Action was taken by the Board against three boys in 1902 as these examples testify:

- March 3: *a boy readmitted into this school today after spending a term of three-months at the Quakers Yard Truant School.*

- April 28: *a boy was sent away to Quakers Yard Truant School for a term of three-months.*
- May 13: *a noted truant admitted to school this morning from Quakers Yard Truant School.*

Unfortunately the problem remained: between 1902 and 1906, the names of 12 truants (eight boys and four girls) were recorded, summoned, and some taken away to Quakers Yard.

Children sometimes missed school for a variety of reasons other than illness, truancy or inclement weather as illustrated by the following extracts from the log book:

- May 7 1900: *A Singing Festival with the Baptists of this valley affects the attendance at school today.*
- August 27 1900: *Poor attendance this afternoon due to a Carnival held in the village.*
- September 3 1900: *The attendance today is poor owing to the Bedwellty Agricultural Show at Rhymney and not just children; three assistant teachers requested permission to visit the show.*
- October 30 1905: *No school this afternoon due to the laying of the foundation stone of a New Church at this place.*
- February 28 1906: *Eleven Catholic children were withdrawn from school this afternoon to attend a Religious Service.*
- November 5 1909: *The attendance this week has fallen a little owing I believe to one of the old school boys being killed at the Darran explosion.*
- July 13 1911: *Prince of Wales Investiture at Caernarfon holiday for the scholars.*
- May 1 1913: *The school was closed this afternoon owing to the Bargoed May Day Show.*
- October 16 1914: *About half-a-dozen scholars have been away hop-picking.*

Any form of outside entertainment was welcomed by local people. For the week ending June 23 1899 the headmaster wrote:

the attendances this week has been far from satisfactory – the chief cause I attribute to the presence of Barnum and Bailey's Great Show in Cardiff; many of the children and their parents visited the show.

While half-day and one-day holidays were granted by the Board for local events, Royal occasions attracted a week's holiday as in the following instances:

- June 21 to 26 1897 -- Queen Victoria's Diamond Jubilee, the first such jubilee for a British monarch.
- June 23 to 27 1902 -- Coronation celebrations continued even though Edward VII's ill-health meant the coronation ceremony was postponed to August. *Merthyr Express*, July 5 1902 carried this report on the Coronation Treat:

*On Thursday, June 26, the school children attending Brithdir Board
School, to the number of about 400, were regaled with a sumptuous tea,
provided by the Gelligaer District Council in commemoration of
Coronation Day. The headmaster, Mr. Samuel Davies, in conjunction with
an energetic committee of local gentlemen, worked hard to make the treat
a thorough success. The schools were tastefully decorated for the
occasion. A procession was formed, headed by the committee, and the
principal streets were paraded. The procession presented a very pretty
sight, the children waving flags of all description, and singing marches
suitable to the occasion. At frequent intervals, too, they sang patriotic
songs, under the conductorship of Mr. H. Williams, assistant master.
Afterwards they sat down to a splendid tea. Each child on leaving was
presented with the Coronation mug, and some fruit. After the tea, sports
were held on Spion Kop Field. A pleasant day was brought to a close by a
splendid display of fireworks and the igniting of the bonfire on the
mountain top.*

- June 16 to 21 1911 -- Coronation of King George V.

Some reasons for absences were seasonal, as in the case of wimberry and
blackberry picking, or nut-gathering. Sometimes such absences seem to have
been condoned, while on other occasions Samuel Davies punished boys who
left school to pick wimberries during school hours. Sunday School treats and
outings, as well as those organised by other groups linked with the places of
worship, usually merited a half or full day closure as, for instance:

May 11 1898: *this afternoon we were obliged to give a half holiday on
account of a Tea-party belonging to the Band of Hope.*

Samuel Davies was concerned about providing the best for his pupils:

May 1 1899: *Martha J Whale an Assistant Mistress here taking charge of
Standard I has been transferred to the Infants School - and a Monitor a
young lad about 13 years of age appointed in her place. That a transfer
should take place now at the end of the school year is very detrimental to
the success of this class at the time of the Examination. I have no one to
take charge of the class except a 1st Year Pupil Teacher or a Candidate. It
is my intention to make an appeal by the next Board to have the
appointment – either rescinded or postponed until after the Examination.*

His entry of June 1 suggests the Board rescinded their decision:

*Miss M.J. Whale has again been transferred from the Infants to the Mixed
School.*

Throughout his time in charge, Samuel Davies strived to make not only his
school but also the local community better. In 1898, he taught French in
evening class. In November 1900, a night school was held on Tuesday,
Wednesday and Thursday evenings, whilst on Saturday evenings a shorthand
class was taught by assistant teacher Mr. F. J. Williams.

Samuel Davies was gratified by pupil successes as illustrated by this log book entry of October 10 1905 in which he underlined three names as if to emphasise their success.

Frank Gerrish a 5th Standard boy gained a Scholarship at the Gelligaer Intermediate School.

Florrie M. Williams a 6th Standard girl gained a Scholarship at Hengoed Intermediate School.

Walter Cooper a pupil from this school has gained a Scholarship at the Pengam Intermediate School (a fifth Standard boy).

From the start Samuel Davies tried to improve attendances and in May 1897 introduced his Attendance Banner. It would appear many scholars bought into the idea as the entry in the log for May 28 1897 revealed:

The 4th Standard after securing the Attendance Banner for a fortnight – had to deliver it up to Standard I, who made a percentage of 94 for the week.

Annual prizes were awarded for regular attendance and even in difficult periods of colliery disputes improvements were made. Gelligaer School Board adopted a similar practice as witnessed by this entry in the log book:

January 27 1902: *The Board at their meeting yesterday adopted a Prize Scheme for attendance which will come into operation upon the resumption of school after the Mid-Summer Holidays. The Prizes are to be distributed annually after the holidays.*

The following examples also show improvements continued as the school moved from Board to LEA control:

- March 7 1902: *the attendance this week has reached its highest climax the percentage for the week 92% of the number on books.*
- September 23 1904: *the attendance this week has been very good on the whole - the percentage being 93, the highest we have had yet.*
- December 4 1904: *attendances were exceedingly good reaching 94%.*

The Inspection report for July 1905 noted *This School well maintains its reputation for good discipline and thoroughness of the instruction. The children attend with great regularity and punctuality.* And further log book entries refer to attendance:

- December 15 1905: *the attendance (always in past years very irregular during the approach of Christmas Holidays) is wonderfully good.*
- February 9 1906: *this is I believe the record week for attendance being 96.7% with the monthly attendance record of 96.3%.*
- March 30 1906: *only one pupil absent for the whole week (out of 181 on the registers) being 97.1% a record attendance for this year.*
- April 12 1906: *the percentage of attendance 98.6, the record weekly attendance to date.*

To further encourage good attendance, the LEA initiated monthly attendance half-day holidays, which the children made gallant attempts to secure – and achieved on numerous occasions. This extract from *Bargoed Journal*, May 21 1908, shows how seriously some took school attendance:

> *Hilda Bennett, who attended Brithdir School for five years and only missed one half-day, has been stricken with illness and after persuading her mother to carry her to school for a week was compelled to give up.*

In 1907, foreseeing possible problems from the addition of about one hundred new houses in the village, Samuel Davies wrote to LEA Primary Inspector on September 2 *alerting him that the building of the new houses would necessitate an increased accommodation shortly.* The influx of newcomers affected attendances, as the following two examples from 1910 show:

> April 22: *the attendance is unsatisfactory according to the high percentage we have been able to maintain during the past years. The reason I attributed to the influx of new children into the school.*

> May 6: *the migratory population which has come to occupy some of the new houses here has had an evil effect on the attendance of the school. The children of the old established inhabitants attend regularly and punctually- as has been the case for the last few years.*

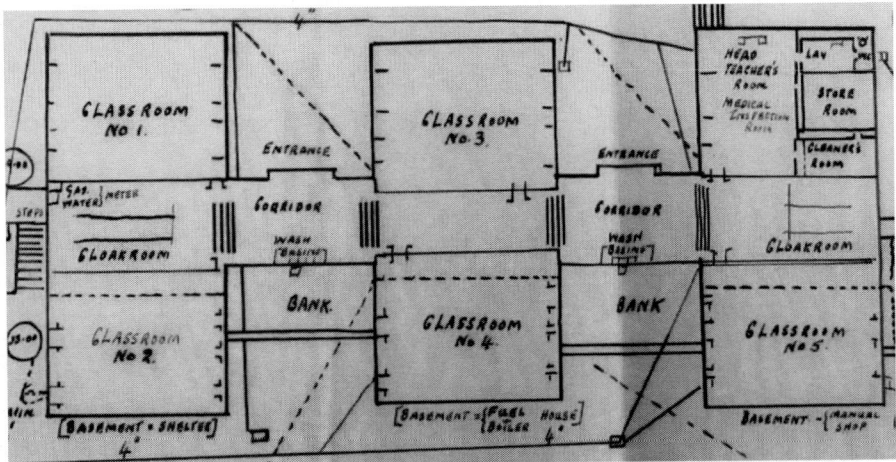

Brithdir Boys' School (plan of school taken from School Compendium of 1930s. Courtesy Glamorgan Archives), built at a cost of £4,960, and with accommodation for 250 boys, opened August 30 1915 with Samuel Davies as headmaster. The official opening, on Monday, August 30 1915, by Kathleen Vaughan of Dromore, Tredegar, deputising for her brother, Lieutenant (Dr.) E. W. Sydney Martin, who was on war service in Malta, was reported in *Merthyr Express*. Mrs. Vaughan, using the gold key presented to her by the contractors, opened the doors to allow guests into the new building. They gathered in its spacious hall where County Councillor Sydney Jones spoke of the skill of county architect, D. Pugh Jones, in designing such a wonderful building on a very difficult site. He paid particular attention to its arrangement with tier above tier like the entrance to some great institution. Pupils celebrated with a half day holiday and a tea, paid for by Dr. Martin, on the following day.

Initially, the steep approach to the school was just earth and stones that, within a few years, became a heap of stones. Children had to clamber over the stones on their way to and from school, and in the winter, with ice and snow, it was nothing short of dangerous. The steps, constructed 1926, made the route far less hazardous not only for school children but also for many older people who used the hill to reach the main road at the top.

The school was built on a steep gradient as shown in this photograph of John Moore at the bottom of the flight of steps constructed up *school hill* in April 1926.
Courtesy his sister, Jacqueline Amy Tiernan.

Samuel Davies's activities were not confined to the school room, for he was an energetic worker in other spheres. He was deacon and treasurer of Libanus Church, Cwmsyfiog, for many years. Elected unopposed on each occasion, he served fifteen years on Merthyr Board of Guardians. He held the position of president and treasurer of Gelligaer Association of National Union of Teachers. On several occasions he was elected a vice-president of Rhymney Valley Cricket League and was president of Brithdir Cricket Club.

As noted previously, Samuel Davies valued good attendance, and this section on the Boys' School is rounded off with reference to the remarkable attendance records of two boys listed in local press reports on attendance prizes. John Williams, 11 Herbert Street, left school in 1925 with a record of six years'

The date on the board is unclear but the watches, medallions and books suggest a prize giving presentation for good attendance. Samuel Davies, sitting centre, retired as headmaster September 30 1926, and Henry R. Judd, sitting right, replaced him November 9 - possibly Mr. Davies was invited to award the prizes. Also included are teachers Francis (Frank) West, standing far right, and Tommy Davies, standing second left.
Courtesy Ivor Lewis

unbroken attendance in Brithdir Boys' School. Over the years, his awards were - 1st year, book (value 2s 6d); 2nd year, book (value 5s); 3rd year, Glamorgan Education Committee's medal; 4th year, a set of mathematical instruments; 5th year, silver watch; 6th year, unknown at time of press report. However, his fine record was surpassed by Milsom Mutlow, 4 Herbert Street, who left the school December 1928 (if he had stayed in school to March 1929, he could have reached nine years) with an unbroken record of eight years' perfect attendance, for which he was awarded an inscribed solid silver watch.

On September 30, 1926, Samuel Davies wrote *Terminated my service at this school today, after 30 years' employment in this village.* Henry R. Judd served as headmaster in Brithdir Boys' from November 9 1926 to March 1939. Tommy Davies, formerly senior assistant (and son to Samuel Davies), took charge until April 22 1940 when Daniel Jones commenced duties as headmaster.

Brithdir Infants' School (1925 onwards)

Muriel Davies, began her apprenticeship as a pupil teacher under the guidance of Agnes Davies in 1913. Three years later, September 1 1916, she began teaching at Brithdir Girls' School. Succeeding Agnes Davies, she took charge of Infants' Department January 5 1925. At the end of November 1941, after sixteen years in charge at Brithdir Infants', she resigned the teaching profession to be married.

Muriel Davies seated, with (L-R) her sister Olwen, Joan Rees (Tir y ferch Gryno) and unknown.
Courtesy Sian Hayworth

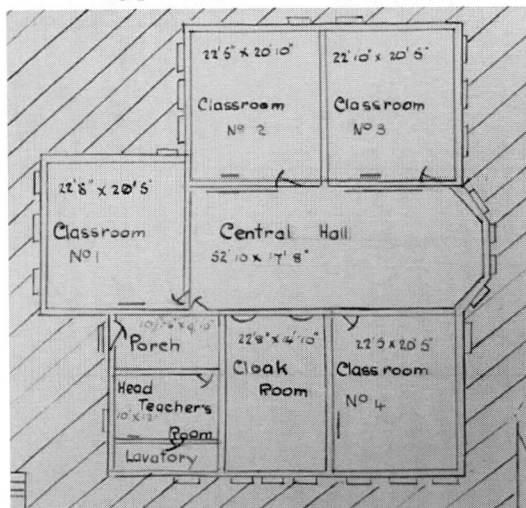

Plan of Brithdir Infants' taken from School compendium of 1930s.   Courtesy Glamorgan Archives

Daughter of Samuel Davies, Muriel Davies was, as reported in *Merthyr Express*, November 22 1941, well known throughout the area through her keen interest in the religious, drama and social activities of the district. She had been the local secretary of the National War Savings Association since its inception.

Brithdir Infants Class 3 circa 1925, (courtesy Glenys Price, née Williams)
Front Row: L-R: Phyllis Hayes (cuddling her doll), unknown, Glenys Williams (marked X),
Beryl Williams.   2nd Row: David Price (fish shop) directly behind the board, John
Jenkins, killed flying Spitfire twenty years later, kneels behind with hand on Glenys's
shoulder. 3rd Row: Peggy Hillman (2nd from left), Emmy Evans (3rd from left), Margaret
Sheasby (7th from left) and Mabel James (right end of row). 4th Row: Freda Wynn (far
left) and Sadie Thomas (far right). Back Row: teacher, Olwen Davies, Moses Price (6th
from left) Ron Goodwyn (far right).

Brithdir Infants School circa 1928 - Muriel Davies with Class 4; the two lads in the back
row right are Don West and Mel Davies.   Courtesy Millie Davies

Brithdir Infants School - Olwen Davies, with her class. Courtesy Millie Davies

Brithdir Infants 1949.   Courtesy Mel Williams
Front row left to right: Sheila Ashley, Mel Williams, Sandra James, unknown, Peter
Williams, Alun Williams, Derek Bennett and Keith Williams. Back row left to right:
Leonora Brain, Mavis Ashley, Royston Smith, Jean Ferguson, unknown

After ten years as certificated assistant at Tirphil School, Eluned Williams
(left) was appointed headmistress of Brithdir Infants'
School in 1941. Much of the information about her
family and career is taken from reports in *Merthyr
Express*. Born in Brithdir, daughter of teacher Henry
(Harry) Williams and his wife Catherine, of Church
Villa, Eluned was educated first in Brithdir before
attending Bargoed Secondary and, on Thursday,
October 10 1929, she started professional training at
Bangor Training College. On returning home for the
Christmas vacation (1929-1930) she was presented with
an ebony clock with silver plate inscribed *Presented to Miss E. Williams by the*

100

Congregational Sunday School as a token of esteem for the services rendered as secretary of this school.

From *Merthyr Express*, October 29 1949:

Brithdir Board Mixed Department, built 1893. It became Brithdir Council Mixed Department when handed over to LEA. It housed the Girls' Department from 1915 to 1954, after which it was used as Youth Club.

At Brithdir Infants' School on Friday, parting tributes were paid to Miss Freda Price, who had been a member of the staff for nine years, on the occasion of her departure for Exhall Training College, Coventry. Miss Eluned Williams, head-mistress, thanked Miss Price for the excellent services rendered during her period among them. On behalf of the scholars Sandra James and Christine Harding presented Miss Price with a beautiful bouquet, and she received handkerchiefs from Stephen Pritchard and Gerald Harris. Miss Olwen Davies made a presentation to their colleague from members of the staff, while Mrs. Dan Jones presented a personal gift from herself and Mr. Jones, headmaster of the boys' school. At the time of leaving Miss Price had been organist at St. David's Church for a number of years and she was a member of the Masque Players, Bargoed.

Brithdir Girls' School 1915-1954

When, on August 30 1915, school re-opened after the mid-summer vacation, the boys reported to their new building while the girls assembled in the former Mixed Department premises. *Staff: Martha C. Price, Head Teacher; Margaret Davies, Certificated Teacher; Marian Lewis, Certificated Teacher; Muriel Davies, Temporary Uncertificated; number on Roll 163.*

Most pages in the school log book contained entries spanning days, weeks or even months, but, in July 1916, Martha Price filled a whole page with just one topic, examination results (below) which suggested a feeling of pride whilst writing the entry.

Entrance Examination to Bargoed Higher Elementary School: The following pupils were presented for examination, and have been accepted as pupils at the above school from August 28 1916:
Ethel Sprague, Hannah Jenkins, Violet Jones, Maggie Thomas, Maisie Williams, Katie Lewis and Valerie Howard.

On December 22 1916, Martha C. Price resigned her post and, when the girls re-assembled on January 8 1917, they were greeted by the new head mistress, Mary L. John.

Staff and pupils in Brithdir Girls' School were rightly proud of their achievements in needlework. Miss Ellis of Board of Education, visiting on

March 6 1918, examined all the classes in handwork and needlework and was very pleased with the work. An entry by Mary John on April 15 1918 noted a receipt from County Accountant for £6. 14s 4d, money from the previous term's needlework sales. The school's successful inaugural *Parents Day*, on December 22 1920, was thoroughly enjoyed by parents, children and visitors. Almost every parent attended, visiting the classrooms to see the girls at work at the various lessons and examining (and sometimes buying) some of the girls' needlework and handwork displayed on tables.

It was during the headship of Mary John that the school acquired a piano. On November 1 1921, she logged, no doubt with satisfaction, *on Tuesday and Wednesday evenings of last week we held our Concerts. We had a second success and are able to buy a piano and pay cash down for it.* A balance sheet of accounts (dated November 15) showed £46 2s 6d *was taken at the concerts and a very good second-hand piano cost £42 10s 6d (with £2 10s 6d allowed for cash payment).*

Both Joan and Olwen Rees (of Tir y ferch Gryno) taught in the village schools. Joan started as a student teacher in the Girls' Department on August 27 1917. An entry in the school log for April 4 1922 reads *Miss Rees was absent today – snowed up as a result of the severe snowstorms of Friday night and all day Monday.* The headmistress also remarked *this is the first time Miss Rees has been absent since her appointment.*

The last entry made by Mary John on November 19 1923 makes sober reading: *The necessity has arisen for me to take an operation (internal) and I am entering a Nursing Home for that purpose tomorrow. I may be absent for some weeks, and am informing the Education Committee so that they may send extra help for my class.*

Sadly, after an apparently *successful operation performed in a Cardiff Nursing Home, Mary John suffered a cardiac weakness and passed away on the morning of November 25. According to her wishes, the Department was closed November 29 1923 for her funeral, a private burial at Gelligaer Cemetery.* The staff shortfall was initially filled by Vida John, temporary uncertificated assistant. Mair E. Davies was appointed as the next head, and she served until retiring February 28 1951.

Samuel Davies had recognised the importance of regular attendance at school and similar good attendance

Brithdir Girls' School Cookery and Domestic Science Class 1928. Cookery courses had started December 5 1918 with a class of 18 girls.
Courtesy Henrietta Jones

102

was encouraged in the Girls' School. Good attendance figures of 98 per cent and above were noted in the Girls' School log during May, June, July, October and November of 1924, earning the school an attendance half-holiday each month.

An attendance awards ceremony was held December 1 1927 when County Councillor W. Hammond and J. H. Stone, local manager, Gelligaer Group of Schools, presented awards to deserving scholars.

The board reads: *Brithdir Girls School 100% Attendance last seven weeks, Class VII. November 1924.* Joan Rees proudly poses with her class after being awarded the *Good Attendance* pennant. Ida Brown is the young girl in the white smock on the teacher's left. Behind her, 2nd from right is Edith Hewitt. Back row L-R: Annie Maud Evans, unknown, Louise Jones. (Image courtesy Henrietta Jones, and details from Nellie Dando)

The full list of the awards for the following year, 1928, the last year in which the LEA gave such awards, was:

- Ceridwen Whitefoot, 8 years' perfect attendance awarded lady's dressing case.
- Marjorie Williams, 7 years' perfect attendance, awarded lady's suitcase.
- Eileen Startup, 6 years' perfect attendance, inscribed gold medal.
- Elsie Gerrish. 5 years' perfect attendance, wristlet watch, suitably inscribed.
- The following pupils each with 4 years' perfect attendance were awarded a work basket: Margaret McCarthy, Brenda James, Nellie Hewitt, Emma Mutlow, Thelma James, Freda Williams, Edith Hewitt, Agnes Jones, Mavis Fry, Violet Gore, Cavell Miles, Lily and Myra Williams.
- Maud Edmunds and Alice M. Davies each received a lady's dressing case for 3 years' perfect attendance.
- Book prizes were given for 2 years' and 1 year perfect attendance.
- Certificates for 99% and 98% attendance.

When, in 1930, Ceridwen Whitefoot, daughter of Mr and Mrs Tom Whitefoot, left Brithdir Girls' School, she did so with a record nine years and three months perfect attendance. Violet Gore, Salisbury Terrace, completed nine years unbroken attendance in 1932. With such records it is not surprising that over a 11 year period (1924-35) Brithdir Girls' School had a record annual average attendance of over 95%. In April 1935, with 98.6 they were the highest in the district.

Nellie Hewitt's silver medal.

Brithdir Council Junior Girls' School 1954

L - R - Front row: Ann Duggan, Jean Porter, Mavis Ashley, Enfys Morgan, Irene Williams, Camilla Jenkins, Gaynor Baker, Margaret Williams, Elaine Moore, Margaret Bevan, Maureen Lewis, Vera Golding. 2nd Row: Janine Winstone, Ann Morris, Myrtle Williams, Christine Gabb, Linda Williams, Marie Winmill, Miss Evans, Miss Thomas, Miss Rees, Sandra James, Yvonne Evans, Dorothy Evans, Rosemary Inseal, Kay Gardner. 3rd Row: Jennifer Harding, Sandra Maggs, Janet Gardner, Yvonne Rawle, Carolann James, Margarette Jones, Jeanette Green, Jean Gibbs, Anita Norman, Alice Carey, Jeanette Hook, Valerie Cox, Emiah Howells. Back Row: Diane Way, Sheila Ashley, Leonora Brain, Mary Tilley, Jean George, Sheila Way, Maureen Williams, Phyllis Dunne, Sandra Duggan, Marlene Davies, Jean Ferguson, Christine Harding, Marjorie Golding, Blodwen Hill, June Howells.

Courtesy Georgina Greaney, names courtesy Sandra Evans

Pupils of Brithdir Girls' School acquitted themselves well in the competition for the cup at Pontlottyn sports in July 1935. The girls, Ruth Gardner, Eileen White, Beatrice Williams, Vida Pudge, Evelyn White, Mildred Harris, Marion White, Beryl Williams, Pearl Williams, Vera Davies, Florrie Harris and Jenny Brewer, won 13 events.

BRITHDIR

" THE SLEEPING BEAUTY ' —Before the August holidays pupils of Brithdir Girls' School gave performances on Thursday of " The Sleeping Beauty," arranged as a play, before audiences of their schoolmates. Miss E. Evans was the producer, and parts were taken by: King, Gillian West; Queen, Maureen Davies; Prince, Pauline Evans ; Princess, Linda Harrison ; Witch, Henrietta Bonney ; Fairies, Linda Startup, Mavis Brown, Ceinwen Evans, Yvonne Gardner, Myrtle Smith, Sybil Williams and Ann Harding; Goody, Valerie Pritchard; Old Men, Dorothy Higgs and Mary Williams; Lords and Ladies, Vera Nicholls, Joyce Underwood, Kathleen Watts.

Merthyr Express, August 6 1949.

July 16 1954 was the last day for staff and pupils of Brithdir Council Junior Girls' School. From September 1 1954, the Boys' and Girls' Departments joined in the former Boys' School to become Brithdir Junior Mixed School. After that, the school canteen was housed in the former Girls' School and local Youth Clubs and further education classes were also held there.

The final attainments by scholars of the Girls' School prior to its closure:

June 17 1954 - *The Scholarship Result arrived. 100% passes.*

Camilla Jenkins

Arithmetic 133 + English 125 = 258;

Gaynor Baker 111 + 121 = 232;

Irene Williams 126 + 97 = 223;

Enfys Morgan 103 + 96 = 199;   Margaret Williams 115 + 71 = 186

Brithdir schools post World War II

On September 1 1954 Ernest Browning commenced duties in charge of Brithdir Junior Mixed School with staff Tommy Davies, Joan John, née Rees, and Miss Evelyn Evans. In the post-war era, falling rolls meant reorganisation, and the village schools amalgamated when, on September 5 1960, the village's Junior Mixed and Infants' School opened (in the former Infants' School) with 97 pupils on roll and Eluned Williams, former headteacher of Brithdir Infants' School in charge.

R Zecca, headteacher in the late 1980s, left in April 1993, to take charge of Elliots Town Primary School in New Tredegar. Deputy headteacher Maralyn Olsen was appointed first acting headteacher before becoming headteacher on June 27 1994. Gill Hopkins was appointed deputy head on April 24 1995. The front page of *South Wales Echo*, July 21 1998, carried a report of the end of an era in Brithdir when its 94 year old school building closed as a school. As from September 1998, the 28 Brithdir pupils transferred to schools outside the community.

Brithdir Primary School Staff circa 1996. Back row L-R, Ann Duggan (dinner lady), Kay Kwiewinski (nursery nurse), Sylvia Evans (dinner lady), Mark Forward (caretaker), Jan Asarati (school clerk) and Enid Bennett (dinner lady). Front row L-R Veronica Eynon (crossing patrol), Gill Hopkins (deputy head), Maralyn Olsen (headteacher), Janet Evans (dinner lady) and Adele Powell (teacher).

Courtesy Morfydd Olsen

The present position

For 119 years, Brithdir had at least one school but, at the time of writing there is no school in Brithdir, and its young people attend schools outside the community, not just for secondary, further and higher education as in the past, but for all levels of their education.

- In 1988, the 95 year old building that served the community as Mixed Department, Girls' School, and Youth Club, was demolished and, by late 1990, a modern brick building, *Brithdir Residential Care Home*, was erected on its School Street site.

Brithdir Junior Mixed School staff L-R Front row: Mrs. J.M. John, Ernest Browning, headteacher, and Tommy Davies, deputy head. Back row: Lydia Davies and Anita Goode.

Courtesy Anita Goode née Shorey

- Brithdir Boys' School has also been demolished and now a small community garden with a stone pillar bearing this plaque marks the place where I and countless other Brithdir boys honed our skills in all manner of classroom and other activities.

TO COMMEMORATE THE OPENING OF
BRITHDIR COMMUNITY GARDEN
ON THE 16TH NOVEMBER 2002
ON THE SITE OF THE FORMER
BRITHDIR BOYS COUNCIL SCHOOL
1914 - 1998

- In 1998, the final bell was sounded at a building that served the community well when the community's last school, the former Infants' School which ended its school days as a Primary School, closed its doors for the last time.

Chris Jones purchased it in autumn 2002. He has (as shown left) retained its outward appearance, but has modernised the interior into a very beautiful family home. The neighbouring headmaster's house, later school caretaker's house, is also a private home.

No doubt, decisions to close the schools were based on financial considerations and perceived advantages of education in larger schools housed in more modern premises. However, they leave the community poorer for the loss of its schools.

Brithdir Brownies: Maralyn Olsen (left) and sister Morfydd Olsen (centre) with back row L-R. Linda Bennett, Raydene Spencer, Alison Jones, Vicki Morgan, Darlene Britten, Helen Jenkins. Samantha Jones, Teresa Morris, Debbie Landrygan and Julie Davies. Front row Karen Roberts. Julie Humphries, Andrea Jones, Lisa Cullum and Teresa Williams. Photo courtesy Morfydd Olsen, names courtesy Christine Davies.

CHAPTER 8 SHOPS AND SERVICES

Over the years, there have been a number of shops in Brithdir. The majority of these were front room shops, often run by widows or wives trying to supplement the family income after breadwinner-husbands suffered accident or sickness. Most such shops sold basic commodities, often home-made, including toffee dabs, toffee apples, sweets, Spanish root, liquorice sticks, paraffin and sand. There were other shops and businesses – butchers, bakers, drapers, grocers, general stores, fish and chip shops, barber shops, cobblers, as well as the post office -- which provided almost everything needed in Brithdir's households. What follows is based on sources such as census returns, trade directories and GUDC minutes as well as the memories of myself and others who grew up in Brithdir.

KELLY'S - MONMOUTHSHIRE & SOUTH WALES DIRECTORY, 1895
COMMERCIAL

Mrs Jane Brown, greengrocer
Buchan & Co. grocers
Arthur Davies, tailor
David Davies, builder
Jacob Gabriel, draper & boot dealer
James George & Son, boot makers
Marks Harris, draper & boot dealer
David Jones, boot maker
Thomas Jones, butcher
Dr. William Jones, surgeon
Joseph King, grocer
John Lloyd, shopkeeper
Alfred Phillips, grocer
Charles James Price, provision dealer
Walter Price, draper
Mrs Eliza Protheroe, ironmonger
Martin Luther Thomas, general dealer & beer retailer (off license)
Israel Williams, baker

Businesses listed 1901 census
Station Terrace,

No 9 John Christopher Phillips, grocer
No 10 Company Shop, lock-up,
No 11 Miss Sarah Foward, dressmaker
No 23 Thomas Jones, grocer
No 24 Miss Miriam Davies, grocer
No 31 Aubrey Lionel Sherwin, clothier and boot dealer
No 33 Mrs. Mary Jane Jones, coffee tavern
No 33 Ernest Lacey, photographers
Bridge Shop, Miss Elizabeth Watkins, confectionery & baker
Old Post Office, Martin Luther Thomas, draper; Mrs. Thomas, confectionery & baker

Elsewhere

15 Charles St, Ann Reed, dressmaker
12 Herbert St, Mrs. Sarah Ann Coombs, dressmaker
28 Herbert St, Mrs. Elizabeth Bufton, greengrocer
13 James St, Mrs. Lucy E. Hallett, dressmaker
3 The Villas, Robert Morris, surgeon
School St, Walter Price, post office
School St, Margaret Wray, dressmaker
Railway Shop, Thomas Howard, grocer
Half Way House, Emily Francis Jones, dressmaker

The range of businesses in Brithdir in the late nineteenth and early twentieth centuries is evident in these lists based on Kelly's Directories 1895 and 1901 and census return. According to *Monmouth Guardian and Bargoed and Caerphilly Observer*, October 30 1914, Andrew Buchan's Brithdir Company

Shop, a lock-up facility at 10 Station Terrace, was managed by William Jones of Bryn Glas, George Hill, for some four decades, He had retired by the time of the 1911 census and he died 1914. Readers interested in further information about Andrew Buchan, a Scot who arrived in the upper Rhymney Valley at the start of the second quarter of the nineteenth century, are referred to websites such as www.butetownhistory.info/en/interesting-characters/andrew-buchan/ and Marion Evans' book (published 2007) *The history of Andrew Buchan's Rhymney Brewery*. John Christopher Phillips's grocery shop was in No 9, and, on William Jones's retirement, he combined the two shops but the venture failed and *London Gazette* April 9 and 12 1912 shows he filed for bankruptcy.

As Brithdir grew, so did the number of small retail businesses in the village. A report in B*argoed, Caerphilly and New Tredegar Journal*, August 6 1905, noted that two gentlemen from Pontlottyn had recently opened shops opposite the railway station: Thomas Owen was a butcher while James Lewis ran a Fish & Potato Establishment.

By the time the 1911 census was taken, Brithdir had the company shop (mentioned above), George Inn Hotel, post office, 9 grocers, 2 general dealers, confectionery shop, barber, shoe-maker, outfitter, milk vendor and 9 dress-makers all working on their own account. Thomas Howard, had moved from Railway Shop to 19 Bristol Terrace; Edwin Bufton had taken over the shop in Railway Terrace. Grocers Jacob Tonkiy and John Davies had new businesses in Station Terrace. Jacob Tonkiy, the grocer at number 29 was, like his parents and all but one of his siblings, born in Russia – his sister Rachel was born in 1908 in Abertysswg, and the family moved to Brithdir soon after. John Davies, a Welsh-speaking native of New Quay, Cardiganshire, opened his grocery business at No 31. Adam Watkins, licensed hawker of Bridge Shop was described as *partly at home and partly hawking* while his spinster sister Elizabeth tended to the confectionery and bakery business. Gwladys May Gwynne of The Villas was a music teacher and Dr. Martin's surgery was in East View. John Griffiths (Ivy Row) a furniture remover and general contractor would have made a pretty sight with his cart and pair, *Jack* and *Stout,* at that year's Bargoed and District May Day Show, where, according to report in the local press, he won two 1st prizes with *Stout* and second prize with *Jack* and *Stout* in the Best Pair competition. By 1912, according to minutes of GUDC meeting September 20 1912, Brithdir had 20 shops and 1 licensed house.

In September 1919 GUDC received the following six licence applications:
    L. J. Jenkins, 7 School Street, applied for a milk vendor's license – granted.
    R.C. Hale, 2 James Street, wanted to sell faggots, peas and potatoes – granted.
    Edgar William Every, 31a Station Terrace, applied to sell fresh fish, grocery
        and greengrocery - granted.
    W. F. Hares, Post Office, applied for a confectionery, tobacco and stationery
        license - granted.
    H Cox, 5 Harcourt Terrace, retail sweet business – not granted.
    J Cacase, 28 Station Terrace, temperance bar - not granted.

Memories of Brithdir's shops: While written sources about Brithdir's shops are sparse, there is still much in the memories of Brithdirites about the retail scene.

I start this journey around Brithdir's shops with Station Terrace establishments. Mrs. Fry sold freshly baked bread from her home in No. 2. From 1893, No. 28 was home to Edward and Mary Ann Thomas and there they raised their 7 children. The family was still there when the 1911 census was taken but it is not clear when the property passed to J. Cacase who, in 1919, applied to GUDC for a licence to open a temperance bar there. His application was refused on the grounds that there was already one in the district. However, the photograph (c.1912) used in the story of Rifleman Jones shows *Temperance* across the shop boarding. By the time the information was being collected for Kelly's 1923 directory, Antonio Roffi, confectioner, occupied No 28. Many Brithdirites remember him travelling to neighbouring villages with his horse (Dick) and cart to sell his delicious ice-cream. Inside the shop, behind the counter, the rows of sweet jars, lined up as if on parade, kept many a youngster in the 1940s and 1950s spellbound, eyes roving from jar to jar until deciding. Then it was usually 2ozs in a small triangular paper bag. Leno Roffi took over on his father's retirement and people of my generation remember how, on wintry evenings in the 1950s, we enjoyed hot Oxo served in glass tumblers, while listening to the latest hit records on a small table-top juke-box. Today, the shop is known as *Brithdir Stores*. Also in Station Terrace, next to the old club was Jones's fish and chip shop.

When the 1911 census was taken, outfitter John Levine, born in Germany, lived in rooms at 12 East View. By 1913 he had moved to 32 Station Terrace where, until 1943, he carried on business as outfitter and boot and shoe dealer.

Henry Jones's grocery shop, known locally as *Jones Henrys,* was next at No 32. After he retired as grocer, Connie his daughter operated a School of Motoring from there. Bryan and Pat Bennett became the proprietors about 1965, and, for some 35 years, ran a fish and chip shop and also sold newspapers.

Brithdir Co-op and Butchers, a branch of New Tredegar Co-operative Society, opened before World War I. A report in *Cardiff Times*, January 30 1909, noted that a

Three shops that served Brithdir well.
The detached property (left) is Bridge House, formerly Bridge Shop. The double bay fronted shop (centre) is *Jones Henrys*, No 32 Station Terrace. The car is parked outside the former Co-op store and butcher, now St. David's Church.
Courtesy Pat Bennett

branch in Brithdir was being considered and a report in *Monmouthshire Guardian, Bargoed and Caerphilly Observer*, May 22 1914 shows it was in operation by then. It was managed by D.O. Davies for many years and, when he was transferred to Ystrad Mynach in 1932, his former senior assistant, Iestyn Havard, replaced him. Later managers included Dennis Arundel (Tirphil), Billy Chandler, Stan Smith (Russell Street) and Aneurin Williams who lived in Ystrad Mynach and was manager at Brithdir and Gilfach. The

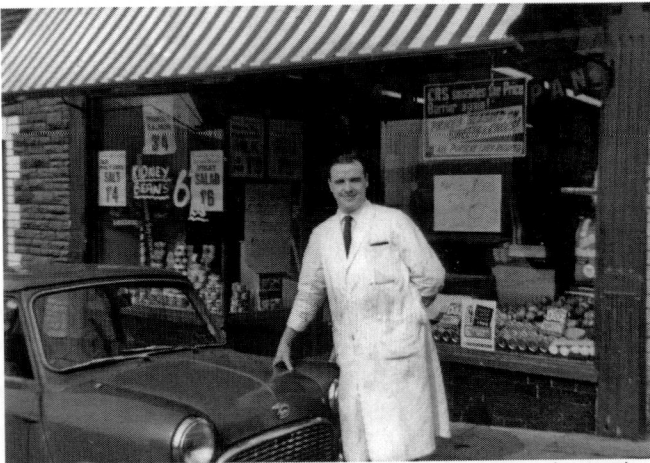

following are some of the staff who over the years worked in the shop - Mrs. Davies, Janet Harris, Pauline Thomas, Lettice Chard, Sonia Williams and Mary Williams (James Street), while Mel Williams, Ivor Williams, and John Thomas were part-time delivery boys.

Dennis Arundel former manager at Brithdir pictured outside Cwmsyfiog branch shop.

I recall two shops, Davey's sweet shop at No. 19 and Mabel George's grocery shop at No. 20, in Charles Street. Herbert Street had, at No.1 barber Jimmy Mellens, at No. 9 newsagent Maggie Place (where we bought our comics and

110

fireworks), at No. 12 Henry French sold Sunday newspapers, at No. 17 Jimmy James's sweet shop, and No. 28 was Bromage's fish and chip shop. Opposite the bottom of Herbert Street was Bridge Shop, where once Adam Watkins had a confectionery and bakery business, before, in the 1930s and 1940s, William Gibbs had a grocery shop there. Moving to James Street: No 5 was Maggie Clark's post office, and there were two fish and chip shops, Mary Price at No 19 and in No 28 Martha Thomas.

There were a number of businesses in School Street. No. 1 was, at various times, post office, greengrocery and Charles *Cobbler* Williams's boot and shoe repair shop. Central Stores (grocer and general dealer) was at No. 12, the top of the street. First opened by Samuel Henry Sprague of New Tredegar soon after he married Rosalie Gunter of Cardiff in 1901, it went on to serve the community for about five decades. Sadly, Rosalie died in 1910, and with the help of general servant Gwladys Frodd (Cardiff), Samuel carried on running the store until the mid-1920s when he moved to Hengoed. Sisters Doris and Minnie Paviour of New Tredegar took over the store and after their marriages (in 1940), Antonio Roffi bought it and gifted it to daughter Rena who, with her husband, Doug Rogers, ran the shop.

Railway Shop at No. 3 Railway Terrace was grocer Thomas Howard's Supply Stores before Edwin Bufton operated Bufton's Stores. Older Brithdir residents remember them delivering bread by horse and cart. In later years George Olsen traded there. Butcher William Hodges ran his business at No. 2 Russell Street.

Frank Goode sold a wide range of goods from his converted *front room* shop at No. 5 Wellington Terrace. The goods were not confined to the front room as the passage was full of stock, and the family living quarters were further confined as Mrs. Goode had a drapery business in the middle room and kept rolls and rolls of material. Also in Wellington Terrace was McLeod's small sweet shop at No. 16, while in No. 21, Les Britton made lead soldiers to sell and Mrs. Britton made toffee apples.

There was another sweet shop run by Polly Hallett at No 6 Tennyson Terrace and, in 1939, in No 7, Mary Hallett had a small general shop. George Bingham, cobbler, operated at No. 13 Tennyson Terrace. Mrs. Rogers, agent for stores such as Bargoed's Emporium and George, Rees and Jones, lived in Milton Terrace, and Lily May Coles had a small shop at No. 5 Nelson Terrace.

Tommy Williams, shown right with son Charles (courtesy Laura Williams), arrived in Brithdir in 1924 and started his cobbling business near the workmen's club in Station Terrace. Later, the family moved to 1 School Street (see above) and set up their front room shop. Tommy died in 1952, working on a pair of shoes for Elvad Williams: he was knocking in the last tack when he collapsed and died. Charles took over

the business on his father's demise and continued repairing our boots and shoes until 1955.

Brithdir had its fair share of fish and chip shops over the years but the one I remember most is Mary Price's at 19 James Street, for me her chips were the best. Mary and husband Richard William (Bill) Price are shown left courtesy of granddaughter Chrissy Price

John and Martha Thomas, (shown right courtesy grandson John Thomas), had their fish and chip shop at 28 James Street, the exact date of them taking up residence there is not known, however they were listed there on 1939 register.

Decades ago, most of the needs of Brithdir people were satisfied by the shops within the community supplemented by occasional visits to the large and prosperous shopping streets of Bargoed. The shopping landscape has changed since my youth and today Brithdir has just one shop, *Brithdir Stores*, 28 Station Terrace, while Bargoed, victim of social and economic change, no longer attracts many shoppers. At the time of writing, local people are just as likely as contemporaries across the globe to shop in large supermarkets and online.

Service (or tertiary) industries

Such industries embrace a wide range of activities with no tangible end-product, but aim to improve the lives and well-being of their users. In the pre-industrial era, most service needs were met locally - within the family, community or, in the cases of poverty and roads and from the sixteenth century onwards, by the parish (acting in its civil role). As, not only were such arrangements proving grossly inadequate by the second quarter of the nineteenth century, and the range of needs was expanding, statutory elected bodies were created to ensure uniform provision of some services across the country. For the Brithdir area:

From 1834 onwards, Merthyr Tydfil Poor Law Union, was responsible for dealing with the problems of poverty in parishes around that new industrial town.

Roads were the responsibility of Glamorgan Highway Board after 1844.

Glamorgan Constabulary (established 1841) helped ensure law and order across the county.

From the mid-nineteenth century onwards, new urban issues, especially those relating to public health, were under locally elected bodies, Boards of Health and, later, Sanitary Districts (coterminous with Poor Law Board).

Gelligaer School Board, established in the wake of 1870 legislation, ensured provision of statutory elementary education.

As society's needs became increasingly complex, locally-elected councils administered a wider range of statutory and non-statutory services. Glamorgan County Council, elected following 1888 legislation, assumed a wide range of responsibilities including, after the legislation of 1902, education. On the second tier of local government, G&R RDC, created 1894, was replaced by GUDC in 1908. GUDC established its fire service (as outlined in *Gelligaer Urban District Fire Brigade*, in *Gelligaer* vol. 20, 2013). Matters such as street lighting and cleaning, refuse collection and disposal, as well as water supply and sewerage, together with gas and electricity supplies, were subject to more formal arrangements. Parallel to all this, was medical care and the role of the local doctor. Volunteers, including groups such as Brithdir Division St. John Ambulance Brigade (see pages 330-335) and committees running Workmen's Institute or local sports fields and playgrounds, also played a part in providing services.

The lamplighter

This cameo study is an example of how a service impacted on life in Brithdir. When Brithdir community started to develop, night meant darkness relieved by moonlight, the flickering flame of candles and, for those who could afford them, oil lamps. How did Rachel Morgan and Alice Bevan, the coal miners' wives enumerated in their new little homes in Bryn Tawel in 1861, manage their chores in the short winter days? And, what about Ellen Isgeas, 17 year old dressmaker who, in 1871, was enumerated in one of the new properties at Bryn Tawel. How these people would have marvelled if they lived long enough to see gas supplies (and even electricity) reach Brithdir.

In September 1895, G&R RDC accepted the tender (£2 a lamp) submitted by Taliesin Isaac (then living near George Inn Hotel). According to the local press, Brithdir's first lamp posts were erected in 1898, the first near the river bridge, then one on George Hill crossroads and another on top of School Street. GUDC minutes show that, in September 1912, a Blanchard lamp was erected on the path to Bute Terrace and one small lamp near the railway station. Every evening the lamplighter made his rounds, lighting these lamps individually, and in the early morning he travelled his route again, to extinguish the lights.

In 1898, the council clerk placed an advertisement for a *competent man at Brithdir to attend to sewage tanks and works, and light, clean and repair lamps, wages 24s a week*. The identity of the man appointed in unclear, but, when the 1911 census was taken, 33 year old Frank Barton of 2 Harcourt Terrace, was working on *street lighting and sewerage* for GUDC. Local vandalism was a problem, as GUDC surveyor's report shows that, on February 18 1910, Frank Barton, reporting Charles Howells, New Houses, and Alfred Willie James of Cwmsyfiog, for breaking three panes of glass in public lamps at Brithdir, said that, since Christmas 1909, 25 panes of glass had been broken in lamps and six panes in the windows of his shed. Parental responsibility was invoked as finance committee minutes show the meeting on March 8 instructed the clerk to write to the father of Albert Neil, 32 Station Terrace, accepting his offer to pay for the damage done by his son to a street lamp at Brithdir. Benjamin Jordan, a 63 year old widower, living in rooms in 4 Herbert Street at the time of the 1911 census, was described as a *lamplighter* employed by Bedwellty UDC.

According to GUDC minutes, although Brithdir had a gas supply by September 1915, there were no gas lamps then. By March 1928, Brithdir had electric lighting both in the homes and the streets. Before the end of August 1939, the road between Brithdir and the Puzzle House (Factory Road, Bargoed), was lit by electric lights, especially welcome in view of the increasing number of accidents there in the previous few years.

Henry Samuel Fry and wife Gwladys May née Jones outside their home in Station Terrace. As mentioned on page 109 Gwladys used to sell freshly made bread from her home. For a number of years in 1970s Henry was chairman of Brithdir OAP Association. Henry and Gwladys married at Bedwellty Church in 1915, he was the son of James W Fry and Hannah Maria née Short of Rhymney. Gwladys May was the daughter of ostler William Jones and Anne of 2 Ivy Row, Brithdir, and the sister of Rifleman William Davies Jones commemorated on Brithdir Memorial (see story on page 193).

L-R Gwladys and Henry Fry with Amy McGraw, Alice Webb and Harriet Harris enjoy an outing with the pensioners association.

CHAPTER 9 SOCIAL LIFE

Up to at least the middle of the twentieth century, people in Brithdir, in common with those in many other villages, had an active and varied social life within or near their community. Brithdir's people not only shared their dependence on the coal industry, but also socialised together. For some families, much of that social activity was associated with their place of worship, and for others, especially young men, it was linked with their sporting activities. However, as illustrated by the following, some events, societies and places bonded people across the community.

Carnivals

The following collection of photographs of carnival queens and characters gives a flavour of Brithdir people and carnivals. The patriotic nature of those in the mid-century reflects local response to contemporary national and international events.

Hazel Hughes (right courtesy Bill Pollock) was *Queen of the Welsh Hills* at the 1938 Bargoed Carnival.

Eileen Williams, 18 year old daughter of Mr. and Mrs. W. Williams, 11 Tennyson Terrace, was *Queen of Brithdir Stay at Home Week* in 1944. She was *Queen of Victory in Europe* in 1945 carnival.

In her court were lady in waiting Dorothy Jones (below left courtesy Dorothy Hawkesford née Jones), and flower girl Maureen James (below right courtesy Angela Arlotte, her daughter).

Barbara Richards was *Queen of the Festival of Britain 1951*. In her court were - left group: Leonard Mutlow [black outfit], Mel Williams and Myrtle Smith behind, them Pat Harris, Gaynor Baker and Margareta Jones - right group: Ann Harding, Sybil Williams, Derek Nicholls, Mildred Ford and Maureen Lewis. (Courtesy Thomas (Mel) Williams).

Joining the Queen and her court below are: back row L-R: George Godfrey, unknown, Bob Major, Betty George and Kath Bennett (centre). Megan Hyatt is holding baby Fay, Pam Dobbs has her faced blackened, Mrs. Stenner (standing behind Wilf Bennett in stripped blazer), Bryn Harris and Rollie Hughes. Ben Watkins sitting left and Mary Hobby seated far right.

Richie Hennessy, marked with a star, among a group of his peers as Zulu warriors.
Courtesy Nita Smith.

The village carnival was a colourful affair with floats (lorries on loan decorated in a theme). In the year I was *Roy Rogers*, not on *Trigger*, but my cousin's horse *Paddy*, the Bennett boys, plastered with gravy browning were jungle natives.

Community spirit was all-important in making a successful carnival. It was an opportunity for the village's characters to entertain, and the following photographs show how this was done in Brithdir.

*Hick*y Bennett, one of Brithdir's characters, in carriage pushed by Fanny Bale.
Courtesy Billy Bennett.

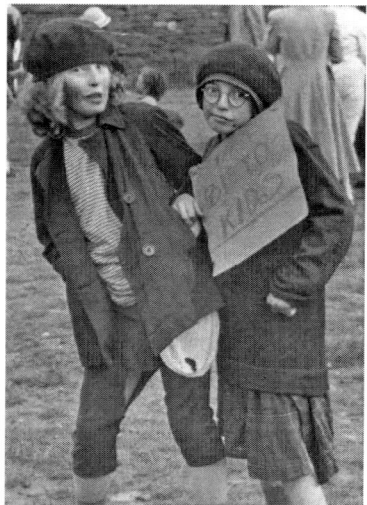

Friends Mavis Brown and Merle Thorne, as Bisto Kids.
Courtesy John Brown.

117

A pair of tough tackling
fullbacks - Alice Griffiths
(Arsenal) and Mary Price
(Fulham).
Courtesy Sandra Evans.

Papoose Paula Bevan proves you are never too young
to join in the fun as she rides with Gaynor mama
squaw Eynon and Billy the Kid Bevan on *Brandy*.
Courtesy Mike Bevan.

Village celebrations to mark the investiture of the Prince of Wales in 1969.
Carnival Queen Elaine Rogers accompanied by Julie Williams, Sian John, Julie Thomas,
Michelle Olsen, Cheryl Williams, Myra Olsen and Debbi Brewer.
courtesy Morfydd Olsen

Social Venues

As the community developed, the built environment comprised not just dwelling houses for the inhabitants but also public buildings. There were shops, places of worship and education, and social venues - George Inn, Constitutional Club, Workmen's Institute and Library - that helped make it a lively community.

118

George Inn Hotel

According to the date of lease given on *Schedule of Properties forming portions of Cefn Brithdir Farm and Brithdir Ganol Farm* (see page 33) Jonah Meredith, formerly farmer at Brithdir, was probably George Inn Hotel's first licensee. His application, at Merthyr Police Court in 1859, for a new licence was refused on account of its close proximity to a house already licensed. Why the application was refused is unclear as it appears to have been the only such establishment in the area.

When the 1861 census was taken, Jonah Meredith headed a household of five at George Inn. Both Jonah and his 28 year old son were described as hauliers. It is not clear

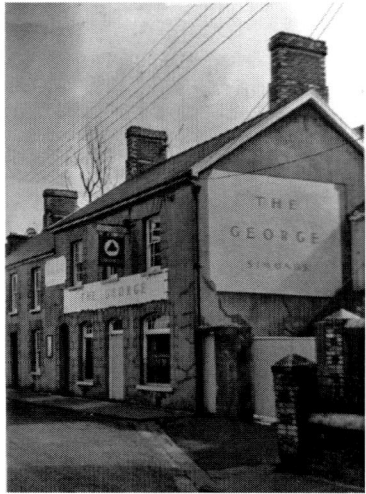

George Inn Hotel post 1954.
Courtesy Lee and Helena Bennett
(landlords at the time of writing)

if his wife ran the bar when Jonah was hauling, but his 16 year old daughter was a barmaid, presumably serving thirsty miners. The fifth member of the household was a lodger, working as a wood cutter.

Early in 1861, Jonah Meredith fell foul of the law. On Tuesday, January 14 1862, Constable Lewis, P.C. 99, entering the premises at half-past midnight, found *fifteen present and eleven drinking vessels containing liquor on the table.* Jonah Meredith was charged with selling beer during prohibited hours and fined 5s plus costs. He was charged with committing a similar breach of the law on the following Wednesday night, and he was fined heavily - 20s and costs.

According to the 1871 census return, Jonah Meredith, by then 67 years old, was *general labourer and beer house keeper*, and his son was a coal miner. Whether or not his son took over on his death is unclear, but a local press report shows that, on February 28 1881, the licence was transferred to James Harry. Head of the household of nine at George Inn at the time of the 1881 census, James Harry was described as *stationary engine driver*, and, presumably, the bar was run by his wife, older children and domestic servant.

Widow, Louisa Davies, moved to George Inn following the death of her husband at Cilhaul Colliery about 1883. In 1888, she married John Thomas, formerly landlord of a Swansea public house. Under their stewardship, *the George*, the community's sole public building, became a busy place. Louisa's son, Joseph Davies, was a young boy when he moved with his mother to George Inn, and he remained there until he was about 20 years old. Aged 93, in 1973, Joseph (see page 271) recalled his formative years in the 1880s and 1890s:

the atmosphere in the public house in those days was very noisy and there was a lot of singing. The intoxicating liquor promoted many fights that took place outside on a square in front of the pub and on a Saturday night there was a room kept especially for women.

119

In August 1891, on his application for a full licence to sell *on* and *off* the premises, tenant John Thomas declared George Inn's owner as David Harris, builder, of Bryn Ivor Villa, Mountain Ash, and RIC as lessee. That full licence was granted by early October 1891. Louisa died in 1896, and, in 1898, John Thomas married Rowena Jones, daughter of Evan Jones, Bute Arms, Rhymney. John Thomas continued as landlord until retiring autumn 1904.

The next tenants, Mr and Mrs Llewellyn Lewis, formerly of Black Swan, Newport, remained at George Inn until about 1909 when Elizabeth Morgan, with a decade of experience at Pontymister Inn, Risca, arrived. Thomas Phillips's Brewery of Dock Road, Newport became owners in 1912. Sadly, Elizabeth Morgan lost two sons, Arthur and Charles, in World War I. Whether or not such losses influenced her decision to relinquish her licence is uncertain. She remained in the community and is included in photographs on page 328. Successive registers of licences show that her

Charlie Davies holding court in *the George* bar.
Courtesy Dilwyn Rees

son, Edmund James Morgan, who had the licence from July 26 1918, remained there until February 3 1950. His son, Augustus Treharne Morgan, was landlord 1950-1953. Ivor Maurice Davies took over in 1953 and stayed just twelve months, possibly leaving when owners Phillips sold out to H. and G. Simonds of Reading in 1954. He was followed by William Webb (1954-63). Thomas Childs, Patrick O'Brien and Lionel Rea were among those to run the pub 1964-1968. James (Jim) and Marge White took over in February 1969. In 1976, they were followed by Malcolm and Linda Winmill who, during their tenure, made many alterations before retiring from the pub in 1982. They were followed by Dave and Annette Braun, Ron and Susan

Mr. Jones, Cemetery House enjoying the banter.
Courtesy Tom Jones

Edwards, Gary and Linda Woods before Mark Lewis and Gaynor Eynon ran the pub between 1989 and 1995. There was a succession of landlords - Ray and Jill Withers, Des and Brenda Britton, Arthur and Kath Gough, Neil and Elizabeth Edwards and Carl Brewer and Kevin (surname unknown) - before *The George* closed about 2010. With its windows boarded up, many residents feared their village pub was destined for permanent closure. Lee and Helena Bennett, landlords at time of writing, opened it in time for Christmas 2011. *The George* has served the people of Brithdir for over 165 years, and hopefully it will continue to do so in the future.

George Inn and its sign, 2016. Prior to alterations while Malcolm and Linda Winmill were landlords, the main entrance, a pair of double doors, was midway between the two windows (below the hanging pub sign). Inside the double doors was a passage-way with doors leading, left, into bar with big coal stove in the middle, and, right, to a big room and a snug bar for female patrons.

Older residents may remember the original Hop Leaf pub sign. The present pub sign, coal miner with mandrel, evokes the local mining heritage.

Courtesy John Grayson.

When built, George Inn was the only building in the village with rooms big enough to accommodate a large number of people for meetings and events of all sorts. Until Public Health Act of 1875, there were no public mortuaries and in the event of a sudden or unnatural death, inquests were often held in the nearest public house. The upstairs assembly room of *The George* was used for such occasions.   And, I imagine, a common scene outside the pub for decades was deliveries by horse drawn drays.

Workmen's Institute and Library – *The 'Stute*

On Saturday, May 10 1924, with John Godfrey presiding, the foundation stones of Brithdir's Workmen's Institute and Library were laid. Mrs. Jones, of Bargoed, laid the first stone on behalf of her son, Morgan Jones M.P. and other stones were laid by Samuel Davies of Brithdir Boys' School, Rt. Hon. Thomas Richards, F.N. Witzel (on behalf of Finlay Gibson of Monmouthshire and South Wales Coal Owners Association), Walter Lewis J.P., miners' agent, Bargoed, and Harry Brown, Institute committee chairman. The ceremony concluded when architect, Mr Routledge, presented each of those who laid stones with an inscribed silver trowel. Building work proceeded and, under the supervision of architect Routledge, much of the unskilled work was carried out by local unemployed.

By the mid-1890s, New Tredegar Workmen's Institute and Library had branch reading rooms in several other communities, including Brithdir. Maintained by

Silver trowel presented to Walter Lewis. Courtesy Jen Pritchard, his great granddaughter

121

miners' contributions and subscriptions from tradesmen, they were valued and well used by local people who went there to read local and national daily and weekly newspapers as well as books on economics and politics.

This advertisement appeared in *Merthyr Express,* June 12 1909.

Brithdir's first reading room was simply a room in a house before it moved to temporary accommodation in a corrugated iron building, near the bottom of Herbert Street. But, intent on substantial purpose-built premises, the first Library and Institute committee meeting was held on April 4 1894. It was chaired by Harry Brown, later appointed librarian. Harry Brown had a long association with the Institute and was its committee chairman for many years. The building fund grew slowly over the years and the 1910 balance sheet showed a yearly profit of nearly £50, and, with a fund of £230, a substantial stone building was being considered.

> **Brithdir Workmen's Library.**
>
> A GRAND
>
> # Competitive Concert
>
> will be held on
>
> **WEDNESDAY, AUGUST 4th, 1909,**
>
> at the
>
> **NEW HALL, NEW TREDEGAR.**
>
> Prize Solos £2 2s. each.
> Two Champion Solos (male and female) £2 2s.
> each and two massive Silver Cups, value £2 2s.
> Recitations and Juvenile Solos,
>
> PROGRAMMES 1d. each, to be had of the Joint
> Secretaries, Mr. Hy. Brown, 26, Herbert Street,
> and Harry Williams, 5, Station Terrace, Brithdir.

The concert room, New Hall as it became known, at the rear of the 'Stute, had a seating capacity of 450, large stage and dressing rooms, and was officially opened Wednesday, September 19 1923. As noted on page 264, one of the first public entertainments was Aeolian Concert Party's performance in support of a local man unable to work for some months.

The Institute, largely financed through weekly deductions from miners' wages, was erected, at a cost of £5,000, as part of Miners' Welfare Scheme. With library, reading rooms, and recreational facilities (including snooker hall, opened Saturday, February 28 1925 and equipped with five full size tables), it soon became the village's focal point, catering for both intellectual and social needs.

At the general meeting in June 1925, most of the committee retired so opening the way for the next batch of dedicated workers. Isaac Jones was elected chairman, W. Davies vice-chairman, Harry Williams secretary and Sam Foward treasurer, while J. Harris (senior), J. Harris (junior), Abe Rees, Roland West, D. John, W. Cooper, Frank Goode, W. Hughes, W. Davies, G. Godfrey, E. Davey, T. Coles, D. Thomas, D. Mellins, H. Morgan, W. Hughes (senior), E. George, Hopkin Morgan and Phil Willets (senior) were committee members.

The 'Stute, with a full calendar of operettas, cantatas, concerts, dramas, dances and much more, was at the heart of the community.

Eisteddfodau were especially popular in the inter-war era and Brithdir Workmen's Institute general and entertainment committees were responsible for a very successful first eisteddfod on September 6 1930 in aid of 'Stute funds. There were over 150 competitors across a range of competitions. Brithdir boy, Melville Davies (see page 293) sang *The Land where the Roses never fade* to win the under 12 boys' solo, while his sisters, Ceridwen and Mildred won the under 14 duet. The event was successful and further annual fundraising eisteddfodau were organised.

With Ben Watkins, chairman, supported by David Davies (treasurer) and Charles Young (secretary), presiding at the annual meeting in February 1939, the committee decided that two portraits should be placed in the committee room. On Saturday evening, May 6 1939, the portraits of the honoured gentlemen were unveiled by former Brithdir schoolteacher, William Bartlett, Penarth, and Albert Thomas JP, miners' agent. One was of secretary

A group of Brithdir starlets photographed by Samuel Cresswell on stage at New Hall c.1925. Zoe Cresswell (see page 287) and Donald Bird are standing to the right. In front are Ira Bevan (left) and Lilian Butler (right).
Courtesy Georgina Greaney.

Charles Young, then 70 years old, in appreciation of his life-long interest and seven years' service as secretary. Fifty years a miner as well as village postmaster, Charles Young was a well-read man who had earned respect within the community. The other portrait was a posthumous token of gratitude to Councillor John Godfrey for his service both to the Institute and to the wider Brithdir community. Councillor Stanley Baldwin of Bargoed said *Councillor Godfrey was one of the pioneers of the Independent Labour Party before the war. He was a faithful, honest and conscientious worker and was one of the greatest fighters in the working class movement.*

The 'Stute committee was forward-looking and, in August 1939, they ensured a new maple floor was installed in the concert hall ready for the winter season of dances. Jean Hill (née Wells) remembers the floor was purchased from Capitol Theatre, Cardiff. This improvement meant that the dance floor soon earned the reputation for being among the finest in the valley, and it was on this dance floor that many Brithdir romances developed. Weekly dances were enjoyed by all at New Hall. The photograph (courtesy Barbara Morgan née Brewer) shows three pretty Brithdir girls, left to right Barbara Brewer, Margaret Morris and Sheila Williams.

In the 1940s, when Horace Brown was caretaker, the 'Stute was a busy place. Time on the five full size snooker tables had to be booked. Each half hour game cost 3d. The series of educational films shown at the 'Stute in June 1941 was well attended, and children's matinee performances were shown to *full houses*.

The history of institutes in general reflects that of coal mining, and post-World War II social, economic and political changes ushered in the demise of institutes. Their educational functions passed to more formal, and often better-funded, bodies, and changes, such as television in the home, as well as pit closures, meant that, at best, some halls and institutes were converted into miners' clubs.

A group of lads who, in the early 1950s, helped to keep Brithdir 'Stute open by raising funds through organising their own tanner hop - dancing to their own records. Left to right: Stan Gibbs, Peter Bennett, Terry Gibbs and unknown.

Courtesy Phil Davies.

By the late 1950s and early 1960s, my generation tried to keep the 'Stute going by running a weekly dance. Our efforts were rewarded when Bryn Harris and the 'Stute committee arranged a visit to Bristol studios and *Discs-A-GoGo*, a TWW production set in a fictional coffee bar and hosted by Kent Walton. As part of a studio audience for that lost pop show, a forerunner of *Top of the Pops*, we represented club-goers and jived with our girlfriends around the set to music from a fake juke box. The guesting *live acts*, miming to their latest records, included Lorne Green (Ben Cartwright in the western series *Bonanza*), Danny Williams (Moon River), Scottish singer Lena Martell, Al Martino (of *Spanish Eyes* fame) and Vince Eager in his best gold lamé suit.

Generations of Brithdir folk found their entertainment in the Workmen's Institute with its concert hall and snooker hall, and every person who passed through its doors will have their own memory. Each generation had its volunteers who worked tirelessly to keep the venue open for the benefit of the village. The last big event held in the hall was in April 1990 when villagers, concerned about their future, organized the exhibition *The Past, Present and Future*, celebrating the history of this former mining village. The exhibition was opened by BBC radio presenter Roy Noble, and other speakers included Ted Rowlands, MP, and Roy Davies, Bishop of Llandaff. Brithdir Community Centre (as it was known by then) was teeming with residents, former residents and visitors. Morfydd Williams, who had lived all her life in the family home in Bristol Terrace, attended with her sister Zoe Cresswell, a former resident who travelled from her home in Penarth. Brithdir Primary School's retired deputy head teacher, Effie Davies of Fochriw, also visited the exhibition. Fast

Brithdir Workmen's Institute, Management Committee – 1947-48
Back row: L-R Dave Thomas, Ivor Harris, Don West, Edgar Jones, Ernie Hayes. Middle row: T.J. Edwards, S. George, I. Jones, W. Davies (trustee), W. Hughes (trustee), D.O. Davies (trustee), J. Harris (trustee), Horace Butts, Sam Foward, Ivor Dando, David Hughes. Front row: Les Williams, Eddy Bevan, Isaac Jones (caretaker), Bryn Harris (secretary), Rollie Hughes (chairman), William Harris (treasurer), Phyllis Jones (assistant caretaker), Phil Willetts senior (vice-chairman), Councillor Harry Williams, Ben Watkins.
Courtesy Bill Thomas.

forward to today, the building, Brithdir Workmen's Hall and Institute, with its windows boarded, stands abandoned and decorated with a *for sale* sign.

Brithdir Constitutional Club

Brithdir Constitutional Club was founded by a small group of local Conservatives seeking to counteract Socialist influence in a Labour stronghold. Anecdotal evidence has it that, after a few beers in George Inn, these pioneers formed Brithdir's first Conservative Committee and proceeded to promote their philosophy through setting up the club.

Starting at 30 Station Terrace, a small house opposite the railway station, formerly in possession of Martin Luther Thomas, the club prospered over the decades. Comprising just a refreshment bar, reading room and billiard room, the club was formally opened on Thursday, December 17 1903, with over 100 members already enrolled. The premises could accommodate over 200 persons. Its first committee was chaired by F. Sims, vice-chairman was W. Thomas, treasurer, William Speake, and secretary, Martin Luther Thomas. Evan Lewis formerly of Hengoed Junction Hotel was appointed steward of the new club.

Over the years, its officials steered this club from humble beginnings to a heyday in the early 1970s. While surviving records do not name all who have served, it would not be invidious to mention a few who deserve credit. John

Hill MM, treasurer in 1949, gave 40 years' club service. Members of the Bennett family have had a long association with the club, giving excellent service over many years: George Bennett, president in 1930s, was supported by his sons, Wilfred as vice-president and Rupert (*Pete*) served as secretary for at least twelve years. By the end of the 1930s, George stepped down and was succeeded by Wilfred as president. Harry James, John Bron, Doug Major and Geoffrey (Geoff) Brewer deserve mention as chairmen at various times, as do treasurers Harry Gwynne and Edgar Jones, and secretaries Gethin Jones (honoured by a plaque on the lounge wall) and Bill Ellis. According to Kelly's Directory (date in brackets is the year of the directory) the following served as club stewards: Evan Lewis (1903); Abel Howard (1906); W.T. Phillips (1910); Joseph Cole and wife Lily (1911); John Brown (1914 and 1920); Charles John Moore (1923); Israel Williams (1926-34) and Thomas Davies (1934).

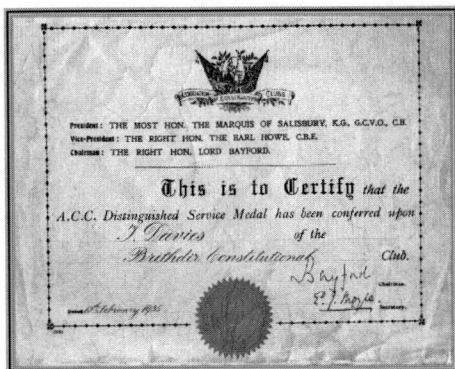

Conservative Clubs' Gazette, March 1935, shows that club steward, Thomas Davies, 15 Charles Street, was awarded Association Conservative Clubs' Roll of Honour certificate (shown left courtesy John Rawle) and Distinguished Service Medal (5 years) on February 15 1935, in recognition of his work on behalf of the Conservative Club movement.

IN GRATITUDE FOR LOYAL SERVICE
TO
Mr. G.E. JONES
SECRETARY FROM 1957 TO 1969

Past service by Dr. O'Shea, club president for about 30 years (see pages 303-309 about his work as doctor in the community for 54 years) and secretary Gethin Jones, is recognized by plaques on the wall of the lounge.

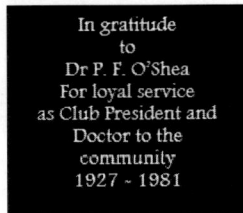

In gratitude
to
Dr P. F. O'Shea
For loyal service
as Club President and
Doctor to the
community
1927 - 1981

Club officers, committee and members were quick to appreciate those members who served in the Armed Forces, as was the case on April 29 1933, when, as reported in *Merthyr Express*, May 6 1933, about 150 members were present at a *welcome home social* for seven young men recently returned from service in India and China. John Green (Sgt), John Lewis, John Woods, John Ferguson, Will Coles, Charles Young and Bert Turner had returned after six years' service in 2nd Welsh Regiment. The evening, presided over by Israel Williams, started with a supper and that was followed by a concert. The programme included performances by The *Cyril* Band, Tom Lewis (DCM.) Tom Lewis (junior) W. and O. Williams, Harry Jones, E. Hammond, T. Beynon, Ben Long, Don Bird and W. Harries. The success of the evening owed much to the efforts of Wilf Bennett (vice-president) and Israel and Mrs. Williams (steward and stewardess).

126

Members' children were treated to an annual Christmas party. An example is the event of 1934, when 120 children sat down to enjoy a fruit tea. After the tables were cleared, George Bennett, assisted by vice president Wilf, presided over the entertainment by the children and, on leaving, each child was given a novelty prize, orange and mince pie. Members and families also enjoyed annual outings arranged by the club.

Doug and Grace Major behind the bar in 1973 (right courtesy Philip Smith). Doug was a popular chairman (1966-71) and steward (1971-77). They left in 1977 to take over Troedrhiwfuwch Inn. After about five years there, Doug retired and Grace worked in George Olsen's shop, in Railway Terrace, until it closed

Geoff Brewer, vice-chairman to Doug Major, took over the reins in 1971 and held the post of chairman for 12 years. During his tenure, the club purchased Honeysuckle cottage (between Roffi's shop and the club), demolished the building and used the space for car parking. Today it is an outdoor seating area. Whilst vice-chairman, Geoff, was also entertainment secretary. On one occasion, in 1975, he booked well-known entertainer Max Boyce. I remember it well. My wife Jen had just come home from hospital after the birth of our son Robert, so my ticket for the show, gave me an opportunity to *wet the baby's head*. On arriving at the

Constitutional Club outing to Dublin (Ireland v Wales 1960)
Back row L-R: Len George, Ron Edwards, Jack Hook, Bill Howells, Dai Thomas.
Middle row L-R: Ivor Lewis, Edgar Inseal, Gethin Jones, Jack Cartwright, Elvad Williams,
Front row L-R: Tom Inseal, Bill Jones (*Postman*), Dai Price (*Half Past Nine*), Arthur Williams (*Fields*), Bill Sheasby.   Courtesy Glenys Price née Williams.

127

Brithdir Constitutional Club Committee 1973.
Front row L-R: Ned Rees (vice-chairman), Bill Ellis (secretary), Geoff Brewer (chairman), Edgar Jones (treasurer). Back row L-R: Will 'W.O' Jones, Bill Hayes, Denis Baines, Les Britton and Bill Cullum (assistant secretary). Courtesy Geoff Brewer.

club, I found Geoff more agitated than usual, telling me *the artist hasn't turned up*. I popped downstairs to see if there was any sign of him, and found Max enjoying a pint at the bar. *Come on Max*, I said, *the chairman's doing his nut*, to which Max calmly replied *I'll be there now in a minute*. But Max carried on sipping his pint. Eventually, I accompanied him up the stairs to the landing where Les Britton was greeting visitors. Through the window overlooking the Cwmsyfiog side of the valley, Max spotted a small chapel and, resting his arms on the bannister, started reminiscing about how he loved the valleys, and their little chapels. Finally, he entered the concert hall and made his way to the stage dressing room. A short while later, his *Oggy Oggy Oggy* rung out, and Max emerged carrying his giant leek. *I Know 'Cos I Was There.*

The club has a tradition of friendliness, with a good night out guaranteed (without a swear word if ladies were present) at the weekend shows. The Christmas morning sing-song at the club was an enjoyable morning, sometimes attracting former residents. One such former resident, knowing the tradition, was Don Watkins, who travelled from his home in Swansea fully prepared. When asked to give a song, like a magician pulling a rabbit out of the hat, Don drew

Party time at Brithdir club with L-R: Henry Chamberlain, Joyce Edwards, Marlene Sims, Violet Howells, Grace Major, unknown, Dai Hughes and Johnny Howells.
Courtesy Geraldine Cook.

sheet-music from an inside pocket, made his way to the stage and accompanied himself on the piano. And of course club favourite, Ned Rees (see page 295), was always entertaining.

The club's darts players, men and women, participated in local leagues. In the mid-1970s, the club's darts team was runner-up in Tirphil and District Sunday Night League Cup. Not to be undone, the ladies too were champions with the arrows.

L-R: Gerald Harris, Jeff Inseal, Barry Jenkins, Robert Jones, Barry Spencer, Richard Bennett and Elvad Williams. In the front are doubles winners, Wayne Cook (left) and Dai Price.
Courtesy Pat Jones.

Back row L-R: Jackie Howells, Glenys Lloyd, Annie Davis, Marge White. Front L-R: Mrs. Kietch, Doreen Hayes, Joan Maggs and Ruth Gardner with Councillor Bryn Harris.
Courtesy Rita White.

Such clubs played a central role in working-class leisure during their heyday to the early 1970s, but many now have an uncertain future. In 2017 Brithdir club still functions, but what of its future? It does not have a *working committee* and, at the time of writing, it is open due to the efforts of man and wife team, Brian and Judith Landrygan, chairman and secretary.

The club had a very strong ladies section for many years and in this photograph are some familiar faces: Marjorie Cullum, Mrs Harrison, Annie Redwood, Cissie Bennett, Eileen Hayes, Cath Bennett, Elizabeth Jones. Gaynor Eynon, Chrissy Price, Vi Ryan, Ivy Gibbs, Joan Stenner, Margaret Eynon.
Courtesy Chrissy Price.

Constitutional Club members at Worcester Race Meeting.
Amongst this happy crowd are Roy and Marlene Sims, Lyndon Davies (behind Marlene), Rachel Dunn, Bill and Eileen Hayes, Margaret Harris, Norma Davies, Maureen Kedwood, Ernie and Doreen Hayes, Vi Harris, Ann Harding, Charles and Laura Williams, Tom and Vi Ryan, Cissy Gardner, Kate Bevan, Vi Chamberlain, Ivor Dando, Brinley Harris, Tom and Emma Edwards. Kneeling in front are Ivor Dunn, Ronnie Harris, Eddy Bevan, Edgar Inseal and Hendry Chamberlain.   Courtesy Hendry Chamberlain.

Societies and organisations

Over the decades, there were a number of societies and organisations that offered not just social activities but also opportunities for members to develop skills in a range of activities especially in the performing arts. Some of these groups were organised by the local places of worship, others associated with social venues such as New Hall. In some cases their success depended on the contribution of the leaders involved including people such as members of the West family as well as local clergy and school teachers. It was not uncommon for individuals to belong to a number of local groups. Two such groups active in the mid 1940s were Brithdir Dramatic Society and Brithdir Welfare Players.

As noted elsewhere in this volume, there were numerous local sporting groups, especially fostering soccer and boxing, in Brithdir. And, for those people who wanted a less physical form of sport, there were groups to support pigeon fanciers.

Almost as soon as the village of Brithdir developed, the interest in ambulance work was evident, an interest born of the realisation of the importance of first aid in the workplace below ground as well as in the home, There is further information on Brithdir Division St. John Ambulance Brigade on pages 330-335.

Brithdir Dramatic Society

A large audience at New Hall on February 3 1944 witnessed Brithdir Dramatic Society's first public performance, *Cold Coal*, a play by E. Eynon

130

Evans. The actors included Stan Williams, Gertrude Davies, Glenys Jones, Stanley West, Ivor Astley, Joe Harris, Roland (Rollie) Hughes, Freda Price, Leslie Williams, Ivor John, Ivor Harris, Nesta Price, Emlyn Foward, Mabel Williams and Mary Evans. It was produced by Frank West and Stan Williams, while Tommy Davies and Bryn Maxey were stage managers, Eddie Bevan was responsible for lighting, and Heather Jones for makeup. The secretary was T. Harris of 3 Harcourt Terrace.

NEW HALL · BRITHDIR

Souvenir Programme of

BRITHDIR DRAMATIC SOCIETY'S FIRST PERFORMANCE

COLD COAL
E. EYNON EVANS

Thursday, February 3rd, 1944

UNRESERVED SEAT · 1/3

NO CHILDREN ADMITTED WITHOUT PARENTS

PROCEEDS IN AID OF ABOVE SOCIETY

Brithdir Welfare Players

On January 21 1944, Brithdir Welfare Players performed *The Joneses*, a three act play by Emlyn Y. Jenkins. The venue was New Hall. Produced by Stanley Williams, the cast included Ivor John, Ivor Harris, Roland Hughes, Gertrude Davies, Nesta Price, Emlyn Foward, Mabel Williams, Glenys Jones, Ivor Stanley Williams, May Evans and Leslie Williams. (Courtesy Pauline Evans.)

Shown on stage (right) are Arwyn Davies, Mabel Williams (armchair), Rollie Hughes (white coat), Glenys Jones, Ivor John with Rene Roffi and Stan Williams seated on the settee. (Courtesy Morfydd Olsen)

In 1950 *Merthyr Express* reported that, having won McTaggart-Short Cup with Emlyn Williams's *Night Must Fall*, Brithdir Welfare Players performed it again at the Workmen's Institute in aid of local Old Age Pensioners Association Funds. (Courtesy CCBC Winding House Museum)

131

Annual Outing

The annual outing, often associated with the places of worship, the local school or local social club, was once one of the highlights of many people's calendars. Over the years, the form of transport changed, reflecting the era. By the 1970s, social and economic changes, especially the increase in the number of families with a private car, meant that such outings were no longer attractive or viable.

Merthyr Express, June 11 1898, reported on one of the earliest such outings from the Brithdir community. Early on Whit-Monday morning, forty teachers and friends of Brithdir Board School, all dressed in their best clothes, clambered into large brakes, supplied by E. J. Jones, Elliots Town, and, with provisions supplied by William Jones, Company Shop, on board, they started the journey to Crickhowell amid the blowing of bugles. After a good journey in fine weather, the brakes arrived at their destination at 12 noon. The trippers dined at Canal House, Llangattock, and enjoyed a day of boating and cricket before setting out from Crickhowell at 7.30 to arrive home, happy and tired, at 11 p.m..

Imagine the scene the party made departing the village: four brakes filled with teachers and friends dressed in their best attire, setting off to the sound of bugles. This typical photograph (courtesy Rob Orland of Historical Coventry via Simon Shaw and June Gibson of Wyken) illustrates travel at that time

Sometimes, as on August 7 1906, Brithdir people joined the wider Rhymney Valley community for an outing. *Cardiff Times*, August 11 1906, reported that some 1400 Rhymney Valley people enjoyed the inaugural annual outing of Rhymney Valley Constitutional Clubs. Two special trains conveyed people from Fochriw, Pontlottyn, Tirphil, Brithdir, Deri, Bargoed, Gilfach, Pengam, Hengoed, Llanbradach, Caerphilly, and Senghenydd to Cardiff, from where White Funnel steamers took them to Weston-super-Mare. Similar outings followed from time to time until the cross-channel steamer service ceased in early 1980s. Records show that secretary Rupert Bennett arranged trips to Barry Island for members, their wives and children (each child receiving a railway ticket and 1 shilling pocket money).

Harry Williams, teacher, David Morgan (known to many as *Dai Concertina* and lived in Ty Coch) and Lewis Bevan captured by the resident photographer as they alight on the Old Pier at Weston.
Courtesy Idwal Morgan Kavanagh

The inter-war era was the heyday of the charabanc for organised outings of Sunday Schools, public houses, social/sports clubs and workmen's groups. Trips on the early charabancs, with cast-iron wheels, and limited to 12 mph, may have been more of an ordeal than a pleasant journey. Brithdir folk embraced the charabanc as the following extracts from *Merthyr Express* reveal:

- September 5 1925: *The annual outing of the Young People's Society took place on August 29, by charabanc, the venue being Cheltenham. The weather was ideal, and the trippers spent an ideal day. Halts were called at Monmouth and Ross, thus giving the party an opportunity to view these historic places.*

- July 2 1927: *A charabanc outing to Barry Island, organised by the Baptist Chapel, took place on June 25, when a large number of people made the journey and spent a pleasant day at the seaside. Twelve vehicles were chartered.*

Caps and bonnets were the order of the day for this group departing Brithdir – date unknown, probably late 1920s.
Courtesy Margaret Sarlais.

- September 3 1927: *Sisterhood of Wesley Church held its outing on Monday, a charabanc trip to Porthcawl,*

- September 1 1928: *On Saturday August 25 the home cricket team played their annual fixture with Clydach near Abergavenny. They made the trip by charabanc.*

- August 24 1929: *Members of Wesley Sisterhood held annual outing on Saturday by charabanc to Swansea.*

No account of annual outings from communities like that in Brithdir would be complete without mention of the annual trip to Barry Island, which goes back as long as memory allows. Special non-stop trains were organised jointly by the local Sunday Schools, and the trips are illustrated by these examples from *Merthyr Express* in the 1920s:

- August 1 1925: *Libanus Sunday School, Cwmsyfiog and Wesleyan Sunday School, Brithdir jointly organised a special non-stop train that, with 600 adults and children on board, left Brithdir on Saturday July 25 for Barry Island. They enjoyed a beautiful day by the seaside and Brithdir Aeolian Party provided music on the sands.*

- July 20 1929: *The annual outing to Barry Island meant that Brithdir was almost deserted on July 11 when Sunday School teachers, friends and 500 scholars of all denominations travelled to the seaside on a special non-stop train.*

For those growing up in the 1950s, the Conservative Club's annual trip to Barry Island was eagerly anticipated. Whether it was by steam train or coach (usually Evans Coaches of New Tredegar), the club committee saw that all youngsters had a little brown envelope containing pocket money for the day. If travelling by train, we passed the pit ponies enjoying a summer break in fields at Llanbradach farm. The highlight of a coach journey was community singing, *Roll a Silver Dollar, Ten Green Bottles, She'll be Coming round the Mountain ... ...* until the mighty cry *I Can See the Sea* rang out. Then, journey over, a quick check of the number displayed on the coach windscreen, before, in the fashion of the Great Oklahoma Land Rush, the dash to the beach to secure the family beach space, where mothers erected a circle of deckchairs, children spread towels and fathers put up windbreakers. For the youngsters, when it was time for a dip, it seemed the tide was always out, and the trek, around the fortified deckchair circles, dodging sand-castles and numerous bodies buried in the sand, took all the skill of negotiating a minefield. Having reached the sea, the intrepid would-be bather put a foot in to test the water, then slowly moved forward until the water was knee-high, before stepping forward on tiptoes so that cold water would not hit the chest. After a quick dip, it was a race back to the family's camp and a feast of cucumber (and sand) sandwiches. Then, time for the funfair before heading to the station or coach

park for the homeward journey. The sun always seemed to shine in those days and the day at the seaside was enjoyed by all, children, teenagers, mums and dads and grandparents.

Barry Island 1950: Idris Jones, wife Elizabeth and daughter Catherine with friends Elsie Harris, Lol Bevan and Mrs. Megraw,
Courtesy Elizabeth Jones.

Porthcawl c.1955: My grandmother *Nana* Brewer (glasses), relaxes on the sand with daughters Jenny (Smith), Barbara and Lol (Garner), son Geoffrey, grandchildren Yvonne and Janet Garner, Christine and Pauline Smith and sons-in-law Phil Garner (trilby) and Doug Smith.

Taking a donkey ride are Kath Harris and niece Olga Watkins.
Courtesy Kay Dennis.

Enjoying a stroll in the sunshine are George and Ethel Astley.
Courtesy Mavis Mahoney.

Ronald and Lilian Winston relaxing on the beach at Barry (1950) while keeping an eye on the children.
Courtesy Diane Heath

Seaweed Queens for the day: Mary Ann Price centre with Ethel Astley on the end.
Courtesy Chrissy Price.

Camping in Hereford - Joe and Ken Maggs, Charles and Keith Williams, Pete Bennett with sons Jim, Derek and Richard and nephew David Bennett and Ernie Hayes

135

CHAPTER 10 SPORT

Introduction

Sporting activities became increasingly popular among the populations of new mining communities like Brithdir from the later nineteenth century onwards. Children, especially boys, honed their ball skills by playing wherever they could, whether on the street or playing field. In the summer, they played cricket, while football was a year-round activity. As the boys matured into young men, many of them looked forward to playing for a local team whenever their working shift in the pit allowed. Boxing also found favour in Brithdir. Sources studied to date have not uncovered the identity of any local bare-fist, mountain boxers, but by the second decade of the twentieth century, some local boxers were making a name for themselves in the ring. From time to time, some villagers flirted with other sports such as quoits (see page 316), but these are included with other pastimes enjoyed by villagers over the decades. What follows deals with association football, rugby union and boxing.

Association Football

Brithdir was a football, rather than a rugby, village and this series of cameo studies relating to soccer in Brithdir over the decades is based on local press (mainly *Merthyr Express*) reports and photographs. While the majority of this section is about men and boys who played football, it is interesting to note that in 1921, Brithdir Ladies were photographed.

Before football leagues were formed, soccer games were

Brithdir Ladies A.F.C. 1921
Lily May, née Gauden, is sitting next to the lady in the white blouse on right. Her husband, Richard John Coles (brother of World War I casualty Ivor – see page 200) is centre back row.

friendly fixtures arranged by club secretaries. Reports in the local press show that during the 1897-98 season, both Brithdir Rovers and Brithdir Stars played regular games against local rivals New Tredegar Albions and Albions Reserve. The turn of the century saw football flourish in the Rhymney Valley and, as new clubs were formed, a league system was necessary. Harry Williams (see pp 146-7) was a driving force, ensuring the new Rhymney Valley and District

136

Soccer League was in place by the start of the 1904-05 season. Brithdir AFC (presumably Rovers and Stars united with a new name to join the league) was accepted into Division Two, with a reserve team in Division Three. Their ground was the distant and rather inaccessible *Spion Kop*, on Cefn y Brithdir farm.

Although the newly-formed junior team, captained by Stephen Davies and with an attractive fixture list in 1906, suggested a promising future for the sport in the locality, the absence of a good playing field near the community was a serious drawback. The committee sought permission from the landowner regarding waste land near the river. However, not only did the area have to be cleared of tree stumps to make it playable, it was also necessary to obtain permission to make a path between Coed y Moeth Colliery and B&MR line. The end result was, according to *Merthyr Express,* September 29 1906, *one of the nicest and most convenient little football grounds in the valley.*

River Field is on the U shaped piece of land to east of river.
Sam Hughes was usually on duty with a large net to rescue balls kicked in the river.

By the end of the twentieth century's first decade, soccer was gaining in popularity in many communities and Brithdir was no exception. Its 1909-10 season, with former player Tom Davies as chairman, and Alf Chard, secretary, was successful. Brithdir was among local teams in Gilfach's Easter Holiday Football Tournament, when, after despatching Penrhiwceiber and Aberbargoed, they lost in the final to New Tredegar Strattons. The Strattons won the silver cup, and runners-up, Brithdir, received medals. Just a few days later, Brithdir hosted a Glamorgan League representative match, North v South, refereed by Harry Williams and with three Brithdir lads, A. Davies (goal), J. Jarvis (half-back) and J. Jones (forward), selected for South team. Brithdir, playing in Second, Third and Fourth Divisions, opted to run teams in Third and Fifth Divisions in the new season.

The 1910-11 season saw League changes. The Third Division divided, with 12 Rhymney Valley clubs forming one group and 12 clubs from Aberdare and Merthyr Valleys in the other, and, before the end of the season, group winners would meet on neutral territory to decide the championship. The Fourth Division consisted of Reserve teams, with an age limit of 23, and the Fifth Division (Old Boys Rhymney Valley Section) had upper age limit of 19.

Brithdir Association Team 1910 (photograph right) comprised Mick Hughes (goalkeeper), W. Welsh and Harry Williams (backs), Will Stephens, A. Green and Tom Williams (halves). The forward line consisted of Jack Rogers, Israel Williams, J. Organ, Dan Dudley and Arthur Canton (son of Police Inspector Canton, Bargoed). The local club tried to enhance the spectator experience. On October 15 Brithdir entertained Troedrhiwfuwch in a Junior Cup tie and the newly-formed Brithdir and Cwmsyfiog Brass Band played the teams to the field. After that, the large crowd watched an exciting match with Brithdir winning 6:4. The season finished with no less excitement. After 17 games, Brithdir headed Third Division, two points clear of second placed Gilfach. Gilfach, taking advantage of their two games in hand, headed the table by the time they arrived at *Spion Kop* for a thrilling end-of-season clash which resulted in a draw and Gilfach capturing the trophy.

In 1910, and under the banner *Mainly About Players*, *Evening Express Football Edition* featured players of both codes - soccer and rugby football. This is what the columnist had to say about some Brithdir soccer players:

November 12: TOM WILLIAMS *better known as "Brecon," is undoubtedly the best half-back playing in the third division. Both his attack and defence this season are above reproach.*

November 19: SID ASTON, *Brithdir's clever centre-forward, is at present showing his best form. He is fast, clever and resourceful, and the ball is always safe when manipulated by him. And, on December 10, he proved his merit again last Saturday by scoring the two goals which vanquished Cwmsyfiog.*

November 19: W. WELSH, *Brithdir, although not yet out of his teens, promises to develop into a classy player. His clever heading is one of the features of his play.*

November 26: J. ROGERS, *Brithdir's outside right is top scorer this season. He hails from Bristol, and, although the midget of the team, has a terrific shot for goal.*

December 3: DUDLEY, *Brithdir's eighteen year old forward, is one of the most promising sharp-shooters in the valley. Goalkeepers dread his well-known daisy-cutters. LAWES, Gilfach, has taken the law into his own hands and tied himself to Brithdir.*

December 10: A. CANTON (photograph) *proved a deadly wing against Cwmsyfiog, his scintillating runs and centres generally spelling disaster.* MICK HUGHES, *Brithdir's clever goalie, played one of his best games this season last Saturday. On one occasion he fisted a shot to nearly half-way.*

December 24: W. DAVIES, *Brithdir's clever full-back was missed at Gilfach last Saturday.* W. ABSALOM, *Bargoed Athletic's clever diminutive forward, is returning to Brithdir Reserves, his old club.*

December 31: HARRY WILLIAMS, *Brithdir, has tied himself to Cwmsyfiog. Probably the salubrious air on Spion Kop is exercising a beneficial influence, hence the many migrations to Cwmsyfiog.* JIMMY MORGAN, *Brithdir's centre-half is a never-say-die kind of player. His defence is without reproach, while he is continually endeavouring to set his forwards moving.*

And not just the players:

November 19: ALF CHARD, *Brithdir, is one of the best in the Rhymney Valley.* Alf Chard, pictured (courtesy Marlene Shaw) with wife Louisa, was the loyal and hard-working secretary, re-elected for many seasons.

November 26: WALTER JARVIS *is justly described as the father of the club. He is, undoubtedly, one of the most loyal supporters connected with the club.*

Not surprisingly, weather was a factor in some football games as witnessed by 1912-13's South Wales Junior Cup Final when Brithdir faced Aberaman Athletic on April 26 at Troedyrhiw under wretched conditions. Although referee Lewis declared the ground unfit, both teams decided to play. Perhaps Brithdir's willingness to start the game was influenced by the expense laid out on hiring a special supporters' train. The wind and rain were in Brithdir's favour in the first half. Only four Brithdir players returned to the field of play after the interval, the others refusing to resume. With the score line standing at 0–0, South Wales and Monmouthshire Association awarded the match to Aberaman: cup and winners medals went to Cynon Valley while the four Brithdir players who remained on the field took home runners-up medals.

Brithdir started 1913-14, the last football season before the war, with ambitious plans to apply for admission to Welsh League Second Division, but was advised, probably in their long-term interests, to remain in Glamorgan League for the coming season. Apart from Dan Dudley, who had transferred to Gilfach, all 1912-13 Brithdir players were available and went on to win the league in style. From the first game of the season, they showed their intent with a convincing 4-0 win over Bargoed Thursdays. By early October Brithdir team was playing like champions: Jimmy Morgan, centre-half and D. Jones and Roberts, at full back, rock-like in defence, while at forward, the Gardner

139

brothers, Wilcox and Turner proved a splendid vanguard. By late November, Dukestown was challenging Brithdir's supremacy and the closely contested November 22 Brithdir v Dukestown match, resulting in Brithdir win 2:1, was deemed by the press to be *one of the best games played at Brithdir for many moons*. Brithdir went on to become league champions without losing a single game and finished thirteen points ahead of runners-up, Pengam. Their stats for the season read P20, W17, L0, D3, F74, A12, Pts 37.

During the same season, Brithdir school team won Upper Rhymney Valley Schools League Championship by a single point (ahead of New Tredegar School) to win the new Dr. Percy Jones Shield. Stats read: P18, W14, D1, L3, F56, A16, Pts29. After a selection trial in October 1913, five Brithdir players (full-backs Mellins and T. Harris, Septimus Harris, half-back, and forwards Harrington and Hallett) were selected to represent the League in Shield competition at Cardiff.

World War I had a major impact on all aspects of society and this was reflected in football in Brithdir. Having played eight games, Brithdir topped the league in January 1915, but, as players left for war service, it was difficult to field a team and the season ended with Pontlottyn as champions. Brithdir was just one of several clubs not to field a team in the 1915-16 and some of their players turned to other clubs. Early in 1915-16 season, four Brithdir players (Albert Jarvis, Ernie Turner, Jack Jarvis and W.O. Jones) took the field for Bargoed Town when

they met Barry in a Welsh League fixture. However, local football resumed: Brithdir was 1916-1917 Rhymney Valley League champions (and this image shows a winners medal) and runners-up 1917-18. In 1919 they reached the final of Glamorgan Knock-Out cup and, as the local press revealed in November, *Brithdir Wesleyans are going well, and, so far, have won all their matches. At Phillipstown they won by 3 goals to 1. Turner scored two of the goals.*

As Brithdir moved into the 1920s, its football future looked promising under a new management team (D. Mellins as chairman, R. Godfrey, treasurer, and W. Walsh, secretary) and with a range of skilful and experienced players available. Players included veteran Dan Dudley, Ernie Turner (formerly of Bargoed Town), Tommy Davies (teacher, captain Caerleon College team 1919-20), Frank West (teacher, captain Bristol College 1920-21), T. Edwards (formerly of Aberaman), Mick Hughes (veteran goalie, still considered among the best), F. Moore, R. Hughes, Ted George, Godfrey brothers, W. Bevan, W. Walsh and Septimus Harris. In addition, Ben Hallett returned from Constantinople a vastly improved player. Albert and Jack Jarvis had returned home, and with House, Morgan, Welsh and Tom Gardner, there was plenty of talent for selection.

There was also a team of youngsters attached to Brithdir Division St. John Ambulance Brigade, a pool of recruits for the future. In the mid 1920s, an U21 side was formed with R. Hughes as chairman, W. Nutt treasurer and D. Dudley secretary. In 1927, local schoolboys gained plaudits with Bert Hayes, Emrys and Elwyn Thomas, John Webb and Charlie Howells praised as *outstanding boys*. St. Paul's Sunday School Football Team, Second Division champions of inaugural New Tredegar and District Sunday School Union Football League in 1927, owed some of its success to the efficiencies of secretary W. Harris, and support of W. Gerrish and B. Chard. Only beaten on two occasions, the boys were prolific goal scorers, netting 33 goals in one week in three matches. The image shows the medal presented to Bill MacDonald in 1927. The boys who received medals were Eddy Bevan (captain), W. Thomas, C. Turner, C. Megraw, W. Barlow, C. Hewitt, Ivor Williams, C. Gerrish, G. Whiting, Reg Williams and Richard Beynon.

Brithdir Boys' School finished 1928-29 as runners-up in Aberbargoed Hospital Cup competition and winners (for the second time) of Rhymney Valley Schoolboys' League's Dr. Percy Jones Shield. But, for the school and village football, the pinnacle was Bert Hayes's selection for International honours.

Brithdir Bluebirds (Brithdir U21s) had a very successful 1930-31 season, as illustrated by games against the strong Abertridwr Stars, and by securing a place in two finals. By April 1931, Abertridwr Stars, a formidable side heading Rhymney Valley League Second Division by a substantial margin, had lost only one League match during the season and had not been beaten on their own ground for two years. Brithdir Bluebirds defeated them twice that season: victors not only in the only League match Abertridwr Stars lost in the season, but also in a cup round. Thus, Abertridwr Stars v Brithdir Bluebirds on Saturday, April 9 1931 was important to both sides. Brithdir was one goal down at half-time, but M. Whiting scored twice in the second half to give them victory. Full of pride, they returned to Brithdir as the only team to beat Abertridwr (three times) in the season and break their opponent's two year ground record.

As reported in the local press, Brithdir Bluebirds made history by reaching the final in two competitions in 1930-31 season, so facing two important games on consecutive days in mid-May. Although they lost both games, the experiences helped strengthen them for the future. On Friday they travelled to Rhymney to face Abertridwr Stars in final of Rhymney Hospital Junior Cup, but lost 1-0. The next day, they faced Trelewis Welfare Juniors (top of League for second year in succession) at Trelyn Park (Fleur de Lys) in Rhymney Valley Junior Cup Final. Trelewis, the stronger side, won the cup they had failed to win in the previous year's final, and Brithdir players had the runners-up medals.

During 1931-32 season, representatives of some premier clubs were watching several Brithdir Bluebirds. Billy Bassett had a trial for Swansea Town and, on February 11, he played in the Welsh League team against Penrhiwceiber on

Brithdir Bluebirds 1931-32, courtesy Sandra Evans.
Back row L-R: Dave Thomas, Harry James (treasurer), Bryn Harris (secretary), Hubert Brown, Ernie Davies, Mr. Davies and Albert (Bert) Bennett. Middle: Rupert (Pete) Bennett (chairman), Reg Williams, Ivor Harris, Joe Cooper, Elwyn Thomas, M. Whiting, Bert Hayes, Wilfred (Hickey) Bennett. Front: Ivor Dando, W. Williams, Bill Bassett (captain) C. Turner and Day Harris.

Vetch Field. Although Swansea lost, Bassett impressed and was offered a further trial. In the same season, Brithdir had two successful football teams: Brithdir United played friendly matches and gained some notable conquests, while Brithdir Bluebirds earned honours in both league and cup engagements. As there was much speculation as to which was the better team, on Monday, May 16 1932, they met on River Field, where Bluebirds won 5 goals to 2. This table summarises Brithdir Bluebirds' honours in League and Cup competitions:

1931-32	R.V. League Knock-out Cup R.V. League Division II	League Cup medal Runners-up medal	Bill Bassett, W. Williams, Ivor Harris, Bert Hayes, C. Turner, Ivor Dando, Day Harris, Reg Williams, G. Whiting, Elwyn Thomas, C. Slade, Emrys Thomas, L. Godfrey, C. Megraw and Joe Cooper
1932-33	Abertysswg Hospital Cup	Cup winners	Trevor Bassett, W. Williams, C. Turner, Edward Bevan, Bill Bassett, Rod Jones, Bert Hayes, Stan Young, W. O. Jones, C. Megraw and B. Hillman
1932-33	Gilfach Tournament	Cup winners	Slade, C. Megraw, A. Holder, Taylor, D. Harris, Bill Bassett, Elwyn Thomas, Bert Hayes, Turner, Idris Bassett and Rhodes.
1932-33	R.V. Junior League	Winners medal	Rhodes, Idris Bassett, C. Turner, Bert Hayes, Taylor, Elwyn Thomas, D. Harris, L. Godfrey, A Holder, C. Megraw, C. Smaile, R. Davey.
1932-33	R.V. Hospital Cup	Runners-up medal	Bill Bassett, Bert Hayes, W. Williams, C. Turner, Elwyn Thomas, Ivor Harris, B. Slade, M Whiting, Day Harris.
1933-34	R.V. League Division II	Runners-up medal	Trevor Bassett, W. Williams, C. Turner, Edward Bevan, W. Bassett, M. James, J. Ferguson, W.O. Jones, Stan Young, B. Hillman, Ernie Turner.
1933-34	R.V. Knock-out Cup	Runners-up medal	E. Mathews, M. James, A. Holder, Bert Hayes, B. Hillman, E. Martin, C. Megraw, W.O. Jones, Edward Bevan, C. Turner, W. Williams and Trevor Bassett.

Medals awarded to Elwyn Thomas,
Top: Rhymney Valley District League Second Division winners 1932-33.
Bottom left: Rhymney Hospital Junior Cup 1931.
Bottom right: Rhymney Valley and District Football League Junior Cup runners-up 1931-32.

Courtesy son John Thomas.

Brithdir United A.F.C. 1931-32.
Dr. P. F. O'Shea (president), Edmund J Morgan and Haydn Sprague (vice presidents), F. Rogers (chairman), Edwin Howells (treasurer) and Edward Rogers (secretary). Standing centre back row is Richard (*Richie*) Hennessy (goalie) with D. Jones (captain), front centre.
Courtesy Nita Smith

Several local footballers went on to have careers in football. The club gave Billy Bassett to Cardiff City, Bert Turner to Charlton Athletic, Idris Bassett to West Bromwich Albion, and Ernie Turner to Southampton. Bert Hayes played for Wolverhampton Wanderers (Wolves) and Wrexham. Charles Turner had trials with Chelsea. Trevor Bassett played for Cardiff City 'A' team. W.O. Jones scored two goals in a trial for Cardiff City but was sent home as he was too young. All from the little village of Brithdir.

In their first year in the League, Brithdir Boys' Club football team defeated Aberbargoed Boys' Club, League champions two years in succession and cup

Brithdir Boys' Club football team 1945-46. Photograph, courtesy Ivor Lewis, includes Roy Jones, R Gough, H. McIntosh, S Jenkins, Roy Jones (captain), Maldwyn Jones, Trevor Hyatt, Dennis Parry, H Bradley, D Regan and Ivor Harris.

143

Brithdir Boys' Club football team 1947-48, courtesy Ivor Harris.
Back row L-R: Edgar Jones, John Mantle, Stan Evans, Roy Jones, Les Cushion, Trevor Hyatt, Don Watkins, George Wall and Les Williams. Front: Howell McIntosh, Ian Evans, Ivor Harris (captain), Brian Holifield and Maldwyn Jones.

holders, by 3 goals to 2 in Rhymney Valley Boys' Club Junior League cup final on Bargoed's McDonnell Ground, Wednesday, May 8 1946.

A former pupil of Lewis School, Pengam, Norman Perry, then 18, son of Mr. and Mrs. Tom Perry, 2, Harcourt Terrace, had just left Saltley College, Birmingham, when he had two Cardiff City trial matches in August 1947. He had previously played for Brithdir Boys' Club and his college teams, and although his usual position was right-back, he played a sound game at centre-half, opposed by Billy James, a Cardiff seasoned forward.

Photograph, courtesy Malcolm Winmill, showing players, committee members and friends of Brithdir Welfare A.F.C. at first annual dinner, concert and dance, Saturday, June 4 1949. Back row includes T. Williams, Rachel Jones, P. Williams, H. Morgan, Lil and Iris West, Ben Watkins, Kate Bevan, Margaret Harris, Violet Ryan, Mary Foward, Rena Roffi and Sylvia Jones with Phil L. Willetts on end of row. In 3rd row Bill Thomas (left), Teddy Woods and Phil Davies 3rd and 2nd from right. 2nd row, Dave Thomas, Sheasby (RAF uniform), Terry Wheeler, John Mantle, Bryn Harris and Glyn Morris. Front row L-R unknown, Ivor Harris (treasurer) Will (W.O.) Jones, Keitch, centre Donald West (chairman) and Arthur Williams (secretary).

At the end of 1940s, Brithdir Welfare A.F.C. played in Rhymney Valley First Division under great difficulties. As River Field was partly covered by a landslide, and there was no other ground available, all their matches were played away. In 1951, Councillor Bryn Harris formed U16 team to play in Rhymney Valley League. When, in 1954, they lost to Ystrad Mynach Boys' Club in cup final Brithdir team included Allan Rogers (goalkeeper), Lyndon Davies and Tommy Hill (full backs), Dai Morris, Ken Dando, Norman Harris (half backs), Albert and Derek Evans, Dilwyn Davies, Lawrence Rogers (centre forward) and Roy Jarvis (forwards). John Hook and Malcolm Jarvis were also playing members at the time. Allan Rogers was selected for South Wales and Monmouthshire against rest of Wales in Welsh Youth International Trial and also invited to two Cardiff City trials. Lawrence Rogers had trials with Cardiff City and played for their Colts team.

Brithdir Welfare A.F.C, courtesy Paul Waite collection.
Michael Edmunds, Henry Chamberlain, Malcolm Jarvis, Dave Thomas, Tommy Hill, Royston Rawle, Ken Davies, D. March, Brian Mahoney, Derek Evans, Norman Perry (captain), Billy Bennett, Gerald Harris, Keith Bennett, Lyndon Davies, Tony Mahoney, Dai Morris, Roy Sims, Glyn Jones, Ivor Rolfe, Roger Henderson, Bill Hayes, Glyn Morris, Mr. Evans, Bryn Harris, Rollie Hughes, Gethin Jones, Terry Wheeler, Elwyn Thomas and B. Kite.

Left: Celebrating cup win are John Evans, Joe Maggs, Phil Davies, Billy Bennett, Royston Smith, Jeff Ferguson, Tony Mahoney, Ken Davies, Ivor Dunn, Tommy Hill, Roy Farr, Ivor Roach, Brian Mahoney, Lewis Edwards, Don Osborne, Roy Sims, Glyn Jones, Derek Evans, Norman Perry, Lyndon Davies and Gerald Harris.

Derek Evans (left), Roy Sims (centre) and Brian Mahoney (right) with Glyn Jones and Royston Rawle, Brithdir Institute in the background.
courtesy Derek Evans

Two cups presented to R. Smith: Right: 1962-63 Rhymney Valley and District Football League Victory Cup Winners and Senior Cup Runners-up. Left: 1963-64 Rhymney Valley and District Football League, League Winners.

An early Brithdir football team outside George Inn. Terry Wheeler, sitting right of front row, is the only player identified. Below left Brithdir team 1945 with Terry named in the side; sadly, later he lost a leg in mining accident.

DRAWN GAME.—Deri Boys' Club were the visitors to the River Field this week, and a drawn game resulted. Brithdir were represented by: E. Rees, T. Wall, T. Wheeler, H. Hughes, D. Williams, Doug Morgan, T. Price, I. Williams, A. Rogers, N. Perry and S. John.

The saddest day in the club's history, January 3 1970, when 23 year old Brian Chard (right), Brithdir's goal-keeper died after playing a game.

Henry (*Harry*) Williams of Church Villa

Born at Pontlottyn in 1874, and educated at Lewis School Pengam, Harry Williams started his teaching career, aged 14, as a pupil teacher in Deri. Having qualified, he taught in Brithdir and Aberbargoed before retiring after a teaching career spanning over four decades. While Harry was an inspiring and respected teacher, he was also influential in local musical, drama and sporting circles.

146

Harry Williams with his children Eluned (1941 became headmistress Infants' School), Dilys, Talfryn and Eirlys and housekeeper Miss Owen.
Courtesy Millie Evans née Davies

His was an era when league football was developing, and he was at the heart of it locally and nationally. He was instrumental in forming Rhymney Valley League and Glamorgan League and in shaping Welsh League. He was a member of South Wales and Monmouthshire Football Association for 21 years, and its chairman for two years. He was elected vice-president of Welsh Football Association, and served as a member of its international selection committee for many years. He was also a member of Welsh Schools' F.A. selection committee. A referee for over 25 years, he had such understanding of the game and he was in great demand, officiating in national and South Wales Senior Cup matches as well in English League and Cup competitions. Eager to share his knowledge and enthusiasm for his sport, he also found time to act as Rhymney Valley League football correspondent for *Merthyr Express* for a few years.

Harry's contributions in other fields are worthy of mention. He gave much to music in local Congregational chapels: having been precentor at Rhymney's Nazareth, he was for 20 years precentor at Libanus in Cwmsyfiog, directing a number of cantatas and operas. He also enjoyed drama, and, as the Baron in Bont Dramatic Society's production of *The Melting Pot*, he earned great plaudits from press and public. He was regularly in demand as an adjudicator in literary competitions in eisteddfodau at Brithdir and other places including Markham, Abertysswg and Ystrad Mynach.

Ernest *Ernie* Turner

Professional soccer player, Ernie Turner came from a footballing family: his father Alf was considered the best full back in the area, whilst his brother Herbert (Bert) played for Charlton Athletic and Wales, and brother Charles had trials with Chelsea. On leaving school Ernie played left-wing for Brithdir and in season 1913-14 was regular member of the team that became Glamorgan League Division 1 Champions. The following season he transferred to Bargoed, playing in their Welsh League side. He was back at Brithdir for 1920-21 season and subsequently joined Merthyr Town in May 1922. On November 11 1923 at Cyfarthfa, Ernie married Margaret May, daughter of Jemima Rees, publican of Old Tanyard Inn, Bethesda Street, Merthyr Tydfil. A regular in Merthyr's league side for three seasons, he scored 32 goals in 110 appearances. Ernie represented Welsh F.A. on several

occasions before, in preparation for 1925-26 season, he was one of three new forwards signed by Southampton. Equally at home at inside or centre-forward, Ernie featured regularly in the first team during 1925-26 season but unexpectedly left the Dell to emigrate to Australia.

Southampton 1925-26; Ernest Turner is right of second row. This image, free in *Boy's Magazine*, courtesy Duncan Holley,

On March 9 1926, Margaret May Turner left London on board *Benalla* bound for Adelaide, and Ernie followed, leaving May 25 on board *Esperance Bay*. However, in November 1926, they both returned to UK on board *Balranald*. On both journeys, Ernie was listed in the ships manifest as *professional footballer*. Aged 36, Ernie finished his football career in 1933-34 season where it all started, playing in a Brithdir team.

Herbert (*Bert*) Gwyn Turner (1909 –1981)

Bert Turner, Charlton Athletic's Welsh International right back.

Bert, as he was known, played professional football for Wales and Charlton Athletic. Born June 19 1909, son of Alfred and Ella Turner of 13 Charles Street, he joined Welsh Regiment on leaving school and served six years in India and China with 'B' Company, 2nd Battalion, part of Shanghai Defence Force. There he developed into an all-round sportsman, winning medals with army teams in football (soccer and rugby), cross-country running and hockey. Within two years of taking up rugby he was picked for his battalion's First XV and awarded a cap in 1930. The following year he was in the winning team in All-India Rugby Tournament Cup Final against Durham Light Infantry.

Welsh Regiment 2nd Battalion soccer team Singapore 1928-1931. Bert Turner is seated front row, second left. Courtesy Bo Roswall, Bert Turner's son-in-law.

On leaving the army in 1933 his commanding officer wrote in the Regiment's journal:
Private Turner, who since he took up Rugby in 1928 in addition to Soccer has been a steadily improving player. With some first class football at home, if he gets it, his weight, height, speed and sure hands in

148

the pack may put him in the running for some higher honours.

Bert returned to Brithdir and made four appearances for the village team before having a trial with Charlton Athletic. He signed for the London club in August 1933. Bert was a powerful defensive player, predominately a centre-half, but he also filled both full back and half back berths. His time with the club coincided with one of its most successful periods. In 1933-34 season he made 20 league appearances in the side that finished fifth in Third Division South before winning the title and promotion the following year. Playing in Second Division, Charlton finished second, a single point behind Manchester United, but enough for promotion to First Division for the first time in their history.

Back-to-back promotion was followed by remarkable year-on-year progress and Charlton challenged for the title. Manchester City claimed the First Division trophy, with Charlton runners-up, while Manchester United, who had pipped Charlton for Second Division title a year previously, was relegated. In the three seasons before suspension of league football during World War II, Bert Turner's Charlton was the most consistent team in the top flight of English football, not once finishing outside the league's top four. On February 12 1938 they attracted one of the biggest attendances in English footballing history with 75,031 turning up at the Valley to watch them play Aston Villa in FA Cup 5th Round.

Charlton Athletic team of 1930s. Bert Turner stands second from left, next to goal keeper Sam Bartram.

During this pre-war period, Bert's club form brought him to attention of Welsh selectors and he appeared eight times for Wales. He made his debut in 1936 Home Championship 2-1 victory against England at Ninian Park on October 17, and he went on to play in all three 1936-37 Home Championship games. Wales won all three games that season to seal a fourth Championship triumph in ten years. Bert also played throughout 1937-38 tournament when Wales finished last. They began with a 2-1 win at Cardiff over Scotland, but were defeated by the same score when Bert captained his side against England at Middlesborough. Wales travelled to Belfast for the final game against Ireland and lost 1-0. Bert played two further full internationals for Wales; against Ireland in a 3-1 win in 1939 Championship and in a 1939 friendly defeat by France.

Football changed after the outbreak of World War II as club sides were depleted when players left for war service, as shown in Jack Rollin's *Soccer at War 1939-45*. Bert, conscripted and joining RAF, was one of over 60 Charlton Athletic players to leave. Clubs survived by fielding guest players in regional league competitions and Football League War Cup matches. Some football matches were arranged to raise money for war-time charities. Bert, selected for Red Cross Wales v England, was not released from war duties in time to get to Wrexham on November 18 1939, but played in the return match before a crowd of 30,000 at Wembley April 13 1940. Bert had eight pre-war international caps but his eight wartime appearances for Wales did not count as full internationals. During the war he played for RAF, including RAF v Nottingham Forest at City Ground November 9 1940, RAF v FA at Aston Gate, Bristol November 22 1941 and the return fixture at Leeds December 13. Although selected for RAF v Scotland at Newcastle-on-Tyne on February 7 1942, Bert had to withdraw from the team.

A prized family heirloom: Bert Turner, Wales captain, introduces his team to King George VI before 1943 international against England at Wembley, in support of Red Cross Prisoners of War and Aid to Russia funds.

Courtesy Bo Roswall.

Professional footballers in the forces could play as guests for a club near their base. Bert played just 18 wartime games for Charlton Athletic but, from the start of 1943 season, he was a regular for Lovell's Athletic FC (Newport sweet factory team), then premier Newport team as Newport County's Somerton Park was given over to the war effort. Lovell's was in second place (behind Liverpool, but ahead of Man City, Aston Villa, Sheffield Wednesday and Man United) in North Second Championship of 1942-43. Lovell's attracted

WELSH SERVICES' XI.

The Welsh Services' XI. to meet the British Police in a charity match at Ninian Park, Cardiff, this afternoon—kick-off 3.0—will be:— Griffiths (Cardiff City); Turner (Charlton), Whatley (Tottenham); Hollyman (Cardiff City), Walters (Chester), Witcomb (West Bromwich A.); (from) Rogers (Swansea T.), Lowrie (Coventry), Lucas (Swindon), Perry (Doncaster), Green (Charlton), Edwards (Swansea T.).

Western Mail, May 23 1942.

CHURCHMAN'S CIGARETTES

H. TURNER (CHARLTON ATHLETIC)

footballers stationed at RAF St. Athan, including Bill Shankly (Preston North End and Scotland wing-half), Doug Witcomb (West Bromwich Albion and Wales) and South African Berry Nieuwenhuys (played for Liverpool in First Division).

There was no full league football in 1945-46, so FA Cup was the main competition. Charlton Athletic met Derby at Wembley when Bert became the first player to score for both teams in a cup final! In the 81st minute he deflected a shot into his own net and then in the 82nd minute equalised with a 25 yard free kick. These were the only goals in normal time but Derby scored three in extra time to lift the Cup with a 4-1 victory.

Although Bert played one more season with Charlton, he was no longer a regular choice, and was used as cover for Peter Croker at right back or Herbert Johnson at right-half. In 1947, after a 13 year (and 196 games) Charlton career, Bert retired from league football to become player-coach at Dartford in Southern League.

Bert Turner, manager/coach (left) and his Malmo 1953 double-winners

After his playing days were over, Bert coached Swedish club Malmö FF (1951-54). In his first season, Malmö, losing just one game throughout the campaign, won league title, and secured a domestic double by defeating Djurgårdens (managed by Welshman, David *Dai* John Astley, Bert's brother-in-law) to win Svenska Cup. Bert and Dai had married sisters Ena and Muriel James. A native of Dowlais, Dai Astley, played for Merthyr, Charlton Athletic, Aston Villa, Derby County, Blackpool and Metz before moving into management in Italy and Sweden. In 1951-52 season, Bert and Malmö were unable to retain their title, finishing second in the league but success returned in 1952-53 season with Malmö recording a fifth Allsvenskan triumph, and second in three years under Bert. He left Malmo FF. in 1954 to manage Swedish club Kalmar FF.

Bert Turner returned to UK in 1956 and settled in Kent where, for 23 years to 1980, he was landlord of Jolly Farmer Inn in Manston. On June 8 1981, Bert Turner, aged 71, died at his Birchington home.

Bert Turner with two trophies: in his right hand International Soccer Championship and Triple Crown trophy won by Wales 1936-37. The trophy in his left hand is from his time in Stockholm as a trainer. Courtesy son in law Bo Roswall.

Albert *Bertie* Hayes – Brithdir's first soccer International

On Saturday, March 23 1929, Brithdir people gathered at the railway station to welcome Bertie, Boys' School centre-forward, who, playing in Schoolboys' International Wales v Scotland at Swansea, became the first local boy to gain international honours on the soccer field. He emerged from the station and was chaired by enthusiastic admirers who, to the accompaniment of much cheering, carried him to the family home. When those

who had travelled with him announced he had scored all three goals to give Wales the victory, there were renewed cheers and in response to repeated demands, he was forced to wear his cap and display his jersey. Amid cries of *Good Old Bertie* and *Cymru am Byth* the hero was allowed to escape into his home.

Bertie had taken part in three trial matches. The first was on February 9 at Treharris. In the second trial at Barry on February 23, he played a splendid game and scored the two goals, the first a beautiful header and the second a solo effort from almost half-way. He was then selected to play for Probables in a final trial at Briton Ferry on March 8. Although he was not included in the team to play Scotland in Swansea announced a few days later, he was selected as first reserve. Owing to illness of P. Bosse of Cardiff, Bertie played, going into his first international as a reserve and coming out with three goals, giving Wales a first victory over Scotland for ten years. The general opinion was that the entire Welsh team was worthy of selection, but the Brithdir lad, and especially his third goal which earned a huge ovation from the crowd, deserved special credit. The next school day, Henry R Judd, logged:

Saturday March 23: Owing to the indisposition of a selected player, Albert Hayes of this Department played his first International Match on the Vetch Field Swansea today. Coming into the team as First Reserve he created a few records. He was the first Reserve ever to score 3 goals in one match; first Reserve ever to score 2 goals in one minute; first schoolboy International to perform the "Hat-trick." This credit is accentuated by the fact that Albert is the top boy of Form II; has complete attendance; and is quite kindly sociable and gentlemanly in his manner.

On Friday, April 19 1929, Bertie, accompanied by teacher Tommy Davies and headmaster Henry Judd, travelled to Bournemouth where he played in Wales v England game. Although the Wales score sheet was blank, Bertie had the ball in the net on one occasion, but the referee ruled him offside. Bertie was the only Wales team member to score in the first two internationals, yet he was dropped, not even included among the reserves, for Wales team in the third international.

Brithdir people were proud of their young footballer and, on May 4, teachers, schoolmates, parents and villagers, packed New Hall to see him presented with a gold watch and chain. On receiving a bouquet his mother, Mary Ann, (right) said *I am the proudest mother in Brithdir tonight and thank you all for what you have done for my boy.*

On June 2 1933, Bertie was presented with a framed photograph of himself wearing his international cap and jersey, and inscribed *In Highest Appreciation of Albert Hayes (champion scholar and footballer) presented to Brithdir Boys' School by the staff and scholars, 1929.* A similar photograph was also presented to the school by teacher Tommy Davies who, having worked hard on schoolboy football for seven years, was proud of this star player.

When Rhymney Valley League team entertained Bristol City at Fleur de Lys on April 1 1935, Bertie played right half, and took his place between the *sticks* when the home goal-keeper was injured. After he left school, Bertie played for Brithdir Bluebirds, and Cardiff City A team before joining Aberdare Town. He was a professional on Wolverhampton Wanderers' books in season 1935-6. He returned to Wales but Wolves signed him again in February 1939. He had a spell with Wrexham prior to playing for Tredomen Works team in Welsh League. He ended his playing days with Brithdir AFC and was team captain in 1948.

William *Billy* Bassett

The Bassett brothers, William (Billy), Trevor and Idris, learned the rudiments of soccer under school teacher Tommy Davies, trainer of the local school team. For two seasons Billy captained Rhymney Valley Schoolboys and played in several international trial matches. Captain of Brithdir Bluebirds, Billy was one of a number of players watched by some well-known clubs. In 1932, Swansea Town gave centre-half Billy his first big chance when he appeared for them in Welsh League and London Combination matches as an amateur. He also played for Aberaman and, as a youngster, he was with

Bill Bassett 1935

Major Buckley at Wolves (1933-1934). In summer 1934 he arrived at Ninian Park (Cardiff City) where he made centre-half position his own.

Signed by City manager Ben Watts-Jones, Billy's debut game, on the opening day of 1934–35 season, was a 2–1 victory over Charlton Athletic (and Bert Turner). The report in *South Wales Football Echo*, August 25 1934, declared *Bassett Outstanding*. That season Billy played in 39 league games including the 2-1 win over Bournemouth and 3-3 draw with Bristol City -- both at Ninian Park. The following extracts from contemporary local newspapers shed light on what were Billy's only two goals in 154 league appearances in his five year Cardiff City career to May 1939:

South Wales Football Echo, October 6 1934, Cardiff City v Bournemouth: *A corner had been forced and the ball partially cleared. It went straight to Bassett, who was not more than about 10 yards inside the visitors' half. He let fly a terrific shot, which hit the inside of the post and crashed into the net.*
South Wales Football Echo, December 22 1934, Cardiff City v Bristol City: *Bassett picked up a pass on the halfway line and finding he could advance; he strode forward about 15 yards and then delivered an amazing left-foot shot which simply streaked into the net - the cheers that greeted this effort were truly ear-splitting.*

In his first season in Division 1 South, Billy attracted the attention of First Division clubs, and their scouts were present when City visited Clapton Orient December 1 1934. In City's game against Crystal Palace, January 5 1935, Billy's solid game provoked the comment *There is no doubt Cardiff City has a great capture in this player.* His supporters in Brithdir enjoyed reading press headlines such as *Bassett best player* and *Bassett by far best of City's defenders.* He was known in Wales as *the Ironclad,* and *the man with the indian-rubber neck.*

Cardiff City 1936-37 Third Division South
Bill Bassett right of back row.   Courtesy Cardiff City F.C.

Richard Shepherd (of Cardiff City FC) sent me this memory of Billy:

An abiding memory of the 1930s is of Bill Bassett's mud-covered bald head glistening in the rain as he swooped, arms flapping, like some great eagle to head away yet another cannonball.

Billy did not forget his Brithdir roots and his former school, Brithdir Boys'. A school log book entry for March 12 1938 notes that headmaster, Henry Judd, and six senior boys were Billy's guests at Cardiff City FC v Watford match the previous Saturday. Neither did Brithdir forget Billy as his footballing achievements merited him a place in Joyce Jones's memories in *Your Rhymney Valley Express* March 20 1998. In response the newspaper published this letter April 17 1998:

What happy memories the report in the Express on the Brithdir Boys going to Cardiff brought back. I was one of the six boys chosen on the invitation of Big Bill Bassett to watch Cardiff play Watford. What a day! Down on the train in the morning, dinner in Cardiff, then out to Ninian Park followed by an introduction to both teams, then up in the big stand to see the game. Bill made six schoolboys so very happy that day – I don't think any of us had been to see Cardiff City play before. The day still lives on in my memory thanks to the kindness of this generous man.

Mick Rogers, West Street, Bargoed.

Billy joined Crystal Palace in 1939 and like fellow Brithdirite, Bert Turner, his football career was disrupted by outbreak of war. Billy re-joined Crystal Palace in September 1942, debuting in an 8-1 win at Brighton, before going on to play 34 wartime games for the club. A Welsh Guard, Billy was wounded while on war service in Italy, but he recovered sufficiently to appear in several army representative sides and to play regularly for Palace in second part of 1945-46 season, before becoming Palace's first post-war captain in 1946-47. His height (six foot) and build (12 stone) meant Billy was ideal centre-half, and he was a fine header of the ball. On the heavy grounds of second half of seasons, he often left the field with his bald pate covered in mud, a fearsome sight for spectators! His experience meant he was unhurried and unruffled, even during the fiercest moments of a match, a model centre-half of the post-war era, on a par with sweepers half a century later.

Western Daily Press reported on Bristol Rovers mid-week visit to Selhurst Park, September 8 1948, when Billy, Crystal Palace's veteran centre-half, blotting out Lambden, Bristol Rovers' prolific goal-scoring centre-forward, ensured his side gained a one goal victory. Billy made 74 post-war league appearances for Crystal Palace before returning to Wales as player-coach at Porthmadog in 1949.

View from terraces recorded on Crystal Palace Supporters website:

Bassett was always known as 'Baldy' among us and it is clear to see why. He was a good, old-fashioned centre half with, so far as I recall, the height to get above most opposing centre forwards when the ball was curled in from the wings. He could head it a considerable distance, especially remembering how heavy one of those old leather balls could be, especially when wet. He always seemed a good judge of a ball's flight, though one thing one of my mates recalls is that he would usually put it out for a throw in rather than risk giving it to one of the five opposing forwards.

Crystal Palace team before match against Cardiff City, at Selhurst Park, November 23 1946. Bill Bassett back row far right.   Courtesy Crystal Palace A.F.C.

Crystal Palace v Watford, February 15 1947; Bill Bassett far right watching Palace goalkeeper Dick Graham punch clear. Courtesy Crystal Palace A.F.C.

Idris Charles Henry Bassett

Idris, the youngest sibling, also played league football. Born in Brithdir on March 12 1915, and like his older brothers, Trevor and Billy, Idris was a product of Brithdir school and junior teams. He played in a school team alongside Raymond White, Kelvin Moore, David Gwynne, Willie John, Willie Redwood, Glyn Harris, Willie Hayes, Leslie Wallis, Tal Williams, Bertie Hayes,

Idris Bassett c.1941

Alfred Holder and Robbie Davey, that won 1928-29 Rhymney Valley Schoolboys League Shield (see above). When, in 1929, Ystrad Mynach Schoolboys met Cardiff Boys on opening of Ystrad Welfare Ground, both Bertie Hayes and Idris Bassett, were in Ystrad Mynach side.

Starting his football career at Sutton Town in 1933, Idris joined West Bromwich Albion (WBA, *Baggies*) as a professional in October 1936. He made his full League debut for WBA against Wolves at Molineux in May 1938, as WBA were about to be relegated. Idris's career was also affected by the outbreak of war. He was a strong-tackling

West Bromwich Albion team 1941; Idris Bassett back row, third from left, next to goal-keeper.
Courtesy Laurence Rampling

uncompromising full back, who made the most of his 100 wartime appearances for the club. He also made 55 appearances, scoring one goal, for the reserves in Central League. Full back Idris played when, at The Hawthorns on Saturday, November 1 1941, WBA faced a touring Czechoslovak Army team. Driven from their homeland, their team included several Czechoslovak Internationals, with excellent *close-passing* game. Idris Bassett retired from football due to injury in January 1944. He died, aged 64, in Birmingham, September 7 1979.

Rugby Union

Local soccer flourished, but the same cannot be said for rugby. Brithdir Boys' School had a brief flirtation with the oval ball in the 1930s. They started in November 1934, not by playing matches, but by raising money to equip the school rugby team. Local people responded generously, and on Saturday, October 12 1935 Brithdir schoolboys played their first rugby match. Most Rhymney Valley schools already played rugby, and a schools' league was in place. Brithdir team, trained by W. Hughes, joined that league. Although the local press report on a match they lost 16-0 noted that boys Emrys Williams, Jimmy Thomas and Austin Morgan showed distinct promise, they did not progress much further.

Keith Alun Rowlands (1936-2006)

Son of P.C. Reginald Rowlands and his wife Edith, Keith was born in Brithdir Police Station House on February 7 1936 but just short of his first birthday, his father was transferred to Pontlottyn. Thus Keith's link to Brithdir was brief. Websites such as www.abgs.org.uk shed light on his rugby career, as player and administrator, that spanned nearly five decades.

Cartoon courtesy Carmarthenshire Archive Service

William *Billy* James Thomas

Billy was capped for Wales at rugby at schoolboy, youth and senior level. Born 1933 in Factory Road, Bargoed, he was son of William (also known as

Billy) Thomas, former middle weight boxing champion of Wales, remembered by many as Groesfaen Colliery pithead baths superintendent. Billy (junior) married Brithdir girl Maureen James on July 16 1955 and, when daughter Angela was born in 1959, they lived in Bronhaulwen, East View. I recall seeing a tracksuited Billy on many training runs along Aberbargoed Road. The family moved to Bedwas about 1963.

Billy and Maureen at St. Gwladys Church, Bargoed, with the bride's parents William and Matilda James

A product of Lewis School Pengam, Billy played for the school's junior and senior teams and, playing for Rhymney Valley Schoolboys in 1948-49 season, he gained Wales Secondary Schools caps against England (left) and Scotland in 1949. On March 26, at Bristol, Wales (Under 15) Schoolboys defeated England 41-8, their highest total since matches began in 1904. At Cardiff Arms Park in April they overwhelmed Scottish Border Union XV 40-0.

On leaving school, Billy played for Bargoed Youth before joining Newport Athletic Youth in 1951. During 1950-51 season, he was capped twice (against Ireland and France) and he played for Wales Youth (Under 18) against Welsh Secondary Schools U18 XV. In 1952, Billy captained both Newport Athletic Youth XV and Welsh Youth side against Ireland.

In two seasons with Newport senior side Billy made just three 1st XV appearances as Bryn Meredith was the club's first choice hooker. Thus, with little opportunity for first team rugby at Newport, Billy transferred to Abertillery RFC where he was a popular player in his four seasons there. In February 1957, while on the books of Abertillery RFC, Billy was conscripted and, stationed at Brecon, he was Sergeant Drill Instructor in SWB. Making the most of every game of rugby, he helped Brecon Borderers in Army Cup. As he was stationed at Brecon, he could sometimes play for Abertillery and, just six weeks into his service, he was in the Abertillery side facing a Cliff Morgan star-studded international team. He gained further honours when, on Wednesday, January 8 1958, he played in combined Abertillery-Ebbw Vale side that defeated touring Australian Wallabies 6-5 at Abertillery Park. At the start of 1958-59 season, Billy, still in the army, joined Cardiff RFC, and during that season he played twelve 1st XV games, was awarded his Athletics cap and selected to play for Crawshay's XV on Monday, September 15 1958 against Devonport Services. On Wednesday, February 11 1959 he played, possibly his last game for SWB, in a semi-final of Army Rugby Union Challenge Cup at Aldershot Military Stadium, in which SWB lost to 1st

Training Regiment, Royal Signals (who went on to win the cup). During 1959-60 season, Billy, Cardiff's first team hooker, played in 30 games and was awarded his first team cap.

Playing for SWB and Cardiff brought Billy to the attention of Scottish selectors - he was eligible for Scotland via his Scottish mother -- but with a Wales Schoolboy cap and Wales Youth cap, he was keen to make it a hat-trick. However, in late 1950s and early 1960s, Wales Selectors put their faith in Newport's Bryn Meredith, selecting him 34 times for Wales between 1954 and 1962. In 1961, Billy was selected reserve for internationals against Scotland and Ireland, but, as Meredith was unavailable when Wales played France on March 25, Billy ran out onto Stade Colombes (Paris) to win his first Wales cap in a game in which both sides scored two tries, but France kicked one conversion to win the match 8-6 and become Five Nations Champions, with Wales runner-up.

Billy, one of the fastest strikers in the game, and Bryn Meredith's sternest challenger for Wales team, was selected reserve for five internationals in 1962-63. He received the card (right) from Bill Clement, WRU Secretary, informing of his selection for Wales v France in Paris March 23 1963.

The Committee of the Welsh Rugby Union has pleasure in informing

W. J. Thomas.

that he has been selected to play for Wales against France at Paris on Saturday, 23rd March 1963.

Yours faithfully,

SECRETARY

Billy played a key role for Cardiff in 1966 Snellings Sevens final against Newport at Cardiff Arms Park. With the sides level at 20-20, the game entered extra time. A late scrum formed to Newport's advantage but Billy made the tournament's most important strike, taking the ball against the head for team-mate Tony Williams to run 60 yards to score the vital try, Cardiff triumphed 23-20.

Cardiff RFC Sevens Team L-R: John Williams, Billy Thomas, captain Billy Hullin with Snelling Cup, Tony Pender, Maurice Richards, Tony Williams and Lyn Baxter.

Over nine seasons, Billy played 268 games for Cardiff RFC and, for eight of those seasons, he was first choice hooker, playing against South African Springboks, New Zealand All Blacks, Old Rugby Roma of Italy (team comprising representatives from France, Romania and Czechoslovakia), West Germany XV and Australia as well as five times against the Barbarians. His pride in being a Barbarian was clear. He played with and against some of the greatest players. On November 23 1963 he was in the Cardiff team to face New Zealand All Blacks, captained

158

by Wilson Whineray, and including Colin Meads (Pine Tree) and Don Clarke. The game ended 5-6 in favour of All Blacks.

Billy retired in 1967, having played 35 games for Cardiff in his last season, an eventful season during which he played with rising stars Gerald Davies and Gareth Edwards. On November 5 1966, he helped Cardiff defeat the Australia touring side by 14 points to 8. He was selected (alongside fellow Welshmen Billy Hullin, John Dawes and Barry John) for Barbarians v East Midlands in a Mobbs Memorial match at Franklin's Gardens, Northampton on March 2 1967. In May 1967 the Cardiff team flew into Jan Smuts airport for a five-match tour of South Africa, during which he played in four of the games, including captaining the team to victory (23:12) in the second match against North-Western Cape.

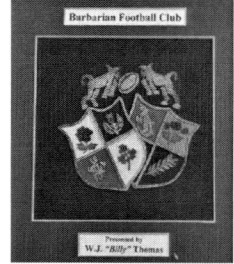

When his playing days were over, Billy coached Bedwas Rugby Club, and he presented his caps and blazer badges to that club. However, some despicable person stole the Baa-Baas badge which, in September 2015, was sold at Mullock's Auctions. The family, having lost Billy in 2013, was outraged.

Neil Webb

Neil Webb was a young boy when, in the mid 1950s, he arrived in Brithdir as his father William *Bill* Webb became landlord of George Inn Hotel. Neil learned the rudiments of rugby football while a pupil at Bargoed Boys' County Secondary School (commonly referred to as *Bargoed North*).

Bargoed North School Class 2a Rugby Team on McDonnell rugby field in 1957 L-R Back Row: Paul James, Tyrone Evans, Brian Bufton, John Sheasby, Ron Cannon. Middle Row: Gerald Harris (Brithdir), Alan Powell, Gareth Fortune, John Forest, Philip Curtis (Tirphil). Front Row: Dennis Burrows, Terry Callaghan, Neil Webb (Brithdir) (captain), Billy Bennett (Brithdir), Alan Evans (Brithdir).

Joining Bargoed RFC in 1964-65 season, he played junior rugby there before transferring to Rhymney RFC where, for reasons no one knows, he became

159

Swansea 1973-74 in their Centenary colours v Australia - Back row: Roger Blyth, Neil Webb, Phil Llewellyn, Mervyn Davies and Geoff Wheel. Others (not in order) are Trevor Evans, Barry Clegg, Mark Keyworth, G. Jones, D. Cole, M. Yandle, G. Higgins, D. Protheroe, R. Dyer (Captain) A. Mages and T.M. Davies. Courtesy David Price, formerly Hon Secretary and President, Swansea RFC, who provided details of Neil's time at Swansea

known as *Ben*. He was mentioned as *new talent* in 1965-66 season, and was part of Rhymney RFC's French tours in spring 1966 and spring 1967. A good player, he was valued highly at the club. He left Rhymney RFC for a short period (possibly due to his job as Brewery rep.) but returned for season 1970-71, playing a dozen games before moving to Newbridge RFC. He made his debut for Newbridge, in a match against Abertillery at Abertillery Park on December

French Tour 1967; Neil Webb far right, back row

9 1970; Newbridge won 18-6. He made 12 appearances in season 1970-71 (all as prop) and in 1971-72 season he played 35 matches (34 as prop, 1 as lock) and scored 2 tries. In *An Illustrated History of Newbridge R.F.C.* Terry Powell described Neil as *six foot, sixteen stone and with a fine sense of humour, had strength, courage and speed.* Neil left Newbridge RFC to join Swansea RFC in season 1972-73. He played 112 1st XV games for Swansea between 1972-3 and 1975-6 seasons as prop-forward. David Price (formerly Hon. Secretary, and President Swansea RFC) described him as *a strong robust player who took no prisoners.* Neil was a key player in Swansea RFC's centenary season, 1973-74: he played in games against touring Australians and Fijians at St. Helens and was part of the side that, winning 31 out of 47

Neil back row 4th from left in this Swansea 1974-75 team.
Courtesy David Dow, Archives, Swansea RFC

160

Neil (left) on a trip to London with friends John Brown and Malcolm Winmill.
Courtesy Malcolm Winmill.

fixtures, was Welsh Merit Table Champion.

At the start of 1975-76 season Neil took over captaincy as new captain Mervyn Davies was one of the club's five Wales players touring Hong Kong and Japan. Mervyn Davies returned as captain but after he collapsed on the pitch during 1976 Welsh Cup semi-final against Pontypool at Cardiff, Neil became Swansea RFC captain, skippering Swansea in 1976 Welsh Cup Final against Llanelli (Llanelli won 16-4).

Boxing

The stories of some of Brithdir's notable boxers are based on correspondence with their families, information on websites such as www.boxinghistory.org.uk (which includes research using the weekly trade paper *Boxing News*), and, especially as many contests were not published in the trade paper, reports in the local press.

Stephen (*Steve*) Kavanagh

Steve Kavanagh, active in the ring between 1915 and 1926, took part in 43 professional contests, and to date, I have studied details of 30 of those contests. Boxing at flyweight, he met and shared honours with some of the best flyweights in the country, and, according to *Merthyr Express*, May 3 1919, was crowned *pit boy champion*.

A native of Cardiff, Steve was son of Irish immigrant, William Kavanagh, and Beatrice Mahoney. He served in the army during the war, (and boxed for the army). His service records have not

Steve Kavanagh and Beatrice née Morgans
Courtesy Idwal Kavanagh

Steve Kavanagh (seated) with committee members Phil Willetts and Hopkin Morgan

survived but his medal index card shows he served in SWB and Cheshire Regiment as Private 31836 and 53264, respectively. On May 5 1917 he married Beatrice Morgan, daughter of David and Elizabeth Morgan, Ty Coch.

When, in 1927, Brithdir Athletic Club was formed to foster boxing, its organiser and instructor, Steve Kavanagh was encouraged to find 120 lads enrolled as members. Dr. O'Shea was president of the club and vice-presidents were Councillor C.A.M.

Steve Kavanagh, front centre, with colleagues at Bargoed Ambulance Station. Brothers Mick and Doug Rogers are either end of front row, and David Willetts third right in back row.
Courtesy Idwal Kavanagh

Cattermole, E.D. Rees, H. R. Judd and J. Hill. Its chairman was T. Bufton, while S. Davey was secretary and E. J. Morgan, treasurer, and the committee comprised A. Rees, D. Jones, J. Harris, W Macdonald, Phil Willetts and Hopkin Morgan.

Merthyr Express, October 22 1927, carried a report on a series of no-decision bouts held on Friday, 14 October, at George Hotel -- four-round contests *between J. Davies and B Barlowe; B. Williams and H. Baldwin; F. Bufton and A. Watkins; R. Thomas and C. Bolton. 3-rounds between E. Pritchard and T. White; M. James and J. Buckley; R Mond* (Maund) *and J. Abraham.* The evening concluded with a 6-round exhibition between Albert Pipe and Bob Mahoney.

Albert Edwin Pipe

Albert Edwin, son of Henry and Mary Jane Pipe of 7 Bristol Terrace, was born in Brithdir in 1909. Active as a professional boxer between 1925 and 1938, he boxed at flyweight, bantamweight, featherweight, and lightweight. To date, I have found details of 64 of Albert Pipe's 100 professional contests, and they show him as *a clever boxer and an expert at dodging blows, who carried a tremendous punch in his right glove.* He met and beat some of the best in the country at his weight, including Terence Morgan and Phineas John.

This photograph, (courtesy British Boxing Board of Control), was attached to Albert Pipe's Professional Boxer's Licence, No 3053, April 11 1931. At the time his address was given as Robin Hood, Gosport, and his manager named as W.T. Gascoyne, Star Hotel, Gosport.

162

Reports in *Portsmouth Evening News* shed light on Pipe's boxing career during his time in Gosport. By defeating Kid Connor of Portsmouth over ten-rounds at Connaught Drill Hall, Pipe became Hampshire's bantam-weight champion in autumn 1930. He endeared himself to his fans when he boxed in aid of charities such as Gosport War Memorial Hospital, Victoria Nursing Association, Gosport and Alverstoke branch of British Legion, and his reputation was enhanced further when, in spring 1931, he was victorious over a boxer of the calibre of Fred Watts of London. By the time he renewed his boxing licence, August 22 1932, he was back at the family home in Bristol Terrace.

Penuel Chapel Whitsun tea party c1920; the two on (right) end of back row are Mary Whitefoot and Mary Price.
Courtesy Chrissy Price

Church outing 1920s.
Courtesy Finnuola Eardley née O'Shea

CHAPTER 11 BRITHDIR AT HOME 1900-1939

As the nineteenth gave way to the twentieth century, Brithdir was an expanding village: new terraces of dwellings were built on land of Cefn y Brithdir in the 1890s, with more terraces erected further north during the new century's first decade. Although some local men were fighting in the South African War, there was no anticipation that most of the next half century or so would be dominated by rumours of war, war and post war readjustment. The agglomeration of incomers was melding into a vibrant and confident community, eager to meet their own spiritual, cultural and leisure needs. Brithdir already had its places of worship by the turn of the century, with, as in many other similar communities, nonconformist chapels in the vanguard, reflecting not only the inclinations of the incomers but also the Anglican church's belated response to the challenges of industrialisation and urbanisation. The school, like the Anglican church, was a creation of an outside agency, and its history is outlined in the chapter on education.   George Inn Hotel, predating the community itself, had satisfied the thirsts of coal miners since the early Victorian era, but was not enough for twentieth century Brithdir people. As a result of the efforts of local people, the new century saw social facilities expand with the opening of both Constitutional Club and Workmen's Institute, the latter with library, hall (New Hall) and games facilities.

What follows in this chapter deals primarily with life in Brithdir in the first four decades of the twentieth century, and succeeding chapters deal with Brithdir people who served their country away from Brithdir.

World War I era

Brithdir's community feeling was maturing in the early years of the century only for it to be shattered by the trauma of World War I. See Chapter 12 for some details relating to local people who served their country during that conflict.

Life for those at home during the war years was difficult. While some menfolk remained at home working in the coal industry, many families faced hardships and worries as fathers, sons and brothers left to serve their country. Most of what follows on Brithdir's home front is based on entries in the log books of the local schools.

World War I and Brithdir schools

This study of World War I and Brithdir Schools is based mainly on entries in Brithdir school log books, and especially those of Samuel Davies whose photograph appears on the left.

As the pupils returned to school after 1914 summer holiday, Samuel Davies did not mention the hostilities with Germany, perhaps thinking the war would be *over by Christmas*. Although he recorded the absence of teacher William Barker on

September 9, to attend examination by military doctor for war service with RFA, he appeared to be more concerned about absenteeism due to the annual hop-picking season and an epidemic of scarlet fever. William Barker was not the only young male member of the profession to enlist for war service, leaving schools like Brithdir Boys' especially vulnerable to staffing difficulties. Others who left Brithdir Boys' included Frank West (see West family pages 347-356) and David Thomas Emrys Davies (known as Tommy) son to Samuel Davies. Towards the end of 1915, the impact was clear. During 1915-1916, Martha C. Price of Brithdir Girls' logged numerous occasions when one, or more, of her female teachers was temporarily redirected to cover staffing shortfalls in the Boys' Department. One female teacher so deployed was Elizabeth Isaacs, transferred from Brithdir Girls' for a week's temporary cover in the Boys' Department on January 27 1916, and again on May 23 1916.

The problem continued as the war progressed and in April 1917 Samuel Davies noted that *W. G. Williams, an uncertificated teacher in Brithdir Boys' School, left for the army on April 2 1917*. William Glyndwr Williams started his teaching career in Tirphil early in 1916, and attended Army Medical Board in Cardiff on the afternoon of September 1 1916. It is likely that he was one of the teachers moved to fill gaps when Brithdir teachers enlisted early in the war.

February and March 1917 were difficult months for headmaster Samuel Davies, with the illness and subsequent death of his wife. The following extracts from the Girls' Department log outline events:

February 23 1917: *Miss Muriel Davies was absent today. Her brother (Tom Davies) arrived suddenly from the French front owing to the illness of their mother, Mrs Davies.*

March 19 1917: *Miss Muriel and Miss Olwen Davies are absent. The death of the mother Mrs Davies will necessitate the absence of these two teachers during the whole of this week.*

March 22 1917 *Mrs Davies the wife of the headmaster of the Boys' Dept. is buried today. The three School Departments have been granted closure this afternoon.*

On his return to duty on April 4, Samuel wrote *Samuel Davies, headmaster, absent from school for 5 weeks (Feb 16 - Mar 30) through the death of his wife and personal illness.*

Samuel Davies logged the sad news that *2nd Lt Tom S Jones killed in France, enlisted April 14 1916.* He lived at 7 Coedcae, Tirphil, with his parents, Stephen and Mary Jones. A pupil teacher, he was transferred from Pontlottyn Boys' School to Brithdir on September 16 1912 and served under Samuel Davies until September 30 1913 when he left for Bangor College. Thomas enlisted as Private 23646 in Royal Welsh Fusiliers 13th Battalion in 1915 and was in France by December 1. He was twice wounded, on successive days, July 10 and 11 1916, at Mametz Wood. He returned to UK, attended a cadets' school and was commissioned as Second Lieutenant on March 27 1917 into 3rd

Battalion Royal Welsh Fusiliers. Serving with 10th Battalion Royal Welsh Fusiliers at third battle of Ypres (Passchendaele), he was killed September 26 1917, aged just 25.

Log Book entry October 18 1918: *received the sad news today that Willie Phillips, a former pupil of this school has been killed in the fighting for Cambrai.* William Phillips (right courtesy Paul Williams), son of Albert and Mary Phillips, 16 Charles Street, private in Royal Welsh Fusiliers, was killed on October 8, age 20.

On February 22 1918 news of a bravery award was recorded in the log: *Private Thomas J. Green has won the DCM in France. Green is an old Brithdir schoolboy.* Born 1895 in Brithdir, Thomas John Green was son of Caleb and Sarah Green of 5 Salisbury Terrace. The citation for his DCM, gazetted February 2 1918 for an action on November 19 1917, reads:

> *For conspicuous gallantry and devotion to duty. When the advance was held up by a group of enemy strong points, he led a party forward and captured them, together with two machine-guns and a large number of prisoners. Later he located an enemy post and single handed compelled the enemy to retire from it. He set a magnificent example to his men.*

A Lance Corporal in Welsh Regiment when he was awarded the DCM, Thomas Green later became Corporal. He remained in the army post-war and was awarded the Indian General Service Medal with Wazirstan Clasp (1920-24) to add to his Great War medals.

Headmaster Samuel Davies regularly recorded visitors to the school and his log book entry for April 16 1918 noted the visit of a soldier of the Australian Army: *The school visited this morning by Private Emrys Morgan of Newcastle, N.S.W. prior to leaving for Australia.* Emrys Morgan, born in Fleur de Lys was 11 years old when, in 1887, his family emigrated to Australia. At the time of his visit to the school he was stationed at Australian Command Depot in Weymouth, and, according to Australian Imperial Force service papers he was medically unfit, and repatriated to Australia on May 12 1918 for discharge. It is not clear why he visited Samuel Davies and the school. Sources searched to date show no evidence that he was a former pupil of the village schools. However, it is possible that he was simply paying a courtesy call on behalf of his father, John Morgan, who before emigrating, may have been a close associate of Samuel Davies. They were both Welsh speakers, interested in Welsh language, traditions and folk-lore, and devout worshippers in local chapels. Prior to emigrating, John Morgan had been a member of Caersalem Baptist Chapel, Aberbargoed, while Samuel Davies was a deacon and treasurer of Libanus CM Chapel, Cwmsyfiog. Thus it is highly likely that the paths of these two Christian Welshmen had crossed regularly.

On June 11 1918, a former teacher of the school paid a visit prompting Samuel to write: *2nd Lieutenant J.D. Jones, Royal Garrison Artillery, an old assistant at this school called to see us today. Mr Jones previous to serving was the headmaster of Fochriw Council School to which post he hopes to return after the war.* A native of Camrose, Pembrokeshire, John David Jones came to Brithdir via Park School, Aberdare, in June 1903 and served under Samuel Davies in the Mixed Department for over six years before being appointed headmaster of Fochriw Council School, October 1909.

Samuel Davies, frustrated by staff shortages, wrote on October 1 1918: *the staff at present is very inadequate, only head-teacher, one certified* [sic] *assistant and one untrained teacher taking charge of six classes. This is undoubtedly the case owing to the great lack of teachers.*

To help with the shortage of qualified teachers, the school managers appointed returning ex-soldiers. David Jenkins Jones, a discharged soldier, commenced duties as uncertificated teacher on March 11 1918. D. Jones, also a discharged soldier, arrived on March 18 as supplementary teacher. The headmaster had cause to remark on more than one occasion how the two discharged wounded soldiers were suffering from their leg wounds. David Jenkins Jones was from Pontlottyn. A student at Caerleon Training College prior to the war, he returned there to complete his training before, on July 12 1920, joining the staff of Brithdir Boys' as a certificated assistant, the same day as Tommy Davies, the headmaster's son. David Jones was newly demobilised, after being on active service in Mesopotamia for over 3 years, when he commenced duties as certificated assistant. It is likely that he was the 15 year old pupil teacher David Jones, living with his parents, John and Harriet, in Station Terrace, when the 1901 census was taken. Before the next census, David Jones had married, and moved to the Roath district of Cardiff to take a post as assistant schoolmaster.

Samuel Davies felt great personal relief when, on January 6 1919 he penned the safe return of his son Tommy after 3 years' active service in France. Tommy had started his apprenticeship in the Mixed Department in 1912. He left for Caerleon Training College in September 1915, but, his training was put on hold when he enlisted into Royal Welsh Fusiliers. It was headmaster and worried father who wrote the entry in the school diary on June 2 1917 - *Pte Davies RWF severely wounded in both legs at Ypres.* Shipped back to UK, Tommy was admitted to 2nd Eastern General Hospital in Brighton on June 29 1917. He remained with the colours until January 1919 and on demobilisation, reported back to complete his college training. Newly qualified, on July 12 1920, he became certificated assistant in the Boys' Department, where he remained until retirement on July 24 1959.

World War I government fundraising

Six Mark IV tanks toured towns and cities across UK to promote the sale of government war bonds and war savings certificates. Pupils of Brithdir's schools were granted half-day holidays on July 1 1918 to attend *Tank Day* at Pontlottyn, and again, on July 5, for *Tank Day* at Bargoed. *Merthyr Express*, July 13 1918, reported *'Egbert' the famous warrior tank brought its South*

Wales money-collecting tour to a triumphant close at Bargoed, whose contributions passed £141,500 and might now perhaps be registered at about £145,000. (Photograph *Egbert* courtesy Jeff Alden, Cowbridge)

THE TANK 'EGBERT' AND ITS CREW

End of the war

The end of the war was recorded factually in Brithdir Boys' log book:
November 11 1918: Declaration of Armistice of the Great World War.

Whereas the entry in the Girls' School log was a little more emotive:
We close school today for the remainder of the week, owing to the good news we have received – The War is ended.

The fighting may have ceased but it took months, and even years, before some fathers, brothers and sons returned. Samuel Davies's log on November 29 1918 shows the importance of older boys to mothers:
A number of the older boys are staying away on Friday especially, to obtain the family ration of food for the week.

The Boys' School log for July 19 1919 describes the peace celebrations thus:
Today is the Great Peace Demonstration - a day of joy and thanksgiving. The scholars and demobilised soldiers formed a huge procession preceded by the Brithdir United Choir, Ministers of the Gospel and Members of Public Bodies. The whole village was gay with bunting and the children carried miniature Union Jacks. After a tour of the village, the children were regaled with an excellent tea at the Girls' School. Sports followed for the school children and demobilised soldiers.

Inter-war years

Much has been written about post-World War I adjustment and the hardships of the 1920s and 1930s in UK and beyond. As servicemen returned after the war, they had a month's paid leave before demobilisation and realisation that life and work in Britain (and Brithdir) was different from that they had left on enlistment. Some national conflicts impinged on life in Brithdir as illustrated by Samuel Davies's log book entry for September 29 to October 6 1919 which read *Great National Strike of Railwaymen - school kept and all the teachers from a distance turned up.* By contrast Muriel Price of Cardiff, assistant teacher in Girls' Department, was unable to get to school for two days.

Brithdir, a coal mining community, was affected by contemporary difficulties in that industry. In the face of foreign competition, mine owners sought to cut miners' wages and extend their working day, and the miners went on strike from April 15 1921. The weeks of strike inevitably meant hardship and, as witnessed by these log book entries, local children received meals in school:
April 27: The feeding of Children's Act (Provision of School Meals) brought into operation today owing to the coal strike.

June 19: *The feeding of children came to an end today. The strike lasted about 14 weeks. The scholars whose fathers had not re-started in their previous occupations were fed in the local Canteen Establishment.*

Hardships continued as reflected in this log book entry:

January 9 1925: *The attendance suffered a good deal this week owing to the absence of many boys who were sent by their parents to carry away soiled goods from the Railway Accident at Coedcae, Tirphil.*

The accident, on Saturday, January 3, involved GWR's Abergavenny to Cardiff train. The engine and sixteen wagons toppled over the embankment leaving the guard's van and nine wagons on the line. The engine driver and fireman were killed as the wreckage covered the engine.

Worse followed with General Strike (1926) and industrial depression and unemployment in coalfield communities in the later 1920s spilling over to the 1930s. Some individuals and families left the area, seeking work in other parts of UK or overseas. However, it was also a time when the community showed its mettle: hardship strengthened community feeling, pulling people together in the face of adversity. It was a time when individuals and groups of people took the lead in ensuring, as far as possible, the physical and social well-being of all sectors within the community.

General Strike 1926

The causes, events and results of the General Strike 1926 have been chronicled elsewhere, so what follows are some specifics about Brithdir.

During the General Strike, Brithdir's local strike committee was busy, raising money (totalling nearly £170) and meeting the needs of local people. While men like Isaac Jones, organiser and treasurer, and Tom Jenkins, secretary, worked hard to ensure sound administration, they were backed by strong support from across the community. Many people worked tirelessly in the

Staff of Brithdir communal kitchen, seated far right front row is Amy Jones (née White), her husband John Jones in back row third from right. Second row Maud Jones (standing directly behind the lady seated second left), her husband Simon Jones next.
Courtesy John Rawle

communal kitchen and elsewhere, to ensure Brithdir people, particularly children, were not only fed, but also able to enjoy as contented and happy a life as possible under the circumstances. School log books narrate the story of the *feeding of necessitous children*, and the communal kitchen, in New Hall, served three meals a day to a large number of local people in need. The communal kitchen committee was chaired by John Godfrey and R. Perryman was its secretary. Extant canteen accounts show the chief sources of income were concerts (raising £80 after expenses), dances (£17 12s 6d), donations (nearly £17) and a fundraising tour by Knibs Outing Club (£35).

Brithdir School Canteen 1926 provided breakfast, dinner and tea in the school's Cookery Centre during the strike. The only person identified in this photograph is Amy Jones (née White) middle row, 3rd from left.
Courtesy Jacqueline Tiernan her great-granddaughter.

The concert committee with W. Bowles as chairman and treasurer, D. Davies as secretary, Evan Davey responsible for dances, and P.L. Willetts for whist drives, was busy organising events. This was an era when a community made its own entertainment and reports in the local press show that as many as three popular and rewarding social and fundraising activities were held in a week. At first, such events were free, but soon a small charge was made, and the takings handed over to the canteen fund. As described on page 265, some of the entertainment during the strike months was provided by local organisations, including Young People's Society (YPS), groups attached to places of worship and societies devoted to performing arts, while performers from many neighbouring communities also visited Brithdir. The weekly Saturday night whist drives were popular, attracting 20 tables. The idle days of the strike saw a revival of the game of quoits, and matches between local teams (Bute Terrace, Constitutional Club, New Houses, Mr. Roffi's team and Tirphil) drew large crowds.

Outing Clubs

Contrary to what their names suggest, Knibs Outing Club and Brithdir Swan Outing Club were not concerned primarily with arranging trips, rather the focus was on raising money for good causes before, during and after the strike months.

Brithdir Swan Outing Club originated in the early 1920s with Wilfred Nutt, president, and Bryn Harris, secretary. Its main aim

170

Knibs Glee Party in Exeter during 1926 strike fundraising tour.
Back row L-R: Ivor Davey (Charles Street) with Les West and Stan West far right. Seated right is David Davies (School Street, father of Melville, boy soprano, Millie and Ceridwen). This group toured Cornwall in 1928 (as described in the diary below).
Courtesy Millie Evans née Davies

was to help local children and pensioners. The club helped local pensioners by organising social evenings and dances in local venues, to raise funds for pensioners' Christmas treat, a dinner and social evening for all male pensioners. It was still in existence in 1934 when Ben Morris was chairman, Brinley Harris, secretary and Rupert Bennett, treasurer. However, although it lapsed about 1944, a meeting in George Inn Hotel, saw it re-formed in March 1950 with Bert Bennett as chairman, Bryn Harris, secretary, and Phil Willetts, treasurer. It held weekly (Saturday) meetings at the hotel.

Sometimes members of Swan and Knibs Outing Clubs united. For example, in February 1934, they organised a dance in New Hall to raise funds for a tea for children (under 14 years), and, in November of the same year, members of the two clubs were stewards at a dance at Workmen's Hall organised by the local branch of NSPCC with Wilf Bennet as one of three M.C.s for the evening. At that time, Knibs Outing Club officers were B. Gerrish, chairman, Clifford Hewitt, secretary, and W. Mortimer treasurer, with Jim Mellins,

Brithdir Swan O.C. circa 1930. Back row L-R; unknown, Rupert Bennett, Albert Bennett, Horace Brown, unknown. Front row L-R; Wilfred Bennett, Bryn Harris, others unknown.
Courtesy Pete Bennett.

171

Hubert Brown, Phil Willetts and O. Hewitt serving on the committee.

Stan West was secretary, treasurer and diarist of Knibs 1928 tour of Cornwall, and the following extracts from the diary, courtesy his daughter, Gillian Pritchard, née West, outline the story of that tour:

April Tues 24	*Went to Constantine via Falmouth. Wrote post card on prom. Fine concert here. School packed out some turned away. Enos and I slept at Mrs. Roberts.*
Wed 25	*Stayed night at Constantine. Went to Swan Vale, seven in a Ford car, a lovely village, recently built. Fair attendance.*
Thurs 26	*Walked from Truro to Baldhu. Good crowd, Ray and I went home with Mr. Roberts in his car and had a good time on his farm.*
Mon 30	*Left Camborne at 4 o'clock. Went by train to Marazion and walked from there to Goldsithney. Waited at hall till nearly 7.30 and rest of party turned up one by one. Failed to get digs after concert so walked back to Penzance, arrived there at midnight. Met policeman who knocked up a hotel keeper for us and dug in there. Poor Bill Hulin slept all night in GWR road bus.*
May Tues 1	*No concert booked so started busking at Long Rock, near Penzance, from there to Marazion. Walked back to Penzance for dinner, then went Newlyn and sang. Newlyn is a large fishing town, hundreds of fishing boats, terrible smell. Went to Labour meeting and slept the night at Long Rock.*
Wed 2	*Finished busking at Newlyn, then we went to Mousehole. Very large fishing village, hundreds of trawlers and boats kept here. Did fairly well there, finished singing about 7 o'clock, then came back to Penzance, where we went to a Labour Social and sang a few songs there. Met Jack Probert of Blaina, who has the job of bandmaster of Penzance Independent Band, and he was very pleased to see some Welshmen.*
Thurs 3	*Went down to Riviera Beach, Eastern Green, to make arrangements for concert on Friday. Sat down and wrote handbills till my fingers were stiff. Arranged to meet rest of the boys at Penzance Station at 2 o'clock, all turned up except George, who was about an hour behind as usual. Instead of going to St. Just to sing as we intended, sang in streets of Penzance and made over £4 in 3 hours (not bad day's work)*
Fri 4	*Had concert at Riviera Beach, Eastern Green. Intended holding it on the open beach, but it started to rain, so we held it in the café. Held one in the afternoon at 3.30 and one in the night. However it rained so heavily we had poor crowds, but quite enjoyed ourselves.*
Sat 5	*Left Long Rock and on to Helston and Porthleven for concert, but such few turned up, cancelled show and busked the streets, did very well. Ray & I stayed at Will's Café.*
Sun 6	*Wesleyan chapel in evening where Ray & George sang 'Watchman'. After chapel, we had a concert in the park, and held our platform on the bridge over the lake. It was like standing on a funnel of a ship and singing to the sea. However, we had a good show and made a fine collection.*
Mon 7	*Sang in the cattle market at Helston, but between the lowing of the cattle and the meanness of the farmers, we didn't do much there. Sang the streets in the afternoon.*
Tues 8	*Today is Flora Day, we sang in the streets, outside the hall, sang for Fox's Pathes Gazette.*

Wed 9 Left Helston for Falmouth. Went to a Unionist meeting on the square and started singing there. Started singing Cwm Rhondda in Welsh after the meeting and two fellows there said we were singing the Red Flag.

Thurs 10 Stayed the night at Falmouth, went to Penryn this morning and sang there, did very well and ordered 2/9 tin of cream to be sent home and also sent registered letter home. Left Falmouth for Penzance at 6, via Helston, arrived Penzance at 8.30 pm stayed at Mrs Courtneys in James Street.

Fri 11 Had two concerts and a dance on Riviera Beach, Eastern Green, but didn't make a great success of it, as all the arrangements had been muddled. Stayed the night with Mrs Duran at Long Rock.

Sat 12 Left Penzance for Camborne, and drop bag off at Mrs Mitchells, went to Redruth in the evening and did very well there.

Sun 13 Stayed at the Mitchells over the weekend and on Sun afternoon we all went to Vogueboth to the S S Anniversary. Went to Chapel in the night, walked back home to Camborne.

Mon 14 Concert at Stithians, near Redruth. Fine concert and the vicar was quite astounded with the show we put up and gave us a hearty invite to return. After show the vicar gave us all a cigar each and went back to Camborne in a car, 'like proper pros'

Tues 15 Went to Lanner and Chasewater and did fairly well, singing on the road. All came back to Redruth, George and I went straight from there to Falmouth where we dug in at Richardsons. Ray went to Camborne and Enos and Bill stayed at Redruth.

Wed 16 Went to Swan Vale, lovely little village set out like a garden. In the afternoon went to Flushing just across the bay by motor-launch. When we arrived found out that a party had already been there so we returned to Falmouth.

Thurs 17 Left Falmouth by steamer for St. Mawes, had to land in a small boat, did very well there and left again by boat for Portscatho, didn't do very well there, met an old professional cello player who was on holiday who gave us tea, very impressed with our singing. After tea walked to Veryan when it started to rain, got in a cart-shed and started practicing Arabella, Row Boatman etc. Rain cleared up, started tramping again. Walked about a mile when it rained terrible, thought we would be drowned, when along came a car which stopped and picked us all up, five of us, bags and all, and away we went like Lords. Except George who had all our bags stacked up on top of him. It was lucky for us that the driver's boss's wife had died and he had been taking the Registrar back in the car, or we shouldn't have met him. Arrived at Veryan and started to sing but everyone thought we were Germans or burglars, they wouldn't have anything to do with us. Started to rain, Enos and I went to look for lodgings for the party but couldn't get in anywhere. Went and had a chat with the bobby and his wife went out and found room for two, they were all afraid of us. However, we finished up by all going to the Butchers house and dug in there. Had a sing-song till about 12.30 and the PC, his wife and five friends came to listen to us. Had a good time and the PC gave us 2/6d

Fri 18 Left Veryan this morning by chara for Mevagissey. It was a lovely trip and we travelled through some wonderful country and saw some lovely sights. Saw and passed right by Praze Castle, where squire Williams, Lord Lieutenant of Cornwell, lives and it is a glorious spot. We passed right along the Cornish coast and in some places through the heart of the country. In

173

fact there are no trains, and the chara we went in was passenger-bus, goods-train, post-office, produce-carrier, errand boy, furniture remover, all combined in one. What amused me was a servant girl stopped the bus and asked the driver, would he take a portmanteau to St. Austell for them? He said he would, and went to fetch it. He returned after about half-hour and informed us that when he arrived at the house, they were just starting to pack it. George remarked that it looked more like a cargo for the ship than a portmanteau. About 4 miles further on, a lady wanted him to take a big armchair for her. The chara was packed, (about 18 of us in a 14 seater) I was in the back seat and had about half-a-ton of farm-produce etc all around me, so he had to tie it on top of his engine. We looked well. However we arrived safely, and sang there and left a good impression there.

Sat 19	*Left Mevagissey for St. Austell at 10.30. Arranged to meet George at 1 o'clock, as usual he didn't arrive until 4. Started singing and met some friends who invited us to spend the week-end with them. Ray & I went to Mrs Thomas at Par Green and we had a nice hot bath.*
Mon 21	*Left Par Green for Plymouth, sang in the streets but didn't do much.*
Tues 22	*Our daily programme whilst at Plymouth is: Sing from 10 till 1 o'clock, then an hour or two in the afternoon.*
Thurs 24	*Laira, sang morning and afternoon and had an engagement at the Cat and Rat Club in the night at 10.30.*
Fri 25	*Sang in the morning at Mutley Plain, finished about 3 o'clock.*
Sat 26	*This morning we are having a spell, as it is a big strain on our voices, but they are all sticking it well.*
Sun 27	*Still at Plymouth, went to Docker's Hall in Trevel street to Christian Socialist Church and gave a few songs. Went to church in the evening.*
Mon 28	*Whit-Monday. All arrangements made for us to go to Bovisands to sing and have a picnic, by the young members of the Christian Socialist Church. Went by motor-boat. When the time came for us to sing, George could not be found, but after looking for him for about 2 hours, he strolled back. He had been sitting just above us writing letters. Sang for about one-and-half hours and took £2.10.0. Walked back over the cliffs.*
Tues 29	*Busked Laira and did fairly well, spent best part of the afternoon writing letters.*
Wed 30	*Busked at Keyham, did well.*
June Fri 1	*Sung at Devonport Dockyard gates and did well. Sang about 20 tunes without a stop.*
Mon 4	*Left Plymouth for Newton Abbot. This terminated a very happy time during our fortnight's stay and I shall hold many fond memories of Plymouth. Arrived at Newton and started singing straight away. Put up in Welsh's Temperance Hotel*
Tues 5	*Went to Torquay to sing but not many visitors there, so went on to Paignton, not many there either, however did fairly well and returned to Torquay to sing coming out of the theatres but police stopped us.*
Wed 6	*Went to Teignmouth to sing, did well.*
Thurs 7	*Left for Exeter and arrived at 1.30. Sang at St. Thomas, Enos and I stayed with Mrs Bastin [where the Knibs stayed in 1926].*

The importance of individual efforts

Brithdir's social life, so important during years of depression, owed much to a small but active group of leaders including Rupert (*Pete*), Albert (*Bert*) and Wilfred (*Hickey*) Bennett, Horace Brown and Bryn Harris. The Bennett family was involved with Brithdir Swan Outing Club and the village soccer team benefitted from their management skills.

Wilfred Bennett, was a popular village character who linked with all generations in the community and had a unique way of fundraising. He was involved in a wide range of local activities from being elected treasurer of Brithdir's testimonial to schoolboy soccer international Bertie Hayes (see page 151) to acting as M.C. at events such as the annual social evening, organised by Brithdir branch British Legion. The Legion's 1932 event was held in Ambulance Hall in November 1932, and Royal Paget Dance Band provided the music. In February 1933, Wilf and Harry James arranged the entertainment at the Legion's annual children's tea. Later, in 1958, I was among the group of boys travelling in an open-back lorry (tent, gear and boys piled on the back) on his

Wilf and Rachel 'Lily' Bennett

camping trip to a farm in Madley, Hereford. On arrival, we pitched our camp in an apple-orchard, and, with bales of hay from the barn, we soon had home comforts (tables and chairs).

This is my photograph (Kodak box camera) of back row L-R; John Brown, Malcolm Winmill, Derek Bennett, Keith Williams with Dennis Williams and Billy Bennett in front, on a visit to Hereford Cathedral and cattle market – Malcolm Jarvis, John Lear, Stephen Pritchard and Roy Bennett were also on the trip.

Outward migration

Brithdir developed as incomers, especially young men, many with wives and children, arrived in search of work in the coal industry. By the inter-war period, economic and social factors turned the flow of migration and some individuals and families left the area, seeking work in other parts of UK or overseas.

Harvest Excursions

Farming in Canada was, like contemporary farming in UK, labour-intensive in the inter-war era, and prairie harvests needed large workforces for a short working season. In 1928, Canadian Government Harvester's Scheme (paying passage and promising short-term harvest jobs) attracted over 8,000 unemployed UK coal miners, and some of these were from Brithdir.

Brithdir people who travelled to Canada as Harvesters						
Name	Age	Dept.	Port	Arr	Port/Ship	Stay
Albert Cooper	19	1928 03.08	Liverpool	1928 12.08	Quebec/Calgaric	settled
David Morgan	28				Quebec	
Graham Hugden Price	25					5½ wks
Baden Powell Price	28	11.08.	Southampton	19.08.	Megantic	17 wks
Francis Windsor Williams	18					8½ wks
David John Thomas	30					4 mths
Ivor Leslie Davey	24	18.08.	Liverpool	25.08	Halifax/Adriatic	16 wks
William S. George	28					6 wks
Richard Smith	27					6 wks
Pharoah J. Nicholls	26					3½ yrs
Christopher Harold	23	1929 16.03	Liverpool	1929 24.03	Halifax/Andania	?
William McDonald	27					3½ yrs
David Morgan	26					?
Francis Windsor Williams	19					settled
Francis Williams	43	21.03	Southampton	30.03	Halifax/Alaunia	8 mths

Francis Windsor Williams (right) is listed twice. Youngest of four children born to Francis and Ruth, 11 School Street, he went to Canada: in 1928, for two months, and in March 1929, he returned to Canada and settled there. He started as a farm hand before moving to Crow's Nest Pass, Alberta, to work in a coal mine. Later, he moved to Saskatchewan and settled in Regina where he met and married farmer's daughter, Violet Rachel McKechnie, and they raised five children. He started working for *Sears Canada*, a large retail and mail order company, and when he retired, 44 years later, he held a senior management position.

Although he settled in Canada, Francis Windsor Williams maintained contact with his family in Wales. In 1957 and 1966, he and his wife travelled to meet his family in Wales, and on a visit in 1971 he was accompanied by his son, Ron (who has supplied much of the family detail as well as the photographs). After his wife's death, his sister Muriel and her husband John visited him in Regina, and his sister Edna visited on several occasions. Such trans-Atlantic visits gave his Canadian children and

Western Plainsmen Singers c.1938: Francis Windsor Williams is in the back row, 2nd from right.

grandchildren opportunities to get to know their Welsh relatives. His son Ron, spoke of his father's wonderful singing voice and his love of singing, and it is clear that the exile, Francis Windsor Williams, gave his Canadian family the impression that music was very special to the Welsh.

I can shut my eyes and imagine the sounds of Welsh coal miners singing on their way home at the conclusion of their shift. After Dad settled in Regina, he became a member of Regina Male Voice Choir.

Other emigrants

George Gibbs, collier, of 18 Nelson Terrace, migrated to Scranton, Pennsylvania on *SS Cameronia.* Accompanied by his wife May and son Charlie, they departed Liverpool for New York on October 25 1925. George found employment in a coal mine. News of his accident and death, aged just 37, was reported in *Merthyr Express*, July 20 1929.

Wilfred Meyrick, son of Rees Meyrick superintendent of Gwaelod y Brithdir Cemetery, and brother to musician Morfydd, was a passenger on *SS Aquitania* departing Southampton on October 31 1925 bound for New York. He settled in *Perkville* a few miles north of Scranton.

William Godfrey,
Merthyr Express, January 1 1927:

Farewell Concert: - A musical evening was provided at the New Hall, Brithdir, on Wednesday last, the occasion being to give a public send-off to Mr William Godfrey of 24 Herbert Street, on his departure to Australia. The musical items were provided by the Savannah Minstrels, assisted by the White Ribbon Orchestra. The soloists were E. Davey, H. Brown, P. Moore, J. Williams and O. Jones. Miss Zoe Cresswell also gave solos and Mr. Ivor Davey sang 'Absent'. Mr. John Jones was chosen to make the presentation to Mr Godfrey, but in his absence this was performed by Miss Cresswell, who wished him all success and all good things in his new land. With the compliments of the party, she handed him a wallet. Mr. Harry Williams, who was the chairman, supplemented these remarks. Mr. Godfrey thanked the party for their great kindness. The audience rose and sang 'Auld Lang Syne' and the Chairman called for three cheers, which were lustily given.

Twenty year-old miner, William *Bill* Godfrey (nephew to Gomer Absalom who had emigrated to America in 1909) sailed from London on Christmas Eve 1926 on Royal Mail liner *Orvieto* and arrived in Brisbane February 10 1927. Friend John Miller said of him *He was a very highly respected Mine Manager. One of his daughters married a good mate of mine. I remember Bill as a very softly spoken man who loved his 'Rum and Coke'.*

Reginald Arundel was born in Tirphil and saw active service during the war, holding the rank of sergeant-major. He was well known in upper Rhymney Valley boxing circles as the trainer of Tirphil's Danny Morgan, lightweight champion boxer of Wales. Having moved to Brithdir in 1923 after his marriage to Emily Jenkins of 6 Ivy Row, Reginald felt he could make a better future for himself and his family in South Africa. He was among the third-class passengers on board Union Castle Steamship Company's *Durham Castle* bound for Natal when the liner departed Port of London on December 13 1928 for a voyage expected to take 33 days. A mechanic by occupation, he found employment on the railway and harbour clerical staff at Durban. On January 23 1930 his wife and 4 year old son, John, embarked on Union Castle Mail Steamship Company's *Dunluse Castle* from Tilbury Dock to join him. He died in 1953 in Natal.

Going into Service

Many Brithdir girls were among the countless girls for whom *going into service* came between school and married life in the decades prior to World War II. Having learned domestic

Reginald Arundel seated.
Courtesy Dennis Arundel

skills in school as well as in the home, most young girls were equipped for little other than domestic work, and, apart from shop work, there were few other openings for them. Sometimes girls found service near home, in the household of a local businessman or farmer, but in the inter-war years many were forced to leave home and family in Brithdir. There are as many different stories as there were girls who went into *service*, but the following illustrate the experience.

Both my mother, Eileen Brewer, and her sister, Jenny, went into *service* with Lady Paynter of Chavenage near Tetbury, Gloucestershire. Having interviewed Eileen at the Brewer home, then Harcourt Terrace, in 1933, Lady Paynter

Postcard (original in colour) of the Elizabethan Chavenage House found in my mother's possessions. Eagle-eyed fans of BBC drama may recognise Chavenage House as Trenwith, Poldark family home.

returned to Chavenage, and wrote to Eileen's mother offering to take young Eileen as a domestic servant. Thus, on her 14th birthday, Eileen left family, home and Brithdir and arrived at Gloucester railway station to be met by Lady Paynter. Young Eileen probably made a good impression as, soon after, Lady Paynter offered a similar position to her younger sister, Jenny, and they spent several years working in Manor Farm House adjacent to Chavenage House.

Colonel William Paterson Paynter. Courtesy his grandson Major-General Anthony Leask.

Eileen and Jenny were employed by Colonel Paynter of the Royal Horse Artillery, then recently retired from the army and renting Manor Farm House from George Lowsley-Williams, owner of Chavenage. Eileen and Jenny were treated very kindly by the Paynters. Eileen, started off as a kitchen help but eventually became cook, while Jenny cleaned the silver and served at the table when they entertained visitors.

My mother's memories of life in service, were interesting. Although primarily employed in the kitchen of Manor Farm House, Eileen and Jenny had other tasks from time to time, especially when the estate had important visitors. Princess Marie Louise, granddaughter of Queen Victoria, was a frequent visitor to Chavenage, and on such visits, Eileen and Jenny had to ensure they had a clean uniform when they helped out in Chavenage. The entire household lined up outside the house to await the arrival of Her Highness. My mother also remembered the Colonel's love for his horses. He had served in South Africa, India and France and went through all the battles with two horses *Lady Mac* and *Bob*. (This has been confirmed by Caroline Lowsley-Williams).

Jenny (seated) and Eileen frequently cycled to Tetbury where this photograph was taken

When my wife, Jen, and I visited Chavenage House, walking in the footsteps of my mother and aunty, we enjoyed the guided tour by owner David Lowsley-Williams who took us through the house and outlined its history. We passed through Cromwell's room, Ballroom and Oak Room (its oak panels date from 1590), and ended up in the private family chapel – the very chapel where Eileen, Jenny and other estate workers sat for Sunday morning services, behind the Hall people seated in their named pews in the front. It was there that on September 3 1939, the vicar gave the news *We are at war with Germany*. Eileen and Jenny, along with countless other domestic servants across the country, had to leave their employment to take up war work. They packed their

Private Jenny Brewer

Private Eileen Brewer

belongings and returned to Brithdir. As factory work did not appeal to them, they joined Auxiliary Territorial Service, and, after training, they were transferred to Royal Artillery Barracks, Shoeburyness, where the siblings met their future husbands: Blodwen Jane (Jenny) married Douglas Smith and Eileen married Robert Anthony Smith (no relation).

Lorraine Bevan was just 17 when she went into service at Longdon Hall, Gloucestershire, a mile south of Longdon village near Tewksbury, and within sight of the Malvern Hills. The earliest part of the house was built by the Parker family in the fifteenth century. In Elizabethan times it was a coaching inn and later a farmhouse. Home to the Unwin family since 1914, the large house, with ten bedrooms, several grand fireplaces and numerous oak ceiling beams, was surrounded by several hundred acres of farmland. Outside there was an old cider house with mill and press, a half timbered barn for over wintering cattle, formerly used as a stable with intact Victorian loose boxes, and a large hay loft above. Next to this was a detached brick-built coach house with groom's cottage. Lorraine was employed by Frederick and Valerie Unwin. Gardeners will recognise this family name and may well have purchased packets of Unwins Seeds. Frederick Unwin ran a successful horse and carriage business between Cheltenham

Bertie Baker and Lorraine Bevan in 1934 possibly on their wedding day at Merthyr Tydfil Registry Office. Photographs and details courtesy Georgina Greaney née Baker.

and London. His groom, Bertie Baker, became Lorraine's husband, and sadly, a name on Brithdir war memorial.

Olga Watkins daughter of Ben and Florrie Watkins, Harcourt Terrace, was another Brithdir girl to go into service at 14. She was in service in The Wallops, Test Valley, Hampshire. The area, near Andover, contained many old thatched cottages, a stark contrast to the coal blackened valley she knew as home.

Olga met her future husband, Ivor Wilcox, in London's Hyde Park. A native of Pembrokeshire he was in the Welsh Guards, stationed at the Tower of London. They married in 1937 and, while her husband was in service, Olga moved back to the family home in Brithdir where daughter Kay was born in 1938. Olga and Kay stayed in Brithdir until Ivor returned home. When he left the

army, November 21 1945, Ivor, Olga and 7 year old Kay, moved to Luton.

Left: Olga with her sister, Muriel, and baby, Kay, photographed on the slopes of Cefn Brithdir with the top-end terraces behind and the valley in the background.

All images courtesy Kay Dennis

Not all young girls went into service in distant places or large houses. Gwladys Hughes of Wellington Terrace is shown left in uniform outside Llanederyn Road, Cardiff where she worked and right in centre with two friends (courtesy Ivor Harris)

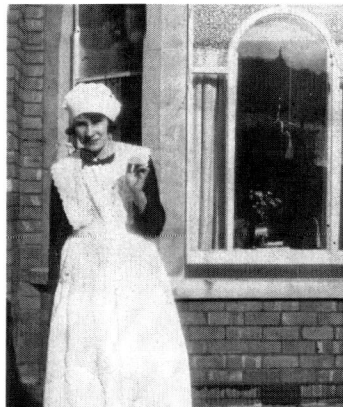

Enjoying the sunshine in Old Bristol Terrace – typical Welsh valley terrace housing Francis Crimp and wife Glynys, formerly Moore, née Cresswell, standing at their front door No 17, next door is her mother Catherine Cresswell in wheelchair and standing right her sister Morfydd Williams née Cresswell. Courtesy Jacqueline Tiernan née Moore

181

CHAPTER 12 WAR SERVICE 1900-1919

Over the decades, Brithdir families experienced the agonies of war and sadly, as witnessed by names inscribed on memorials to individuals as well as the war memorial, some of those who served did not return.

Indian Mutiny Veteran

Monmouthshire Guardian, November 23 1917:

Mr. Charles Newberry, of 8, Wellington Terrace, Brithdir, celebrated his 88ᵗʰ birthday on Saturday last. He is the oldest of the four remaining Mutiny veterans in South Wales. He is in good health, and retains his mental faculties to a wonderful degree; he has a retentive memory, is able to read and write without the aid of glasses, and can move about like a man more than a dozen years his junior. Mr Newberry now resides with his daughter, Mrs Morgan.

Merthyr Express, August 24 1918:

The death has occurred at Brithdir, at the age of 88 years, of Mr. Charles Newberry, one of the oldest surviving veterans of the Indian Mutiny. Mr. Newberry who resided in Hirwain Street, Cardiff for some years, joined the Navy in 1846 when only 12 years of age, and then joined the 9th Lancers, being wounded at the storming of Delhi, and the bullet that injured him he carried in his body to the day of his death.

Anglo-Boer War (South African War) 1899-1902

South Wales Daily News, February 3 1900:

. . . a large number of the 3ʳᵈ Militia, hailing from Brithdir, New Tredegar and other districts proceeded to the barracks Brecon by the first morning Brecon and Merthyr train on Friday.

Western Daily Press, January 21 1902, (extract from C. N. MᶜKay's letter to *Standard*:

. . . the little village of Brithdir, in the Rhymney Valley, sent nine sons to the front. Seven of them have perished by bullets or disease. The two left, W. Davies and J. Thomas, will, if nothing further intervenes, divide upon their return £200, being the accumulation of two-pence per week, subscribed by each of the inhabitants of their native place during the absence of these brave young fellows.

Research to date has revealed information about casualties David Thomas and John Thomas, but not the identities of other local men who endured the war's harsh conditions. Of the two men mentioned by name in MᶜKay's letter, it is not clear who J. Thomas was (a typical difficulty given the number of local men with similar names), but W. Davies survived the war and was later a Mametz casualty. It also seems that there were other local survivors.

Casualty David Thomas -- This advertisement in *Evening Express*, May 5 1898, suggests David Thomas, farmer of Tir y ferch Gryno, was preparing for his departure:

Wanted; a man and wife without encumbrance (middle-aged preferred); wife to attend small dairy and do plain cooking, with the husband to work on the farm.

Whether or not that elicited much response is unclear but he placed a further advertisement in the same newspaper on February 11 1899 for *a general servant for farmhouse, able to milk.*

David Thomas (photograph right courtesy Sian Hayworth) left the farm in December 1899. As Private 5615, 3rd Imperial Yeomanry Company (Gloucestershire) 1st Battalion, he left Liverpool on board *Cymric* February 28 1900 and arrived at Cape Town March 19 1900. During their 18 months in South Africa, 3rd Gloucesters lost 2 killed in action, 1 died of wounds, and 7 others, including this Brithdir farmer who died of enteric fever at Elandsfontein (the railway station around which the new town of Germiston was then being developed) in May 1901.

On Sunday, October 20 1901, one of four windows unveiled at a special service conducted by Rev. T.J. Jones, Rector of Gelligaer, in St. Gwladys Church, Bargoed, was dedicated to the memory of Private D. Thomas, Tir y ferch Gryno. The window (shown left) bears the words *In grateful memory of David Thomas Tiryferchgryno who whilst serving his country in the South African war died at Germinston May 8th 1901.*

Later, on a very snowy Sunday, January 26 1902, a large congregation attended a service in Gelligaer parish church for the unveiling of the tablet shown right. He is also commemorated on South African War Memorial in Cardiff and Gloucester County memorial in Gloucester Cathedral. His service earned him Queen's South Africa medal with clasps Wittebergen, Cape Colony, Transvaal and South Africa 1901.

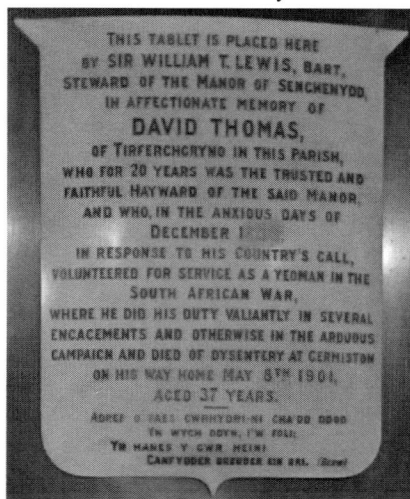

183

Casualty John Thomas -- On Thursday evening, January 21 1904, Brithdir's Mission Church was full when Colonel Lindsay unveiled the marble wall tablet inscribed with gold lettering, commemorating John Thomas, Station Terrace. Just two years later the tablet was inserted into the masonry of St. Paul's Church, but what became of the tablet when that building was demolished is uncertain.

> In Loving Memory
> Of
> Corporal John Thomas
> Beloved son of Ann Thomas, Brithdir
> Died at Hoopstad
> September 11 1900
> Whilst serving his Queen and
> Country
> with the
> Third South Wales Borderers in
> South Africa,
> aged 19 years, buried in Hoopstad

Born in Railway Row, Cwmsyfiog, John Thomas was youngest of four children of John and Ann Thomas. The family moved to Station Terrace before the 1891 census was taken, and young John attended Sunday School at the nearby mission church. On April 13 1898, aged 17, he volunteered for the militia. Just 5ft 3⅞ inches tall, weighing 7 stone 12lbs, and described by the medical officer as *under weight, otherwise fit,* he became Private 6805 3rd Battalion SWB. The progress of the battalion during the following months, in Brecon and Dublin, can be traced in newspaper reports and military archives, until, with thick snow on the ground, on the morning of February 14, its 28 officers and 750 men of all ranks and under command of Colonel Charles Healey, entrained at Knightsbridge Terminus for the 180 mile journey to Queenstown, where they embarked on *SS Cheshire* which arrived in Cape Town March 8 1900.

Sources studied to date have not shed much light on what happened to Lance Corporal Thomas before, like so many of those fighting with him, he died of disease September 11 1900 at Hoopstad. He was buried at Frankfort, a small farming town near Wilge River in Free State province. His body was later exhumed and reburied at Hoopstad cemetery where his grave is marked with a metal cross. His service entitled him to Queen's South Africa Medal, with at least one clasp (Cape Colony, but possibly also Orange Free State and/or Transvaal.

Western Mail, September 8 1900 reported under headline *A Mother's Sad Blow at Brithdir*:

Joy and sorrow have alternated quickly at Brithdir, in the Rhymney Valley. A week ago the widowed mother of Lance Corporal John Thomas, 3rd Welsh (Brecon) Militia, received intimation that her son had died from enteric fever at the Kroonstad Hospital. Inquiries were made at the War Office, and the authorities there replied that the John Thomas referred to was not the same man. The old lady naturally became much elated at this good news, but her joy was turned to sorrow three days later, when she was officially informed that the deceased man was, after all, her son.

John Thomas is not forgotten: he is remembered both on South African War Memorial, Cardiff and plaque to 3rd Battalion, SWB in Brecon Cathedral, but as the 1904 marble tablet has gone, not in Brithdir.

184

Returning safe -- Evidence about those who returned safely to Brithdir is based largely on reports in the local press. The headline *Men receive a Welcome at their Homes, Evening Express*, March 26 1902, was followed by *at Brithdir ten men arrived, and there were enthusiastic scenes. A vote of condolence was passed with the relatives of two others who had been killed in action.*

Merthyr Express, July 5 1902:

> *Private William Jones, 3rd Battalion, South Wales Borderers, who did not arrive home the same time as the other men of his battalion owing to illness, was presented with his watch on Tuesday, the 13th inst, in the presence of the Brithdir Conservative Club committee.*

It is not clear when South Africa veterans Andrew McLeod and John Hill lived in Brithdir, but press reports show they lived in the community in the 1940s: according to his obituary (*Merthyr Express*, March 8 1941), Andrew McLeod lived in 16 Wellington Terrace, while John Hill of 6 Charles Street was mentioned in a report (*Merthyr Express*, March 11 1944) on a presentation to his son. There is more information about returnees George Gambling and Alfred Wells.

Born in 1880 in Pyle, Bridgend, George was third of seven children of police constable Thomas Gambling and wife Mary. Young George probably arrived in Brithdir in the mid 1890s, and, aged 18, joined the militia, taking the oath at Blackwood April 13 1898, the same day as Brithdir lad, John Thomas. After medical examination the next day, he was appointed to 3rd Battalion SWB as Private 6789. Volunteering for active service, he embarked for South Africa on February 14 1900. He returned in 1902 with Queen's South Africa medal, with clasps for Cape Colony, Orange Free State and Transvaal, and King's South Africa medal, with clasps for 1901 and 1902. During World War I, George Gambling served in Royal Field Artillery. According to his obituary in *Merthyr Express*, March 4 1944, George Gambling was, for nearly 50 years, lodger with William George and his wife at 21 Charles Street.

Soon after Alfred Wells was born, in 1880 in St. Michael's Southampton, the family moved to Ebbw Vale. His father, Alfred, died in 1884, and his widowed mother, Elizabeth married widower George Coombs in 1886. Sometime between the 1891 and 1901 censuses, the family arrived in Brithdir and made their home in Charles Street. In March 1898, Alfred, a collier who had already seen service in Cardigan Artillery Militia, enlisted into SWB. Weighing just 7st 11 lbs and with chest measuring 32½ inches, his medical record notes *under weight and chest measurement, otherwise fit*. On Saturday afternoon, January 13 1900, Private Wells 5892 of 2nd SWB, was in Southampton on board transport ship *Bavarian*, one of the new vessels of Allan Line, chartered to take troops to South Africa. The liner steamed out of port amidst great noise and ceremony, ships bedecked with flags saluted with steam whistles and the 3,000-strong crowd (including veteran officers remembering 2nd SWB's heroic stand against the Zulus) cheered enthusiastically. After arriving at Cape Town

185

February 3, 2nd Battalion was sent to join Lord Roberts' force on Modder River, and their first engagement started on February 15. Private Wells served 1 year and 166 days, returning to UK June 27 1901 with Queen's South Africa Medal, with 4 clasps, Johannesburg, Cape Colony, Orange Free State and South Africa 1901. After that, he served almost 4 years in India, attaining rank of Corporal. On returning to UK in December 1905, he was transferred to Army Reserve. In 1909, he married Rachel Harding, and the couple lived in 21 James Street (1911 census return) and 3 Salisbury Terrace. He saw further service during World War I, reaching rank of Sergeant Major, and he was a Special Constable during World War II.

World War 1

Brithdir men responded to the call to arms and the stories of their brave exploits are myriad. George Young and James Harding, two young railway employees, are mentioned in the chapter on transport. What follows are a few accounts of the wartime experiences of some other Brithdir men.

Captain Edwin William Sidney Martin

South Wales Echo, Tuesday, February 20 1917:

Death of Brithdir Doctor
News was received last night that Dr. E.W.S. Martin, Brithdir, who was on active service with the Royal Army Medical Corps, had died in Mesopotamia. Dr. Martin had a large practice in New Tredegar, Brithdir and Cwmsyfiog, and was medical officer for the urban district. He was highly esteemed, and his death is deeply regretted.

The second of four children, Edwin William Sidney Martin was born September 18 1874, to grocer John Edgar Martin JP and his wife, Margaret, née Guiney, of 41 Church Street, Dromore, Banbridge District, County Down. Sidney, as he was known, received his early education at Dromore National and Intermediate Schools before studying at Queen's College, Belfast. Matriculating in 1892, he enrolled for Physics, Chemistry, Zoology, Biology, Anatomy and Practical Biology courses and, in his last year he studied Sanitary Science and Midwifery. He graduated in 1899 taking the degrees of Bachelor of Medicine, Bachelor of Chemistry, with Bachelor of the Art of Obstetrics. UK Medical Registers show the newly qualified young doctor went to Wales, starting at Tynewydd, Ogmore Valley, as assistant to Dr. Williams, Bryn Siriol. He soon became very popular within that mining community, and, when he left in 1903, both workmen and officials of Aber, Wyndham, Tynewydd and Ocean collieries acknowledged his popularity at a presentation in Workmen's Hall, Tynewydd. According to a report in *Merthyr Express*, September 26, his gifts included steriliser (in morocco leather bag) for instruments and dressings, a case of knives, microscope with oil immersion lens, a purse of sovereigns, an amputating case, aspirator, tonsil guillotine, stomach pump, laryngoscope and artery forceps, as well as an obstetric bag and instruments, a personal present from Dr. R. A. Williams. The presentation, valued in today's prices in excess of £7,000, showed the high regard in which he was held.

When Dr. Martin arrived in Rhymney Valley, he made his home in *Leargaidh*, East View, and his surgery was at the back of the house.

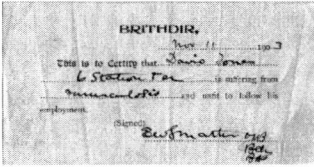

This doctor's slip, dated November 11 1903, was sent to headmaster, Samuel Davies, to cover David Jones's three day absence due to illness. According to the school log book, David was then 3rd year pupil teacher.

Dr. Martin built the practice into a large industrial one with additional surgeries at Cwmsyfiog and New Tredegar. Although one of the busiest practitioners in the area, Dr. Martin studied for and was awarded the prestigious Cambridge Diploma of Public Health in October 1905. During his 15 years in Brithdir, Dr. Martin became very popular and his active involvement in community life earned him much respect. As the local doctor, he played a significant role in forming and training Brithdir Division St. John Ambulance Brigade. He represented Brithdir ward on Glamorgan County Council, was a Gelligaer School Governor, Medical Officer of Health to Bedwellty Council and Medical Officer to Bedwellty Board of Guardians for New Tredegar District.

His medal record card shows he enlisted in 1915 with the rank of Lieutenant. He was first stationed at St. George's Hospital in Malta, He was promoted to Captain on attachment to 9th Battalion Worcestershire Regiment. He went to Gallipoli, and was present at the evacuation of Suvla Bay, before moving on to Egypt and Mesopotamia.

Worcestershire Regiment History: Vol 2, page 223:

*On February 15th the Battalion Medical Officer, Captain E.W.S. Martin was killed on the banks of the River Tigris about 4 miles west of Kut. He was killed going to the aid of a fallen fellow officer, 2nd Lieutenant W.B. Busby who was mortally wounded. No medical officer we ever had was more beloved by all, from the C.O. to the last joined sweeper of the native establishment, no trouble was ever too much for him, no risk to himself ever affected him........*written by a senior officer.

Mentioned in despatches, Captain Martin was entitled to wear the bronze oak leaf on ribbon of his Victory Medal. The emblem and his medals were issued to his sister Mrs Vaughan of Dromore House, Tredegar. Captain Edwin William Sidney Martin lies in plot XX1. L. 11, in Amara War Cemetery in Iraq. He is also remembered on the following war memorials -- Dromore, (birthplace), Queen's University, Belfast (where he trained to be a doctor), Brithdir (his place of residence), New Tredegar (Cwmsyfiog and New Tredegar were part of his Brithdir practice), Tredegar (where his sister lived) and Lewis School Pengam (where he had been a school governor).

As reported in *Rhymney, Bargoed and Caerphilly Observer*, the following tributes were paid to Dr. E.W.S. Martin at Bedwellty Council meeting of February 27 1917:

Joshua Tillott, JP chairman: *A more loyal servant the council had never had. He was admired by all, and cherished by those who came in contact with him. Very many in New Tredegar and district would always honour his memory.*

Edgar Davies endorsed the chairman's views and added: *He took a deep interest in the work of the council and the district in general. He was always particularly keen upon the health of the people. They had lost a most valuable officer.*

R. J. Jones: *There was no better officer in the whole of the valley or one who took a keener interest in the welfare of the people than Dr. Martin had done.*

Isaac Jones: *The neighbourhood in general had lost something more than a doctor. The district had sustained a loss which could not well be replaced. He had many traits in his character which could well be emulated by others. In times of extreme pressure or other circumstances he never rose his voice above its even tenor and was at all times most guarded in his statements.*

An extract from a letter his father received from Lieut-Colonel W.D. Gibbon of Worcestershire Regiment quoted in *Monmouth Guardian*, April 27 1917:

Hearing that Lieutenant Busby had been hit and was lying out in the front; Captain Martin unattended went out to succour him. When at his side, he was shot through his head. He never recovered consciousness, and died in the field ambulance the next day. Captain Martin, or the M.O. as we always affectionately called him, had been with us since June of last year. By officers and men alike he was respected and admired. He never spared himself when his help was required.

The Battle of Mametz

A magnificent Red Dragon monument to the Welsh Division at Mametz is the most striking memorial I have ever seen. Standing atop a granite plinth and clutching strands of barbed wire in its claws, the dragon glares in defiance facing Mametz Wood. In 2012, I visited the site with my grandson Morgan, then twelve years old, and as we walked across the fields towards

Mametz Wood, conscious we were walking in footsteps of heroes, my thoughts turned to Brithdir men who fought there.

After eight months training in North Wales, 16th (Cardiff City) Battalion moved to Winchester in August 1915 with other units of 38th (Welsh Division). In November, ready for active service, 38th Division was inspected by Her Majesty, The

Cardiff City Battalion marching through Cardiff before a parade at Arms Park.

Queen, on Salisbury Plain before they boarded the train for Cardiff. They had a rousing reception from relatives and friends. After a ceremonial march past, the men had 24 hours leave before returning to Winchester and the movement order for France.

William Davies, son of iron miner Thomas and Ann Davies was born in Blaenavon. On the death of his father in 1892, twelve year old William became the family's breadwinner, supporting himself, his widowed mother and three younger siblings. Later, the family moved to Brithdir and made their home at 10 James Street. William joined the Territorial Army and served in the South African Campaign qualifying for Queen's South Africa Medal and King's South Africa Medal. He enlisted at Bargoed in November 1914 and joined the newly-formed Cardiff City Battalion, appointed to 'D' Company, as Private 24302.

Matilda Davies, devoted sister.
Courtesy Linda Winmill.

On December 4 1915 at Southampton, 30 officers and 995 other ranks of Cardiff City Battalion embarked on paddle steamer *La Marquerite* for France. Private Davies was one of that number. The battalion experienced major losses in the battle for Mametz Wood, with most casualties on July 7 1916. After two more failed attacks, orders were given to cease operations. Battalion Losses: *6 Officers killed, 6 wounded, 268 Other Ranks killed, missing and wounded.*

Private William Davies was one of the thirty killed on July 7 when, under heavy machine gun fire from Flatiron Copse and Sabot Copse, the battalion was forced back. Family members, including his sister Matilda, shown in photograph above, may have derived some comfort not only from the fact that, unlike the majority of his fellow

Flatiron Copse Cemetery, Plot X, Row E, Grave 7. 24302 Private W. Davies Welsh Regiment 7 July 1916.

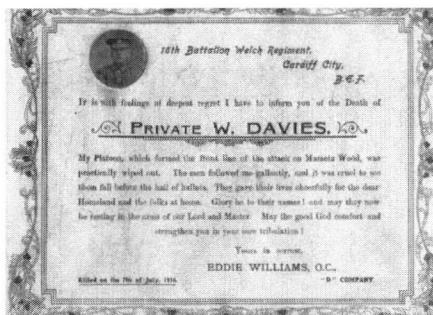

casualties, William Davies had a grave, but also from the beautiful decorated condolence scroll sent by his commanding officer, Eddie Williams

David John Williams, aka *Dai Brithdir*, came to Brithdir from Bedlinog. In 1901, he was a 14 year old coal hewer living with his grandparents at 5 Station Terrace. Having married Brithdir girl Lily Coombs of 7 Charles Street in 1906, they made their home at No 10, a few doors from her parental home. They had three children, Winifred (1907), David (1908) and Aubrey born

June 1914. Leaving this young family, David John Williams enlisted on January 18 1915 and as Private 24051 joined Cardiff City Battalion in Colwyn Bay the next day.

David John Williams and his wife celebrating their Diamond Wedding Anniversary in 1966.
Courtesy daughter Lily Williams.

David John Williams had been in France just three months when in March 1916, whilst in the trenches at Festubert his right eye became inflamed and, according to his army casualty sheet, he had *trouble with conjuctivitus on and off ever since*. Appointed Lance Corporal on March 23 1916, he was with his battalion at the hell that was Mametz. Although costly, the battalion, together with other units of the Division, through five days of hard fighting, cleared the Germans from the greater part of the wood.

After eleven months' service in France, Private Williams was posted back to UK and reported to Welsh Regiment Depot on November 25 1916.

On February 16 1917, he was deemed more valuable to the country in civil than military employment and, posted to Army Reserve Class W, he was sent back to his old job at the colliery. On May 31, a Cardiff medical board deemed his disability to be the result of exposure whilst on active service and recommended his transfer to Class P of the Army Reserve – he was finally discharged from the army on August 25 1918. David Williams returned to Brithdir and lived in Charles Street for the remainder of his life. He received his Silver War Badge No 243611 and Certificate, denoting honourable discharge due to wounds or sickness during World War 1.

According to his memorial scroll **Private 23221 Stephen Williams** lived in Brithdir and, enlisting in Bargoed, joined Cardiff City Battalion. His service records do not survive. He was wounded, possibly on July 7, and hospitalised in Rouen, where he died, July 17 1916, and was buried in St. Sever Cemetery, Rouen.

Two Mametz survivors

John James Price survived the battle but died of wounds received in action in April 1918. This photograph, together with much of the information that follows is courtesy his granddaughter, Audrey Smith.

Born 1875 in Upper Square, Beaufort, the fourth of five children of Samuel and Margaret Price, he started work, aged 13, as a coal miner. In 1891, he was a 17 year old lodger in the Mountain Ash household of Henry and Louisa Tucher. It was there he met Sarah Elizabeth Butt,

190

who, on Christmas Day 1894, became his wife. For the next decade they lived in 13 Napier Street, Mountain Ash, where their children Margaret, William, Samuel and Henry were born. Prior to 1908, the family moved to 15 Charles Street, their home when daughter, Olwen, and son, Thomas James, were born.

Thomas James, the youngest child was just twenty-one months old when his father attested at Cardiff on October 26 1914 and, the following day, enlisted at New Tredegar and joined the Welsh Regiment 13th (Service) Battalion (2nd Rhondda Pals) as Private 21444. Posted to France with BEF, he landed at Le Havre December 2 1915. What records survive reveal very little about Private 21444. He survived Mametz and, according to the field service report, he died of wounds received in action in 1918. The battalion war diary for April 22-24 1918 records *casualties on the 22nd were considerable - and enemy activity on the 24th resulted in 20 casualties.* Private Price wounded in the action, died in the field hospital at Millencourt on April 24 and was buried in Plot 2 Row E Grave 41 in Millencourt Communal Cemetery Extension on April 26 1918. (courtesy britishwargraves.co.uk)

When, in November 1915, Private Price applied for separation allowance, the family home was 15 Charles Street. By the time of his death, wife Sarah and children had moved to 11 Salisbury Terrace. On June 20 1920, his widow received his memorial scroll, memorial plaque and war medals.

Private Thomas Lewis, a coal miner, known as *Silver Tenor* because of his passion for singing, was awarded a medal second only to the Victoria Cross for an act of gallantry. This is his story, as told by his granddaughter, Nita Smith, née Campbell, and great grandsons, Major Howard Campbell Smith and Philip Campbell Smith, with additional information from War Diary 2nd Battalion Welsh Regiment, Vol 21, September 1916.

Thomas Lewis was born 1878 in Pentre, Rhondda. One of six children, he was son of an iron moulder and grandson of a Cardiganshire Baptist minister. His working life in the colliery started when he was 11 years old, as a colliery door boy. When he was 14, he started manual mining. He lived and worked in the Pentre area for most of his formative years and married Mary Kavanagh in Ss Gabriel and Raphael Church, Tonypandy in 1900. Sometime after the 1911 census was taken, Thomas and Mary Lewis and their five children, moved to Brithdir, and made a home in 6 Tennyson Terrace. Thomas worked at Elliot Colliery.

Thomas, then 38 years old, volunteered on October 1 1914 and joined 2nd Battalion, Welsh Regiment as Private Lewis 36123. It is not clear whether he volunteered for financial benefit (soldiers were paid slightly more than miners) or out of a sense of duty to his country. His medal index card shows he landed in France on May 5 1915, 7 months and 5 days after he enlisted.

On September 8 at High Wood, Thomas earned the Distinguished Conduct Medal. A soldier of SWB lay wounded and dying in no man's land. Courageously, Thomas Lewis left the comparative safety of the trench and, in spite of intense and accurate enemy rifle and machine gun fire, went to rescue him. He picked him up and returned him to the safety of the British front line. On November 14 1916 the following appeared in Supplement to *The London Gazette*, page 11095:

Private T. Lewis 36123 - Welsh Regiment
For conspicuous gallantry and devotion in voluntarily going out 100 yards in front of a line and bringing a wounded man of another regiment, who had been lying out for four days, under observation of numerous enemy snipers. Private Lewis was heavily fired on the whole time.

Thomas Lewis was transferred to Labour Corps and given number 510282. Sometime later, in a subsequent action during the battle of Flers, he was wounded, and he had also been subjected to a mustard gas attack. As a result of his injuries, he was evacuated to Kinmel Park for medical treatment before, on February 17 1919, no longer physically fit for war service, he was discharged. He was issued with Silver War Badge No B/136498 and certificate on March 28 1919.

On his return to Brithdir, Thomas Lewis was treated as a local hero. He had a civic welcome and a street party was organised. As a result of a collection amongst villagers and work colleagues, he was presented with a gold hunter watch inscribed *Presented to Thomas Lewis DCM - By the inhabitants of New Tredegar & District - In appreciation of his bravery on the battlefield, 1916.*

Thomas Lewis returned to coal mining. When his grandchildren asked him to tell the story of how he won his DCM, he joked that he had shot the cook because he did not like his food.

Thomas lived at Brithdir for the remainder of his life. When he died, July 1944, he had a military funeral, with members of Brithdir and Tirphil Home Guard on parade. Brithdir Home Guard, under Sgt. R. Major, provided the firing party which comprised Corporal I. Williams, Privates T. Willetts, H. Brown, T. James, H. Hughes, T. Wall, S. Keitch and W. McDonald. Corporal E. Watts was pacemaker. M. Barry was in charge of Tirphil Platoon, who acted as escort and bearers. Thomas Lewis DCM was buried in Gwaelod y Brithdir cemetery. His medals were gifted by the family to Welsh Regiment Museum's trustees. They have been loaned to, and, at the time of writing, are on display in *Firing Line – The Story of The Welsh Soldier, Cardiff Castle.*

Private William Davies Jones's parents, anxious for news of their son missing in action, turned to the readers of *Merthyr Express*, December 14 1918.

Mr. & Mrs. William Jones, 2 Ivy Row, Brithdir, would be glad if any prisoner of war from Germany could give them any tidings of their son Rifleman William Davies Jones, Kings Royal Rifles Corps, who was reported missing on November 30th following operations at Cambrai. Rifleman Jones is 23 years of age and a letter from his officer at the time he was reported missing stated there was a possibility that he had been taken prisoner.

According to his medal card, Rifleman R/3531 Jones, 10th Battalion, arrived in France on July 30 1915 and was officially declared *killed in action* on November 30 1917 during a German counter attack at Cambrai. Rifleman Jones is commemorated on Brithdir war memorial and on Panel 9 Cambrai War Memorial.

The young lad on the cart is William Davies Jones, helping his uncle Thomas Jones deliver milk before the war. Courtesy Jeanette Laslett, née Green.

William Davies Jones senior, former ostler Elliot Colliery,

and wife Anna, 2 Ivy Row, parents of Rifleman W. D. Jones.

Cousins go to war.

The names of cousins George Frederick Watkins and David Robert Cleary appear on this gravestone in Gwaleod y Brithdir Cemetery.

To The Memory of
Private George Frederick Watkins
(2nd Welsh Regt) son of
Mary M. and the late George F. Watkins
Rose Hill Cottage, Brithdir
Who fell in action at Ypres, Flanders
November 16 1914, aged 26 years
Also L/Corporal David Robert Cleary
(2nd Welsh Regt) son of
David and Elizabeth A. Cleary
West Street, Bargoed
Who fell in action at the Battle of the Aisne,
September 14 1914 aged 20 years

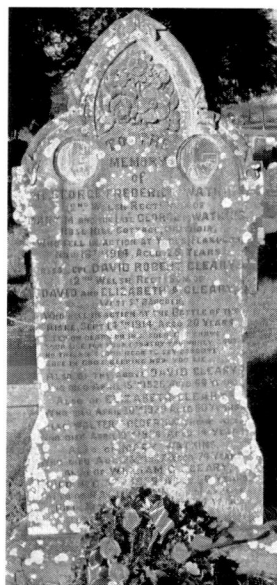

193

George Frederick Watkins, Rose Hill Cottage, and his cousin, **David Robert Cleary**, formerly of James Street, enlisted together. They joined 2nd Battalion Welsh Regiment, and arrived in France on August 13 1914. Sadly, they were killed in action within 53 days of each other. Lance Corporal 10923 Cleary died September 14 1914, at Battle of Aisne and his name is on La Ferte-sous-Jouarre Memorial. Private 9525 Watkins died in action at Ypres on November 6 1914 (CWGC difers from gravestone), and his name is on Ypres Menin Gate Memorial. Both young men were named on local war memorials; George Watkins in Brithdir and Robert Cleary in Bargoed.

The Clearys - father and two sons
Left Father Private 314, David Cleary, 1st Battalion, Welsh Regiment, was awarded Egypt Medal with clasp for Gemaizah 1888, and Khedives Star for serving in Sudan *Middle* Charles Lewis Cleary was 1st class stoker on HMS Queen Mary, although when he served is unclear. HMS Queen Mary was sunk May 31 1916 at Jutland with the loss of 57 officers and 1,209 men. His name is not listed amongst those killed nor the 20 survivors.
Right Lance Corporal David Robert Cleary.

David Cleary, senior, a native of Pontypool, and his wife Elizabeth, from Herefordshire, with sons Charles aged 3 and Robert aged 2, moved to Brithdir about 1895. They lived with Walter and Rose Nash in 19 James Street - where daughters Margaret and Rose were born, 1896 and 1899 respectively. Son Willie was born in 1901. By 1906 the family had moved to West Street, Bargoed.

Lieutenant William Richard Barker

Generally known as Billy Barker, son of timber merchant Frederick Barker, he was born September 7 1893 in Aston, Warwickshire. By the time the 1911 census was taken, 17 year old Billy was a student teacher boarding in 28 Edmund Street, Pontlottyn. He taught in Brithdir Mixed School from August 26 1912 to September 21 1914 before leaving for war service. On demobilisation from the army, Billy returned to teaching at Brithdir Schools, but not in his old position at the Mixed Department. Whilst he was away on active service a new Boys' School had been built, Samuel Davies, his old mentor, was its headmaster and it was there Billy resumed his duties.

Samuel Davies entered his return in the school log: *May 1 1919; Mr W. R. Barker returned to duty today after over four years military service. Mr Barker joined the army voluntarily at the outbreak of the Great War in October 1914. He secured rapid promotion and obtained his commission in the South Wales*

194

Borderers in 1916. He has been on active service for three years in Mesopotamia gaining his Military Cross for conspicuous bravery. A further entry on June 5 1919 revealed *Mr. W.R. Barker called to London by Royal Command - to attend Buckingham Palace on Saturday June 6 – for the Investiture of his Military Cross by His Majesty the King.* On August 31 1919, twelve weeks after receiving his award, Billy left Brithdir Boys' School. His departure, perhaps a disappointment to Samuel Davies was recorded briefly: *Mr. W.R. Barker left here today.*

Billy Barker received a commission as temporary Second Lieutenant in South Wales Borderers on August 7 1915 (gazetted London Gazette August 12 1915, page 8003). He was awarded Military Cross for distinguished services in operations in Mesopotamia (gazetted February 7 1918, page 1301). The award being approved on January 1 1918, was technically a New Year's Honour, hence no published citation of the deed which earned him the medal. His medal index card reveals he had been *Commissioned*

Lt William Richard Barker's Military Cross, British War Medal and Victoria Medal. Courtesy Regimental Museum of Royal Welsh.

Lieutenant in SWB 4th Battalion and first entered Mesopotamia on June 9 1916. Additional details on the back of the card show a change of address with 28 Edmund Street, Pontlottyn crossed through, and Canynge Hall, White Ladies Road, Clifton, Bristol, added. Thus, like fellow young teacher Frank West, it seems he went to Bristol to study for a teaching qualification.

Monmouth Guardian and Bargoed and Caerphilly Observer, September 5 1919, reported that Pontlottyn Church Lads' Brigade, meeting in St.Tyfaelog's Schoolroom on Tuesday, September 2, presented their Commanding Officer (Captain W.R. Barker, MC) with a silver mounted ebony walking stick. On making the presentation, Rev. W. Brazell referred *to the energy displayed by Captain Barker, and the deep interest taken by him in the company since its*

formation four months ago. He was now leaving to take up an important commercial position in London.

Billy Barker returned in 1922 for an important date with the vicar and Rachel Elizabeth Hughes, daughter of grocer and baker Councillor Benjamin Hughes, Farm Road, Pontlottyn. The couple exchanged vows in St. Tyfaelog's on August 8. Later, they lived at 53 Park Road, Bargoed, where daughter Marion Elizabeth was born in August 1927. The birth certificate shows his occupation was elementary school teacher. Today, some people remember him as headmaster at Deri. (Photograph courtesy Dave Williams)

During World War Two he held the rank of Major in Deri Home Guard and in that capacity he attended the military funeral of Percy Cartwright of Brithdir platoon in October 1943.

On his retirement as headmaster at Deri, William and Rachel continued to live in Bargoed at 24 Hillside Park. He died on December 17 1972 in Cardiff Royal Infirmary and was cremated at Thornhill (Cardiff) on December 20; the cremation records show he was a resident of Bargoed and his wife was the informant.   Rachel died in St. Peters Convent, Plympton, Plymouth in September 1983 and her death was registered by her daughter Marion Elizabeth.

Daniel Dudley DCM and Bar.

The village of Brithdir had its second DCM with Dan Dudley. Born in Cwmaman near Aberdare in 1891, the son of William and Margaret Dudley, Dan moved to Brithdir prior to 1910. He worked as a coal miner and was a boarder in the household of Mark Mellens at 1 Herbert Street. He was well-known as a talented footballer who played regularly for Brithdir Bluebirds.

According to his medal index card, Dan Dudley, formerly infantryman in Welsh Regiment, first went overseas to France on May 4 1915. He later transferred to Machine Gun Corps and went to Machine Gun Training Centre, Belton Park, Grantham, before returning to BEF in France with 236 Company on April 25 1917. He may have had further training in trench warfare at base depot at Camiers before being posted. Lance Corporal 19404 Dudley was awarded Distinguished Conduct Medal for bravery with B Company, 3rd Battalion Machine Gun Corps at Heninel on March 28 1918 and the citation reads:

For conspicuous gallantry and devotion to duty. Under a heavy artillery barrage he kept his gun in action, inflicting severe losses on the enemy. When they several times got within bombing distance he successfully drove them off. On his gun being damaged by a shell, he took his rifle and killed several of the enemy at close range, then got his gun away, repaired it, and came into action again.

Promoted to Sergeant, Dudley performed a second gallantry act at Seranvillers on October 8 1918 and was awarded a Bar to his DCM. The citation gazetted February 18 1919 reads:

His section was heavily shelled in its assembly positions, and the section officer and section sergeant became casualties. He immediately took command of the section and, despite the intensity of the hostile barrage, moved forward with his men and limber in support of the attacking infantry. The objective gained, he led his section to the position assigned to them for consolidation and got his guns into action, assisting greatly in beating off the enemy counter-attack.

Dan Dudley left the army February 22 1919, and returned to Brithdir. He was soon back scoring goals for the village team and hailed as the star forward on many occasions by *Merthyr Express* reporters. On retiring from playing, he became secretary of the newly formed U21 team in 1926.

Astley brothers win gallantry medals
Charles Raymond Astley MM and John Seymour Astley DCM MM

The Astley family originated from Newtown, Montgomeryshire, where, for generations, the family had worked in the woollen industry. Thomas and Annie Astley, and all but one of their children worked at Cambrian Woollen Mill. Thomas died in 1899, leaving Annie a widow with seven children between 13 and 2 years old. When, in 1912, Cambrian Mill was destroyed by fire, its former workers had to seek work elsewhere. Annie and married daughter, Emily, remained in Newtown, whilst, over time, six Astley siblings headed for the coalmining valleys of South Wales: Frederick to Upper North Road, Bargoed, Alfred and John to Ystrad Rhondda, while George and his youngest sister Susan, settled at Brithdir. George Cecil Astley married Brithdir girl, Ethel May, daughter of Edwin and Hannah Edwards, 7 James Street, on April 16 1914 and, soon after, they made their home a few doors away in No 11. While George joined RAF towards the end of hostilities, his brothers, Thomas Frederick, Alfred Edward, Charles Raymond and John Seymour, volunteered for the army. Both Frederick, killed in action with SWB at Battle of Aubers on May 9 1915, and Alfred, lost his life in action at Gallipoli with South Lancashire Regiment on June 9 1915, are remembered on Newtown war memorial. Astley family details are from family members – Mavis Mahoney, née Astley, of Brithdir, Paul Astley of Deri and Paul Astley of Nelson – while service records shed light on the brothers' wartime experiences.

Charles Raymond Astley, aged 18½, enlisted at Cardiff on July 20 1908 and joined Welsh Regiment (Special Reserve). On December 31 1909, he enlisted into the regular army, joining Welsh Regiment as Private 10263. His service records portray a colourful character, guilty of a number of misdemeanours. At Pembroke Dock, on January 10 1911, he received 56 days' detention for absenting himself without leave and losing, by neglect, his clothing and regimental necessaries. Then, on March 25, for committing wilful damage, he was sentenced to 2 months at HM Carmarthen Prison. Whilst at Cairo and Khartoum, he was reported on several occasions for being drunk, incurring fines and confinement to barracks for total of 68 days. On other occasions, a dirty rifle on duty and dirty boots on palace guard earned him 4 extra turns on guard duty; for other misdemeanours he was punished with forfeits (loss of pay) and detention.

The battalion returned to England on December 22 1914 and moved to Hursley Camp, Winchester, before landing, with BEF at Le Havre, January 18 1915. Receiving a gunshot wound to the scalp on May 7 1915, he was admitted to Versailles Hospital before being shipped back to England on May 11. He re-joined his battalion and BEF in December 1915. In 1916, in the space of six months, rapid promotion propelled him to the rank of Sergeant. He was awarded Military Medal in the field (gazetted December 12 1917):

Sergt. Charles Astley, of Newtown, has been awarded the Military Medal in the field for gallant work in France. During an engagement two officers were killed and another wounded; the commanding officer ordered Astley to get his company into shell holes, and, immediately afterwards was killed. Sergeant Astley then took command and acquitted himself so creditably that he received the above award. On the outbreak of war, he was in India, having enlisted at the age of 15 as a drummer.

He was wounded a second time on April 12 1918, buried when a shell burst near him. Repatriated, he arrived at Leith on December 13 1918 and was posted to Welsh Regiment Depot, Cardiff. After his discharge, April 9 1919, Charles Astley MM made his home with brother George at 11 James Street. Apart from the gallantry medal, he was awarded 1914-15 Star, British War Medal, Victory Medal and Silver War Badge (No 4731030). On April 6 1921 he re-enlisted in 1st Battalion Monmouth Regiment (TA).

I came to know of John Seymour Astley through the pages of *Merthyr Express*. Royal Welsh Fusilier, Private 290188 John Seymour Astley was a courageous soldier who was awarded two of his country's highest awards for gallantry. On February 25 1918, Distinguished Conduct Medal:

For conspicuous gallantry and devotion to duty in carrying wounded during an action under heavy machine-gun and rifle fire. He set a splendid example of courage and self-sacrifice.

and, a month later, Military Medal *for bravery in the Field.* Also mentioned in dispatches to the Secretary of War by Sir Archibald Murray, Commander in Chief, he was entitled to wear emblem of bronze oak leaf on the ribbon of his Victory Medal. Apart from his gallantry medals (DCM, MM) he was also awarded Victory Medal, British Medal and 1914-1915 Star.

> **BRITHDIR DCM AND MM WINNER**
> **SENT TO PRISON.**
>
> John Seymour Astley and William Redwood, colliers, Brithdir, were charged with being drunk and disorderly and refusing to quit the Railway Hotel, Caerphilly.
> A scuffle en route to the police station led to the two police constables being kicked in the leg and for that the defendants were sent down for a month.
> Merthyr Express September 1920

Private Astley's service records have not survived. but his medal index card (shown below) makes interesting reading. His service number 915 suggests he was a long-serving territorial force soldier with service dating from soon after the creation of the force in 1908. His division sailed from Devonport on July 19 1915 for Gallipoli. His battalion stayed in the Middle East – Egypt (1916) and Palestine (1917 and 1918) until the end of the war. Discharged in February 1919 he later re-enlisted in the Territorial Force to complete 12 years' service, so qualifying for Territorial Efficiency Medal.

The soldier in the photograph left, a family keepsake, (courtesy Mavis Mahoney née Astley), is unidentified. As the cap badge is that of Royal Welsh Fusiliers, it may be Private John Seymour Astley. It is not clear how long he lived in Brithdir, but it was long enough to make an impression as a hard man. Anecdotal evidence has it that he was known throughout Wales for his bare-knuckle prowess, and that the toughest of men in George Pub would tremble when he visited. At some point John Seymour returned to Newtown, married and raised a family.

Military and boxing interests have carried through the generations as many of the Astleys have been soldiers and boxers. George and Ethel's great grandson Paul Astley (barber in Nelson), formerly a boxer, now has his own gym and trains others. In 2013, 14 year old Conor Mahoney (Mavis and Tony's grandson), won WABA Welsh schoolboy boxing championship (36kg weight) just two years after taking up the sport. About two years ago he enlisted into the army and, at the time of writing, is stationed in Dorset.

John Robert Tilley, Rifleman 25/1026 3rd Battalion, C Company New Zealand Rifle Brigade. 1st New Zealand Expeditionary Force

A report on heavy losses sustained by New Zealand Brigade in France during September 1916 in *New Zealand Herald*, October 3 1916 included reference to a soldier with a Brithdir connection. Listed among the wounded embarking for England on September 19 was Rifleman Tilley, whose next of kin, his mother Sarah Ann Tilley, lived at 7 Bute Terrace. Research shows John Robert Tilley was born November 14 1891 in Canton, and baptised on January 20 1892 in Parish Church of St. John, Cardiff. According to information in 1901 census return, John Robert was oldest of five children, all born in Cardiff, to Frederick and Sarah Ann Tilley. While father Frederick, then a labourer at Cardiff Docks, was born in Cardiff, mother Sarah Ann hailed from Cwmsyfiog. As son Clifford Lewis was born in Brithdir about 1905, it is likely the family had moved there by then, possibly living in Bute Terrace, home of Sarah Ann and two of her children when the 1911 census was taken. It is not clear when John Robert set sail for New Zealand, but he had arrived there in time to register for the vote in New Zealand's General Election, December 10 1914. Having attested at Trentham on October 14 1915, he underwent training in New Zealand before sailing, via Suez Canal, for France, and he joined his unit in the field May 21 1916. He received wounds to head and right knee during action September 15 1916 and was

shipped to England where he was hospitalised before invalided to New Zealand January 13 1917 where, no longer physically fit for service, he was discharged

April 25 1917. It is not clear if he returned to UK after that but he died February 26 1935 at Dunedin, New Zealand.

Lost and found - Private Ivor Coles

In 2008, I began to research the names on Brithdir war memorial. I found information about the majority of the 42 World War One casualties, but 7 remained unidentified and were confined to a file marked *Lost Souls*, lost and remembered in name only. Private I. Coles was one such *lost soul*. His service papers had not survived, a check on 1911 census returns revealed John and Rhoda Cole at 7 Salisbury Terrace, with 13 year old son, Ivor. Not only was the name on the war memorial marked Coles, not Cole, but also he would have been too young to join the army, unless he had lied about his age. Several years later, during a search of old newspapers for details on other casualties, the *In Memoriam* shown right caught my eye. Published in *Western Mail*, September 18 1916, it referred to *Private Coles of Brithdir killed in France, September 15 1915.*

> **IN MEMORIAM.**
> **COLES.**—Mrs. S. Gauden and Family, 11, Milton - terrace, Brithdir. — In Loving Memory of Private Coles, of Brithdir, killed in France, September 15. 1915.
> "Somewhere in France' a body lies,
>   Amid the battle's din,
> But a spirit freed death's power denies,
>   And leaves a world of sin.
> Somewhere at home a tear is shed,
>   And sorrow rends the breast;
> But a trusting soul, by pure faith fed,
>   Just whispers, "God knows best."

I had found Private Coles! At least, that was what I thought but Commonwealth War Graves Commission database did not list anyone of that name killed on September 15, although there was Private 12788, Ivor Cole, 9th Battalion Welsh Regiment with date of death, September 25 1915. Unfortunately, this entry had no additional information, so Private Coles returned briefly to my *Lost Souls* file. In a search for Mrs. Gauden, I discovered Ivor Coles's story written by Chris Stone - who has given permission to share his work.

Meet Ivor Goodacre Coles, a Brithdir *Tommy* killed in action in September 1915, lost, and now found again. It is a great story, one that is common to so many people, so many families in Britain had that or similar experiences because so many people, were lost in that war. Chris has given a story of a young man who mattered. He has placed Private Ivor Coles in history among his comrades.

We're Here Because We're Here,
A soldier's death in Vieille-Chapelle, September 1915 - C.J. Stone

It was the song they sang as they marched to the trenches *We're Here Because We're Here*. It was sung to the tune of Auld Lang Syne, a sardonic joke sung in full-throated defiance of death. *We're here because we're here because we're here because we're here.* But underlying that song there is a question: a question to which the song gives no answer, stark in its simplicity. *Why are we here?* In this article, C.J. Stone attempts to answer the question, not for every man who died, but for one man at least.

There's a grainy old sepia photograph of Ivor Coles standing in front of a shop. He's maybe 12 or 13 years old, wearing a flat cap and a donkey jacket with leather patches on the shoulders, with knee-length breeches and woollen socks, with these huge shiny black leather clod-hoppers on his feet. They are far too big for him, clogs rather than shoes, with wooden soles turned up at the toe. The clothes are functional and sturdy, heavy duty work-clothes. A miner's uniform. Perhaps they are his new work clothes. Perhaps he's just about to start his first job, down the pit. He was the right age. He's got one hand in front of him, the thumb hovering around his waistcoat pocket as if he's about to hook it in; the other hand is tucked into his jacket as if he's about to take something out. He's leaning on the windowsill, one leg cocked forward, totally at his ease, with this cheeky look on his face, grinning broadly at the camera from under the brim of his cap, which is pulled down tight over his ears. It's obviously the fashion. A young boy with a cheeky-monkey grin on the threshold of his future with everything to look forward to. Within six years he would be dead. His name is Ivor Coles, and the picture was taken sometime in the early 1900s - 1908 or 1909 - and he died of wounds sometime in September 1915 near a town called Vieille-Chapelle in France on the Western Front.

He had an older brother, Richard Coles (right). Richard was also stationed on the Western Front, but survived. He later married Lily May. Lily May lived on till she was over a hundred. It is Lily May who is the thread who holds this story together. As it turns out, if you look at the dates, Ivor must have been underage when he joined up. He was born on June 24 1897. He was less than three months into his eighteenth year when he died so he must have joined the army before the proper age of recruitment at 18. Also, according to Richard - who would tell the story in later years - Ivor was only a few days away from moving to Richard's regiment, on compassionate grounds. The British Army usually allowed members of the same family to serve together. But then the big push came, the move never happened, and Ivor Coles died as a private in 9th Battalion of Welsh Regiment. There's not a lot more you can say about him. He died anonymously, another anonymous death in a war where death was the norm, routine and unavoidable. A conveyor belt of death. A death factory in full-production.

Years later, Richard went back to find him. He scoured the cemeteries of the Western Front looking for his name, but it wasn't there. He thought he saw it on the Menin Gate Memorial, where all the missing are listed. The ones without bodies. The ones whose bodies had been blown to bits, smashed and pulped into a goulash soup and absorbed into the earth. There was one name there which resembled his brother's. Ivan Coles, rather than Ivor. Maybe they just got the spelling wrong. Anyhow, it was enough to satisfy Richard, enough for him to say to himself, *well I've found my brother now*, to pay his respects and then to leave. And that's how the story stood. An old story. As old as time. As old as history. One of those stories that most families are familiar with, like a thread from the past left dangling in the present. A story without an end or without resolution, like a detective novel with the last pages missing.

Later again Richard's granddaughter, Vanessa, went to the Menin Gate to check the story out, scanning the thousands of names to find the one that her grandfather had seen. It wasn't there. There was no I. Coles listed on the Menin Gate. So the mystery deepened. Ivor Coles had just disappeared from history, lost without a trace. He had no grave, no memorial, nothing to mark his passing in the great river of time, nothing to show that he had ever been here, that he had ever mattered. Nothing but an old grainy photograph tucked away in a biscuit tin in someone's bottom drawer, all but forgotten.

Except for Lily May, that is. Lily May who had married Ivor's brother. Richard sometimes spoke about him, about his lost brother, and Lily May always remembered this, even after Richard had died. That's how the thread of history is kept alive. It's in the minds of the living. In the minds of the people who remember. Lily May never met Ivor Coles, but she shared his surname, and she remembered the stories her beloved husband had told her about their childhood together in South Wales, remembered even when she was a hundred years old and had great-great grandchildren who would play around her ankles while she snoozed away her last few months, delicate and brittle like an old clock.

And who was Ivor Coles anyway? His life was so short it could hardly have impacted on this earth. He was here, and then he was gone, along with a whole generation of young men. He left no progeny. He left no mark. He added little to the world's store. Had he lived he would have gone back to being a miner, feeding the power industry with his sweat and his muscle, digging the coal deep underground. But he never went back. And who's to say? Maybe he never even

Richard Coles and Lily May

fired a shot while he was on the frontline. Maybe his only contribution to the factory of death was his own body, swallowed by the mud in the mangled earth.

But Lily May had a secret. All those years she kept it. It was a tightly wrapped bundle which went everywhere with her. From the South Wales valleys where she started out, to the Weald of Kent, where the family eventually settled, miner following miner across the landscape of Britain in the search for work, miner's families following on behind. And that's how Lily May got here with her bundle.

It was a simple brown paper bundle, tightly wrapped in sellotape, wrapped and wrapped, tighter than a nun's wimple and containing just as many secrets. She called it *the crown jewels*.

Don't open it till something happens to me, she'd say, in her broad South Wales accent. *That there's very precious.* And she'd brandish it about with a flourish, with a twinkle, enjoying the mystery. Everyone thought it must contain diamonds at least. Or pearls. Gold and silver. Ancient artefacts from the mysterious East. It turned out to be mainly paper. Little more. Nothing of obvious value. So it was passed on to Warren, Vanessa's brother, as the family historian after Lily May died. *Here,* they said. *You might like this.* And it was in here that Warren found the clues that lead us back to Ivor, to finding him again.

The bundle was full of paper. Old faded sheets of time, folded, brown and musty with age. The usual things. Birth certificates. Death certificates. Marriage certificates. People's wills. Most of it was hardly surprising. But there were a couple of new things in there: one a verification notice, sent to Richard and Ivor's parents, John and Rhoda, by Commonwealth War Graves Commission. It contained the name of a cemetery, with a plot number, a row and a grave number, plus an army number, only it was made out in the name of T. Coles giving the date of his death as September 25 1915. *T* rather than *I* - a simple clerical error, a typing error. That's all it takes to lose a human being - a typing error. It was a printed form part filled in, in pencil. You were supposed to correct the details and send them back. Only no one ever did.

Later Warren checked the army number against an identity disc which they'd found behind the glass in a picture frame tucked behind a wardrobe in Lily May's house. The picture was of Lily May's brother, but the identity disc was Ivor's. The number on the verification document and the number on the disc matched. The family had found the whereabouts of Ivor's grave at last. All the information was on the document.

And there was something else in the bundle too, something even more precious. The bundle didn't contain jewellery; it contained a work of art - Ivor's memorial from a fellow soldier. It was a small package, the size of a man's outstretched hand, wrapped in brown paper. Inside the brown paper was a yellowing cotton cloth, and inside that, a layer of tissue paper. And inside the tissue paper, wrapped up like a sacred relic, like Tutankhamen's remains, there lay a simple chalk cross. It's about nine inches by seven. The cross is carved from a single lump of chalk, possibly with a penknife. The rear side of the object is a plain, smoothed surface, but on the other side the cross stands out in relief from a flat background, resting upon a plinth of steps. It is meant to be displayed in an upright position, facing forward to give the impression of a cemetery cross standing upon a platform of ascending steps. And all across the cross, in elaborate, ornate, copperplate lettering, in ink, using a fountain pen, written so that they too form the shape of a cross, are the following words:

> *R.I.P.*
> *In*
> *Loving Memory*
> *of*
> *Private Ivor Coles*
> *Killed In Action*
> *At*
> *Givenchy*
> *FRANCE*
> *September 15 1915*
> *He Gave His Life for England's Honour to Save*
> *Now he Lies in a Soldier's Grave.*

It is poignant in its simplicity. This plain, simple cross made from the bones of the soil, from the very chalk landscape that had swallowed Ivor's body, that had drank his blood and consumed his flesh, maybe even from the trench in which he lay shivering, afraid, in the muck, with the stench of death in the air, just before he was sent over the top to be chewed up by the teeth of the guns in no man's land, snared upon a wire to die, to give up his young life for some abstract cause; this cross carved with slow care and dedication in the weeks and months following by a comrade-in-arms, by a man who had watched him die perhaps, and who had wrenched this lump of rock from the living earth and carved it in his memory, so that Ivor's name would not be forgotten. *In Loving Memory*, he wrote. He meant every word of it.

This was the great secret that Lily May had kept all these years, wrapped up in a bundle, a memorial to her long-lost brother-in-law, a message from history. Not that this cross or this bundle answer all the questions. In fact, they bring to light new ones. There are discrepancies. The dates for a start. The cross has it that he died on September 15, while the verification document delays it until the 25. Perhaps he was wounded on the 15 and died in hospital ten days later on the 25. Except that there was a big offensive on the 25 - the so-called 2nd Battle of Loos - in which Ivor's regiment took part. Before that an uneasy stalemate had existed across the front line, an eerie peace broken only by the occasional skirmish. On September 25, thousands of men had died, mown down by the enemy guns, or gassed by their own side, or blown to smithereens by the artillery-fire while ducking for cover in no man's land. It was much more likely to be that day. Or perhaps he had taken part in a skirmish on 15, been killed by a sniper's bullet, but in the mass of deaths ten days later, in the confusion of slaughter, this one lone private's death had got muddled up. Who knows? It's a mystery.

And then the other great mystery. Why, when he received the verification document didn't Ivor's father return it with the amended information, the *I* instead of the *T*, and acknowledge his son's resting place? What father wouldn't want to know the place of his son's burial? Perhaps he couldn't read?

And why was the location of Ivor's grave kept hidden, even from his own brother? Mysteries on mysteries, and questions to which we will probably never have answers. But it's the questions that bring Ivor to life again. It's as if, in the anonymity of his death he planted a seed. A seed in history. And in the moment of remembering Ivor Coles, so long forgotten, we remember all the others who died in that carnage - *the war to end all wars* - and in that moment, too, remember the futility of war, its meaninglessness, and by that give meaning to Ivor Coles's death.

So, after 90 years the family had finally found the burial place of Great Uncle Ivor. All the information was in Commonwealth War Graves Commission's letter, and in 2006 Warren and Vanessa and their respective partners went to lay a wreath of poppies on his grave, to pay their respects. They had solved the mystery and brought Ivor Coles back into the bosom of their family once more. Now all that is needed is to get the grave re-carved so that it reads I. Coles instead of T. Cole, as it should. When that day comes there will be a dedication ceremony at the grave.

Post script

- Under the pen *name C J Stone*, Chris is an accomplished author, columnist and feature writer best known for his columns in *Guardian Weekend* and *The Big Issue*. He regularly features on the web-site *HubPages* where I first located his story of Ivor Coles. (hubpages.com/education/Were-Here-Because-Were-Here)

- Sarah Gauden, the lady who posted the *In Memoriam* was the mother of Lily May. Before he joined the army, Ivor's elder brother, Richard Coles was lodging with Sarah Gauden at Milton Terrace, and he married Lily May when home on leave from France in 1918. Sarah died August 17 1924 at 5 Nelson Terrace.

Sarah Gauden, née Cartwright, with son Frederick.

- Since found, the family has made several visits to the memorial (Menin Gate) and, at the time of writing, plans are in hand to take Warren's oldest grandson on the next family visit. I am indebted

Warren Hughes at the grave of his great-uncle Ivor Coles

to Warren Hughes for sharing his notes, family documents and photographs. Also to his mother Beryl Hughes (daughter of Richard and Lily May Coles) who, then in her 91st year, patiently answered the many questions put to her. She recalled that when her mother went on holidays Beryl was entrusted to look after the bundle. Never questioning its contents, she simply thought it was a bundle of insurance papers. On the demise of her mother, the bundle with its secrets came to Beryl who in turn handed it to Warren. There are still unanswered questions, the date of Ivor's death still a mystery, recorded as September 25 1915 yet on the chalk cross sculptured by a surviving comrade in the trenches, the date is September 15.

On receipt of proof, the Commission's records have now been partially amended to read Ivor Cole; however, the family await the replacement headstone.   To this day, the discrepancy of the surname has carried on throughout the family with part of the family using Cole and other family members using Coles.

Letters Home

Letters sent home from the trenches provide eyewitness accounts and a unique view of life in the trenches. Sadly, some were final letters, written just before the soldier died. The following are extracted from wartime issues of *Monmouth Guardian and Bargoed and Caerphilly Observer*.

The Great Battle of Loos - **December 3 1915**

Councillor Joseph Morgan, formerly of Tirphil, of Llanishen, received this graphic description by his nephew of the great Battle of Loos:

I am going to give you a description of the battle of Loos and Hill 70 the best way I can. The artillery started an intense bombardment on the Germans on Tuesday and kept it up continually for days—until the Saturday or Sunday, I am not sure, which. I think it was on the Saturday we let go the gas and our infantry followed it on and walked into the German trenches. Try and picture the battlefield on our front that day, thus: Our artillery in action in a line running parallel behind Williams's Farm at Graig Rhymney, and facing Brithdir; our front, two trenches, in front of Coedcae, and the German trenches in front of the new houses, Brithdir, facing Coedcae, with their artillery somewhere behind Brithdir. That's about the best description I can give of that. Well, we bombarded their trenches and the woods behind where we thought their guns to be, and the roads, to stop their reinforcements coming up we sent the 'physic' over for them. When they saw the gas coming, the dogs were reaching over the trenches putting petrol on top of their parapets and setting fire to it. That is their remedy for lifting the gas up; but it didn't come off. They didn't have enough petrol, or something, because there was not much wind, and the gas was going over dreadfully slow in a great cloud - too slow. Anyway, their fires went out, and our boys were going mad in the trenches to go over the top. They were like coursing dogs on leashes. Mad they were, and went over the top, more's the pity, a lot too soon for some, for the first batch ran headlong into hell - into the gas before it had gone far enough. It was the courage of madness. The remainder took a lesson and held back awhile, and they simply walked over the trenches. When the first regiment went over the first trench, their orders were to jump it and go on. There were a few of the Huns left in that trench holding up their arms and shouting for mercy, but our lads took no notice but left them for the next lot of men coming up from behind. After being spared, the dogs opened fire into the backs of the leading lads that spared their lives; but not for long they were wiped out. After running over the trenches, Loos (Brithdir) was to be taken at the point of the bayonet, because of the civilian population there. It was dreadful work—bloody work. After taking Loos (picture it as Brithdir and you will follow me better), and while our infantry was attacking the village, most of their field guns had retired, but we got a fair haul. Then came Hill 70. The Hill was taken, but was given up again as their big guns were playing havoc on it. In the meantime, the Guards had arrived on the scene; and the order came that the Guards were to retake Hill 70. That is where the Welsh Guards made their name. It was a competition between them and the Grenadiers - but the Taffies won. They tried to go over the Hill and down the other side, but it was pure suicide to go over, so they dug themselves in on this side of the Hill; and there we are still - holding it. That is about the best idea I can give of it, and I hope I have not bored you. We are now in front of a place called Auchy-la-Bassee. It is dreadfully wet here now, and it would break many a poor soul's heart to see the state of the boys; but I don't think our boys are ever happier than when they are up to their necks in mud - and up to our necks we are. Fancy digging yourselves in by the side of the gun down to a depth of about five feet, and old trees and mud thrown on the top for shelter. Well, the rain has soaked through, and our home from home isn't very comfortable at present with the continual drip, drip, drip. It's fun to see us.

A brilliant local application of the scene of the fighting which enabled readers to grasp in an instant the full position of the opposing armies.

Bargoed Boy's Last Letter – October 22 1915

Private Albert (Bert) Trotman of the South Wales Borderers, a young man of Bargoed, after 12 months' thrilling experiences at the front in France, was home on five days leave. On his return to the front he was killed in the great drive. On September 22, a few days before the great attack, he wrote his last letter to his widowed mother. He said he was quite well at the time. Dear mother, he added, I am writing now because I don't know when I will have a chance again. They have started the bombardment for the big attack. It is nothing but one roar, but it is nothing to what we are going to give them. We are going to send ten times as many shells at them, and if it is a success, I hope the next time I write we will be a lot nearer Berlin. Everybody seems to think it will be a success. I will tell you a bit about myself. I have been in the trenches since I came from home. I have not had a shave, have only once washed, and have not taken my boots off, so I can tell you I am looking well, and I wish you could see me now. We have got to be ready for the big attack, so I must wish myself the best of luck, and if I have it as have always had, I shall be alright.

Private Trotman was killed in action on September 26 1915, four days after writing his letter. Bert Trotman, son of George and Elizabeth Trotman, was born in 1891 in Bute Terrace. The family moved to Bargoed sometime before 1911. His older brother George Trotman is remembered on Brithdir war memorial.

Slackers Made To Have Some.
A Brithdir non-com at the Dardanelles - 12 November 1915
(Note – several instances of censorship in this letter.)

Mr. T. B. Fisher, the respected manager of the Brithdir Pit, Bargoed, received the following interesting letter on October 20 1915, from Lance-Corpl. Jenkin Jenkins, a young married man of Brithdir, with the British Mediterranean Expeditionary Force at the Dardanelles, he says:

I was very pleased to receive your letter this week and glad to know that although out of sight one is not out of mind. I am pleased to say I am quite well, although the conditions have been very rough, but when one thinks of the cause, he seems to gain encouragement, and the burden is somewhat lightened. My first experience of war was on August 9, when we landed on censored *at 2.30 am, and after about two or three hours rest we were told to move on about 500 yards over the crest of the hill. We had just finished breakfast when there came a whistling, screeching noise, and then, bang! One of the enemy's shells had burst in our midst, but our boys were as cool and collected as if they had been in the midst of shells for a lifetime. After that, the order came to advance, and I can tell you the boys were more than eager to get into grips with the enemy. We advanced across* censored *right through the open, no cover of any description - with bullets and shrapnel flying around like hail. I don't think that any of us will ever forget that experience, which only comes one's way once in a lifetime - and I assure you it is quite sufficient. Our casualties the first few days were very heavy, as I have no doubt you have seen in the papers. Our officers proved themselves men of the right calibre, but I'm sorry to say we lost a good many of them. For the first 18 days it was very hard digging trenches day and night, and after finishing one lot, advancing under cover of darkness to dig more, and I may say it was a sight to see men and officers working like beings possessed to get under cover before darkness left us. I think our battalion can say without exaggerating that we were the first to dig proper trenches on this part of the Peninsula. The weather the first six weeks was very hot by day and cold by night, which severely tried one's constitution. The winter has now set in and by what I can see of things we are in for a rougher time than we had in the beginning. What with the cold and rainy season, we have been out of the firing line for a month, but don't know the minute when we'll have to return. We are being supplied with new clothing in preparation for the winter season. I think that is enough of grumbling now, so I will write of something more cheerful. Joe Mellens* [son of Mr. and Mrs. Mellens, 1 Herbert Street] *is here with me. We have been together ever since our enlistment, and although we lost each other for four days, we met again, and it gave us both more spirit to find one another, when each thought the other was gone. The meeting was like one of persons meeting after being separated years. We have stuck to each other since. I am glad to hear that things are going about the same; and when one begins to think of the things in England and we in such a big crisis, I think it shows*

208

our superiority on land and sea. The young able-bodied man that can stay at home in ease while thousands of his fellow countrymen are roughing it, ought to be made to have SOME, as numbers will win this war. As a preference, I would rather be under the "droppers" of Killarney Level than out here, and I live in hopes of coming back to Bargoed Brithdir Pit—and that before very long. I think the beginning of a great and decisive victory has set in, and I think the sooner the better for everyone concerned. I was very sorry to hear of Dr. Clarke's death, [doctor in Aberbargoed who died of wounds at Suvla Bay October 9 1915] *although I never knew he was out in these parts until I had your letter. Dr. Martin* [Brithdir doctor] *is at Malta, so the people at home write to tell me. Our stretcher bearers have done some great work bringing in the wounded from what one may describe as a* censored. *Well, I don't think there is any more now, only to thank you once more for your encouraging letter. With best respects and thanks from one of your boys.*

Jenkin Jenkins, born in Cwmsyfiog in 1893, was son of David and Emma Jenkins, 28 James Street. He enlisted at Brithdir and joined 1/5th Welsh as Private 2870. In February 1915 his battalion was sent to Forth and Tay defences and later, on July 19, sailed from Devonport to arrive at Suvla Bay on August 9. Evacuated from Gallipoli on December 11, the battalion moved to Egypt. On March 1 1917, Jenkins had new number, 241094. His medal card shows he attained the rank of Sergeant. Killed in action December 12 1917 aged 24, he was buried in grave M. 24. Jerusalem Cemetery.

A Tribute to Capt. Rowley and an Appeal - April 7 1916

Sir, - I hope you will be able to find space in your valuable paper for this letter and appeal. It comes from some of the local boys, who, at present, are using their time "somewhere in France." Since our advent into the zone of war some three months ago, our work has been of an arduous nature, and we have been very busy. We have taken over trenches in which there is often a plentiful supply of water, only it is under our feet. This has not tended to make the boys comfortable by any means. Indeed, but for the unconquerable spirit they possess they would have been a very miserable set. However, I claim we have been fairly happy in spite of the odds. One thing has been missing, and that is a bit of music. I am now taking the liberty of appealing through the media of the "Journal" for a melodeon to enliven and cheer the boys from Bargoed, Brithdir and Pengam. Our section is almost entirely composed of chaps from Bargoed and its suburbs. As many of your readers are aware, we have one local officer, that is Capt. and Adjt. Rowley, the most popular officer in the Battalion, beloved by all ranks, and those of us who hail from the Bargoed district are proud of him, and we know that he is proud of his boys. I should mention that we have two first-class players of the instrument required. Wishing your paper every success and "cheer-ho" to all your readers, - On behalf of the boys

Pte. HARRY WEST (Brithdir) 16th Batt, Welsh Regt.

209

CHAPTER 13 BRITHDIR WAR MEMORIAL

Brithdir, like so many other communities in Rhymney Valley and beyond, was traumatised by the Great War. Many of its sons went to serve and, sadly, the names of 42 Brithdir men who did not return are inscribed on the village war memorial.

World War I casualties named on Brithdir war memorial

BENDALL J.
Alfred John Bendall, Private 10969, Devonshire Regiment, 8th Battalion. Died November 9 1915, age 38, buried at Gorre British and Indian Cemetery, Pas de Calais. Son of Thomas Bendall and Fanny (later Jones).

BENDALL T.
Thomas Bendall, Sergeant 9772, SWB, 2nd Battalion. Died October 21 1916. Commemorated Pier and Face 4 Thiepval Memorial, Somme. Previously served with Welsh Regiment 3rd Battalion (militia) as Private 5264. Younger brother of Alfred John Bendall.

BENNETT H.
Harry Bennett, Sergeant 23914, Welsh Regiment 15th Battalion. Died May 10 1918, buried at Varennes Military Cemetery, Somme. Son of John and Sarah Bennett. Husband of Hannah Bennett (née Mellens) 1 Herbert Street.

BUTLER W.
Not identified at the time of writing.

CONOLLY J.
(as spelled on the memorial)
Jeremiah (Jerry) Connelly, Private 12054, Welsh Regiment, 8th Battalion. Died August 8 1915, age 20. Commemorated Panel 140 to 144; Helles Memorial, Turkey. Son of John and Mary Connelly.

COLES I. — Ivor Coles, Private 12788, Welsh Regiment, 9th Battalion. Died September 25 1915, buried Vieille-Chapelle New Military Cemetery, Lacouture, Pas de Calais. Son of John and Rhoda Coles, 7 Salisbury Terrace.

DAVIES W. — William Davies, Private 24302, Welsh Regiment, 16th (Cardiff City) Battalion. Previously served in South Africa. Died July 7 1916, buried Flatiron Copse Cemetery, Mametz, Somme. Son of Thomas and Ann Davies, 10 James Street.

DAVIES S. — Stephen Davies, Corporal 241090, Welsh Regiment, 5th Battalion. Died March 10 1918, buried Jerusalem War Cemetery. Husband of Gertrude Davies, 26 James Street.

DAVIES T. — Not identified at the time of writing.

EVANS B. — Benjamin Evans, son of Joseph and Mary Evans, Bristol Terrace. (His military record has not survived)

GUMMER W. — William Gummer, Driver 40015, Royal Field Artillery. Died August 1 1916. Commemorated Face B Kirkee War Memorial (Kirkee War Cemetery), Bombay. Son of Samuel Gummer, Church Villa.

GODLEY F. — Frederick Godley, Private 21560, Welsh Regiment, 10th (Rhondda) Battalion, transferred to Company Labour Corps. Died December 5 1917, buried Duisans British Cemetery, Etrun, Pas de Calais. Survived by widow Mary and nine children, 1 Salisbury Terrace.

HARDON S. — Not identified at the time of writing.

HALLET A. — Arthur William Hallett, Gunner 80597, Royal Field Artillery, Died June 10 1917, buried at Reninghelst New Military Cemetery, West-Vlaanderen. Son of Benjamin and Hannah Hallett of Bristol, and brother of Mrs. Edward Rogers, 3 Nelson Terrace.

JAMES A.G. — Alfred George James, Private 28568, Welsh Regiment, 18th Battalion. Died October 18 1916, age 23, buried at Maroc British Cemetery, Grenay, Pas de Calais. Son of James and Mary Jane James (later Mrs Mellens, 1 Charles Street).

JENKINS J. — Jenkin Jenkins, Lance Sergeant 241094, Welsh Regiment, 1/5th Battalion. Died December 12 1917, buried grave M. 24. Jerusalem War Cemetery. Son of David and Emma Jenkins, 28 James Street.

JONES W. — William Davies Jones, Rifleman R/3561, King's Royal Rifle Corps, 10th Battalion. Died November 30 1917, age 23. Commemorated Panel 9 Cambrai Memorial, Louverval. Son of William Davies Jones and Anna, 2 Ivy Row.

LEWIS B. — Bertie Lewis, Private 31818, SWB. Died January 5 1919, age 21. Commemorated Kirkee 1914-18 Memorial, Face 5. Son of James and Helena Lewis, Plas Milfre Farm.

LEWIS T.   Not identified at the time of writing.

LIVINGSTON G.   George Livingstone, Private 18574, Welsh Regiment. Died
(as spelled on the   May 25 1915. Commemorated Panel 37 Ypres (Menin Gate)
memorial)   Memorial, West-Vlaanderen. Son of Mr and Mrs George
Livingstone. Living with Henry and Sarah Evans, 10 Nelson
Terrace at time of 1911 census.

MARTIN E.W.S.   Edwin William Sidney Martin, Captain, RAMC. Died of wounds,
February 16 1917, age 41, buried grave XXI. L. 11. Amara War
Cemetery, Iraq. Son of John E. Martin, JP, Ridgeway, Newport.

MORGAN C.   Charles Ernest Morgan, Rifleman 123, Monmouthshire
Regiment, 1st Battalion. Died April 24 1915. Commemorated
Panel 50, Ypres (Menin Gate) Memorial, West-Vlaanderen.
Son of Elizabeth Morgan, George Inn Hotel.

MORGAN G.   Arthur Augustus Morgan (Gus), Lance Sergeant 19453,
Dorsetshire Regiment, 5th Battalion. Died January 3 1917.
Commemorated Pier and Face 7B Thiepval Memorial, Somme.
Son of Elizabeth Morgan, George Inn Hotel.

NEAL A.   Not identified at the time of writing.

NEWMAN T.G.   George Thomas Newman, Private 18342, Welsh Regiment, 8th
Battalion. Died August 8 1915, age 19. Commemorated Panel
140 to 144; Helles Memorial, Turkey. Son of Fred and Mary
Newman, Station Terrace.

PARRY E.   Edwin Parry, 4 Old Bristol Terrace, husband of Rose Ellen Price
is the only Parry residing in Brithdir of suitable age to have
enlisted. CWGC list just one casualty of that name and he is
14391 Private Edwin Parry, 2nd Battalion SWB. No record
studied identifies him.

PEARCE J.   James Pearce, Lance Corporal 1430, Monmouthshire
Regiment, 3rd Battalion. Died September 29 1915, age 20,
buried at Bard Cottage Cemetery, West-Vlaanderen. Son of
William and Cecilia Pearce, Blaina and husband of Cecilia (later
Sheasby), 26 James Street.

PHILLIPS W.   William Phillips, Private 93735, Royal Welsh Fusiliers, 2nd
Battalion. Died October 8 1918. Commemorated Panel 6 Vis-
en-Artois Memorial, Pas de Calais. Son of Albert and Mary
Phillips, 16 Charles Street.

PORCH L.   Lewis Henry Porch, Private 11019, SWB. Died October 31
1914. Commemorated Panel 22 Ypres (Menin Gate) Memorial,
West-Vlaanderen. Son of Stephen and Sidnea Porch, 12
Nelson Terrace.

PRICE J.   John James Price, Private 21444, Welsh Regiment. Died April
24 1918, buried Millencourt Communal Cemetery Extension,
Somme. Husband of Sarah Elizabeth Price, 11 Salisbury
Terrace.

PRICE E.

Evan Price, Private 24516, Welsh Regiment, 9th Battalion. Died October 2 1915, buried Wimereux Communal Cemetery, Pas de Calais. Son of Rees and Jane Price, 10 School Street.

REED T.

Thomas George Reed, Private 18614, Welsh Regiment, 13th Battalion. Died July 10 1916. Commemorated Pier and Face 7A and 10A Thiepval Memorial, Somme. Son of Thomas and Ann Reed, 17 Station Terrace.

SHEEN R.

Possibly: Reginald (Reggie) Charles Sheen, Private 2876, Welsh Regiment 5th Battalion. Died August 20 1915. Commemorated Panel 140 to 144 Helles Memorial, Turkey. Lived at 21 Charles Street.

SCRIVENS W.

William Scrivens, Private 20868, SWB, 10th Battalion. Died July 31 1917 Battle of Pilkem Ridge. Commemorated Panel 22 Ypres (Menin Gate) Memorial, West-Vlaanderen. Born 1894, son of George and Amelia Scrivens.

SPEAKE J.

Possibly John Herbert Speake, boarder with Charles Hutton at 8 Harcourt Terrace. No sources studied to date confirm identification.

TAYLOR T.

Thomas Robert Taylor, Sergeant 241100, Welsh Regiment, 1/5th Battalion. Died November 3 1917, age 38, buried Beersheba War Cemetery. Husband of Violet Charlotte Taylor, Salem House.

TROTMAN G.

George Trotman, Royal Field Artillery. Died 1922 of disease. Son of George and Elizabeth Trotman formerly 2 Bute Terrace, and later Capel Street, Bargoed.

WATKINS G.

George Frederick Watkins, Private 9525, Welsh Regiment, 2nd Battalion. Died November 6 1914, age 26. Commemorated Panel 37 Ypres (Menin Gate) Memorial, West-Vlaanderen. Son of George and Mary Watkins, Rose Hill Cottage.

WATTS T. J.

Thomas John Watts, Private 8/15973, SWB 8th Battalion. Died December 15 1918 aged 26, buried grave 1747 at Mikra British Cemetery, Kalamaria. Son of John and Margaret Jane Watts, 17 Charles Street.

WILLIAMS F.

Not identified at the time of writing.

WILLIAMS W.

William George Williams, Private 20953, Gloucestershire Regiment. Died September 3 1917, buried at Villers-Faucon Communal Cemetery Extension, Somme. Son of William and Elizabeth Williams, 14 Charles Street.

WILLIAMS A.

Arthur Williams, Private 8831, Royal Welsh Fusiliers, 4th Battalion. Died October 5 1916. Commemorated Pier and Face 4 A Thiepval Memorial, Somme. Son of William and Mary Williams, The Villas.

Unveiling and dedication Brithdir War Memorial.
It was dedicated by Vicar Rev. C.J. Griffith, assisted by Revs. H. Williams and Harry West. Gertrude Davies, secretary, in front of the clergy, read the list of casualties' names. Jack Rees, chairman of memorial committee, is on her left, and, directly behind him, Harry Brown.

Courtesy Fionnuala Eardley

During the 1920s, the community of Brithdir, although numbed by the devastating impact of war and facing a difficult period of economic, social and political re-adjustment, turned its attention to commemorating local casualties. With £87 held in trust for a memorial to those who had made the supreme sacrifice, local people met in George Hotel in September 1930, and elected a small organizing committee to push the project forward. After much deliberation, the preferred site was in Gwaelod y Brithdir Cemetery, and, as reported in *Merthyr Express*, March 18 1933, the committee was disappointed to find that was denied them. After further discussion, a site in front of the Workmen's Institute was chosen. On Sunday, November 22 1936, a large crowd witnessed Captain Lionel Lindsay, Chief Constable of Glamorgan, unveil the memorial, the work of sculptor, Griffith Evans, Treforest.

The school log book records that Henry R. Judd, Brithdir Boys' School, placed a wreath on behalf of all school children of Brithdir on the occasion of the unveiling.

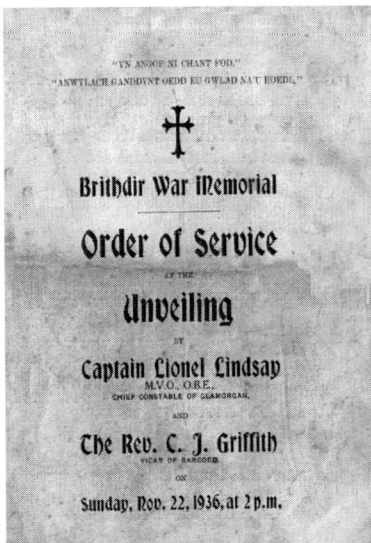

Cover of Order of Service November 22 1936

214

The crowd gathered to witness the unveiling ceremony: Right mid centre is Joe Hayes, on his left wearing a light coloured bonnet is Mrs Harrison. The baby, extreme left and nursed in a white shawl, is Peter Evans. Directly in front of third and fourth constables from left are Granville Brewer and William Powell. Note the attendance of eight police constables.   Courtesy Malcolm Winmill

Brithdir branch of Royal British Legion was formed in 1930, with Edmund Morgan as president, supported by vice presidents Dr. O'Shea, C. Cattermole and John Hill. Its committee was chaired by W. Harris with J. Rees as vice chairman, H Gwynne, secretary, and J. Hill, treasurer. By 1932 progress was such that members considered it fitting they had a standard. Their standard was dedicated at an impressive service, on Sunday, July 10 1932, at St. Paul's Church (then in the Ambulance Hall). Prior to the service, there was a spectacular parade with New Tredegar Silver Band leading nearly 150 people and 17 standards through the village. Branch members, led by John Hill, then president, and Henry Judd, vice-president, marched together with representatives of Tirphil, New Tredegar, Pontlottyn, Abertysswg, Gelligaer, Ystrad Mynach, Bargoed, Pengam and Fleur de Lys branches, as well as Tirphil section of Gelligaer Fire Brigade and Bargoed Cubs. James Way, Union Jack standard bearer, was supported by Mr Morgan and Catherine Cresswell (secretary women's section), while J. Davies, Royal British Legion standard bearer, was supported by Walter Wells and Thomas Bishop (secretary men's section). After the service the procession returned via Bristol Terrace to Legion headquarters (presumably in the former Roman Catholic Church near Ty Coch) for refreshments.

Brithdir War Memorial committee 1936.
Standing L-R: Lucy Davies, Harry Brown (Wesley House), Ben Watkins, T. Lewis, Jack Hill, Thomas Bishop, W. Hares and Mrs. H. Williams.
Seated Mrs. W. Williams, Elizabeth Morgan (George Inn Hotel), Mrs. Webb, Catherine Cresswell, Tommy Davies (schoolteacher and trustee), Gertrude Davies, secretary (wife of Tommy Davies), Thomas Davies (trustee), Mrs. Jeremiah, Mary George and Mrs. T. Woods.   Courtesy Don Watkins

Brithdir British Legion (women's section).
Front row: L-R: Officers, Mrs. O. Woods (chairperson), Mrs. Cresswell (secretary), Elizabeth Morgan (president), and Alice Webb (treasurer). Sitting right of front row is Mary (Mollie) Lewis, née Kavanagh, wife of Thomas Lewis DCM. In the back row third from right is Bridget Mary Campbell née Lewis, daughter of Tom and Mary Lewis.
Courtesy Nita Smith

WAR MEMORIAL. — The committee responsible for the Brithdir War Memorial met at the George Hotel Assembly Room on Wednesday, and Mr. John Hill presided. It has been agreed to add the names of all who made the supreme sacrifice during the 1939-45 war to the existing memorial, and the following names have been supplied : John Jenkins, Vivian Willets, John Ferguson, Wm. Howells, Wm. Williams, Tom Ferguson, G. Baker, Wm. McDonald, Trevor Butts, and R. Phillips. If anyone from Brithdir is not included in this list, please inform Mrs. G. Davies, Brynglas Villa, as soon as possible, as the date for the unveiling is fixed for Sunday, November 9. Valuable assistance has been received from the Institute Committee, Conservative Club, British Legion, and all the churches, and a special effort organised by the ladies realised a considerable amount. The officials are : Mr. John Hill, chairman; Mr. Idris Jones, treasurer; and Mrs. Gertie Davies, secretary.

Sadly, it was necessary to add further names to the memorial after World War II. The extract, left, from *Merthyr Express*, August 30 1947, lists some names - 15 names were later added to the lower side plinths of the memorial. I draw readers' attention to three of those names; namely John and Tom Ferguson, and William Howells. With regards to the family Ferguson, although the family spelled their name with a single s, the mason engraved the name with two. The initial for Private Howells is set in stone on the memorial with the letter J. Anecdotal evidence has it that J. Howells survived the war. *Merthyr Express*, September 16 1944, carried the following report:

BAKER G.	PTE.
BREWER E.	··
BUTTS T.	··
FERCUSSON J.	CPL.
FERCUSSON T.	PTE.
HILL W.T.	P.O.
HOWELLS J.	PTE.

JONES E.T.	F/SGT.
SOUTHAM E.	CPL.
JENKINS J.C.	F/LIEUT.
JONES C.I.	PTE.
MᶜDONALD W.	··
PHILLIPS R.	L/AC.
WILLETTS V.	F/SGT.
WILLIAMS W.C.	PTE.

Two well-known Brithdir soldiers Corporal J.T. Ferguson and Private W. E. Howells have recently met their deaths during the liberation of France. 26 year old Pte William Edwin Howells of 8 Milton Terrace is reported to have died of wounds. A cook in the Army Catering Company, 2nd Monmouthshire Regiment, he had been stationed in Northern Ireland for some time, and had been abroad only a short time. With 5 years' army service, he was formerly employed underground at Elliots Colliery. Two brothers are also serving, Charles in France and Joseph with the Royal Naval (landing craft).

However research to date reveals the following about William Edwin Howells: *Private 3910928, Date of Death: 17/08/1944, Age 26, Army Catering Corps attached to Monmouthshire Regiment. Buried grave VI. D. 18 Banneville-La-Campagne War Cemetery, Son of Thomas and Elizabeth Howells, of Hillingdon, Middlesex.* Does his attachment to Monmouthshire Regiment imply any link with Brithdir?

World War II casualties named on Brithdir War Memorial

BAKER G.   Bertie William George Baker, Private 14767330, Durham Light Infantry. Died 4 April 1945, age 29, buried Reichswald Forest War Cemetery. Husband of Lorraine Baker née Bevan.

BREWER E.   Edward Brewer, Fusilier 4204990, Royal Welsh Fusiliers. Died 12 April 1941, buried Llandudno (Great Orme's Head)

Cemetery. Son of Sylvanus and Margaret Brewer, 1 Wellington Terrace, husband of Winifred Brewer née Appleton, Llandudno.

BUTTS T. Trevor Butts, Gunner 1492701, Royal Artillery, 12th Coastal Regiment. Died 18 December 1941 age 23. Commemorated Column 3 San Wan Memorial, Hong Kong. Son of Herbert and Ethel Butts.

FERGUSSON J. John Thomas Ferguson, Corporal 3954925, Welsh Regiment, (as spelled on the 1/5th Bn. Died 12 August 1944, age 37, buried at Banneville La-memorial) Campagne War Cemetery, Normandy. Son of Emily Cooper.

FERGUSSON T. Thomas Henry Ferguson, Private 3959703, Welsh Regiment 1st (as spelled on the Bn. Died 27 May 1941, age 23, buried at Suda Bay War memorial) Cemetery, Crete. Son of Emily Cooper.

HILL W.T. William Thomas Hill, Petty Officer Stoker D/KX 83585 Royal Navy (H.M.S. Dragonfly). Died 14 February 1942. Commemorated on Panel 9, Column 1 Plymouth Naval Memorial.

HOWELLS J. Not identified at the time of writing.

JENKINS J.G. John Griffith Jenkins, Flight Lieutenant (Pilot) 124463, RAF V. R. Died 24 April 1945, age 23, buried Gwaelod y Brithdir Cemetery. Son of Lewis J. and Sarah Jenkins.

JONES C.I. Clement Idris Jones, Private 3912662, SWB 1st Battalion. Died 19-21 June 1942, age 28. Commemorated Column 62 Alamein Memorial, Egypt. Son of Charles and Harriet Jones, husband of Amelia Jones.

JONES E.T. Ernest Thomas Jones, Flight Sergeant (Pilot) 570004, Royal Air Force, 15 Sqdn. Died May 12 1944, age 24, buried Leuven Communal Cemetery, Vlaams-Brabant. Son of Joseph and Margaret Jones, husband of Sylvia Jones.

McDONALD W. William McDonald, Private 2182010, Pioneer Corps, Aux Mil. Died June 17 1940, age 38, buried Rennes Eastern Communal Cemetery, Bretagne. Son of William and Mary Ann McDonald

PHILLIPS R. Ronald Phillips, Leading Aircraftman 1313723, RAF V.R. Died November 20 1944, age 28 at Hampshire, buried Gwaelod y Brithdir Cemetery. Son of Richard and Claudia Phillips, husband of Gwyneth Phillips, Bargoed.

SOUTHAM E. Ernest Southam, Corporal 7012844, Royal Ulster Rifles 1st (Airborne) Battalion. Died August 23 1944, age 24, buried at Tourgeville Military Cemetery. Son of Richard and May Southam, husband of Amelia Elizabeth Southam.

WILLETTS V. Vivian Alquin Willetts, Flight Sergeant (Navigator) 970524, RAF V.R. Fighter Command 23 Sqdn. Died April 27 1942, age 24. Commemorated Panel 76; Runnymede Memorial. Son of Phillip and Margaret Willetts

WILLIAMS W.G. Not identified at the time of writing.

As a result of discussion in the early 1970s, it was decided to move the war memorial to the village centre site which had lain empty since St. Paul's Church was demolished. The site, at the top of Russell Street, was paved and the base laid about 1973-1974 but the memorial was not moved until a decade later. Margaret Price née Rawle drew my attention to this extract from *Merthyr Express*, Thursday, December 20 1984:

The war dead of the village of Brithdir were remembered at a special service when the St. Paul Memorial Garden was dedicated and the Cenotaph was re-dedicated. The gardens and re-sited cenotaph now occupy a once-derelict site in the village where the old St. Paul's Church formerly stood. The British Legion felt it was an ideal site for the cenotaph and a special scheme was designed by the architects' department of Rhymney Valley Council. The special services were conducted by the Rev. John Oeppen and attended by the chairman of the

Rev. John Oeppen at the service of re-dedication.
Courtesy Phil Davies.

council, Reg Parry; the chairman of Gelligaer Council Roger Edwards; local councillors, residents and representatives of the British Legion.

The rededication of the Brithdir Cenotaph brought back memories for Mrs. Lucy Davies. She is the only person alive who was in a 1936 photograph of the British Legion Committee [on page 216]. Mrs. Davies lives in Charles Street; in the house she came to almost 70 years ago. She is the only survivor of eight children and had five children herself. She now has three daughters left, 14 grandchildren, 20 great grandchildren and two great great grandchildren.

A sprightly Mrs Davies chuckled as she reminisced over the photograph and recognised herself as a forty-year-old, furthest left on the back row. Her husband, Thomas Davies is fourth from the right in the front row. He had been in the Royal Horse Artillery. Mrs Davies recalled what a tall, handsome man he had been. She pointed out Mary Ann George, layer out, known because she laid out the dead in the village, who is also in the photograph. Schoolteacher, D. T. [Tommy] Davies, who may be remembered by many readers, is in the front row. Mrs Morgan, who kept the George, the only pub in Brithdir, is also pictured.

Mr and Mrs Davies took over the Brithdir Constitutional Club, and Mrs Davies became the first and only stewardess there. Later they took over The Pelican in Dowlais and their daughter, now Glenys Smith, was married from there. It was while they were steward and stewardess at the Dowlais Labour Club that Thomas Davies died and his widow returned to her home village.

"My father was very strict, a real military man but it didn't do us children any harm" – recalls Mrs Smith. She left Brithdir and lived in England where she was landlady in several pubs but after being widowed eleven years ago she returned to Brithdir to care for her mother. Now the two have one great ambition. On the wall of their living room hangs a photograph of Mrs Davies's niece, Margaret Elizabeth Thomas. She went into show business and used to make records and appeared regularly on radio using the stage name, Peggy Bailey [see page 292]. She married another singer, Bill Campbell but since the war years has lost touch with her Brithdir relations and they would love to hear from her, or get some news of her. Mrs Davies now looks forward to her 90th birthday on Christmas Day (1984) in the village of Brithdir she loves.

Egypt 1952, Private Peter Bennett of RASCs relaxing on the sands reading his copy of the Rhymney Valley Express.
courtesy Phil Davies

Aden January 1968, Sergeant Thomas Melvyn Williams, RM24505, Royal Marine Commandos. Written on photo *From Aden, love Mel.*

CHAPTER 14 WORLD WAR II

Brithdir's home front during war years

World War II changed the lives not only of people who left the community to serve their country but also of those who remained at home. On September 3 1939, many local people heard the declaration of war on the radio and the older generations realised they would see a second major conflict in their lifetimes. What follows, based on memories as well as sources such as 1939 Register (September 29 1939), local newspapers and school log books, offers some specific Brithdir examples of life on the home front in this part of upper Rhymney Valley.

From early in 1939, the community, although hoping for peace, was preparing for war. During April and May, Air Raid Precautions (ARP) Wardens were busy assembling and fitting respirators to gas masks ready for distribution. Under the guidance of Councillor George Godfrey of 5 James Street and senior warden, Tommy Davies, and working with P.C. Lloyd and Brithdir Division St. John Ambulance Brigade, they were soon ready for distribution. Research to date has revealed the following local ARP wardens: school teachers Francis (Frank) West of 1 The Villas, and Tommy Davies of Bryn Glas, George Hill, were senior wardens, while Steve Kavanagh 2 Bute Terrace, Raymond Smith 16 Station Terrace, Charles Pudge 31a Station Terrace, William Samuel Cresswell 18 Old Bristol Terrace, James Griffin 6 Bristol Terrace, William Davies 3 School Street, Francis Young 10 Harcourt Terrace, William J Williams 11 Tennyson Terrace, David West 13 Nelson Terrace and Edward Wilcox 11 Milton Terrace were ARP wardens.

On the evening of May 14 1940, with the threat of invasion by air and sea imminent, Anthony Eden, Secretary of State for War, asked men aged 17 to 65 who were not engaged in military service to report to local police stations to enrol as Local Defence Volunteers (LDV). It is not clear when and how many Brithdir men responded to this call for what Winston Churchill renamed Home Guard, but there is no doubt local men played their part. The following names appear in sources relating to Brithdir Platoon of Home Guard -- Commander Charles Pudge, Lieutenant Lewis Harding, Sergeants G. Mantle and Samuel Mantle, and Corporals Tom Higgs, P. Moore, B. Stenner, Tom Hughes, Tom Startup, I. Davey, Frank Goode, Tom Davies, Eddie Bevan, Steve

L-R: Morgan Jones, Charles Davies and Horace Butts. The latter served with E Company, 6th Battalion, Brithdir Platoon from beginning to end of its wartime existence
courtesy Morgan Jones

Kavanagh, B. Harris, Dan Jones, Dai *Bocka* Williams, J. Davies, G. Godfrey, E. Jeremiah, A. Rees, G. Gwynne, Charles Williams and Horace Butts.

The following wartime Special Police are named in sources: Idris Jones 4 Station Terrace, Frederick Jones 18 Station Terrace, George Bateman 10 Bristol Terrace, John Davies 2 Charles Street, John Williams 13 Herbert Street, John Curtis 15 James Street, Rupert Bennett 6 School Street, Evan Davey 10 East View, Herbert John Williams 13 Harcourt Terrace, Hubert Brown Church Villa (shown right courtesy John Brown), David Watts 1 Salisbury Terrace, Alfred Wells 3 Salisbury Terrace, John O'Leary 18 Nelson Terrace and Edward Coombs 6 Milton Terrace.

The following (some VAD nurses and others associated with St. John Ambulance Brigade) are named in sources as having responsibility for first aid as and when required: Gertrude Davies (VAD Nursing Superintendent), Catherine Williams 27 Station Terrace, Harriet Bateman 12 Bristol Terrace, Thomas Edwards 10 School Street, Mary Mathias 2 Bryn Cottage East View, Gwilym Price 6 East View, Olive Woods 8 Harcourt Terrace, Alfred Wells 3 Salisbury Terrace, Stanley Wells (son of Alfred) 3 Salisbury Terrace, Arthur Jones 12 Salisbury Terrace, Francis Meredith 9 Tennyson Terrace, Albert Gullick 12 Milton Terrace, and Annie McDonald 15 Milton Terrace.

The establishment of Royal Ordnance Factories (ROF) not only played a crucial role in the war effort but was also significant in the history of women in the workplace. The following are some Brithdir women among those taking sometimes lengthy train or bus journeys to work in the munitions factories:

- ROF Glascoed: My grandmother, Margaret Brewer, Mary Price, Lettice Chard, Gwyneth Chard, Margaret Jones née Sheasby.
- ROF Currans, Grangetown, Cardiff (making shell cases): Nellie Ferguson, Sylvia Pritchard née Rees, Iris Williams and Gladys Eileen Williams née Hopkins.
- ROF 53 Bridgend: Ceinwen Smith.
- Royal Navy Propellant Factory, Caerwent: Marjorie Hughes travelled on one of the 5 coaches taking women from Rhymney Valley.
- ROF Llanishen, Cardiff: Winifred Maggs.

The factories were sometimes dangerous places of work as witnessed by this report of an explosion (revealed in Llanishen Local History Society 2011 weblog to have been at ROF Llanishen) carried by *Western Mail*, March 19 1944:

> *Anti-aircraft shells, one of which exploded in a crowded factory, killing 12 people, including seven women, and injuring as many more, were the chief cause of damage during activity over the South Wales coastal area on Monday night.*

Memories of W. G. Hares (Taunton). His step-father was an engine driver.

I was a young school boy during the Second World War and apart from rationing, we children, living at the very top of the Rhymney Valley knew very little of what was happening in places like London or Cardiff. It was only after my father started taking me on the footplate with him during weekends and school holidays (which of course was contrary to the rules of the railway) that I experienced some of the harsh realities of war. I travelled with him and his regular fireman, Dudley Jones, to stations like Cardiff, Pontypool, Penarth and Dowlais Top.

My very favourite trips, however, were on the evening trains leaving Rhymney taking the night shift workers to the munitions factories at Currans in Cardiff and Glascoed. Here a purpose built platform had been constructed so that the engine could run around the train for the return journey. We then waited to bring the afternoon workers home, returning around midnight.

The journey to Glascoed took us through magnificent scenery from Glamorgan to Monmouthshire starting at Rhymney crossing over west of Bargoed colliery to the Brecon line north of Pengam Monmouthshire station, to join the Pontypool to Neath line just east of the impressive fifteen arch Hengoed viaduct. The journey then continued via Pontllanfraith and over the famous Crumlin viaduct, which sadly has since been dismantled. I remember the thrill I experienced the first time I crossed that magnificent piece of engineering, looking out from the cab of a 2.6.2T 5500 Class locomotive to the valley bottom, 200 feet below – although the feeling was tinged with apprehension as the speed restriction crossing the 1,650 foot span was only 15 mph.

I distinctly remember one evening journey to Currans munition factory, when the whole night sky over Cardiff was lit up like an enormous firework display. This turned out to be the result of a particularly heavy bombing raid by German aircraft on the city docks. On our return journey back up the valley, we were followed by a German plane which had probably strayed from his flight path. We stopped at Cefn-On halt just before the tunnel through to Caerphilly and could hear a faster aircraft in pursuit. The following morning we were told that a German bomber, being chased by one of our fighters had dropped its bombs on the "peak", a local hilltop at New Tredegar. This brought the war to our doorstep

Through summer 1940 Brithdir Women's Voluntary Services (WVS) knitting class made comforts (socks, scarves, hats and gloves) for local men on active service. They sent their first winter parcels early November and hoped that by Christmas all Brithdir service people would have received one.

In 1941, Leonard John Stone, 9 Station Terrace, serving in military police in England, died in an accident sustained while on duty. The funeral, at Gwaelod y Brithdir Cemetery, was a military one with the duties attended by Brithdir Platoon of Home Guard, under Commander C. Pudge. The firing party consisted of Sgt. L. Harding, Sgt. G. Mantle, Corporals Higgs, P. Moore, B. Stenner, T. Hughes, T. Startup and I. Davey. The coffin, draped with the Union

Jack, was carried by Sgt. Cook, Cpl. Jones, L/Cpl. Moore and L/Cpl. Macduff, representatives of the unit to which he belonged. The Last Post was sounded by Sergeant Bugler J. Burkley.

Brithdir participated in national war savings campaigns including Spitfire Fund (1940), War Weapons Week (1941), Warship Week (1942), Wings for Victory Week (1943) and Salute the Soldier Week (1944). The fundraising activities, as illustrated by the events in War Weapons Week, helped bring the community together as they strived to meet their target.

War Weapons Week started with a dance, to music of Bert John's Radiant Dance Band, at the Institute on Saturday, March 29 1941. On Sunday morning there was a grand parade of representatives of New Tredegar Drum and Bugle Band, Brithdir Home Guard Platoon, New Tredegar Ambulance, Lady and Girl Cadets, Boy Cadets, Ex-Servicemen, WVS, members of ARP and Special Police, before a religious service was held at the Institute. There was community singing in the Institute in the evening. On Monday evening, there was another dance to music of Bert John's Band, and on Tuesday and Wednesday evenings there were whist drives. On Wednesday, a darts match, women of Bottom End of the village against those of Top End, took place at George Hotel. Thursday was drama night, and people flocked to the New Hall to see Glyn Dramatic Society (Deri) present *Partners* by Vincent Douglas. Friday evening was for children, and a large number attended the go-as-you-please competition. The week was rounded off on Saturday when concert party *Sunny Side Up*, with the *Sunshine Girls* provided non-stop variety to a full house. *Merthyr Express*, April 12 1941, reported:

> *Over £1,000 had been paid into the Savings Account. £514 11s. 6d from the Infants' School and £47 from Boys' School. The amount handed over to the Government as a free gift was about £75.*

After a similar programme to that of War Weapons Week, the balance sheet of Brithdir's Warship Week, was presented to a meeting held at the Institute on March 2 1942, and a cheque for £55 2s.9d sent as a gift from Brithdir.

Salute the Soldier Week aimed to encourage civilians to invest in Government accounts, such as War Bonds, Savings Bonds, Defence Bonds and Savings Certificates. Parades and exhibitions were organised to inspire people to invest at post offices or banks across the country to help their community reach its financial target. The War Office presented a commemorative plaque to those local savings committees who achieved their target. Councillor H. Williams was president of Brithdir fund committee, Harry Williams was chairman, Idris Jones, secretary and Tommy Davies, treasurer. Idris Jones received the plaque awarded to the village and arranged for Lieutenant Colonel Phillips, Commanding Officer, Swansea Garrison, to present the certificates (with a message of thanks from

P. J. Grigg, Secretary for War) to the following - Tommy Davies (Boys' School), Olwen Davies (Infants' School), A. Greenwood (GWR), Leslie Williams (Methodist Church) and Tom Braine (Salisbury Allotments). Brithdir's Salute the Soldier Week raised £1,212. The whereabouts of Brithdir's plaque has not been ascertained at the time of writing.

David Bryn Maxey, 7 Station Terrace, was Fire Guard Area Captain for Tirphil, Brithdir and Deri in 1943 and 1944. After working a shift as haulage driver underground, he changed into his uniform and walked around his area. Details and certificate courtesy of his daughter Morfydd Olsen née Maxey.

How the war affected Brithdir's schools

During the early months of the war, few log entries related to the war. The Girls' Department had frequent air raid drills. The first air raid warning logged was on July 3 1940, the night Cardiff was bombed. The Girls' Department air raid drill at 10 a.m. had vacated the school in 30 seconds. When the air raid alarm was sounded at 12.22 p.m. the school was vacated in 28 seconds, and *All Clear* came at 12.57 p.m. The times differ slightly in the Boys' Department log book (warning at 12.20 and *All Clear* at 12.45).

The following extracts from Brithdir schools' log books give a flavour of school life during the war years:

May 10 1940 (Boys' Log): *Whitsun Holidays cancelled by order of the Government owing to the sudden invasion of Belgium and Holland by the Germans.*

July 15 1940 (Boys' Log): *Air-raid alarm sounded at 10.20, a number of boys in the school playground were sent home. 'All Clear' given at 10.50, the boys returned to school. From today the Director of Education has ordered all schools to open an hour later for the morning session. This is in the interests of health and education of the scholars owing to loss of sleep due to air raid alarms at night.*

According to the Boys' Log, there were a total of 25 air raid warnings recorded between August 18 and December 11 with four days disrupted twice. It usually gave time warning sounded, and time all clear was given, but the entry for October 1 noted *warning sounded 10.20 and Raiders passed 10.45.*

September 23 1940 (Girls' Log): *Swimming Instruction terminated.*

October 10 1940 (Boys' Log): *Received from County Hall Cardiff, equipment for dealing with incendiary bombs and outbreaks of fire (Stirrup pump and long hose, 2 buckets full of sand, 2 water buckets and a long handle shovel).*

December 1940 (Girls' Log): *Introduction of Oslo Sandwiches to scholars; 6 girls and 5 Brithdir School boys receiving Oslo Sandwiches.*

February 5 1941 (Girls' Log): *Councillor George Godfrey (local school manager) Head ARP Warden demonstrated the use of the Stirrup Pump to all the scholars and Staff.*

April 4 1941 (Boys' Log): *Headmaster's room fitted with blackout curtains in preparation for fire watching. All the windows in the corridor have been made splinter proof. The county council workmen have this week completed the work of building blast walls in front of the doors of the school and also in front of the covered playground. They have also sandbagged all the windows in the corridors and lobbies.*

July 15 1941 (Boys' Log): *Owing to curtailment of petrol supplies Gelligaer Transport Company are no longer able to convey boys to and from Bargoed Baths for Swimming Instruction.*

July 30 1941 (Boys' Log): *Manual Centre (woodwork) closed; Mr Walters, instructor, has received 'call up' papers for the RAF Volunteer Reserve; he is to report on August 9.*

April 20 1942 (Boys' Log): *From tonight on the following men will fire watch the school - Mr. John Rees, Charles Howells and William Hughes. They will fire watch from half-an-hour before blackout to half-an-hour after blackout.*

November 5 1943 (Boys' Log): *Fire watch party withdrawn – School now watched by street party. On 'Alert' Fire Guards will report to school and remain until all clear.*

Evacuees

When arranging Brithdir school's 75th birthday celebrations, Maralyn Olsen, then deputy head in the school, tried to contact former evacuees from

Evacuees arrive at Brithdir Station 1940 (later it was goods' depot opposite George Inn Hotel) L-R: Tommy Davies (trilby hat) and Frank West (bowler hat) both teachers at Brithdir Boys' School, and Idris Jones (trilby hat) welcome evacuees.

Courtesy Henrietta Jones.

Maralyn Olsen
Courtesy Mr and Mrs Olsen

Sheerness Central School. In 2006, in response to my advertisement in *Memory Lane* column of *Sheerness Times Guardian* and a notice in Sheerness library, Rhoda Francis née McCarthy renewed the links between Brithdir and its evacuees. Her letters and telephone calls were full of memories and stories of her war time in Brithdir. Visiting there in 2007, a treat on her 80th birthday, she saw how the community had changed in the 67 years since 13 year old Rhoda had been in Brithdir -- the pit no longer there, the schools closed, chapels gone and childhood friends passed away. Rhoda was thrilled to meet Mavis, great granddaughter of Nan Edwards, the lady she lived with in James Street. The sight of the school steps and the steep valley sides brought back memories as did a walk along the little road to the river bridge that straddles what the evacuees had considered the boundary between Wales and England (Brithdir and Cwmsyfiog). When she returned to Sheerness, Rhoda, a qualified ballroom, old time and sequence dance instructor told *Sheerness Times Guardian* that to *dance in the Con Club was the highlight of my trip, I had my first dance in Brithdir Miners Institute when I was thirteen and I can honestly say it's because of Brithdir that I learnt to love dancing and I have been dancing ever since.*

On Sunday, June 2 1940, Rhoda was one of a number of girls who, leaving their families in Sheerness, took the special evacuees' train for the long journey to upper Rhymney Valley. According to Brithdir Girls' log book June 10 1940, she and Lily Wildish, Maureen Collins, Chrissie Munden, Barbara Roach, Annie Wood, Joyce Dowding and Edna Lawrence, as well as their teacher Miss Howells, from Sheerness Central School, started lessons in Brithdir.

Maureen Collins and Rhoda McCarthy, then 13 years old, were billeted with Nan Edwards at 7 James Street, while Lily Wildish stayed with Mrs. Clark, also in James Street. On weekends Mr. and Mrs. Clark took Lily, Rhoda and Maureen walking on Cefn Brithdir, a real treat for girls who had never seen such landscape before. Rhoda remembered not only visiting the ruined farmhouse (Ganol), Capel y Brithdir and Tegernacus Stone, but also Mr. Clark's interesting stories about each place. He showed them the crags and crannies where sheepdogs and sheep fell into the crevices and told them how Nan Edwards's grandson, with a rope tied round his waist, was lowered into the cracks to rescue the animals.

A selection of Rhoda's Memories

Rhoda Alexandra McCarthy aged 17

I remember the day we left Sheerness; the old steam loco was pulling slowly out of the station when the children at the front of the train started cheering so we all crammed to the windows. Pulling into the station was the longest troop train I have ever seen and as the two trains passed each other we waved to the soldiers. Two weeks later my mother wrote to Nan Edwards and told her that the train we all waved to was full of soldiers rescued from Dunkirk. The town of Sheerness had never seen anything so pitiful as these soldiers and their plight helped take the sadness off the children's departure as naturally all rallied round with tea, coffee, cigs and clothes.

Three weeks before Christmas 1940, Nan Edwards prepared the mixture for four Christmas cakes and asked Maureen and I to take them to Henderson's the baker in School Street, Tirphil. There were about forty people all taking cakes to the baker who cooked for the village. Two weeks later we all returned to collect them; we were all singing as we strolled along, it was such a lovely experience.

I remember an air raid, I hadn't been there long, it was one o'clock in the morning and Nan Edwards called us down stairs and we had to go into a small cupboard that she had prepared. The bombs were dropped in the next village Tirphil, we were joking about it the next day, how we had come to Wales for safety and the Germans were still bombing us.

Another experience I will never forget is when Nan asked us girls to go to Jones Henry's shop and, I was to get 'two gibbons' and Maureen to get '4lb murphys'. On our way we pondered on the names, what on earth were 'gibbons' and 'murphys'. Well first off we struggled to find the shop so we asked a lady, only to find that we were standing directly outside it, we had been looking for Jones Henry's but actually the proper name was Henry Jones's. Then when we found that 'gibbons' were onions and 'murphys' potatoes, Maureen and I sat on the shop step and laughed till we cried.

Iris Devine née Fowler, an evacuee from Birmingham, remembers:

We were taken from Smith Street School in Hockley, Birmingham to Pontlottyn, where we were given food and drinks, separated into small groups and taken to the village where we were to be billeted. I was sent to Brithdir. The most vivid memory I have of Brithdir is the Institute where we were taken; there, a row of people stood waiting for their evacuee. If you can imagine a seven year old seeing a man who had just come from working in the pit in an old mac, I remember so clearly thinking I don't want to go with him. This was Frank Pudge who I got very fond of later, but he was there to deliver me to his brother Charles Pudge and his wife Gladys.

228

When I first arrived we lived in a house behind Eddy Lewis's shop, then Eddy bought a farm and we moved to Station Terrace. I owe the Pudges so much because it was with them I developed a love of books. I read all the books, and there was a lot, in their home. Aunt Gladys would keep me up to listen to Valentine Dyall, "The Man in Black". Looking back I think she was afraid of listening on her own, that's how I got to stay up. Some nights we would hear the German planes going over knowing they were going to Birmingham and Coventry and hoping we would not hear bad news, but my mother was bombed out and lost everything. Mam came to visit us in Brithdir with my two year old sister; my mother was very distressed but was made very welcome and stayed with another family. Strange things stay in your memory like visiting Frank and May Pudge. May's mother, Granny Parry was very old, in my eyes. She was dressed all in black with a lace cap and had long thin fingers. I was scared to death of her when I first met her, yet again she told me stories, helped me with my Welsh language and sorted me out for a Welsh outfit for St. David's Day.

The memory of coal miners early in the morning coming home after night shift, seeing Uncle Charlie as black as soot and having the large tin bath waiting to wash before we got breakfast will always remain with me, especially helping wash his hair which was white when clean. It wasn't a happy time for a child to be parted from her parents, and please God it won't ever happen again, but I had a good home during those years in Brithdir and a lot of the person I am today is because of those guidelines and caring. It is quite noticeable, as my only sister and I are different in so many ways. It can only be because of the years I spent with Charlie and Gladys Pudge and the people of Brithdir.

Charles Pudge and Jane the cat relax outside the family home, Station Terrace, in 1944.

Gladys Pudge on Barry Island beach 1942.

Courtesy Iris Devine née Fowler

While at Brithdir, Iris passed the entrance examination to Hengoed Girls' School, and returned home to Birmingham five years later at the age of twelve. For her 70th birthday Iris, accompanied by her grandson, visited Brithdir. She met up with some old friends including Georgina *Geena* Baker, Dorothy Jones, Pam Davies, Grace Jenkins and Jean Wells.

Other girl evacuees to Brithdir included:

- Sisters Betty and Margaret Fenn, Birmingham, who lived with Mr. and Mrs. Alf Wells (parents to Jean), 23 James Street.
- Some, including Julia Sullivan of St. Anne's Roman Catholic School, Stepney, and Jane and Pamela Somerfield, Anerley Junior Mixed School, arrived in April 1942 and were accompanied by their parents. Their fathers

found employment locally. It seems that the Somerfield family was hosted by Mrs. Hyatt. Pamela married Hugh O'Neil and now lives in New Zealand.

- Named in July 1944, but with no reference to a previous school, was Rosina Wooldridge who stayed with Mrs. Woods.
- An entry on January 17 1945 revealed four London evacuee scholars (unidentified) were still on the Girls' School roll – Middlesex (2), Croydon (1) Kent (1).

Brithdir Boys' School log book notes that June 10 1940 school master F. Jenner and 14 boys from Sheerness Central School were the first evacuees admitted to the school. These boys, aged 11+, were taught in a separate unit with their own teacher. Other masters including W. R. Lang, A. A. Clemaghan who taught Woodwork to evacuee boys in Tirphil on Thursday mornings and evacuee boys in Brithdir on Thursday afternoons, and E. H. Bloxham, arrived in the school later.

Some of the evacuee boys named in the log book:
- Barry Ingram and Jackie Tabrett from Sheerness.
- Donald and Patrick Wilson (identical twins), stayed with Mrs. Pollock in Nelson Terrace. But, they, together with Stanley Hardy, returned to Sheerness after just thirty days in school. Stanley went home to start work while the Wilson twins went back to re-evacuate with their mother to a place nearer to Sheerness.
- Not long after, a log book entry for August 19 1940 noted *Derek Welsh and Eric Green returned to Sheerness to take up employment. There are 9 boys left.*
- October 7 1940, Colin Lambourne and Ronald Kay returned to Sheerness.
- In June 1941, 8 year old evacuee David Richard John Beck from Southall, the great grandson of Mr. and Mrs. Briffett, East View, had an accident leaving school and died at Cardiff Royal Infirmary.
- Peter Harry, evacuee from Cardiff, stayed with the Rogers family at 12 Tennyson Terrace.

Not all evacuees returned home at the end of the war: siblings June and John (in photograph) and sister Pat Blake were evacuated to New Tredegar and remained in Wales.

June's Memories:

It was in 1943 when my family evacuated to New Tredegar from Watford in Hertfordshire. I was just three years old at the time, my sister Pat was five and my baby brother John was eleven months old. My father was fighting in Egypt - he was a Desert Rat. There had been a lot of bombing in our area and my mother thought it would be safer if we came to stay with her aunty in Long Row, New Tredegar. Two incidents stand out from those early days; I can remember being afraid when they sounded the siren

at Elliot Colliery for the men to go to work. It reminded me of the time we heard sirens warning of bombings at home.

It was the time of make do and mend, my mother made all our clothes for us, and she also taught my sister and myself to knit, this was a big help as clothes and materials were on ration, and very hard to come by. I also remember sitting with my aunt making hair ribbons, you couldn't get anything for your hair so you had to make your own. We made lots of items for the home also; we would spend some nights cutting all the odd pieces of materials into strips so my mum could make a rag rug, when they were finished they were all sorts of colours and looked pretty too.

After the war, when I was about ten (right) the headmaster at our school told us that we were going to have a special visitor coming through the village. Later that day, he got all the pupils together and took us to the main street where it seemed that the whole town had turned out and were waiting for something to happen. Shortly a motorcade came along and there was 'Monty', Field Marshall Montgomery, standing up in a jeep, waving. The jeep stopped and he got out and spoke to some of us. He stood right in front of me with a big smile on his face. After speaking to several of the adults, he got back in the jeep and was driven slowly along the street. It was a great moment for a small child.

When my father came home from the war, he had to find work; he was a builder, a bricklayer by trade, unlike all my friends' fathers, who worked in the local pit. He eventually found work on a new housing estate being built in Fochriw which prolonged our stay in Wales.

The pretty young Essex girl eventually caught the eye of a Brithdir lad, and as love bloomed she stayed and, on March 15 1958, June Blake and Geoffrey Brewer exchanged vows at St. Dingats Church, New Tredegar.

Experiences of Brithdir people in the armed services

Stanley West, *Merthyr Express* correspondent

Stan West, then living at 13 Nelson Terrace, was Brithdir's *Merthyr Express* correspondent during the 1940s. His regular meticulous reporting kept readers informed about the fate of local people serving their country away from home. The following are transcribed from 1944 and 1945 reports:

1944 reports:

Jan 22: *Safe Return - Pte Stanley Wells, son of Mr. and Mrs. Alf Wells, 3 Salisbury Terrace has returned home after nearly 4 years abroad. He has served in Abyssinia, Sudan, Palestine, North Africa and Italy. His father served in the Boer War and during the last war he held the rank of Sergeant Major.*

Jan 22: *Prisoner of War - Private Andrew McLeod, SWB, has been a PoW in Italy since July 1941, is now in a prison camp in Germany. His wife is a Sergeant in the ATS. Two of his brothers are also in the services. LAC Denis*

McLeod RAF is in India and signaller Richard McLeod, RN serving abroad. They are the sons of Mrs. McLeod and the late Mr. Andrew McLeod, 16 Wellington Terrace.

Feb 12: *Carols for PoWs - A band of local men went out singing during the Christmas festivities and collected £4.12s. The members of the Cons Club made this up to £7.10s. Five boys of the village in PoW camps will receive a parcel and 30s, which has been handed to the parents. The five prisoners are: Sid Bateman, Tom Astley, Tom Williams, Andrew McLeod and David Harris.*

Mar 11: *Home on Leave - Sgt Ivor Wilcox of the Welsh Guards who is a first-class rugby player was on leave over the weekend. He is married to Olga daughter of Mr. and Mrs. Ben Watkins of Harcourt Terrace. On Saturday he played in an All Star representative match between the Northern Command and the Scottish Services at Headingly Ground, Leeds. Sgt Wilcox plays for London Welsh and the Army.*

April: *Brothers' Battle Front Meeting - Mr. R. Bennett recently received a letter from Sgt. Ron Maund serving with the PLA. describing how his unit had been changing their positions when a message from one of his men reported a motor-cyclist behind them. "Imagine my surprise," he writes, "to see that it was my brother Cecil, who was serving with the Transport." They had a few days together before moving off. He eagerly follows the local news in the Merthyr Express.*

June 10: *On Leave - Charlie Megraw, RN, son of Mr. and Mrs. J Megraw, 3 New Bristol Terrace is home on leave after a period in hospital. He has been in the Navy for three years and has seen considerable overseas duty on convoy work.*

Aug 12: *Met in Jungle - It is said "the world is a small place", this has certainly proved to be true in the case of two Brithdir Boys serving with the forces in India. A letter received by his wife, tells how L/Cpl Leslie Britton, RWF, met "Tonny" Evans in the heart of the jungle, near Poona. L/Cpl Britton has been in the army for 16 years and has served in Egypt, South Africa, France, Persia and Iraq and has been in India for more than 2 years. His wife and two children live at 6 Milton Terrace; "Tonny" Evans is a single man and his home is at 21 James Street.*

Aug 26: *Welcomed Home - Pte Tom Astley, Welch Regiment, 18 months PoW; at the collapse of Italy he succeeded in escaping from Northern Italy and making his way towards the Allied lines in the South, he was befriended by a farmer and his family who fed and concealed him.*

Sept 23: *Wounded in Europe - L/Corpl Elwyn Thomas (3rd Mons)* (right courtesy son John Thomas), *son of Mr. and Mrs. John Thomas of 28, James Street, is now a patient at Whitchurch Hospital, Cardiff. His injuries were received in the European theatre of war, and he spent five days in hospital in Brussels, and was afterwards flown back to this country. He is progressing favourably from shrapnel wounds. His wife and four children live at 3, James Street.*

Sept 23: *Italian Job - Aubrey Glyn Evans, RAMC, of Charles Street, met Verdun Williams of Bristol Terrace, in Italy. Bill Bassett is also with Williams.*

Sept 30: *Hello Don - Donald West, who is in Italy in the Royal Signal Corps, son of Mr. and Mrs. Frank West, 1 The Villas, in a letter received this week, stated that last week part of his duty consisted of driving front-line troops to a rest camp somewhere in Italy. Entering the canteen on Wednesday he was greeted with "Hello Don" from another Brithdir boy, Graham Godfrey. Graham, whose wife lives at 2 Bristol Terrace, is the son of the late Councillor and Mrs. Jack Godfrey. During the 2 years he has been abroad in North Africa, Sicily and Italy, this is the first local boy Donald has met to speak to, although a few weeks ago, attracted by roars of enthusiasm, he found a football match in progress Wales v Yugoslavia, and the chief item of interest on the Welsh side was Bill Bassett, the Brithdir and Cardiff City centre-half. Unfortunately, as the convoy was moved off before the game ended, they were unable to meet.*

Oct 7: *Brothers Meet - C.S.M. Thos. John Abraham son of Mrs and the late Mr. T. Abraham, 6 Harcourt-Terrace, is home on leave after five years abroad. Thirty-nine years old, he has more than 21 years' service in H.M. Forces to his credit, and has been in Italy, Palestine and many parts of the Far and Middle East. He recently met his brother Gnr. Wm. Abraham in the Middle East. He had not seen him for many years. Another brother is David Hayden Abraham.*

Nov 14: *Wounded in Yugo-Slavia - Twenty-four-year-old A/B, C.W. Greencombe-Lewis, only son of Mr. and Mrs T. Lewis, formerly of Brithdir, and now Canton, Cardiff, is at present in hospital at Liverpool. Wounded in Yugo-slavia, his leg was amputated below the knee, and he had been in a Malta hospital for 4 months. A/B, Lewis is the only grandson of Mr. and Mrs. Wm. George, 21 Charles Street, Brithdir and his father was a ticket collector at Bargoed GWR Station for some time.*

Dec 2: *Boys Met Abroad - A letter recently received by Mr. and Mrs. George Astley, 11, James Street, from Private A.G. Evans, serving with the R.A.M.C. C.M.F., tells how he met their son, Alf Astley. Pte Evans is a son of Mr. and Mrs. Walter Evans, Charles Street. He was riding on a lorry into town when he saw Alf standing in the roadway. They got together and started swapping experiences, and it transpired that they had been in the same hospital together, and also the same transit camp. Arthur Keitch, another Brithdir boy, had been with them.*

Dec 16: *Rugby at Brussels - Among Welshmen who played in the services rugby match at Brussels between the Army and RAF on Saturday was Sergeant Ivor Wilcox (Welsh Guards, Army and Wales). Both teams included many well-known players.*

1945 reports:

Feb 10: *Home from Europe - L/Cpl Thomas Baylis, R.E.M.E., is spending a short leave at home after serving with the B.L.A. since D Day. His wife and two children live at 11, Nelson-terrace. His brother, First Class Stoker Harry*

Baylis, R.N. was buried at the Gwaelod y Brithdir Cemetery last week as the result of an accident received at Weston-super-Mare.

April 14: *Certificate from Monty - Home on leave from Europe last week was Sergt W. John then of the Duke of Cornwall's Light Infantry. His wife, formerly Lorraine Cresswell, and their son live at 18 Old Bristol-terrace. A soldier for 14 years, Sgt John took part in the first break-through in France, and he later took part in the epic race to relieve the airborne divisions trapped at Arnhem, being themselves cut off and having to fight their way out. He has been wounded in the head, and a Certificate of Merit was recently received at his home from the 21st Army Group (Field Marshall Montgomery), which reads: "It has been brought to my notice that you have performed outstanding good service and shown great devotion to duty during the campaign in France. I award you this certificate as a token of my appreciation, and I have given instructions that this shall be noted in your record of service." Sergt. John has now returned to Europe.* Image courtesy Jacqueline Amy Tiernan

May 5: *Home on Leave - A soldier for 20 years, who has served in Normandy since D-day, Sergt. John Lewis, Wiltshire Regiment, is spending a short leave with his wife and son at their home, 4, Wellington-terrace. Wounded in Normandy, he was in hospital in this country for some time, returning through Holland to Bremen. Sergt Lewis is a son of Mrs. Lewis, 6 Tennyson-terrace, and the late Tom Lewis, D.C.M.*

May 5: *Wounded in Germany - In one of the first tanks to enter Bremen was Trooper Elwyn H. Fry, R.A.C. (Desert Rats), attached to the Inniskilling Dragoon Guards. He received injuries to the eye when his tank was blown up, and is now in hospital. He had returned from leave in this country twelve days previously. The youngest son of Mr. and Mrs. Harry Fry, 2 Station-terrace, his brother, L/Sergt Wm. Eric Fry, R.A., is also serving abroad.*

June 23: *Monty's Decoration - Phil Willetts, son of Mr. and Mrs. P. L. Willetts, Railway-terrace, has been fortunate in seeing many famous personalities on the Continent. Attached to S.H.A.E.F., he was recently in Frankfurt and had a grandstand view of the great parade, and "Monty's" decoration by General Eisenhower. His brother David is with the RAF in India.*

July 7: *From Italy - Among many local soldiers now on leave is Pte. Reg Winstone (Commandoes)* (right courtesy Louise Winstone), *who arrived from Italy. His wife, Mrs Louise Winstone, is a daughter of Mr. and Mrs. Isaac Jones (librarian), who is a nurse at Bedwellty U.D.C. Isolation Hospital, and they live at Station-terrace. Recently transferred to a Commando unit, he was formerly with the R.A. and fought in the defence of Britain, serving with the ack-ack batteries in the blitz on Swansea. From El Alamein, with the Eighth Army, he travelled through the desert into Italy. He has been*

in the Forces for five years, and his parents are Mr. and Mrs. Winstone, of Jubliee.

July 7: *Escorted King Haakon - Sig Jimmy McLeod, RN, the youngest son of Mrs. McLeod and the late Mr. Andrew McLeod, 16, Wellington-terrace, is spending a leave after being on a Norwegian destroyer some time. He has been on the Russian convoy route, and while patrolling the ports of Norway he witnessed the signing of the surrender terms in several ports. The escort of two cruisers and four destroyers which accompanied King Haakon back to this country was led in by Signaller McLeod's Norwegian destroyer Stord. Twenty-five years old he has served five years; and his two brothers are Pte. Andrew McLeod, repatriated PoW; and L.A.C. Dennis McLeod, RAF.*

Aug 11: *On Leave - In the Forces for four years, Driver James James R.A.S.C., arrived home from Italy this week; and is spending a leave with his wife and daughter at their home, 17 Herbert-street. Abroad for more than three years he has seen extensive service in South Africa, Palestine, Egypt, Tripolitania, Libya and Tunis. He took part in the landings in Sicily and Italy; and his parents are Mr. and Mrs. Morgan James, 14, James-street.*

Aug 11: *His Last Leave - Home on leave from Burma prior to being demobbed is Pte John Rowlands, R.W.F., a married man with two children whose home is at 24 Herbert-street. Overseas for three years, he served in France, North Africa and Sicily.*

Sept 8: *In European Hospital - A local soldier, Sgt. Wm. (Jock) Pollock, Scots Guards, has been in an European hospital for three months. Moved recently to a Red Cross hospital in Cervia, he is now reported to be improving. He has been in the Army since the outbreak of hostilities and took part in the first Allied invasion of Norway and three years ago went overseas and fought through North Africa, Italy and Austria. His wife, Mrs. Lily Pollock, and their son live at 12, Nelson-terrace.* (Photograph courtesy son Bill Pollock.)

Sept 15: *From Malta - A patient at Bighi Hospital, Malta, for five months, Flt-Mec, Gus Morgan, F.A.A., youngest son of Mr. and Mrs. E. J. Morgan, George Hotel, is now home. Two and a half years abroad in Gibraltar, North Africa Tunis and Algeria, he was recently recommended to the Admiral of the Fleet for carrying to safety an officer whose both legs had been severely injured. His brother Fus. Austin Morgan, R.W.F., has been in hospital in India.*

Sept 29: *From Italy - Driver William Hyatt, R.A.S.C., third son of Mr. and Mrs. W. Hyatt, 2 Tennyson-terrace, arrived home last week after three years overseas. He is a survivor from a troopship torpedoed on the way to N. Africa. He served later in Sicily and Italy where he took part in the landing at Salerno, the Anzio beach head, the landing on the Gulf of Genoa and also at Naples. Driver Hyatt received a presentation from the Conservative Club members during the weekend.*

Case studies of local men who served in World War II

Brithdir people responded to the call to arms and the stories of their experiences are many and varied. What follows are a few accounts of the wartime experiences of some local people.

Brithdir station masters

Both James Lock and W. R. Westhead, the first two men to take charge of Brithdir station post-war, saw war service.

James Lock, a man with a splendid record of war service was discharged in June 1945, and was appointed station master at Brithdir to replace A. Pritchard. Born, about 1882, in Jersey where his soldier father William was serving at Fort Regent Barracks, St. Helier, James Lock arrived in Brithdir prior to 1911. On census night 1911, a boarder in the household of James and Sarah Leadbetter at 10 Tennyson Terrace, he was described as colliery assistant timberman. His younger brother Henry was also boarder in the household. It is not clear whether James Lock saw active service during World War I, but brother, Henry, joined Gloucestershire Regiment 1st Battalion and, sadly, was killed October 29 1914 and his name is on Ypres (Menin Gate) Memorial. James Lock was mobilized September 1 1939 in Supplementary Reserves 154 (GW) Railway Operating Convoy, Royal Engineers, and proceeded to France as a sergeant and was evacuated June 17 1940. Commissioned in January 1941, he served as transportation officer in command at various ordnance depots in Wiltshire, Dorset, Shropshire and Hampshire, with the rank of captain. In February 1945, he left UK for India, where he was second in command of the Indian Railway Survey Company at Jullundur, in the Punjab.

On returning from the Forces, after serving with Royal Signals' Airborne Division in the Middle East Mr. W. R. Westhead (Llanbradach) was appointed clerk (not station master) in charge at Brithdir Station in 1949.

Bertie William George Baker

Bertie William George Baker, groom at Longdon Hall, Worcestershire, married domestic servant, Lorraine Bevan in 1934. Their children, Georgina and Edward were born at Longdon, but by the time Lorraine was pregnant with their third child the little family lived in Lorraine's home village. Bertie was called up for war service. The photograph (courtesy his daughter Georgina Greaney née Baker) shows him in the uniform of South Staffordshire Regiment, the regiment he enlisted into.

He was part of the unsuccessful Allied *Operation Market Garden*. On September 17 1944, aiming to secure Holland's river bridges for rapid Allied advance northwards into lowlands of Germany, South Staffordshire Regiment, flown to the battlefield by glider, dropped behind enemy lines. If successful, this attempt to skirt the German Siegfried line, the German defence line, might have ended the war by Christmas 1944. However, the bridge at Arnhem was *a*

bridge too far and, after 10 days of bitter fighting, the operation ended with the evacuation of the remainder of 1st British Airborne Division from the Arnhem

area. The South Staffordshire Regiment went into battle with 47 officers and 820 soldiers of other ranks, but only six officers and 133 enlisted men returned. Bertie Baker survived the battle and, separated from his unit, he avoided capture as a Dutch farming family (left, courtesy Georgina Greaney née Baker) hid him in the farmhouse chimney.

On returning to British lines, Bertie Baker joined 9th Battalion Durham Light Infantry. He was with the *Durhams* on Ibbenburen Ridge, when, on April 4 1945, they were ordered to advance on the town. On the outskirts of Ibbenburen town, they found a row of enemy-occupied houses. As they fought for each house separately, there was heavy sniper fire from German defenders. Pte B. W. G. Baker (listed as George Baker) was one of six killed during this bitter fighting. He was buried in plot 55 grave B13 at Reichswald Forest War Cemetery, Nordrhein-Westfalen, Germany. His name is on Brithdir war memorial and on a brass shield within St. Thomas a Becket Church, Pucklechurch, his village of birth in Gloucestershire.

Edward (Eddie) Brewer

Edward Brewer, known as Eddie, was my mother's oldest brother, an uncle I never knew as he died before I was born. Born 1913 in Pontlottyn, as a young child he lived with his grandparents, who later moved to Llandudno. He married Winifred Appleton in 1938.

Edward Brewer joined 12th (Home Defence) Battalion in July 1940. It was reported in *Whitby Gazette,* April 18 1941, that, on Saturday, April 12 1941, when riding a war department Ariel motorcycle, carrying dispatches from Staithes to Whitby, he crashed into an electric light standard at Hinderwell High Street and was killed. The coroner

recorded a verdict of accidental death. He was buried in the Appleton family plot in Great Orme's Head Cemetery, Llandudno. His name is carved on war memorials in Brithdir, and his wife's home town, Llandudno, and it appears in Book of Remembrance in St. Paul's Church, Llandudno.

Edward Brewer and his wife Winifred.
Courtesy Gwendoline Davies née Appleton

237

Trevor Butts

The following extracts from Trevor's letters home, written whilst stationed on Stonecutters Island, Hong Kong, are evidence of the friendship between Trevor Butts, a coal miner from Brithdir, and Ivor Bevan:

Mam I will never forget the first leave I had while soldiering at Kinmel Park; Ivor Bevan and myself, we were like two little schoolboys, we were so excited.

Mam, Ivor and myself shared one another's birthday by ourselves, just quiet and sober. We are at a little place all by ourselves; of course there are Indians and Master Gunner here, but we have a little bunk of our own, it's just toppin.

A similar theme ran through the letters sent home by Ivor, the former milk roundsman of Pontlottyn, and their close bond of friendship is confirmed in this copy of a painting of the soldier friends that accompanied the letters.

The friendship had started when, in July 1939, they met on the train, at the start of their journey to Kinmel Park Camp for military training prior to being posted to a Royal Artillery Regiment. The following owes much to Tony Banham's publication *Not the Slightest Chance – the Defence of Hong Kong 1941*, as well as to details provided by Margaret Bevan of Llanelli and David Bevan of Birmingham, widow and son of Ivor Bevan, and Margaret Saralis of Brithdir, niece of Trevor Butts.

These young bachelors were militiamen, called up in the aftermath of the Munich Crisis. They were given uniform and civilian clothes and, after a short service, expected to be discharged into the reserves. But the international situation deteriorated and, with the outbreak of war, they were absorbed into the rapidly expanding army.

On October 20 1941, Gunner Trevor Butts and Gunner Ivor Bevan were part of the force sent to defend Hong Kong and the coastal artillery batteries at Stonecutters Island. The Battle of Hong Kong, part of the Pacific campaign, started December 8 1941, when Japanese aircraft struck Kai Tak airfield on Hong Kong mainland, before turning attention to military positions on Stonecutters Island. The British, fighting alongside Canadian and Indian soldiers, were vastly outnumbered by Japanese troops, artillery and aircraft, and were soon forced to retreat to Hong Kong Island. Although initial Japanese attempts to cross the straits were thwarted, the main Japanese force landed on the island's north east coast on the night of December 18, and pushed forward, dividing the defending force which, on December 25 and 26, surrendered to Imperial Japan.

Trevor Butts, son of Herbert James Butts and his wife Ethel, was just 23 when, on December 18 1941, he was killed by a direct hit of enemy shell on his battery position at Pak Sha Wan. Like fellow servicemen in 12 Coast

Regiment Royal Artillery, Trevor Butts, Gunner 1492701, is remembered on Sai Wan Memorial, at entrance to Sai Wan War Cemetery.

Ivor Bevan, captured by the Japanese Army, was initially interned at Sham Shui Po PoW camp in Hong Kong but later transferred to Oeyama PoW Camp in Japan where he was one of nearly 700 fellow PoWs forced to work in the open-pit nickel mine in Kaya and the smelting factory in Iwataki.

Ivor Bevan and fellow PoWs, liberated by the Americans September 9 1945, began the long journey home three days later. The 55 day journey began with the train to Yokohama. Here he joined the troopship *USS Tyron* to Manila. The troopship *General Robert Howze* took him to San Francisco. He crossed the United States and Canada by train and reached Halifax, Nova Scotia on October 31. He joined the troopship *Queen Elizabeth* and reached Southampton on November 5. The next day he was issued with a train warrant, and returned home to Pontlottyn via Cardiff.

Ivor Bevan (right) became a Baptist minister. Although he never spoke of the war, the bond between the soldier pals was such that Trevor's family became his extended family. In later life Ivor took up painting, and although not the most talented of artists, his watercolour (left), based on his memory of his friend, reflects their close bond. Ivor died in 1997.

Flight Sergeant Vivian Alquin Willetts – Navigator

Flight Sergeant Vivian Alquin Willetts (known as Vivian), lost his life when his fighter aircraft was shot down by flak during a night-intruder operation over Dinard on night April 26-27 1942. Having no known grave, he is commemorated on Panel 76 Runneymede Memorial. Locally, he is remembered on his parents' gravestone in Gwaelod y Brithdir Cemetery and his name is on Brithdir war memorial.

Born April 24 1918 at 15 Station Terrace, Vivian was oldest of three children of Philip and Margaret Willetts. He was educated in the village before scholarship success took him to Bargoed Secondary School. He joined RAF on October 28 1939, and, after qualifying as an Air Observer (navigator), he was posted October 6 1940 with the rank of Sergeant, to No 23 Squadron, Fighter Command, at RAF Ford in Sussex. In December 1940, the squadron started their night fighter role, to take the war to the Germans on the near continent. The highly skilled three-man crews worked in co-operation with ground control, carrying out offensive night-intruder operations over enemy territory, using bombs and machine guns, to destroy hostile aircraft and airfields and dislocate enemy flying organisation. Promoted to Flight Sergeant sometime between December 15 1941 and January 22 1942, Vivian flew with three pilots on operations - Flying Officer Robinson (12 sorties), Pilot Officer Simpson (1 sortie) and Sergeant Millard (12 sorties including his last) and, they flew many training sorties.

On the night of April 26-27 1942, Havoc Mk1 Intruder AW398, crewed by pilot Sergeant Millard, Air Observer (Nav) Willetts and Wireless Operator/Air Gunner Robert Moore, took off from RAF Ford, West Sussex. It was one of ten aircraft despatched as part of Operation Circus, to attack Dinard-Pleurtuit airfield in Brittany. According to a letter from his Commanding Officer to his parents, Willetts, one of the best navigators on the Squadron, had done 32 night operations. Havoc Intruder, painted black and equipped with flame-damping exhausts, was hidden in the darkness of the night, but the sound of its engines alerted the enemy to its position. On this sortie, the searchlights went on, and the illuminated Intruder was hit by anti-aircraft fire. Sergeant Millard survived and was taken prisoner. Sergeant Robert Moore was later buried in Bayeaux War Cemetery, but Flt/Sgt. Vivian Willetts, the navigator, had no known grave.

His mother, Margaret Willets, wanting to know what happened to Vivian, wrote to the pilot's mother. When liberated from Stalag 357 at Kopernikus in May 1945, Sergeant John (Jack) Millard was taken to hospital in RAF Cosford. From there, on May 30 1945, he replied to Mrs Willetts thus:

The plane was hit in the fuel tanks by anti-aircraft fire and caught fire. Both Vivian and Bob Moore our gunner elected to stay with the aircraft rather than bale out and as a crew we decided to crash-land in the sea, which meant that Viv had to get his top escape hatch open to be safe because in the Havoc we were all cut off from each other and so can not help each other in case of emergency. Just before we could touch down in the sea Vivian shouted that his hatch was jammed and the next thing I knew I got a crack between the eyes and was knocked unconscious. I do not know what happened after that because when I recovered the aircraft was almost about to sink and Vivian's cabin which is below and in front of mine was completely under water and the waves was washing over me. Only a miracle could have saved him and unfortunately, no miracle happened because I shouted for him and got no answer. The place where we crashed is about 5 to 6 miles out to sea off Dinard.

Olivier Brichet, who investigated the wreckage in 1992, takes up the story:

Millard inflates his dinghy and clambers inside; until morning, he drifts with the currents. The Germans, who occupied the island of Cezembre, saw the burning aircraft land near the fort of La Conchee. They warn by radio the HQ of the Kriegsmarine [German navy] - many German boats leave Cerzembre. At daybreak, fisherman, Jean Cahu, left the anchorage of Solidor, on board the Chilly, a 21-foot fishing cutter. Around 9 o'clock while the fishing boat is 3 miles NW of Cezembre, Jean Cahu sees a guy in flight suit, head and legs projecting from a small dinghy. The man was hoisted on board, the survival craft punctured with a knife and abandoned.

Millard, his head bloodied, explains he was shot down, one of his comrades died in the plane and he has not seen the other crew member. He gives Jean Cahu a handkerchief decorated with Union Jack and the whistle of his survival gear. But it's not over, because the German armada is heading toward Chilly. Sailors of the Kriegsmarine board the boat and find the whistle and handkerchief. They hastily tow the Chilly to Saint-Malo. Millard is taken to hospital while Jean Cahu [left courtesy Daniel Dahiot via Jonathan Ives] is taken to headquarters. After a long interrogation and search of his home, he is released. After the war he received a letter of congratulations from George VI.

The body of Sergeant Robert Paxton Moore was found off St. Malo by French fishermen. He was buried in St. Malo Communal Cemetery on May 5 1942. More than a thousand French people attended the funeral, not only to pay tribute to the brave liberator, but also to show their hostility to their occupiers. In a letter to the Willetts family, March 22 1999, Claude Hellas of Plomelin, described how the angry French crowd tore to pieces the flower wreath the Germans had laid on his grave, and replaced them with flowers they had brought, and the grave was covered in flowers. In consequence, ten Frenchmen were arrested and interned in Germany. After the war the remains of Sergeant Moore were exhumed and reburied in Bayeux War Cemetery.

Sergeant John Edward Millard was haunted by the loss of his crew and inscribed the last page of his log book to the memory of Sgt. R.P. Moore and Flt/Sgt. V.A. Willetts. As pilot he was the captain of the ship, but on Havoc Mk1 Intruder, with the crew members physically separated, there was little chance of them helping each other out of the aircraft.

In his youth, Breton artist Olivier Brichet developed a fascination with the sea, and as he grew up he combined his passion for diving with his artistic talent, producing detailed, photograph-like imagery of underwater wrecks. He video records and photographs his dives and then, in his studio, sketches the wreck in pencil before using acrylic paint and airbrush. Olivier, drawing on his experience as an industrial designer, worked from plans of the boats to ensure accurate representation on canvas of what he considered beautiful wrecks cast off the French coast.

When he discovered Vivian's aircraft was a war memorial and that the navigator had gone down with his aircraft, Olivier contacted Département des Recherches Archéologiques Subaquatiques et Sous-Marines (since 1966, responsible for underwater archaeology), seeking permission to search the wreck for objects or bones to return to Britain for burial. As the administrative procedures were complicated, he abandoned the project, but he was willing to share his knowledge and, in August 2015, I received a copy of his work on the wreck and of associated photographs.

Olivier Brichet's sketch above depicts the Havoc-intruder on the brink of slipping below the waves. Pilot Millard eases his life raft into the water; the Navigator's position, situated in the nose below the pilots' cockpit, is already under water and the hatch of the wireless operator/air-gunner's compartment centre of fuselage is open.

Olivier Brichet photographed at the wreck of the Havoc 1 AW398 aircraft (Vivian's aircraft)

After several years of dedicated research of aircraft and crew-members, Association Bretonne du Souvenir Aèrien 39-45 organised a ceremony on July 18 2017 at St. Malo in honour of the three crew members. There was a service at Rocabey Cemetery and the wreck site was visited. Wreaths were laid and a plaque (right) was attached to an aircraft part on the seabed.

The Ferguson brothers

These two headstones (left, courtesy British War Graves Commission, and right, image courtesy Tim Todd) mark the graves of brothers Private Thomas Henry Ferguson and Corporal John Thomas Ferguson, sons of Emily Cooper. They both served in Welsh Regiment. The former, just 23 when he lost his life on May 27 1941 while serving in Crete, is buried in Suda Bay War Cemetery. Corporal John Thomas Ferguson had some 19 years' service in Far and Middle East including India, Singapore and Shanghai, and was recalled to his unit a few days prior to the war. When he was killed by enemy fire on August 12 1944, he left a widow and four children at 1 Milton Terrace. He was buried in Banneville-la-Campagne War Cemetery, France. According to a letter from his officer: *he was a good NCO, excellent in battle and a soldier that his family may be proud of.*

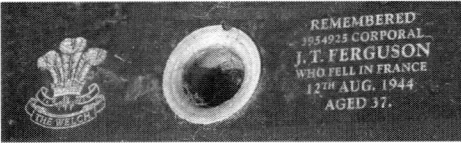

Cpl. Ferguson is remembered on the family grave at Gwaelod y Brithdir Cemetery.

Belongings of Brithdir's First War Casualty Sent Home

Private William (Bill) McDonald, 2182010 Auxiliary Military Pioneer Corps, who died June 17 1940, was Brithdir's first casualty in the war. Four years and eight months later, his family received his personal effects, held by President of Souvenir Francais at Rennes during the German occupation of France, before being passed to British Military Authorities. It was reported in the local press in March 1945, that these effects included a rosary from his sister, Elizabeth Parlor, and an ornamental leaf from a cake sent by neighbour, Mrs. S. Lee.

Born in 3 Rising Sun Row, Troedrhiwfuwch, Bill (Photograph and some details courtesy Colin Parlor, his great nephew) moved to Brithdir about 1908. When the 1911 census was taken, he was enumerated in the family home, 2 Salisbury Terrace, with his parents, William and Mary Anne, and his siblings. It is not clear when the family moved to 22 Herbert Street. Bill was a keen sportsman who played for Brithdir Bluebirds for several seasons. He is listed among the Brithdir men to go to Canada as part of the government harvesters' excursions scheme and for about 3½ years he was a logger on Hillcrest ranch, Lethbridge. War service took him to France where he died from wounds received during a Luftwaffe bombing attack on the railway complex at Rennes. He was buried in plot 1, row A, grave 48 in Rennes Eastern Communal Cemetery.

Spitfires honour Flight Lieutenant John Griffith Jenkins RAFVR

Sunday School teacher, organist, choir conductor and deacon (since a home leave just four weeks prior to his death) at Beulah Baptist Church, Flight

Lieutenant John Griffith Jenkins RAFVR (124463) was just 23 years old when he met his death in a flying accident near Haverfordwest on April 24 1945. Just before his funeral left his home, RAF honoured him with two Spitfires streaking low across the valley. He is buried in Gwaelod y Brithdir Cemetery.

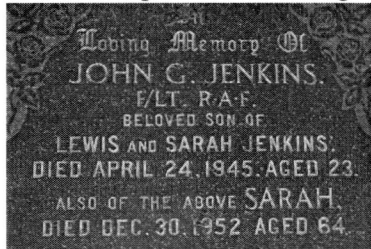

Only son of Lewis John and Sarah Jenkins, 7 School Street, he was educated at Lewis School Pengam before, in 1941, starting undergraduate studies in Cardiff where he joined the First Air Squadron. He left for Toronto, and, on completing his training, became an US Army Air Corps instructor and gunnery officer for eighteen months. He returned to UK briefly before going to the

Middle East. John Jenkins, commissioned Petty Officer on probation June 19 1942, was promoted to Flying Officer on December 19 1942. In June and August 1943, he was involved in training exercises when the undercarriage of the Halifax aircraft collapsed. He later flew a tour with 10 Squadron and was promoted to Flight Lieutenant on June 19 1944. Whilst serving with 8 (Coastal) Operational Training Unit, Haverfordwest, he was killed when his fighter aircraft Spitfire serial number EN666 crashed near Corner Piece Inn, Fishguard Road, three miles north of Haverfordwest.

His memory lived on, not just within the family, but also in his place of worship. At an unveiling and dedication service in Beulah English Baptist Church on Sunday, September 8 1946, a memorial to late Flt/Lt. John Griffith Jenkins was presented by his parents, sister, fiancée, relatives and friends, to the Church and Sunday school. Measuring 24 x 21 inches the wall plaque, imposed on an oak base, was unveiled by Mrs K. Randall and was inscribed:

To the Glory of God.
In honoured memory of John Griffith Jenkins, R.A.F. V.R., who lost his
life in an aircraft accident, April 24 1945, aged 23 years. He faithfully
and devotedly served this church – Beulah – Sunday School, Christian
Endeavour, and latterly as Deacon.
I thank my God upon every remembrance of you.

The John G. Jenkins Shield of Honour was awarded annually to the Sunday School class with the highest number of new scholars, and the names of the class and its teacher were inscribed on one of the miniatures surrounding the centre piece.

Kay's Dad, Sgt. Ivor Wilcox

Dawn Price (left), of Charles Street, was on her way to school when she saw a soldier entering the Harcourt Terrace home of Kay, her best friend. On arriving in school, she said *a soldier has just gone into your house* and Kay raced home, her father was *home on leave*. The image of him in his army uniform that day is the earliest memory Kay Dennis, née Wilcox, has of her dad, Ivor. Much of the information and photographs relating to Ivor Wilcox, son-in-law of Mr. and Mrs. Ben Watkins, Harcourt Terrace, husband of Olga, and father of Kay, are courtesy Kay.

A native of Pembrokeshire, Ivor Wilcox joined Welsh Guards in 1932. Stationed in London prior to the war, he was a Buckingham Palace sentry. His attestation papers show that on enlisting he gave his birth date as February 22 1914, but it was actually 1916.

As a Reservist in Welsh Guards he was called to the colours in 1939 and went to France almost immediately. Serving on the perimeter defences while the great retreat to Dunkirk was in progress, Sgt. Ivor Wilcox, 2733539, 2nd Battalion Welsh Guards was one of the few guardsmen to return. Entering Europe again on D-Day with the Guards Armoured Division, he fought in France, Belgium, Holland and Germany. As the German 15th Army retreated into Belgium and Holland from the Allied advance in August 1944, Hechtel, at the intersection of two main roads, was a key defensive position. The little battle of Hechtel was a serious attempt by the Germans to stop the allied attack in Belgium after the breakthrough in Normandy. On September 8 1944 Welsh Guards, including Lieutenant W. H. Griffiths commanding a Cromwell tank, were engaged by Sattler's forces and events unfolded as described by Major L.F. Ellis in *Welsh Guards at War (1946)*:

Lieutenant William Hugh Griffiths waiting in a wood, let a huge Jag-Panther (easily capable of blasting his tank wide open) pass within a few yards without seeing him and then shot it up from the rear, the gunner being his Troop Sergeant, Ivor Wilcox, who had played rugby in Welsh Trials and for the Army.

Sattler's Jager Panzer was taken to UK for evaluation and testing. Now, part of Imperial War Museum collection, the four hits from the Cromwell in the rear are visible.

The Guards Armoured Division, including Welsh Guards, attacked Hechtel and encircled the town on September 10. On September 12, Allied heavy artillery compelled the Germans to surrender. 150 Germans were killed, 220 wounded, and 500 captured. 92 British troops were killed.

When not on duty Ivor Wilcox was a first-class rugby player who played for London Welsh and as a regular in teams representing Welsh Guards and Army over several years, he won several Army "caps", and is shown left wearing his 1933-34 cap. In 1934 he helped Welsh Guards win Prince of Wales Cup at Richmond. He played for Army v Harlequins at United Services ground Portsmouth and for Army at Twickenham in Inter-Service Championship Finals. Champions 1933, 34, 36 and 37, the Army shared the trophy in 1935. He also represented the Brigade of Guards on many occasions. Stan West mentioned his rugby prowess in his March 11 and December 16 1944 reports.

A set of medals awarded to Sgt. Ivor Wilcox was offered for sale on eBay and purchased by Major Christian Borland, a Canadian collector, who was told they were the medals of a veteran named Wilcox of Welsh Guards. As Ivor Wilcox's grandson, Alan, had visited various internet sites researching his grandfather's military career, Christian, contacted him. Alan explained that it was not the family who had offered them for sale on eBay. Some time ago, two men, posing as municipal workers, arrived at his grandma's flat claiming a water leak under the kitchen sink. As one of them kept grandma occupied in the kitchen, the other rifled through her dresser drawers, and took a number of items, including Ivor's medals. Grandma, embarrassed that she had been taken advantage of, did not report the theft to the police. Later, the medals, on sale in a charity shop, were purchased by the dealer from whom Christian acquired them. The family, having acquired replicas of the medals, allowed Christian to keep the group and in return he shared information from his research, which included the original citation for Ivor's action against the Jaeger Panzer tank – which the family had never seen before.

The original citation for the Croix de Guerre 1940, with palm, which was announced in The London Gazette, December 8 1945. Courtesy Captain Christian Borland.

Prisoners of War

Stan West had informed readers of *Merthyr Express*, February 12 1944, of village lads singing carols during 1943 Christmas festivities to raise money for five PoWs from Brithdir - Tom Astley, Andrew McLeod, David Harris, Sidney Bateman and Tom Williams.

Private Thomas Edward (Tom) Astley, 1st Battalion Welsh Regiment, had been a soldier for seven years and was held captive in a PoW camp in northern Italy for 2½ years before he escaped. He spent twelve months behind enemy lines, making his way towards Allied lines in the south and was befriended by a farmer and his family who fed and concealed him. The second son of Mr. and Mrs. George Astley, 11 James Street, was welcomed home in August 1944. When his younger brother, Alfred Astley, who had been with the Royal West Kent Regiment in Greece for more than three years, arrived home in October 1945, it was the first time for them to meet for nine years.

Private Andrew McLeod, SWB, of 16 Wellington Terrace, was PoW (prisoner number 1764) in Italy from July 1941, and later transferred to Oflag 79 camp at Waggum near Braunschweig, Germany.

As Gunner David Harris was still a Japanese PoW, his street, James Street, did not celebrate VJ Day with a street party like the rest of the village and the rest of the country. They decided to wait and hope for his return. In October, every street in the village put out flags to welcome home Gunner Harris and Gunner Sidney Bateman, both returning Japanese PoWs, and there was a concert and presentation for them and their families at Brithdir Constitutional Club at the weekend. The club, having raised funds through the efforts of Wilf Bennett, Billy Redwood and Harry James (club steward and treasurer), presented each former PoW with £10 and everyone returning from overseas received £2. Gunner Harris not only received his £10 gift, but also gifts of £5 3s. 6d. which had been put to his credit as a club member during his enforced absence.

Gunner David Harris, 1605205, Royal Artillery, 3rd Heavy Ack Ack Regiment was son of David and Martha Harris, 22 James Street. He was captured when Singapore fell to the Japanese on February 15 1942. Like his fellows, he was initially sent to Changi, at the east end of Singapore Island, before being removed to wherever the Japanese war machine needed their labour. Gunner Sidney John Bateman, 5950477, 1st Cambridge Regiment, 18th Division, was the son of Jack and Minnie Bateman, 10 Bristol Terrace.

Private Thomas (Tom) Hayden Williams, 3855306, 2nd Battalion, Loyal Regiment was based in Singapore as part of Singapore Fortress's Malaya Brigade. The battalion was captured by Japanese on February 15 1942 and the survivors became prisoners for the rest of the war - at first they were held at Changi. In April 1942, the Loyals started two month's work building *Victory Road* to a planned memorial commemorating Japanese victories in Malaya.

On August 16 1942, in company with other British and Australian prisoners, Tom Williams embarked on Japanese cargo ship, *Fukkai Maru*, as part of 'B Party' bound for Takao, Formosa (Taiwan). The ship arrived at Takao on August 29. Tom and fellow prisoners

NEWS FROM PoW – A letter received this week by Mr. and Mrs. T. Williams, Ty Coch, Bute Terrace, from Manilla tells of the safety of their second son, Pte Thomas Hayden Williams (Loyal North Lancs) who was a captive in Jap hands from the fall of Singapore. Age 31 he has been a soldier for 13 years; and served in Haifa, Palestine and the Far East. His family has not seen him for ten years. Pte. Williams states they have received terrible treatment from the Japs – more than half his battalion being starved to death because they were not strong enough to work. He has lost a great deal of weight. They are now being well fed and entertained by the US Army while waiting for a boat to come home. He did not receive any mail in the 3½ years of his captivity.

Merthyr Express, October 20 1945

spent two weeks working in the docks to load *Fukkai Maru* with its cargo of rice. Finally, the ship was loaded and set sail on September 15. The PoWs were then taken not to Japan, as first thought, but to Fusan, Korea. There they were made to march for several hours around the streets to jeering crowds, who had turned out in force to witness *the collapse of the mighty British Empire.*

Tom Williams's index card was updated on September 25 1942 - *imprisoned in Chosen OA Keijo Camp.* The Japanese symbols on his index card suggest he was sent to a camp in Osaka, on July 20 1943, but no evidence has been found of this. On May 10 1945, he was moved to Fukuoka 27B Tagawa, a coal mining camp.

Tom's PoW record card. Courtesy The National Archives

Brithdir Celebrates Victory in Europe (VE day)

Daniel Jones, headmaster Brithdir Boys' Department entered in the school log on May 8 1945:

Victory in Europe Day; the boys assembled at 9.30 for a short service before being dismissed for the day and the following day was also granted a holiday.

The community had anticipated the peace announcement and was ready to decorate streets and houses with flags and bunting. Huge flags covered the front of the Institute and the war memorial was floodlit. The two days of celebration started with a soccer match - married men v Boys' Club. A service of thanksgiving was held in St. David's Church, while the three nonconformist congregations united in Beulah for a service. Nearly five hundred people gathered at the Institute Ballroom for the dance, and the day was rounded off when a large crowd assembled at the war memorial for community hymn-singing led by Harry Williams and Frank West. The second day also opened with a soccer match, Tom Braine's team v Sam Price's team, and in the afternoon there was a comic soccer match, ladies v gents, which ended when the referee awarded a penalty against the ladies and they carried him across the field and dropped him in the river. Collections at each of the soccer games provided prizes for the sports that followed. A large audience attended an impromptu concert at the Institute. Harry Williams and Frank West led community singing and the local dramatic society and friends gave a reading of *Shall we join the ladies?*, J.M. Barrie's one-act mystery play. The majority of streets had a tea party for the children. There were bonfires and fireworks and many people danced and sang until well into the morning.

This was followed in August, with two days of carnival and sports at Grove Park, organised jointly by Tirphil, Troedrhiwfuwch and Brithdir Comforts

Funds with a carnival queen selected for each village. Brithdir Institute was full for the crowning ceremony of their queen. The royal procession entered the rear of the hall and the crowing ceremony took place on the decorated stage. As Ceinwen Hodges placed the crown on the queen's head, the throne was illuminated by coloured fairy lights.

Victory in Europe carnival queen, Lettice Chard, with court ladies, Olwen James, Margaret Jones, Morfydd Maxey and Megan Edmunds, flower girls, Eileen Rowlands, Thelma Williams, Gloria Headly and Margaret James. Douglas Williams, page boy, is holding the cushion; herald, Edward (Ned) Rees sitting crossed leg.

courtesy Olwen Woods.

Post World War II

Peace had come but wartime restrictions including rationing continued for some years. People adjusted to post-war life and today's older residents may remember events such as the Coronation in 1953 as well as the many ways in which life changed in the decades that followed.

Charles Street 1953 – perhaps Coronation Day.

Among those in the photograph are - front rows: Lorna Hayes, Lynne Hayes, Gail Hutchins, Janice Hayes, Roy Davey, Robert Winston, Gerald Harris, Royston Smith, Brian Chard, Howard Cullum, Mike Edmunds, with Dawn Price, Maureen Harris, Rita White and Pam Green on end of row.   Standing: Albert and Gwyneth Gullick, Elsie Harold, Gwladys Harris, Albert Gullick, Violet Edmunds formerly Sims, Ernie and Doreen Hayes, Roy Sims, Walter and Jane Evans, William Hayes, Philip and Lettice Hutchings, Ron and Lilian Winston, Margaret Cullum, Marge White, David Williams (aka Dai Brithdir) Lily Williams, Bryn and Margaret Harris.   Courtesy Helen Jones

Constitutional Club Roll of Honour

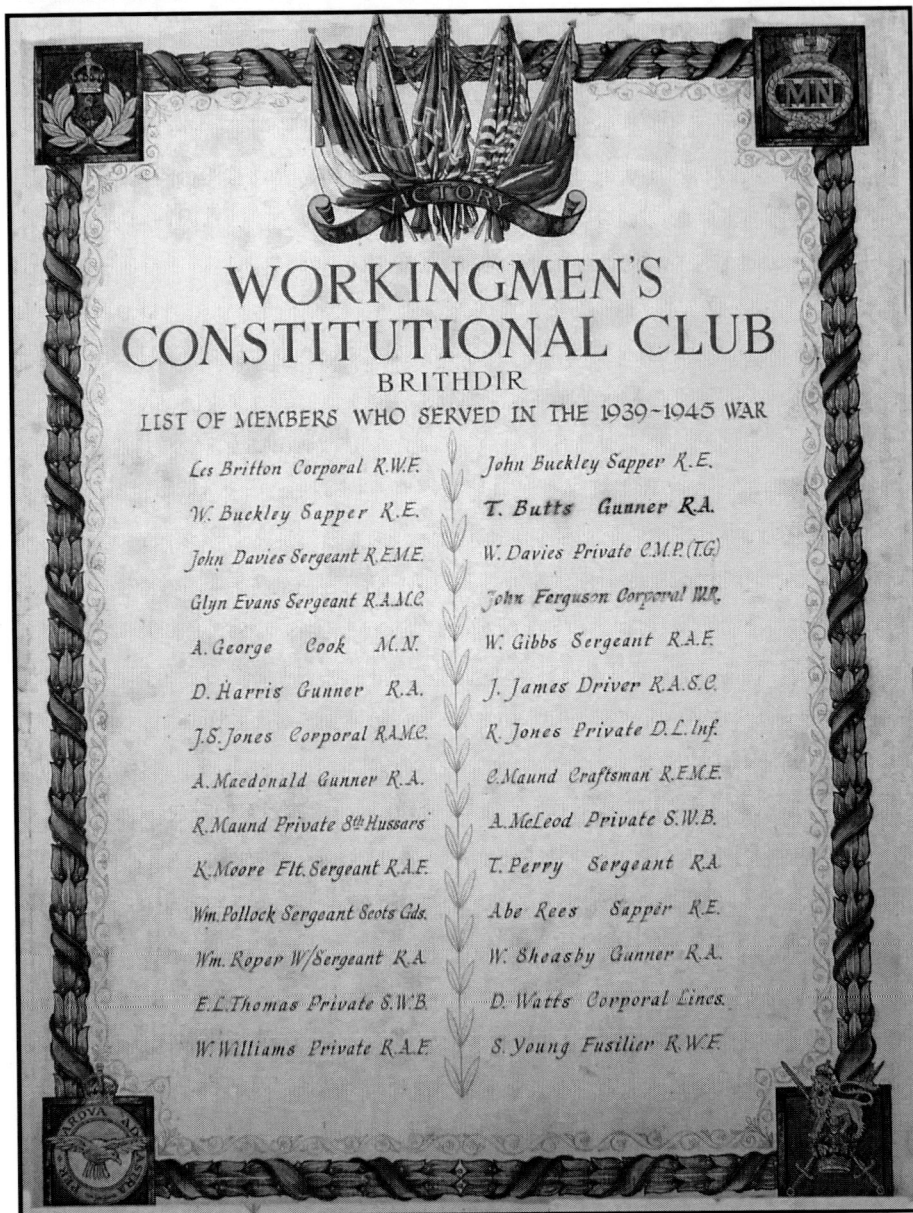

WORKINGMEN'S
CONSTITUTIONAL CLUB
BRITHDIR
LIST OF MEMBERS WHO SERVED IN THE 1939~1945 WAR

Les Britton Corporal R.W.F.	John Buckley Sapper R.E.
W. Buckley Sapper R.E.	**T. Butts Gunner R.A.**
John Davies Sergeant R.E.M.E.	W. Davies Private C.M.P. (T.G.)
Glyn Evans Sergeant R.A.M.C.	John Ferguson Corporal W.R.
A. George Cook M.N.	W. Gibbs Sergeant R.A.F.
D. Harris Gunner R.A.	J. James Driver R.A.S.C.
J.S. Jones Corporal R.A.M.C.	R. Jones Private D.L. Inf.
A. Macdonald Gunner R.A.	C. Maund Craftsman R.E.M.E.
R. Maund Private 8th Hussars	A. McLeod Private S.W.B.
K. Moore Flt. Sergeant R.A.F.	T. Perry Sergeant R.A.
Wm. Pollock Sergeant Scots Gds.	Abe Rees Sapper R.E.
Wm. Roper W/Sergeant R.A.	W. Sheasby Gunner R.A.
E.L. Thomas Private S.W.B.	D. Watts Corporal Lincs.
W. Williams Private R.A.F.	S. Young Fusilier R.W.F.

Roll of Honour, unveiled on Christmas Day 1948 in Brithdir Constitutional Club. Two members, Gunner Trevor Butts, Royal Artillery, and Corporal John Ferguson, Welsh Regiment, made the supreme sacrifice.   Reproduced courtesy Ivor Lewis

IMAGES FROM BRITHDIR'S PAST

Charles Street residents George and Elizabeth Coombes. (Courtesy Lily Williams)

L-R: **Mary Ann MacDonald née Buckley**, of Herbert Street, mother of William MacDonald remembered on the Brithdir War Memorial, (photo by Stan West, courtesy of Mary's great grandson Colin Parlor.) **Maria Cooper** wife of Joe Cooper, Rose Hill Cottages. (Courtesy Sue Opeka) **Beatrice Morgan** formerly of Ty Coch, wife of Steve Kavanagh, (Courtesy son Idwal Kavanagh, whose photo is in the locket around his mother's neck.)

Left: **Mary Matilda Thomas née Bendall** wife of William Thomas, 15 Bristol Terrace. (Courtesy Lynda Hunt).

Right: **Elizabeth Jane Morgan**, daughter of David and Elizabeth Morgan of 7 Station Terrace. She married James Morgan, son of Samuel and Sarah Morgan, 26 James Street. Image and details courtesy nephew Idwal Kavanagh

251

Left: **Isaac Jones and wife Winifred**, of Station Terrace. Courtesy Louise Winstone.
Right: **Gwladys Harris, née Lewis**, wife of Cyril Harris, Charles Street, courtesy Ceinwen Bevan née Harris.

Left: **Eddie Bevan**, one of the stalwarts of the Workmen's Institute in its heyday. courtesy Sandra Evans

Right: A young **Cyril Harris** – a native of Llantarnam, raised in New Tredegar, but it was in the village of Brithdir he lived much of his adult life.
courtesy daughter Ceinwen Bevan

Two former officials of Brithdir Bluebirds Association Football Club in season 1933, **William A. Bonney**, vice-chairman and **Harry James**, treasurer.

Photos courtesy Sandra Evans (née James), and Henrietta Jones (née Bonney).

Family photos: **John and Geoff Brewer with nephew Roy.** (right) **Irene Brewer née Cook and Geoff**. (below) cousins **Christine and Pauline**, daughters of Doug Smith and Jenny née Brewer. Christine was born 17 Wellington Terrace, Pauline born in London. Like many other family members they spent many summer holidays in Brithdir.

Four generations **Nurse Davies** centre

Eddy Baker walking his dogs, Butt, Honey and Bob. Courtesy Georgina Greaney [Baker]. Eddy was never happier than when carrying out his day job of village road sweeper. He whistled while he worked and one could hear him on the job even before catching sight of him. When he was not busy keeping the streets clean he could be found on the mountain with his dogs. Courtesy Georgina Greaney

Left: Two Brithdir characters **Marge White** and **Sylvia Rees**. Marge, holding the bird, liked a flutter on the horses, and Sylvia (Ned's sister) loved animals, her favourite was a pet mouse, which followed her everywhere.

courtesy Pat Jones

Salisbury Terrace, Festival of Britain 1951 courtesy Dorothy Heyworth

Birthday Party on the ground in Russell Street where church used to be and before cenotaph re-sited.   courtesy Kay Dennis née Wilcox

Winifred and Isaac Jones of Station Terrace, former librarian of Brithdir Workmen's Institute with their family; standing L-R are Tudor, Louise, Glanville, Agnes and Maldwyn. Seated either side of their parents are Non and Beryl. Courtesy Louise Winstone.

Mrs. Mabel Davies, of Tennyson Terrace, with Brian, Lyndon, Marlene and Ken. Courtesy Mostyn Davies.

L-R Annie Rees (Nelson Terrace) holding the jug, Mrs. Price (15 Wellington Terrace), Mrs Porter (5 Milton Terrace), Mrs Howells, Mrs Cooper, Mrs Ferguson (3 Nelson Terrace) Lily Cox
Early 1950s
courtesy Pat Jones

London trip 1950s L-R Leonard Edward with pipe, Ron Harris, Ivor Tilley, Phil Davies, Ken Maggs. Terry Wheeler with woman, Terry Woods, Peter Bennett. Front row Kelvin Edward, Ralph Thorne and Ken Jones. The one with dickie bow, the woman and the gent right of front row were locals who came out of the pub with us and joined in the photo for a laugh.   Courtesy Phil Davies

Coventry 1956, Chrissy Price at a cousin's wedding

A young Doreen Tilley. She married Ernie Hayes

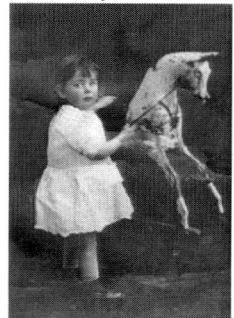

255

In September 2017 Ken and Christine Davies celebrated 50 years of marriage. This photo of guests L-R Sadie Bevan, Rita White (later Mrs Harris), Jennifer (my wife) and Irene (later Mrs Bennett) was taken at their 1967 wedding. Also in the photo is Michael Bevan.

Above: Phil Davies.

Far left: Dave, Vivian and Phil Willetts.

Left: William Davies Jones (see page 193).

Right: Noel 6½ years taken in Cardiff 1942 with parents David W Watts and Gwyneth M Davies. Courtesy Dorothy Heyworth née Higgs.

Below right: David Williams and Iris née French wedding day 9 Feb 1942 courtesy daughter Abbie Williams

Gladys Weatherley, former dinner-lady at Brithdir Infants School and Anne Edwards, neighbours of James Street, on holidays at Happy Valley, Porthcawl in 1964. The person in the middle, someone they befriended, named Val from Tonypandy – image courtesy Alf Weatherley, details Mrs Mary Williams née Edwards.

256

CHAPTER 15 BRITHDIR ALPHABET

Introduction

While everyone who has ever lived and/or worked in, visited or even passed through Brithdir is part of its story, this chapter deals with people and family groups, and some of the developments that concerned them, in more detail.

Some of these people are included because their work made a difference in one way or another, spiritually, materially or culturally, to the lives of other people, whether to people living in or near Brithdir or in other parts of the country and beyond. Others are included here as examples of Brithdir achievers, people who progressed in careers of different sorts, sometimes locally but often in more distant places. There are also narratives of families who remained in Brithdir, families who, over the generations, experienced the changes within the community.

Some of the stories come from memories shared by people who live in or have a connection with Brithdir. The internet, with email, social media and websites connected with family and local history, has made it comparatively easy to contact not only local people but those living in other parts of the country and across the world.

The variety of stories and the talent and dedication displayed by so many has been amazing, and samples are recorded in the following Brithdir alphabet.

A – Allotment holders

While the history of allotments in UK can be traced back to Anglo-Saxon times, the story in Brithdir is more recent. Reports in the local press show that in 1915 some Brithdir residents were petitioning GUDC, requesting the council find land suitable for allotments. The response was slow: not only did Thomas R. Gabe, GUDC deputy surveyor find it difficult to cover the work after surveyor (Frank Read) left for war service, but also local landowners were reluctant, demanding high prices for poor land. Brithdir residents' unwillingness to wait for GUDC and landlords to reach a settlement, plus wartime privations spurred progress:

Merthyr Express, April 29 1916: *Many townships may well follow the movement – patriotic and enterprising – formed in the village of Brithdir. A committee has been organized with Councillor Harry Brown, as chairman and W. Bartlett, as secretary, the object of which is to urge upon the inhabitants the importance of cultivating all the gardens. In order to give all encouragement, the committee intends to approach the P.D. Company to obtain manure and other forms of assistance. The idea of acquiring allotments is also kept in view.*

Merthyr Express, April 21 1917: *After considerable delay owing to prolonged negotiations between the District Council and the estate owner, matters regarding the Brithdir allotments have been adjusted, and the allotees made a start. The piece of land is situated on the side of the Bargoed-road, between Brithdir and Bargoed and fifty-two plots have been planned. The officers of the Brithdir Allotment Committee are Councillor H Brown, chairman, William*

Bute allotments in fields above Rhymney Railway line as it sweeps around the bend south of Brithdir. The allotments stretched from Gwaelod y Brithdir Cemetery gate adjacent to Tir y ferch Gryno farm to the southern end of Bute Terrace
Courtesy Paul Waites collection

Lewis, contractor, vice-chairman, Harry Williams, treasurer and William Bartlett, Gwynne's Cottages, Brithdir, secretary.

Allotment holders formed a society which went from strength to strength and, through hard work by its officers and committee, held its first flower and vegetable show in George Hotel on September 14 1925. Those officers were F. Mutlow, president, Henry Briffett, chairman, James Boddington, general secretary, William Goodwin, financial secretary, Hector Briffett, treasurer, and the committee comprised Messrs Will Gibbs, James Nicholas, M. Price, C. Butler, Edmund J. Morgan, T. Davies, A. Davies, D. Rideout, R. Phillips, John Curtis, James Inseal, W. Greenaway and Tom Perry.

Many of the Brithdir allotment holders were not far removed from their rural backgrounds and seemed to have an in-born feel for the soil. One such man was Danny Darcey (right courtesy Bill Rogers), who, an immigrant from Ireland, arrived in Brithdir as a young man. He found work in a local pit and lodgings with Elizabeth Rogers in 12 Tennyson Terrace, where he stayed, as part of the family, for 60 years. He loved his allotments – one at the Bute and the other alongside the Boys' School behind Salisbury Terrace.

259

Granville Brewer was another local man to derive great pleasure from his allotment. As a 12 year old in 1941, he accepted the offer from allotment secretary, Elwyn Mathews, to take a half-plot. It was not long before he took over the full plot, and later had a second plot also. At the time of writing, Granville, aged 87, is still working the ground.

While, by the later twentieth century, allotment holding fell out of favour across the country, allotments have regained much of their popularity among those seeking both the outdoor life and fresh food, produced organically.

B – Bevan family

The Bevan family merits special attention as it has been represented in the community from the 1850s to the time of writing.

John Bevan moved from Llangyfelach, Swansea, to Mynyddislwyn prior to 1827. Having married Elizabeth Williams, he settled at Pontaberpengam. According to the 1841 and 1851 census returns, seven of their children -- William, Ann, John, Sarah, Henry, David and Thomas -- were born in Mynyddislwyn, while youngest child Mary was born in Bedwellty. On December 31 1851, John Bevan, collier at Glanddu colliery (near present day Tiryberth), was cutting coal when he was killed by a roof fall.

In April 1854, oldest son, William, married Alice, daughter of Llanblethian tailor William Lewis and Jane (née Thomas) at Beulah Welsh Baptist Chapel, Newbridge, Monmouthshire. Alice signed the marriage certificate but William made his mark. It was William and Alice who took the Bevan family to Brithdir and, as noted on page 32, leased land (32 perches, about quarter acre), marked E on Brithdir Estate map 1858. Like John Morgan, lessee of adjoining plot marked F, William Bevan erected a cottage on his plot. Both William Bevan and John Morgan headed households in their cottages when the 1861 census was taken, and both men built two more cottages on their plots within the following decade. This row of six dwellings cut into the mountainside, consisted of two flagstone floored rooms downstairs, with stone stairs leading to two rooms on the upper level. Directly outside the front doors, a flagstone pathway, the length of the row, separated the dwellings from their gardens, beyond which were further buildings, used as stables and, later, as garages. At first the cottages were called Bryn Tawel (Quiet Hill), but when the 1901 census was taken, those erected by William Bevan were recorded as 1, 2 and 3 Ivy Row and the three John Morgan built listed as 4, 5 and 6.

At the time of the 1861 census, William and Alice, together with infants John and Jane, lived at Bryn Tawel. The family grew with four more children, Elizabeth, George David Lewis, William and Alice, born before 1872. A gravestone in Caersalem chapel burial ground, Aberbargoed, records that father, William, died March 5 1876, aged 48. His widow, Alice, continued to live in Brithdir until her death, December 24 1910, and although, on December 28, she was buried at Caersalem, her name does not appear on the gravestone.

260

While his siblings moved to neighbouring villages or further afield, George David Lewis Bevan, known as Lewis (shown right), remained in Brithdir and some of his descendants are still there at the time of writing. Following his 1890 marriage to Sarah, daughter of Thomas and Martha Miles of Cwmsyfiog, Lewis lived with his widowed mother, Alice, at 1 Ivy Row, and there he and Sarah raised 10 children – Martha May, Alice Maud, William Henry, Bronwen, Lewis Trevor, Olwen Sarah, Emily Ira Myfanwy, Edward Thomas, Tyrwen Ceridwen and Elizabeth Lorraine. Although, between 1911 and 1918, Lewis and his family moved to 6 Station Terrace, No. 1 Ivy Row remained in the family. Sadly, Lewis died September 5 1939, in the ambulance bringing him home from a Cardiff hospital. When his widow, Sarah, died April 11 1958, she was buried with him in Gwaelod y Brithdir Cemetery. Although some of the children of Lewis and Sarah, moved from the area, the Bevan line continued in Brithdir.

Sarah Bevan née Miles (seated) with her daughters, left to right: Olwen, Alice, Tyrwen, Bronwen, May, Ira and Lorraine. Sarah was often referred to as *Snow White* because of her daughters' small stature.
Courtesy Georgina Greaney who with Geraint Bevan provided many of the family details.

In 1920, Alice Maud Bevan (born May 1896) married Owen Griffiths. Born in Llandegai, Caernarvonshire, Owen was son of Robert Griffiths and Catherine (née Parry). The Griffiths family was one of a number of families to move from the troubled North Wales slate industry in search of a better future in coal mining. It is not clear when the family arrived in the local area but the birth of daughter Olwen was registered in Bedwellty 1906. When the 1911 census was taken, the family was in Phillips Street (near Tanlan Square), Cwmsyfiog, and father

Brithdir Old Age Pensioners on the occasion of an annual outing. Seated third and fourth from left are sisters Olwen and Alice (née Bevan). Alice was a bubbly character, the life and soul of any party. She played piano and led the singing at pensioners' meetings.

Robert was *building stone quarry foreman* in employ of Powell Duffryn Steam Coal Company while his two oldest sons, Thomas and Robert, were *miners in stone quarry*, and Owen, aged 13, was *apprenticed butcher*.

Owen and Alice started married life in Phillips Street where children Gwynfryn (Gwyn) and Gloria were born, in 1921 and 1924 respectively. After that they lived in Brithdir, first at Co-op House, attached to Co-op Stores, Station Terrace, where Dolores was born, May 23 1928, and Menai, April 29 1930, before moving, in 1931, to Rose Cottages (21 Bristol Terrace) where son Trevor was born July 29 1935. A few years prior to her death in 1980, Alice left Rose Cottages for a new flat in Bristol Terrace - on former gardens to Rose Cottages, where Owen had once worked an allotment.

Aged 18, son Gwyn joined the Royal Navy in 1939. On one occasion, his ship was torpedoed by a German submarine, but although in the water for several hours, he survived. While stationed at Clyde in 1942, he met Patricia Louise McLaughlin at a dance in Greenock Town Hall and, post-war, they married. Gwyn and Pat were living at Rose Cottages when they celebrated 60 years of

marriage in 2006. Their five children, Trevor, Eddie, Margaret, Kathleen and Lynne, grew up in Brithdir. While Trevor, Eddie and Kathleen no longer live within the community, Margaret and Lynne do. Sadly, both Gwyn and Pat passed away in 2009. At the time of writing, their granddaughter, Laura Davies (Kathleen's daughter) lives in the house.

Dolores (left) inherited her mother's singing talent. As a child she loved to sing and from the age of 10 she had singing lessons from Zoe Cresswell. She enjoyed performing in school St. David's Day concerts and, having rehearsed in home of Bryn Maxey who played the piano, she was well prepared for her parts in Penuel Sunday School anniversaries. During the 1960s and 1970s Dolores often entertained in Brithdir Constitutional Club, singing songs from the musicals, her favourite being *This is the Moment*, (*Jekyll and Hyde*). Dolores holidaying with husband William (*Bill*) Prince, won talent shows at Butlins, Minehead, and Pontins Sands Bay, Weston-super-Mare eleven years running (2002-2013). At the time of writing, the petite songstress Dolores is 89 and still singing, performing every Saturday in Trefil Rugby Club's concert room.

While Alice's singing genes passed to Dolores, her humour genes went to youngest son, Trevor, one of the village characters. He married Gillian Gillard in 1955. At the time of writing, Trevor and Gillian live in 1 Wellington Terrace (my grandmother's old home) and their son, David, residing in Harcourt Terrace, is part of yet another generation of the Bevan family in Brithdir.

In 1925, Olwen Sarah, known as *Lol*, married Brithdir-born Harry, son of Morgan and Blanche James of James Street. For about thirty years, Lol and Harry lived in 1 Ivy Row where they raised three children, William (*Bill*), Olwen and Sandra. Later they made their home in 9 Harcourt Terrace, where they celebrated their golden wedding (left). Harry died 1976 and Lol, then 87, in 1993. Daughter Sandra married Michael Evans in 1963, and, at the time of writing, they live in Harcourt Terrace.

Edward Thomas (Eddy) Bevan married Catherine (Kate) Thomas of Rhymney in 1939 and, apart from a brief spell at Rose Cottages, they spent their married life at 1 Bristol Terrace. On the demise of his mother, Sarah, in 1958, Eddy inherited the family home at Ivy Row, and, after a century, it passed out of the family and was sold in 1960. The Bevan name continued in Brithdir with son Michael, shown on right as a young

boy with his parents. He married Sadie Davies in 1966 and they made their home in James Street. Sadly, Mike passed away shortly before this book was published.

Tyrwen (*Tyr*) married Brithdir-born Ivor Harris in 1936. Many youngsters of my era remember her serving our sweets in Roffi's shop. Her kind gesture as the first person to meet and greet the Roffi family when, after a long journey from Bardi, they stepped off the train at Brithdir station, meant the Roffi family employed *Tyr* for many years. On right she is shown with her husband and daughter Pat, Whitsun 1952. Tyrwen passed away 2002 and, at the time of writing, Pat does not live in Brithdir (Family Photographs: Courtesy Sandra Evans née James)

C – Concerts and such like

Reports in the local press show that local people were regularly entertained by public performances of all sorts in the first half of the twentieth century. This was especially so in the inter-war years when they provided much-needed stimulus and activity for people of all ages. New Hall was an ideal venue for such performances, and not only was there no shortage of talent within the community, but also there were people with the ability and dedication to cultivate that talent within the schools, the places of worship as well as the various local groups. While several members of the West family (see details pages 347-356) were ably and actively involved in such training, there were others who also contributed. Rehearsals were social occasions and like the performances they helped many, especially young people, gain confidence in performing in public and in working within a group. Sometimes local people competed, as individuals or as part of groups and choirs, in eisteddfodau in Brithdir and elsewhere. What follows, just a sample of some inter-war concerts and other performances reported in the local press, illustrates the variety in an era when the community not only made its own entertainment but also benefited from the fundraising performances.

Sometimes, local performances were dedicated to helping needy local individuals as in the case of a concert at the newly-opened New Hall on September 22 1924 when Aeolian Concert Party (then comprising Ivor Davey, David Jones, Stan West, Phil Moore, Tom Jones, comedian Will George and pianist-conductor James George), performed to a large audience to raise funds to support H. Whale of Brithdir, who had been unable to work for some months.

For decades, many Brithdir children grew up performing in Sunday School anniversaries in their place of worship and, as young adults, they took part in drama, opera and cantata nurtured by the societies within those places of worship. Groups from St. Paul's Church, Penuel, Wesleyan and Beulah chapels, as well as Congregationalists, performed before large appreciative audiences in New Hall, and guest chairmen were frequently amazed at the high standards and professionalism shown. The principal artists of *The Magic Cup*, Ivor Day (tenor), Zoe Cresswell (soprano) and Will Phillips (baritone), were highly praised by chairman Dr. Gwylim Rhys Pennant, while at another concert Dr. Maunsell (of Tirphil) voiced amazement at the galaxy of talent in Brithdir. Beulah Baptist Choir, under conductor Phil Moore, gave regular performances of the operetta *The Royal Jester*. During the General Strike, a variety concert at New Hall, presented by scholars of Wesleyan Sunday School, attracted large audiences on each of its three nights. The Congregationalists, with choir and orchestra directed by Harry Williams, staged the operetta *The Wishing Cap* in New Hall over two nights in December 1928. The accompanist was Bryn Maxey and the cast included Brithdir girls, Agnes Jones, Louisa Jones, Lorraine Bevan, Mildred and Ceridwen Davies. On another occasion they performed *Zurika, The Gypsy Maid*. St. Paul's Church Choir performed the operetta *The Enchanted Rose* (based on *The Sleeping Beauty*) in which Zoe Cresswell played Princess Charming, and Don Bird was Prince Braveheart.

It is not clear when the local YPS, part of a worldwide interdenominational Christian youth organisation, was formed but it was active in the inter-war years. Through its stimulating activities YPS helped local young people develop their talents and confidence in a difficult period and showed them how they could be useful members of the local community. To help raise money for Brithdir Division, St. John Ambulance Brigade, they performed the operetta *The Magic Cup* on three consecutive evenings in early February 1925 at New Hall. Soon after, they started rehearsals for another performance and in November, again over three nights in New Hall, they entertained with the operetta *The Magic Ruby*. The following year, they performed the operetta *Pearl the Fishermaid*, in aid of the local Boot Fund, and took *The Magic Ruby* to venues in Aberbargoed, Hollybush, Deri, Cefn Forest, Abertysswg, Phillipstown and Tredegar to help raise funds for the local strike committee. As their conductor, Roland West was largely responsible for ensuring that these young people gave of their best. They were supported in performances by his wife, Amelia, at the piano and an orchestra comprising W. Haig, Baden Price, John Connelly, Cyril Hewitt and Morfydd Meyrick.

Just as Brithdir performers visited other communities, groups from other villages entertained in Brithdir. During the year of the General Strike, Brithdir people enjoyed performances by Aberbargoed Glee Party, Brynmawr Troupe of Dancing Children, Bargoed Salvation Army Band, Rees Christy Minstrels of Tredegar, Brithdir Savannah Minstrel Troupe, New Tredegar Choral Society, Ystrad Mynach's Songbirds (a concert party of young soloists) and Bargoed Cambria Gleemen. From time to time, a drama was presented, for example Tredegar Star Dramatic Society performed *The Octoroon Girl*, St. Mary's Dramatic Society of Fochriw entertained with *Simon Lee* and Nazareth Amateur Dramatic Society from Deri gave two dramas *Saved* and *The Factory Girl*.

D – Daffodils for St. David's Day

I could fill this book by recounting the memories of St. David's Day celebrations in Brithdir schools shared with me. I remember the St. David's

Day when I was armed with a silver sword and green shield emblazoned with a red dragon, hand-crafted by a local carpenter. Readers who attended the village schools will have their own memories to add.

The following, taken from reports in *Merthyr Express*, March 5 1935, illustrate how the day was celebrated in all three schools under headteachers Henry Judd, Mair Davies and Muriel Davies in that year.

The morning of St. David's Day 1935 in each of the three schools started with talks about the patron saint before teachers and scholars celebrated in song, recitations and drama. The names of those who took part are listed in the newspaper.

- In the Boys' Department there were pianoforte solos by Norman Cattermole, John Jenkins and Austin Morgan; banjo solos and trios by Sidney Bateman, Willie Harris and Trevor Butts; recitations by Leslie White and Willie Coleman; solos by Willie Williams, Ivor Ashley and Vivian Lloyd, and a mouth organ solo by Ivor Jones. In addition, there were short addresses on *Welsh Ideals* and on the life of Joseph Haydn. One new feature in 1935 was a series of gramophone records of Welsh choral items and national songs. The pupils also sang a number of Welsh songs.

- In the Girls' Department the celebration opened with *Cwm Rhondda*, after which the headmistress spoke about St. David's Day. Girls of Standards 1 and 2 performed Welsh dramas: Standard 1 *Mary Jones and her Bible* and Standard 2 *Tywysog Cyntaf Cymru*. Standards 3 and 4 sang Welsh folk songs. Standard 4 performed the drama *Llewelyn and Pistol*, Standard 5 gave Welsh recitations while senior scholars performed Welsh folk dances.

- In the Infants' Department, the children sang Welsh folk-songs, recited and dramatized nursery rhymes.

The following medley of photographs taken on various St. David's Days captures the atmosphere of the day across the decades.

Sisters Dorothy and Margaret Jones of Cemetery House photographed in 1940 outside Mixed Department. Courtesy Dorothy Hawkersford née Jones. In the same year *Merthyr Express* noted *Every pupil in Brithdir Girls' School dressed in Welsh costume, some of the costumes worn were over 100 years old.*

St. David's Day 1965: Cynthia and Dulcie Porter in their Welsh outfits. Courtesy Bethan Roberts.

266

The smiles tell the story of an enjoyable c1935 St. David's Day at Brithdir School. The two girls out front are Beryl Jones in her Welsh outfit and carrying a stool with Eirwen Maxey; others in the picture are unknown.

Courtesy Ann Louise Winstone

The board, shown in the foreground of this photograph, courtesy Millie Davies, reads:

Ysgol Merched Brithdir

Gwyl Dewi Sant 1928

Brithdir Girls School

St. David's Day 1928

The school building in the background is typical of the local architecture with the light brick decorative features around door and window.

This photograph, courtesy Morfydd Olsen, shows how, in 1938, an imaginative teacher arranged the girls to form the outline of the map of Wales

St. David's Day 1954: L-R Back, Ann Duggan, Lorna Hayes and Myrtle Williams. Front row L-R Ann Morris, Christine Gabb and Linda Williams. Courtesy Anne Machin, names by Ivor Williams.

Below - St. David's Day 1970: From their cheerful smiles it is obvious these pupils of Brithdir Mixed School are proud to be Welsh. Back row, L-R: unknown, Mostyn Davies, Keith Rees, Robert Jones and Donald Williams. The three boys in front of them are Paul Buckley, Gary Bennett and Ian Henderson. 2nd row L-R: Carol Harding, Beverley Taylor, Helen Jones, Beverley Lewis, Danna Hughes, Jill Hodges, Lynne Phillips and Sian John. Front row, L-R: Janet Edwards, Julie Williams, Jackie Clarke, Diane Howells, Wendy Phillips and Angela Brewer. Names courtesy Angela Phillips née Brewer.

E – Equestrian

Yvonne Garner

Born in 1940, Yvonne, daughter of Philip and Lovaine Garner, 17 Wellington Terrace, has a life-long passion for horses. Since childhood, she has filled sketch book after sketch book with hundreds, if not thousands, of drawings of horses. Today, people of the horse world refer to her as *the renowned Welsh equestrian artist Yvonne Garner*.

Yvonne, a self-taught artist and, at the time of writing, living in Aberbargoed, is often, palette in hand, at the easel applying oils onto the current canvas. Her home is her studio, and its walls are covered with framed paintings, ready for dispatch to stud farms across UK, Europe and beyond. Nearer home, her paintings hang on the walls of Gwaelod y Brithdir farm and Cefn Brithdir farm, and there is one in my home.

During the past five years, Yvonne has produced beautiful paintings for The Welsh Pony and Cob Society (WPCS) fundraising auctions.

Welsh mountain pony mares, foals and stallion running on an open hill sold President's Auction at WPCS AGM at Saturday March 28 2015. Brightwells auctioneers secured a sale price of £110.

Five show ring champions, L-R: Nebo Daniel, Llanarth Flying Comet (top), Cyttir Telynor (centre), with Derwen Replica and Parc Welsh Flyer (bottom). Commissioned by WPCS for 2017 auction,

Yvonne's images of ponies roaming free on Welsh hills are a popular series. Those depicting horses in wintry scenes support Hillside Animal Sanctuary of Norwich as they are printed as Christmas cards for sale, and the original paintings are sold with proceeds to the sanctuary.

Nowadays, most of Yvonne's work is commissioned, as for example, the delightful portrait (left), for a lady from Isle of Wight, showing her pony *Isle of Wight Spellbound*. There is no fancy name on the painting (right) which was done purely for the artist's pleasure.

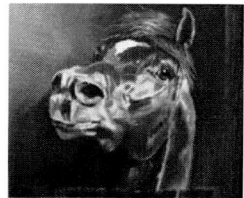

Yvonne Garner's paintings are enjoyed by many, her tally to date is about 3,000 and she has no thoughts of hanging up her paint brush any time soon.

Olympic Boy and *Treason Trial*

This extract from Alan R. Bennet's *Horsewoman: The Extraordinary Mrs. D.* (1979) relates to Louisa *Louie* Dingwall née Foott (1893–1982), one of the first English female racehorse trainers.

Olympic Boy was a yearling colt which had been injured on a flight from Ireland, leaving him concussed and blind. Louie bought him and managed

to restore his sight and nurse him back to health. Amazingly the horse went on to win four races and be placed nineteen times, later retiring to stud. This was the period when the few women trainers in the country were campaigning to be officially recognised. Louie herself was ejected from the weighing area of a racecourse by the Duke of Norfolk, a steward of the Jockey Club, while paying her entry fee for a horse. She had been a trainer for thirty years but was still without status. Finally, in 1966, the Jockey Club conceded to the women and Louie became one of the first female licensed trainers in the country. There were more successes including a triumphant trip to France in 1968 when Treason Trial won the Prix des Anemones and the total prize money was over £6,000.

Elwyn Evans, Nelson Terrace, who supplied photographs and details in this account, was commissioned by Louie to manufacture a pair of wrought iron gates for her stable yard, Yew Tree Stud, Goodworth Clatford, Andover. When he delivered the gates, he found a photographer in the yard preparing to take photographs of *Treason Trial* and *Olympic Boy* for a sales brochure. Observing the smartly dressed Elwyn, Louie asked him to hold *Olympic Boy*. The other person in the photograph is also from Brithdir, Ken Evans of Bristol Terrace, head stable lad at Yew Tree Stud. Louie often teased Elwyn that she had more enquires about him than the horse.

Michael *Mike* Bevan, local jockey

In the mid-1950s, Mike often rode *Crystal* and *Troedy*, owned by Ron Prosser of Troedrhiwfuwch, in the popular Galloway races in Bargoed Show. Many older Brithdirites recall Mike, in the silks of Milton Bradley of Chepstow, on mounts such as *Sunshine*, *Cindy*, *Blue Boy* and the big grey *Silver Dollar*. It was on the latter that Mike competed at a point-to-point meeting at Nelson and, in 1958, won the Empire Games Stakes at Cardiff.

F – Emlyn Foward

Emlyn Foward (left courtesy Pauline Jones, née Evans) was a well-liked, generous man who put much back into his community. A school teacher, rugby player and youth centre officer, he related well with the generation growing up in the village in the 1940s and 50s.

During the war, Emlyn Foward served as a Bevin Boy. Chosen at random to work the *underground front* fuelling Britain's war by mining coal, his uniform comprised boots and hard hat, and his weapon was a shovel. He hated it. Emlyn Foward died before, sixty years later, Bevin Boys were awarded Veterans Badge (right). By profession, Emlyn Foward was a school teacher. He was an effective teacher, liked and respected by both pupils and colleagues. Outside work, his main interest was rugby, a game he was well suited to. He was part of a very successful Bargoed team and its captain 1952-1953 (see *Bargoed RFC 1950-1960 Gelligaer* Journal Volume 20). While he did not secure international honours, he played against men like Roy John, Don Hayward and Rhys Williams who distinguished themselves with Wales as well as British and Irish Lions.

Bargoed RFC Season 1951-52: Emlyn Foward standing behind Glyn Morgan, club chairman who is seated centre front row. To left of Emlyn Foward is Bryn Jenkins, police constable, Brithdir.

Plaque presented to Emlyn on his selection for Welsh rugby trial match. Note incorrect spelling of his surname.
Courtesy Pauline Jones née Evans

BARGOED R.F.C.

PRESENTED TO
EMLYN FORWARD
IN RECOGNITION OF
PLAYING IN
WELSH RUGBY TRIAL
SEASON 1951-1952.

Emlyn Foward, second from left in back row, stands tall among teaching colleagues at Graddfa Secondary Modern, Ystrad Mynach.

Brithdir County Youth Centre opened in the Girls' School on Tuesday evening, March 9 1954 with Emlyn Foward, officer in charge of the club, with Dorothy Jones and Anita Goode providing art and craft classes. There were rules to follow and Emlyn made sure club members did. During the first part of the session there was an interesting and useful range of classes available and he would not allow the playing of records and dancing to start until members had taken part in at least two of the classes.

G – Gambler – Joseph Davies

Joseph Morris Davies, born about 1880, was raised in George Inn village. In 1884, his father, David Davies, under-manager at Cilhaul Pit (near Deri) fell down the mineshaft, leaving widow, Louisa, to bring up their six young children (including Joseph). It is not clear when Louisa and her family moved to George Inn where she kept George Inn Hotel, but, in 1888 she married John Thomas, a locomotive driver at Cilhaul. Some of the following information is based on an audio tape of an interview recorded in 1973 when Joseph Davies was 93 years old, and now held at South Wales Miners' Library.

Aged 13, Joseph Davies started work, striking for a blacksmith in Abernant Colliery. The colliery, sunk by Bargoed Coal Company in 1880, was near Argoed, some 4 miles distant from his home. Thus long, hard days, walking over the mountain, whatever the weather, to and from his shifts, and all for two shillings a week. About two years later, he became the first haulage driver in the new Coed y Moeth Colliery, much closer to his home, and paying him two shillings and eleven pence (2/11). Another two years on, and Joseph secured a job as haulage driver underground at West Elliot Colliery, that paid him three shillings and tu'pence (3/2) a day. Joseph Davies proudly boasted:

Elliot Colliery as seen from top of Cefn Brithdir mountain

Courtesy Paul James, Bargoed

I drove every engine that was in West Elliot Colliery. All the engines that they had; South Engine, the Face Engine, the Princess May, the Middle and the North Engine, I drove them all.

Joseph Davies lived in George Inn Hotel until his mother died when he was 20, after which he drifted from job to job. He was a mining engineer (above ground), living in rooms in 22 Station Terrace when the 1901 census was taken. After a stint in Elliot Colliery, he went north to Newcastle where he found work in Armstrong Whitworth's shipyard, but his sister's illness cut short his stay there and he returned to haulage driving in Elliot Colliery. He married Beatrice Jane, daughter of Edmund and Margaret Richards, Half Way House Inn, Pengam. It is not clear when he left Elliot Colliery, but he and his wife moved to Maesteg where he became landlord of Garne Inn.

Joseph Davies described himself as *the best known gambler in South Wales*, and it was his love of gambling that led to his loss of licence. He forgot to lock the pub doors after *stop tap* and the police walked in on him and another playing a game of crib for £50. Gambling was a crime and with the money on the table, he was caught red-handed. His wife and their two sons moved to her parents in Half Way House Inn and, in 1905, Joseph Davies sailed from Liverpool to Halifax, Canada via St. John's, Newfoundland. After a brief spell in Toronto, he moved to Chicago where he worked for Illinois Steel Company of America. There he met Ed Pendry Williams, a friend and former workmate in West Elliot Colliery. Soon the two of them headed for California, paying their way as hobos. He learned the dangerous art of freight train hopping, hitching a free ride between the buffers, on top of the carriages, sitting on the front of the engine, or, most dangerous of all, riding the rods. He recalls one time being thrown off a train with about a hundred others, and forced to find somewhere in the shade to sleep until the next freight train came along.

He travelled via Kansas City, Denver, Salt Lake City and then into Nevada. At Goldfield, Nevada he found work as an engineman in a goldmine, earning five dollars a day. Readers may be interested to note that Joseph Davies missed out on meeting two of Goldfield's famous residents, Wyatt and Virgil Earp as Virgil died there in 1905 and Wyatt, deputy sheriff in 1904, left Goldfield shortly after.

Joseph Davies found it easy to live on a dollar a day, and the other four dollars went to satisfying his passion for boxing. In Goldfield, on September 3, 1906, Joseph Davies saw one of the classic fights in the history of boxing, the championship fight between two great lightweights. Joe Gans (right) faced Oscar *Battling* Nelson (left) in a 45 round showdown for Gans' lightweight title. The late afternoon fight, starting just after 3 p.m., saw ring temperatures in excess of 100°F. Gans entered the ring carrying an umbrella to shield himself from the hot Nevada sun. In the 42nd round, Nelson hit Gans with a low blow that was quickly ruled a foul and Joe Gans was declared the winner of the fight by disqualification. Images courtesy Martin Bradford, Plano, Texas.

Joseph moved on to Rawhide where, in December 1906, a new gold rush had started. When he arrived, its population was housed in a few tents, but the town grew very rapidly with the population rising to upwards of 5000. He witnessed a gun-fight in the local saloon. When a man came in, the barmaid ducked behind the bar only to reappear brandishing a revolver. The man pulled out his gun and fired, but the barmaid's bullet found its mark first, and she killed him.

Using skills learned in his work in Welsh collieries, Joseph Davies had no trouble finding work. He travelled on, working his way over Emigrant Gap, the steep pass through the Sierra Nevada mountains used by migrant wagon trains. He noted that when he reached San Francisco the scars of the April 1906 earthquake and ensuing destructive fires were still visible.

Exactly what Joseph Davies did over the next few years is unclear. He was a gambler and recalled that *In Reno, Nevada, I put a thousand dollars on the red, in roulette, and it came up black* – when that was is not clear. He mentioned being in Seattle, working as a blacksmith in a lumber camp high up in the Cascade Mountains and accessible only by horse, and also, having been to Montana.

Later he determined to see Jeffreys and Johnson fight for the world heavyweight boxing championship. This was originally scheduled for San Francisco June 1910 but was transferred to Reno. By then, Joseph had had enough: he wanted to go home, but had no money. He wrote to his wife, and she sent him enough money to get back across the Atlantic, first by train to New York and then sea to Glasgow. He says he was back in Wales in 1909 but 1910 seems more likely. Ivor Williams, one of his first colleagues in Elliot Colliery and then engineer at Bedwas Colliery, secured him a job in Bedwas Colliery, and he remained working there until, aged 74, he was forced to retire. In a working life of sixty-one years, Joseph Davies was never out of work, working as winder while new shafts were sunk during the 1912, 1921 and 1926 strikes.

H – Hares family

Ernest Hares (1904-1960)

Stepping on American soil on October 31 1922, Ernest Hares was the first member of the Hares family to take his talent to America. Much of the information as well as many of the photographs in what follows come from his widow, Marion Hares, of St. Louis, and Glynn Hares, his son.

Born in 1904, Ernest, son of David and Hannah Hares, spent his formative years in Herbert Street. He was educated in Brithdir before attending Bargoed Higher Elementary School. His parents bought him a piano when he was young, and he had lessons from Tom Gabriel, Bargoed's well-known composer and music teacher. From childhood he was involved in music and it seemed he never stopped playing the piano. He studied piano and organ in Cardiff and attended Royal Academy of Music in London. Reports in the local press show that in 1916 and 1917, this young musician was very busy competing in eisteddfodau, winning first prizes at Rhymney, Bargoed, Aberbargoed and Pengam. As accompanist for Bargoed's Apollo Male Choir, he went to many concerts, and won prizes at two national eisteddfodau. He took his talents beyond the local area, touring Wales and England as a concert pianist with Royal Welsh Singers for two years and as a soloist and accompanist with Oliver Trio.

Ernest Hares, then 18 years old, left Southampton on board New York-bound White Star's liner RMS *Olympic* on October 25 1922. The ship's log records Ernest's final destination as Indiana Harbour where he was visiting friend Frank Sargent. A steel worker from Blackwood and former vocalist with Gwent Male Glee Singers, Sargent emigrated after touring America with the choir in 1912 and 1915 and, according to Pennsylvania's *New Castle News*, January 22 1924, was a notable concert manager. Possibly, during a visit to his brother William in Newport in August-September 1922, Sargent persuaded Ernest to travel to America. Ernest Hares and David Edgar Davies (also a passenger on board RMS *Olympic*) were part of a quartet calling themselves Royal Welsh Singers who toured America 1922-24.

274

Royal Welsh Singers 1922-1924
L-R: Griffith Howells, Ernest Hares, Gladys Smith and David Edgar Davies.

Right: *The Wilkes-Barre Record*, Pennsylvania, March 14 1924.

Royal Welsh Singers Coming

The Royal Welsh Singers, who are making o tour of the United States, will appear at Moriah Congregational Church on Friday evening, April 4. The quartet is composed of three men and a lady. The mixture of voices, that they blend together in their program, is indeed very entrancing. Their solo and duet work is very pleasing also, and the reader is an artist of exceptional ability.

D. Edgar Davies sings several solos in a rich baritone voice that always captivates the audience. He and Miss Smith sing several duets that are very enjoyable.

Griff Howell has a tenor voice that many would like to listen to a whole evening, if he could continue with the selections he renders. Then the duets given by Mr. Howell and Davies usually take their audience by storm, so captivating is the perfect rendition of their numbers.

Gladys Smith, reader and soprano, delights her audience. She is a superior reader and her numbers gives diversion to the program.

Ernest Hares, the boy pianist, is the delight of the evening. In addition to being the accompanist for the company he plays a number of solos and has a touch that is hard to surpass.

Billed as *Welsh Boy Organist*, Ernest Hares was for three years, solo organist playing the fine organ of Loew State Theatre, New York City. In the days of silent movies, every movie house had a master of ceremonies, a line of *choral kickers*, and an organist who not only played popular tunes but also directed the audience in singing them. While the 1927 movie, *The Jazz Singer*, electrified audiences, it signalled the beginning of the end of the silent film, and therefore of theatre organists like Ernest Hares. However, Ernest Hares, already in

Ernest Hares seated at the beautiful organ of the Loew State Theatre, N.Y.

possession of a master's degree from Michigan University, enrolled for further study in Chicago in 1929, hoping that such qualifications would open the way for a career in musical education. Appointed to supervise music at Soldan High School, St. Louis, in 1931, he encouraged his students to share his all-embracing taste in music.

Amid his success in that post, Ernest Hares found time to spend 1933 summer vacation in Brithdir, and

Merthyr Express, July 15 1933, not only reported the community's pride in his

YMCA Concert Glee Club, St. Louis.
Director Ernest Hares (front centre) 1933-6.

achievements but also relayed good wishes from his parents who, as noted below, had crossed the Atlantic to join their son. By 1937, as Director of Music of St. Louis Public Schools, Ernest Hares had a large all-school band of 800 instrumentalists, an orchestra of 400 and a chorus of 1,000 voices.

As the person responsible for the three biggest musical pageants ever produced in the public schools of America, he, according to report in

St. Louis Daily Globe-Democrate, May 2 1942, became life member in Music Educator's National Conference. These pageants were:

- March 28 1938: *Music Americana -- Music Exhibitors Magazine*, June 1938, provides much information on how, in just two months, Ernest Hares masterminded this dramatic project, a portrayal of 100 years of American music, from Indian war dance to *Rhapsody in Blue*, to celebrate the centennial of the opening of St. Louis' first public school. Having researched the music, written the script, designed stage sets and costumes and arranged dance routines, he directed the cast of more than 2,700 (orchestra, dancing and singing choruses) that performed to an audience of 10,000.

Ernest Hares, Director of Music in St. Louis Public Schools, dressed in band uniform of All City High School Band (comprising the best musicians from 12 different High Schools).

- December 4 1941: *Musical Missouriana --* According to *Missouri Historical Review, Columbia*, April 1942, Ernest Hares directed and produced this unique musical production with a cast of 1,500 pupils of St. Louis public high schools. Its thirteen musical settings reflected the history of Missouri.

- April 1 1942: *Free Men – a musical drama of democracy.*

In addition to his school work, Ernest Hares became widely known for his radio work and this photograph shows him broadcasting *Music in Our Schools*, broadcast weekly on Fridays on KXOK. For six years he entertained as soloist organist and, in spite of reservations by some radio colleagues, his religious programs on the radio proved popular.

276

Music filled Ernest Hares's life and his musical talents spread wide. He was director of music for St. John's Methodist Church and for United Hebrew Temple, as well as Faith Evangelical Lutheran Church's organist, lecturer in music education at St. Louis University and director of Missouri Music Education Association. He was a member of St. Louis Music Guild and he contributed to publications such as *Music Educational National Journal*. These are some of the examples of how Ernest Hares, a boy from Brithdir, was described in the American press:

- St. Louis Optimist Club News, August 6 1942: *We Banish Cares When Hares Shows His Wares - Mr. Hares is a youngish man who really gave us music that we understand. He is a rotund, jovial soul with pudgy fingers, a keen sense of humor and the ability to make the piano trip and dance, weep and laugh, and moan and sing. His love of music simply banished any barriers. Ernest was welcomed and belonged to many organizations; he played at a Jewish Temple, taught at a Catholic School and played at a Methodist Church on Sundays. He could walk into a room full of people, sit down at the piano and hypnotize everyone in earshot.*

- *Missouri Lodge News*, October 1947: Ernest Hares was a freemason and *Lodge News* No 22 advertised their regular monthly meeting at the Regency Room at Hotel Chase thus -- *Have you ever seen a human dynamo in action? If you think you have, brother, you ain't seen nuthin' yet!*

His widow, Marion Hares of St. Louis, recalls: *One time at Christmas when Ernest was playing the organ at the Jewish temple, he played 'Oh Little Town of Bethlehem' in the Temple! He played the song in a different key and the Rabbi actually walked up to him and said 'Oh what a nice piece of music', what was that?*

Ernest Hares and Marion, his wife of 18 years, travelled widely in America, attending parties and entertainments. If there was a piano and a few beers, Ernest was at the keyboard and Marion, an accomplished singer, singing along with him. Ernest Hares died in 1960 and this stone marks his final resting place in Lake Charles Cemetery, St. Louis. The square and set of compasses, symbol of Freemasonry, also appear on the grave stones of his father and his brother.

Ernest's parents and siblings

Brithdir Male Voice Choir gave a farewell concert in George Hotel before David Isaac Hares left Brithdir to join his son Ernest. Barely four months after Ernest sailed for America, his father, accompanied by Ernest's friend, 26 year old James Harrhy from Brithdir (son of Mrs. Harrhy of Crown and Sceptre

David and Hannah Hares
Courtesy John Thomas

277

Hotel, Cwmsyfiog), boarded *Berengaria* in Southampton and arrived in New York eight days later on February 18 1923, before making their way to Ernest's home in Indiana. Six months after David Hares left for America, his wife, Hannah, accompanied by 14 year old son, David Percy, and 17 year old daughter Louisa (former domestic servant) crossed the Atlantic on White Star ocean liner *RMS Majestic*, arriving in Boston August 1 1923, before travelling on to Sharon, Pennsylvania (presumably Ernest and his father were there at the time). Hannah and her sister Margaret had married brothers, thus Hannah's next of kin was named as her sister, Margaret Hares, 14 Herbert Street.

David Percy Hares (1909-1991)

Born in Brithdir, David Percy Hares was just 14 years old when he left Brithdir. For many years he worked as a professional letterer and studied in evening art courses at Washington University. He earned a reputation as one of the leading water colour artists in St. Louis. Starting with Ad-Craft, Inc., an advertising display company, he was, in the late 1930s, account executive and vice president. He also served as president of St. Louis Artists' Guild and was given honorary life membership. Like Ernest, he was a Freemason: he became a Shriner in the early 1950s and for over 35 years, he was chief designer of Moolah Temple Shrine's children's floats for the annual circus parade.

Over the years, David Percy Hares won numerous art competitions, gained awards for his creative works and exhibited widely, as witnessed by the following list:

- In 1956, his was one of about a hundred entries in the fourth annual Christmas card competition (to convey a St. Louis winter scene) sponsored by First National Bank in co-operation with St. Louis Artists' Guild. His painting of a boy pulling another youngster on a sled through an ornamental gateway, near stylized trees won the $250 prize.

- 1967 Purchase Award of Butler Institute of Art, Youngstown, Ohio.

David Percy Hares Exhibition, Clayton 1958; one-man show of 43 paintings in casein and watercolour. The painting at his arm is Maine Harbor Watercolour.
Courtesy Glynn Hares.

- 1967-68 national first award of Birmingham Water Color Society.

- 1968 first award in St. Louis Artists Guild Water Color Exhibit.

- He was invited to exhibit at many prestigious venues including Nelson Gallery, Kansas City; Western Society of Artists, San Francisco; Joslyn Museum, Omaha; Brooks Memorial Gallery, Memphis; Evansville Museum in Indiana; Southwestern Artists, Oklahoma City.

278

Aged 82, David Percy Hares died March 8 1991, at his home in Kirkwood, Missouri after a long illness. He is remembered as his works are in numerous industrial and private collections, including American Telephone and Telegraph Co., New York, First National Bank and McQuay-Norris in St. Louis.

I – Idiosyncrasies

Brithdir, while similar to many other communities, is its own unique place. Its built environment hangs on to a part of the east-facing upper Rhymney Valley slope that is like no other. The people who inhabited its terraced dwellings and worked in the shadow of local pit winding headgears formed a close community in which everyone knew and cared about everyone else. They played and prayed together, and faced life's challenges as a community. While for long, the village's physical face, dominated by pit, chapels and the 'Stute, was grey, its human side was multi-coloured, a patchwork of characters interacting in a multiplicity of ways.

One aspect of this human story is Brithdir's rich collection of nicknames - a feature of many mining communities in the valley and beyond. Given the comparatively small pool of surnames in Wales and the seemingly-smaller range of given names in common use, nicknames often proved useful to distinguish between the different John Williams (for instance) in a community. Readers who grew up in Brithdir will recall some of the following.

There were nicknames derived from people's place of origin. Brithdir was a new community in the mid-nineteenth century and, as people came in from a variety of other places, their place of origin was often a distinguishing feature. Brithdirites would have known the identities of *Dai Brithdir* and *Dai Brecon* without any need for an identifying surname. Sgt. William Pollock of Scots Guards, a native of Motherwell, arrived in Brithdir in 1936, and was simply *Jock* Pollock.

There were many whose alias derived from their occupation. Greengrocer Dan Jones from Tirphil who ran a lock-up shop in School Street, was known to all Brithdirites as *Dan the Ashman* because he worked on the ash cart. Joe Massay, an early missionary of Wesleyan Chapel, was *Joe the Collier*, as he had worked in a coal mine. Road sweeper Leslie Williams was *Les Brush*. Police Constable Joe Evans, policing Brithdir during the war years, was dubbed *Blackout Evans* as he often stepped out of a dark doorway to apprehend a mischief maker. Such appellations were frequently applied across the family: Charles Williams who repaired our boots and shoes was *Charlie Cobbler*, his son Keith inherited the handle, and wife Laura was *Laura Cobbler*.

Some local nicknames have more glamorous origins and the era of films was reflected on Brithdir's streets and playing fields. Ronald Rogers, with a mop of blonde hair, was *Trigger*, after Roy Rogers's horse. Roy Jones, forever throwing himself around as goalkeeper of boys' football team, was *Spider* Jones, named after *Spiderman*, and Ivor Harris's tackling earned him the nickname of *Chopper Harris*.

279

There were interesting and intriguing nicknames with obscure origins, often based on a version of some incident, real or supposed, relating to that person.

This photograph, courtesy Glenys Price, shows *Dai half-past nine* and Glenys Williams on their wedding day. David Price, collier in Markham Colliery, frequented George Inn Hotel to play cards with Cliff Ferguson and Ron Goodwin. When working afternoons and his shift finished early, David's journey from home (even in the darkness of winter) to *The George* took him over Coed y Moeth Common, down the mountain, under Cwmsyfiog railway bridge, up over Jarvis's bank near Brithdir railway station and over the railway track to emerge opposite George Inn Hotel. Regular as clockwork at half-past nine, he entered the pub, hence *Dai half-past nine*.

Some nicknames do not need explanation. William Davies was *Number 10* because he lived in 10 East View. David Morgan was *Dai Pigeon* or *Dai Concertina*, from his hobbies. But, why was Mr. A.B. Harris better known as *Mr. Tom Davies*?

There were nicknames based on physical appearance. Ernie Hayes's very blond hair meant he was known as *Snowflake*. Eddy Lewis, poor fellow, was *Eddy Chin* because of a noticeable facial feature. Billy Thomas of Station Terrace, a signalman at Bargoed North signal box, was dubbed *Billy Bomper* by his workmates, because he always kept his hair cut very short. Tom Evans wore thick rimmed spectacles hence *Tommy glasses,* while his son Ken who loved chocolate wagon wheels became *Wagons*.

The origins of two local nicknames have eluded me. Wilfred Bennett and Derek Bennett have been known respectively as *Hickey* and S*hinkey* for as long as people can remember. Yet, no one seems to be able to recall how or why they came by their aliases.

Without doubt the most entertaining nickname was *Galloping Major*, a nickname Trevor Griffiths earned in his National Service days. When, from time to time, he went AWOL from his unit, the military police visited the village. Trevor, mounted on *Brandy*, would gallop up Cefn Brithdir and look down on them sitting in their jeep, waiting for him. If truth was known, perhaps they enjoyed their regular time out in Brithdir.

Nicknames sometimes changed as events occurred. Terry Wheeler was *Griff* as he lived with the Griffiths family. After he lost a leg in a pit accident, he was given a few more aliases, *Pegleg*, *Hopalong* and even *Sawdust*. Cruel as it might sound, Terry took it all in good fun; after all he was one of the instigators of many of the village nicknames.

Terry was the person to give me my own peculiar handle of *Jinks* or *Meow*. On Saturdays in the 1960s, my friends and I went to the weekly hop at Ystrad Mynach. We met up in Brithdir 'Stute snooker room and often joined Terry at the card table while we waited for others to arrive. On one particular occasion, I was wearing a tan suede jacket (right) and, quick as a flash, Terry dubbed me *Cat* after the television cartoon character *Top Cat*. The name stuck, and over time *Cat* became *TC*, *Jinks*, *Meow* which mutated to *Smeow*. Yes, old *Pegleg* has a lot to answer for.

Nicknames run in families. Ken Davies became *Little Darby*, as older brother Lyndon was *Darby* Davies. Malcolm Jarvis's nickname *Jack* was probably from his notable uncle, footballer Jack Jarvis. Terance Ferguson, the youngest of the Fergie's, was *nipper Ferguson*.

The majority of Brithdir nicknames were attached to males, but a few females also had nicknames. Ceilia (Cissey) Bennett, originally from Deri, became known as *Aunty Cissey Brithdir* to her Deri relations. Maggie Place, who had a newspaper and general shop, was known as *Maggie Damp* because some items purchased were damp.

J – Jones

Jones is a common surname across Wales and, not surprisingly, Brithdir had its share of families with that surname. This section deals with some members of some of those families.

Brothers David Roderick (1929-2006), Howard and John Jones

Brothers David Roderick, Howard and John Jones, sons of Police Sergeant Thomas Jones of 21 Station Terrace, were born in Brithdir. They worked on the railways: David Roderick started his railway career in 1947, Howard in 1949 and John in 1957. The two older brothers worked together for 43 years, and younger brother John was with them for eleven years. Retirement did not diminish their interest in rail transport, as David and Howard took every opportunity to visit steam trains and make excursions on railways. For David in particular, steam trains remained important until his death in January 2006, as witnessed by the following information and photographs provided by his son, Darryl.

David Roderick Jones, born June 12 1929, grew up in an era when the sights, sounds and smells of steam locomotive engines reflected the glory days of travel by train, a time when many young boys aspired to a career driving such locomotives. David not only lived that dream but also went to the top of his trade. He started his working life as a glass blower in a factory on Treforest Industrial Estate, but, in December 1946, the family moved to Tyesley, Birmingham where, April 1947, an 18 year old David started working for GWR as a fireman on steam locomotives. Three months into the job, National Service with the Royal Artillery put his railway career on hold. By the time it was completed, the railways were nationalised and he resumed his job as fireman, then in the employ of British Railways (BR). In 1960 he was promoted to train driver and he remained a dedicated railway employee for 45 years, during which time he was to drive many locomotives including some on prestigious journeys as shown by the examples below:

David Jones (on right) with a fellow member of staff at Army Apprentice School, near Chepstow.

- In 1968, enthusiasts mourned the end of regular steam working on British Rail (as it became 1965) but, on October 4 1971, Great Western 4-6-0 King George V (6000) ran the first *Return to Steam special* on a main line. David Roderick Jones was asked to drive the leg from Birmingham Moor Street Station, to Kensington Olympia, London.
- He had the privilege of driving *Flying Scotsman* on two occasions. Built in Doncaster in 1924, it was the first steam train to crash 100 mph barrier. His certificates show he was driver of Gresley Pacific Locomotive 4472 *Flying Scotsman* on June 9 1973 between Tyesley and Didcot, and on June 9 1974 between Didcot and Tyesley.
- The pinnacle of David Jones's career however was in 1986 when he was asked to drive the Royal Train from Stratford upon Avon to Marylebone. Further research may reveal whether Her Majesty Queen Elizabeth II was on board.

Idris Jones

A native of Trelewis, Idris Jones was just an infant when, in 1908, his father, police constable Albert Jones, was transferred to Brithdir and 20 Station Terrace. Idris began his working life as a railway clerk with GWR and later became deputy stationmaster, which meant he had to stand-in wherever his services were required.

Outside family and working life, Idris derived great satisfaction from his involvement with St. John Ambulance Brigade, and daughter, Elizabeth Jones, has supplied the photograph and information about this aspect of his life. In the mid-1930s he started his first aid classes for Brithdir boys, first, in the Ambulance Hall on the *tump* but later in Workmen's Institute. Appointed Serving Brother of the Venerable Order of the Hospital of St. John of Jerusalem on May 4 1955, later he was appointed Officer Brother. His highest accolade came when, on July 24 1963, he was appointed Area Commissioner for the Caerphilly County Area, Glamorgan. On retiring in October 1969, Idris Jones had completed thirty-five years of ambulance service.

Les Jones

Having served an apprenticeship as a car mechanic with Jaguar dealer Chastons of Blackwood in the 1960s, Les Jones, of The Villas, became mechanical engineer with Welsh Water. Over some four decades, he built seven bodies for Rolls and Bentley chassis.

This photograph shows Les sitting proudly behind the steering wheel of the 20hp Rolls Golfers Coupe which he rebuilt from scratch between 1981 and 1991.   Courtesy son Chris Jones

K – King family

Joseph King was born in Merthyr Tydfil about 1860. He emigrated to America about 1878 and married American-born Mary Ann

King Family clockwise : Maisie, Annie, Lizzie, mum Polly

(known as Polly). Their three daughters, Elizabeth (*Lizzie*), Annie and Mary Ann (known as *Maisie*) were born in America, in 1883, 1888 and 1890 respectively. When Maisie was about 3, father Joseph King inherited an estate in Rhymney and took the family to his native land.

Maisie and her sisters grew up in Wales. After her first husband was killed in a mining accident, Maisie married Walter Cooper – son of Joe and Moira Harris Cooper of Rose Hill Cottages, and they had two daughters, Olga Elizabeth (born 1918) and Moira (born 1920).

Following the death of Joseph King, his widow Polly moved back to America to live near her siblings. Prompted both by the fact that Maisie was suffering with a heart condition and wanted to be near her mother, and the contemporary difficulties in the mining industry, the family decided to emigrate. When *RMS Mauretania* left Southampton on September 29 1923, Walter Cooper (right) and his brother-in-law, John Israel Williams, both of Charles Street, were on board, bound for New York and a fresh start in Girard, Ohio.

Initially, Walter Cooper lived with his mother-in-law. He found work at U.S. Steel Corporation's McDonald Works, and eventually sent for Maisie and the girls. Before she left Brithdir, little Olga gave her teacher, Miss Evans, a photograph of herself as a keepsake.

Passport photograph of Olga and Moira

Maisie, by then quite ill, 8 year old Olga and 6 year old Moira, were on board *Mauretania* which left Southampton on October 9 1926. Olga was seasick throughout the journey and Maisie was too ill to offer her any comfort. On arrival at Ellis Island on October 14, Maisie was transferred to a hospital and the girls were left to fend for themselves. Fortunately, an Irish

283

woman realised their plight and found them a place to sleep and saw they had food. Their father made frantic efforts to get them off Ellis Island, and after about a week, aided partly by Maisie's American birth but more by the efforts of an Ohio senator contacted by Walter, the girls were reunited with their mother and released.

Six months later, Maisie died. Soon after, her oldest sister Elizabeth (Williams) (left) joined them, to help bring up Olga and Moira. Elizabeth, a mine-accident widow, had managed to make a comfortable living for herself, working at Refuge Assurance Company, Bargoed, for 11 years, before running a small grocery shop in her front room at 28 Charles Street, and a *bake house* (where people had large items cooked) behind the house. She sacrificed this for a life in the country in which she was born, caring for her two nieces.

Olga adored her Aunt Lizzie and enjoyed her life in Girard, Ohio, under her care. Olga met her future husband, Louis C. Hoier, at high school, and they were married August 22 1942. They raised three children: Susan (born in 1944), Carol (1947) and David (1950). Older daughter Susan Hoier Opeka has provided the family details as well as the photographs in this account. Olga worked as a medical secretary, first in McDonald and later in Giraud. She was a member of First Baptist Church in Girard, Eastern Star Lodge, and Girard Literary Club.

Although Olga had sent a letter to her Brithdir teacher, Miss Evans, telling of her safe arrival in her new home, she made no further contact with her until the mid-1980s. Alice Maud Evans, daughter of Joseph and Mary Evans, was born, raised and lived her life in 9 Bristol

Alice Maud Bridges, née Evans, holding framed photograph that little Olga had given her as a keepsake in 1926.
Merthyr Express 1985

Terrace. She had attended the local school before teaching there for 24 years, leaving only when she was married. Planning her first visit back to Wales, Olga Hoier, née Cooper, was delighted to discover Miss Evans (by then, Alice Maud Bridges) was alive and living in Brithdir. Olga contacted Florrie Harris (niece of Mrs. Bridges) and arranged that, while visiting relatives in Cardiff, she would call on Mrs. Bridges.

1997 Re-union of old friends. L-R; Lillian Winston (Davey), Olga Hoier (Cooper) and and Morfydd Williams (Meyrick)

Thus, after nearly six decades, Olga met her former teacher. *Merthyr Express* reporter and photographer were present at the reunion.

Olga visited Brithdir again in 1997 when she was accompanied by her daughter Susan. On that occasion, she met former school friend, Lillian Davey (Mrs. Winston of Charles Street).

Olga enjoyed a long life, outliving not only her husband, who died November 25 1987, but also her sister Moira, and Moira's husband, Bob Collins. She died, aged 97, on Tuesday, September 8 2015, at Casa de la Luz Hospice of Tucson, survived by her children, six grandchildren and seven great-grandchildren. Olga was buried at Giraud City Cemetery.

L – Lawes family

Born in County Durham early 1840s, Katharine Elizabeth Victoria Theresa Elliot (right – from image on glass courtesy Sir Bernard Knight), niece to Sir George Elliot, married Robert Morrow Lawes in 1861. Their first three children, Alfred, Edith, and Frederick, were born in the north east, in 1864, 1865 and 1866 respectively. The family moved to South Wales before George was born in Aberdare in 1869 and to Rhymney Valley before 1871 census was taken when the family was in Greenfield Cottages, New Tredegar. Four younger children, Mary (1872), Arthur (1874), Thomas (1876) and Bertha (1877) were born in Gelligaer parish. As noted, page 14, Katherine and seven of her children were at Gwaelod y Brithdir at the time of the 1881 census, but her husband was enumerated in Liverpool, with Sarah Ann, listed as his wife, and an infant daughter. Presumably he had divorced Katherine who later emigrated to Antipodes where, in 1897, she married Valentine Jacob Hermann.

The Elliot family name was often on the lips of several generations of Brithdir people, especially as many of the men worked at Elliot Colliery. There is much information on Sir George Elliot and Elliot Colliery in Leslie Shore's publication listed in the bibliography.

Space does not permit the inclusion of details of the life and work of all Katherine's children but that of George Elliot Lawes follows.

1892
Born in Cwmaman July 1 1869, George Elliot Lawes (left) attended the Welsh School, Ashford, from 1878 to 1880 until, due to ill-health, he was withdrawn and taught by private tutors to 1884. On completing his schooling, he served an apprenticeship under Edmund Mills Hann. When his apprenticeship ended in 1889, he took his skills to South America, working in several Latin American republics before his premature death, aged just 42, after a short bout of yellow fever in 1912.

Much of the information about the career of George Elliot Lawes has come from his family and from *Grace's Guide to British Industrial History*. George Lawes went to Buenos Aires in 1889 and spent five years on the Port Works and with Buenos Aires Great Southern Railway, working as fitter and valve-setter, before becoming a trial engine driver. It was while he was in Buenos Aires that he met Margaret Louise Anthony and they married March 10 1891. Their great granddaughter, Pat Lawes (of Buenos Aires), provided details of their names shown in Spanish on the marriage certificate (issued in Buenos Aires Register Office):

JORGE ELLIOT LAWES, hijo de (son of) ROBERTO LAWES y CATALINA ELLIOT
MARGARITA LOUSE ANTHONY, hija de (daughter of) GUILLERMO E. ANTHONY y MARIA A. PIDDINGTON.

George Elliot Lawes became acting locomotive superintendent of Argentine North East Railway in 1894, and oversaw the introduction of many appliances, including an oil-burner which, eliminating the need to send cold air into the furnace, saved 30% oil compared to other burners. He moved to Paraguay where, in 1904, he became locomotive and stores superintendent of Paraguay Central Railway, and, as the only representative of the Institution of Mechanical Engineers there, he was magistrate, doctor, and chief constable of a little township inhabited by workmen and their families. Three years later, he took an equivalent position with Peruvian Central Railway.

The family was taking a holiday in UK at the time of the 1911 census, when George Elliot Lawes, his wife Margaret, and three of their five children: Herbert, Ellinor and Trevor, were at Rome Farm Cottage, Hampshire (Margaret's family were from this county). He returned to work as stores and locomotive superintendent with Brazil North Eastern Railways but sadly died at Ceara, Brazil, on February 14 1912.

During his career in South America, his contributions to labour relations and technological development were significant, and a credit to himself and his former mentor, E. M. Hann. His knowledge of both the Spanish language and South American customs, combined with experience in so many Latin American republics, ensured he was widely recognized as one of the highest authorities on management of local railway labour. Records show that George Elliot Lawes was member of several professional organisations: in 1904, he became member of Institute of Mechanical Engineers and he was also member of Institute of Engineers of River Plate and of Royal Society of Arts.

M – Music

Local newspaper reports regularly included long lists of local musicians of all ages who passed music (usually piano playing) examinations or performed in chapel anniversaries, concerts and eisteddfodau. While such performers are far too numerous to mention, their talent is acknowledged. This chapter starts by highlighting the musical careers of some Brithdir people with exceptional musical talent who made a name for themselves beyond Brithdir, before continuing to provide more general insight into the range of musical talent and interest within Brithdir over the decades. Although a number of the West family merit a place in this chapter, their musical talents are mentioned elsewhere, alongside their other contributions to the local community.

Madame Zoe Cresswell-Minett – *The Welsh Carmen*

Madame Zoe Cresswell-Minett, the delightful lady shown in this photograph, had a long musical career. Aged about five, Zoe, at ease with tonic sol-fa, excelled in school singing lessons and performed in annual St. David's Day school concerts. Aged 83, she was still on stage when, at a St. David's Day concert in Barry's Memorial Hall, she provided the piano accompaniment for two of her pupils, Suzanne Harris and Jemma Crockford. Much of what follows about the family and Zoe's career, as well as permission to reproduce the various photographs, was from Morfydd Williams née Cresswell, Kay Williams, Jacqueline Tiernan, and Nigel and Joanne Minett.

Born in 1909, Mary Ann Zoe Llynos Cresswell was the second of five girls born to William Samuel Cresswell and his wife, Catherine Ann. Growing up at 18 Old Bristol Terrace, Zoe was amidst four generations of the Cresswell family – her siblings, their parents, grandparents, and great grandparents. She attended the village schools before going to Bargoed Secondary School.

Young Zoe enjoyed music and, by the time she was about ten years old, she started taking piano lessons. Her grandfather, Samuel Cresswell, although he could not play the piano himself, was often at her side and if she played anything wrong, he would stop her, saying *you're not right there you know; that was a wrong note*. He encouraged her, telling her *now half-hour practice, half-hour play*, and, later, when she went on to her diploma studies, it became *one hour practice at least every day*.

The Anglican church played a big part in young Zoe's life: her grandfather was Sunday School superintendent, some family members sang in Brithdir church choir and her piano teacher, organist in St. Gwladys Church, Bargoed,

Seventeen year old Zoe proudly wearing the cap and gown purchased for her by local church members.

287

encouraged her to learn to play the pipe organ. When just fifteen, Zoe was church organist and choir master at St. Paul's Church. Stan West, Brithdir's *Merthyr Express* correspondent, regularly included reports on her progress in his news report, and this extract from January 1 1927 is just one example:

> *Congratulations were in order to Miss Zoe Cresswell who at the recent examination of the London College of Music had passed her degree which entitled her to affix to her name the letters A.L.C.M.*

A conductor of considerable ability, Zoe was involved with several operettas associated with St. Paul's Church, and one such example was reported in *Merthyr Express*, February 14 1925:

> *A grand performance of the operetta "The Magic Cup" was given by the Young People's Society on three consecutive nights at the New Hall, Brithdir; Miss Zoe Cresswell, although still a student at Bargoed Secondary School, enhanced her reputation as a singer. Her voice is young, sweet and powerful, and to her much of the success of the concert was due.*

Zoe Cresswell, front centre, and cast members of *The Magic Cup*, on stage in New Hall, Brithdir, February 1925.

Zoe was well-known in upper Rhymney Valley, especially as she willingly gave her services to many charitable and philanthropic institutions, as illustrated by the following:

- October 19 1925: she was among the artists performing at Brithdir Ambulance Cadet Corps social concert and presentation meeting. Her father, as Superintendent of the Corps, presented certificates to cadets successful in a recent examination.
- Monday, November 16 1925: she was one of numerous local artists singing at a concert in Brithdir New Hall, in aid of St. Peter's Roman Catholic Church, Bargoed.
- July 26 1926: Beulah Baptist Choir, assisted by friends (Zoe was one of three friends to appear in the second half), performed operetta *The Royal Jester* in aid of Canteen Funds.
- Saturday, September 11 1926: in an Eisteddfod in Brithdir in aid of the communal kitchen fund, Zoe, competing with Mary Williams, won open duet competition, and they shared first prize in novice solo competition. The newspaper report noted the commendable gestures of many winners who returned their prizes to the fund.

- Wednesday, December 22 1926: Zoe was one of several artists to perform in New Hall at a farewell concert, a public send-off to William Godfrey, 24 Herbert Street, who was emigrating to Australia.

Zoe's musical career took a large step forward when she sang with Royal Welsh Ladies Choir under the guidance of Madame Clara Davies (mother of Ivor Novello). Young Zoe travelled to and from London for rehearsals and to concerts at venues such as Albert Hall. After a few singing lessons Madame Clara offered her a scholarship, but Zoe realised she could not afford to live in London. However, Madame Freebairn Smith threw Zoe a lifeline, offering not only accommodation in her home outside the city but also, in exchange for some household chores and washing the front door steps, her fare into London. One of the highlights of her time with Royal Welsh Ladies Choir was a command performance at Windsor Castle in May 1928, when the 18 year old from Brithdir sang before H.R.H. King George V, Queen Mary, the Prince of Wales, Princess Royal and the infant Princess Elizabeth (later Queen Elizabeth II). At the end of the concert, Queen Mary and the toddler Princess met and thanked the choir. Just months later, in August 1928, Zoe, a promising young soprano, was a member of Madame Clara Novello's Royal Welsh Party on a two week tour of the Isle of Wight, a preliminary to Madame Clara's projected world tour.

St. David's Church Choir with Zoe Cresswell. Arthur McCraw in back row second from left with Clifford Hewitt in front of him standing left of front row. Kneeling central is Dick Williams

Sometimes Zoe performed nearer home as illustrated by these extracts from *Merthyr Express*, January 26 and April 27 1929:
Miss Zoe Cresswell was one of Madame Clara Novello Davies' sexette [sic] *which gave a concert at the Paget Rooms, Penarth on Friday 18,*

Miss Cresswell had been selected as the chief soprano vocalist in the oratorio "The Prince of Peace" at Newbridge.

About 1932, Zoe not only finished many of the concerts in London and returned to Cardiff, she also parted company with her mentor. Her new scholarship agreement with Madame Teresa Johnson in Cardiff took her to competing at eisteddfodau. Although the schoolgirl Zoe had been successful in eisteddfodau, this was different: in her words *in those days my goodness me there was some beautiful singers, you really had to sing to win.* She competed for about a year before winning a prize. In April 1932 she was placed second at the semi-national at Pontypridd and gained two first prizes in open soprano solo competitions at Pentyrch and Pontyclun. Further successes followed with first prize in soprano solo at Pontlottyn Eisteddfod on September 9 1932, and in open soprano solo at Barry Eisteddfod where she also shared champion solo.

Zoe met her future husband Herbert Minett when he was chorister in St. Gwladys Church and, after an eighteen month courtship, they married at Gelligaer Church on May 19 1934. On October 13 1934, they both competed at Bargoed's 4th Annual Eisteddfod, and *Merthyr Express*, October 20 1934, reported Madam Creswell-Minett won soprano solo and shared champion solo with Madam Grove-Morgan, Newport, while her husband also won two competitions that day.

During the 1940s and 1950s the voice of Zoe Cresswell was heard many times on the radio. Her radio debut was on Christmas Day 1940, singing to the Forces, and, after that, she appeared regularly on such programmes as BBC's variety show *Welsh Rarebit,* produced by Mae Jones. Older readers may recall it also featured Idloes Owen's Lyrian Singers as well as listeners' favourite, *The Adventures of Tommy Trouble*, a story by E. Eynon Evans. Zoe was principal soprano with BBC Welsh Orchestra, singing operettas *The Desert Song, The Student Prince* and *The Vagabond King.* On March 1 1952 she debuted on BBC TV in St. David's Day Festival Concert broadcast from Royal Albert Hall.

ZOE CRESSWELL is a singer with a voice of unusual charm and power. Her many successes in Opera, Radio, Television and the concert platform have brought her high praise and great renown throughout the length and breadth of the country. She is acclaimed a true musician as well as an outstanding singer and artist

Daily Express (Albert Hall Concert)

At 7 o'clock on Thursday, December 2 1943, Zoe Cresswell and Herbert Minett were among twenty-eight people -- students, friends and acquaintances of Idloes Owen -- who met at Cathays Methodist Chapel, Crwys Road, Cardiff. By the

end of the meeting the Welsh National Opera Company (WNO), had come into being. Zoe Cresswell sang in the first concert performance of *Cavalleria Rusticana* in Cardiff Empire Theatre on Sunday, April 23 1944. About eighteen months later, although offered auditions at both Covent Garden and Sadler's Wells, family commitments meant Zoe decided to remain with WNO and, as principal soprano, she took the leading role in a number of their operas. In 1947 she first performed one of the most famous operas in the world and, over some sixteen years, her fiery Gypsy *Carmen* wowed audiences, and she became widely known as *The Welsh Carmen.*

Her final performance with WNO was *Trovatore* in Llandudno during the 1960-61 season. When, the night before opening night, the singer cast as *Leonora* fell ill, Zoe received a phone call at her Cardiff home. Although she had not sung the role for four years, she agreed to help out. Taking the score with her on the train, she arrived in Llandudno in the afternoon, and was given a brief run-through at the theatre with the trio before being whisked off for a costume fitting. An hour later, she was singing what she felt was the best performance she had ever given. The chorus must have thought so too, for, at the end of the performance, they picked her up and carried her off stage. So ended her last appearance with WNO.

The following list of principal roles performed by Zoe Cresswell is taken from Richard Fawkes, *Welsh National Opera*, 1986, (which is also used for other information on WNO).

Role	Opera	Date
Carmen	Carmen	1947
Santuzza	Cavalleria Rusticana	1948
Rosalinda	Fledermaus	1950
Lenora	Trovatore	1951
Cio-Cio-San	Madam Butterfly	1953
Musetta	Bohème	1955
Fenena	Nabucco	1956
Giselda	Lombardi	1957
Viclinda	Lombardi	1957

As well as performing opera and taking part in many concerts, Zoe Cresswell also taught singing at Welsh College of Music and Drama for 35 years. She started teaching in the college in 1950; just three hours at first, extending her hours gradually, and, after she finished opera, it was full time teaching.

Her last public appearance, in Cardiff's St. David's Hall, was April 4 1984, a *Gala Evening – A Celebration of Band, Harpist and Welsh Choirs*, and, during the evening, Zoe conducted the Lyrian Singers.

The Lyrian Singers 1983-84: Zoe Cresswell (centre) was musical director for several years; her husband Herbert is back row 3rd from left. Prior to becoming their musical director, she frequently performed as guest artiste with Lyrian Singers.

A memory shared by her son Nigel Minett:

She went to Covent Garden after she retired and, while in the crush bar having a drink, who should arrive -- none other than Dame Joan Sutherland who, parting everyone in the bar, walked up to where Mum and Dad were standing and said "Good heaven, it's you Zoe. I haven't seen you since I saw you doing Il Lombardi and I came to the show incognito, how lovely you were" so, wow, that was some compliment.

Zoe Cresswell-Minett, *The Welsh Carmen*, passed away, aged 82, on June 3 1992, and was buried in St. Andrews Churchyard, Dinas Powis. On his death December 9 2004, Herbert Minett was buried in the same grave.

Peggy Bailey – Sweet Voice of the West

Readers who grew up before the age of the television remember family entertainment on the wireless (radio), including serials like *Dick Barton - Special Agent*, *Riders of the Range*, and *Journey into Space* on BBC Light Programme. In our household, we gathered by the little Rediffusion box radio in the front room when *Big Bill Campbell and his Rocky Mountain Rhythm* was broadcast. As a lad, Uncle Geoff loved this show, with its girl singer, stage name *Peggy Bailey, Sweet Voice of the West*, singing numbers like *Prairie Rose*. She was born in Brithdir and lived in Charles Street. *The Herald* of Glasgow, April 27 1943, had this to say: *Gracie Fields "fans" will find that their favourite has almost a counterpart, from the vocal standpoint, in Peggy Bailey, who appears this week at the Empire with Big Bill Campbell and the Home Town Mountain Band in "Rocky Mountain Rhythm". This attractive singer fully justifies her radio fame and is the outstanding personality in the show.*

Big Bill Campbell, a Canadian entertainer living in England, helped popularise Western/cowboy music through BBC and Radio Luxemburg cowboy-variety shows, recordings and regular UK tours. I remember Big Bill's *Mighty Fine* after every song and frequent instructions to *Pass around the*

Peggy Bailey (left centre) and Big Bill Campbell and his Rocky Mountain Rhythm.
Courtesy Margaret Fonde.

292

Applejack. Big Bill Campbell and His Rocky Mountain Rhythm was a musical cowboy act which topped the bill in 1940s and 50s music halls the length and breadth of UK. When Big Bill took his show to New Theatre, Cardiff, Malcolm and Linda Winmill were among the coach load of Brithdir fans who travelled to see the local girl.

Melville Ceiriog Davies – boy soprano

By the time he was 10 years old, Melville Davies, School Street, had already made a name for himself through his musical achievements. Often competing above his age group, he was successful in eisteddfodau: aged 12 and competing against about 50 others in the under-14 competition at Neath National Eisteddfod, he reached the final, and he was a semi-national winner at Mountain Ash. By the time he reached his 13th birthday, he had won over 30 prizes, and before another year passed, he was on the road, touring London and the provinces as a soloist with Jack Lewis's *Singing Scholars*, and had appeared at London Palladium with the *Crazy Gang*.

Melville Davies holding cup won at 1935 Abertysswg Eisteddfod

Courtesy Mel's proud sisters, Millie Davies and Ceridwen Evans, (who also provided much of the detail on Mel's career).

Mel with friend from Aberbargoed. They entertained locally as *Ronaldo Brothers*.

His marriage to Dilys Jones of Bargoed at Penuel Chapel in 1952 is mentioned on page 83. A year or so later, when on holiday at Weston-Super-Mare, bystanders were so impressed on hearing Mel recording *I'll walk beside you* and *This day is mine* for his wife, that they urged him to enter an adult talent competition at the resort's Rozell bandstand. Mel won the competition and took part in West regional *Music by the Sea* festival. He not only sang in a cabaret show at Winter Gardens before the end of his holiday, but also at a Sunday concert a few weeks later. Following his broadcast from Weston, Mai Jones, Welsh variety producer, put his name on BBC audition list. Mel sang with Powell Duffryn choir for many years and gave his services to support good causes in Rhymney Valley. Not only blessed with a fine voice he was also a very talented snooker player. After retiring from work on the railway, he became caretaker of Brithdir Workmen's Institute.

Tommy Hennessey -- *Singing Scholar*

During the Easter vacation 1937, Tommy Hennessey, son of Mr. and Mrs. Pat Hennessey, Harcourt Terrace, paid a visit home. A boy soloist with Jack Lewis's *Singing Scholars*, Tommy made such good progress on the stage that he appeared with the *Scholars* in 1937 film *The Penny Pool*.

Morfydd Meyrick – orchestra violinist

Most of this information on the career of Morfydd, the talented daughter of Mr. and Mrs. Rees Meyrick, Cemetery Lodge, Gwaelod y Brithdir, is based on contemporary reports in *Merthyr Express*. She passed Senior Grade in violin playing at London College of Music at the age of 12. At just 17 years old, she was successful in final examination of Associated Board of Royal College of Music and Royal Academy of Music. On her first attempt, and just 18 years old, she won first prize in open violin solo at Llandovery Semi-National Eisteddfod on Whit Tuesday 1930. On March 30 1931, she was awarded a silver medal for viola playing at annual music festival in Bristol's Victoria Rooms. One of the first violins (in orchestra led by Herbert Ware) at a symphony concert in Cardiff's Park Hall, Morfydd Meyrick played under the baton of Sir Thomas Beecham. In May 1931, she gained first prize at Cheltenham, and her successful career continued when she was awarded first prize in open viola solo competition at Port Talbot National Eisteddfod in August 1932. In May 1933 she was chosen to play in Three Valleys Festival orchestra at Mountain Ash. In 1933, following success in Royal College of Music examination in London, she became Associate of Royal College of Music with a teaching diploma.

In spite of her successes, Morfydd Meyrick did not forget Brithdir. She adjudicated orchestral items at Brithdir's 3rd annual eisteddfod, in New Hall, October 1 1932, and she taught music to local youngsters. In later life, renowned composer Alun Hoddinot (born in Bargoed) was proud to say that *he had lessons in Brithdir from Morfydd Meyrick, who still occasionally plays in the BBC Welsh Orchestra. Merthyr Express*, February 13 1937, informed readers that Morfydd Meyrick and her junior orchestra of Brithdir entertained the patients of Talygarn Miners' Convalescent Home on Sunday. There is further information about Morfydd Meyrick's successful musical career after her marriage and move from Brithdir in *Gelligaer* volume XVII.

Ned Rees -- club singer

Ned Rees, (photograph courtesy David Rees), was a native of Brithdir who became known throughout the Rhymney Valley as a popular and talented club singer. Such was his talent that, given sound management and classical voice training, a career on London and world opera stages was not beyond the realms of possibility. To his credit, Ned realised that big city life was not for him, and he returned to Wales. His friends and admirers in his home village and throughout the valley were proud to welcome him back home and Ned was a favourite artist on the Constitutional Club's stage, thrilling listeners with songs he made his own. Ned had a beautiful selection of songs

Ned Rees, centre, doing what came naturally, winning a singing competition.
Courtesy Debra Gypsy Rose Rees

and his renderings of such favourites as *Thora, Ave Maria, I Believe, Ponchinello, Because You're Mine, Love is a Many Splendid Thing, I Reach for the Stars, Girls were made to Love and Kiss, The Story of a Starry Night, She Wears My Ring, Delilah, Funny Familiar Forgotten Feelings and Danny Boy* will be remembered for a long time. Although Ned died young, his voice lives on in our memories, as in the words of one of his favourites, *The Song of My Life:*

Everyone has a song that belongs to their life,
that will go on and on through the years of their life.

★   ★   ★
NELSON British Legion on May 8 presents the Welsh Command Performance all Star Gala. Appearing are: Lennie Leighton, comedian and singing impressionist; The Mimeros, comedy mime plus brilliance; Cyril Perslow, Maureen Paul, Whit Monday, comedian; Carol Baker, Huw Berton, a tenor with greatness; the fabulous Margaret James, Gwyn Davies, outstanding comedian; Chris Bayliss, tenor; wonderful Shirlee Stevens and the fantastic voice of Ned Rees.

The show will be compèred by the famous Les Webb, with Kay Payne, organist, and Leslie Davies, drummer. Produced and directed by Ernie Dowell, the show will be covered by TWW and naturally— the Press.

The Stage, April 27 1967.

TENOR NED REES of Brithdir, near Gwent, can certainly afford to buy a few luxurious presents at Christmas for his wife and family. For in nine minutes flat he won himself the first prize of £100 at the final of a six-week talent competition at THE MARKHAM MINERS' WELFARE CLUB, Markham, near Blackwood. His superb singing of two songs greatly impressed both adjudicators and the capacity audience alike.

Caerphilly songstress LYNNE TAYLOR was a worthy second prizewinner, with another singer, HARRY BREWERS, coming third.

Club Chairman DAI CRADDOCK said afterwards: "This has been a truly wonderful night for the club. We will undoubtedly run another talent competition next year."

The Stage, December 30 1977.

Alan *Spud* Murphy, formerly of Phillipstown, shared this memory of Ned:
I remember Ned had a ten-bob bet with his brother Biffo that he could not hang by his feet from the railway bridge. Sure enough, Biffo climbed the bridge and dangled by his feet, only to find that on getting down, Ned had scampered off with the money.

Piano

The piano was usually first choice for Brithdir parents who wanted their children to learn to play a musical instrument and many local pianists and/or organists offered private lessons, teaching the basics and preparing pupils for examination. Over the decades, local newspapers carried detailed reports that often named the teacher as well as pupils successful in the examinations.

One of the earliest such reports relating to Brithdir folk was that announcing that Marjory Lewis, Brithdir Farm, and Winifred Lewis, Plas Farm, were successful at London College of Music (L.C.M.) examination held at Cardiff in April 1899. The identity of their piano teacher is uncertain.

In 1903, Charles Williams, L.C.M., 4 Bristol Terrace, was successful in the examination of Associate of London College of Music (A.L.C.M.). It is likely that he was the first music teacher in the village.

In January 1904, Gwladys, daughter of Mr. and Mrs. Gwynne, The Villas, and pupil of Charles Williams, gained senior certificate of L.C.M. in piano playing, and, by December 1906, had added certificate of Higher Division of the Associated Board of Royal Academy of Music in piano playing. By 1910, when she passed A.L.C.M, she was a pupil of Mr. D.W. Davies, organist of Bethania, Dowlais. Described as a music teacher when the 1911 census was taken, Gwladys Gwynne prepared Ernest Harris for his success in L.C.M. primary examination in piano playing in 1913.

Tom Gabriel, composer and music teacher of Bargoed, taught some Brithdir pupils including Alfred Powell, James Street, who passed L.C.M. primary examination in 1914, as well as Ernest Hares, Herbert Street, Edith Bufton, daughter of Edwin and Elizabeth Bufton, Railway Shop, and Peris Brown, 12 year old child of Harry and Annie Brown, Station Terrace, three successful candidates in 1917 examinations held at Park Hall, Cardiff. The success of Ernest Hares is detailed on pages 274-277 and, by 1925, Peris Brown was organist at Brithdir Wesleyan chapel.

The identity of the piano teacher of some other Brithdir scholars who passed L.C.M. examinations is unclear, but pupils included Gwladys Jenkins, Maggie Jones, Valerie Howard and Stanley Cole in 1916, Freda Price and Mair West in 1928 and Annie Maud Evans, James Street, passed with honours in 1929.

Wally Jarvis, son of Mr. and Mrs. Walter Jarvis, Russell Street, passed the primary piano, practical and theory examination in 1930 and, gaining 91%, was awarded a first class certificate. In 1931, Wally Jarvis gained an honours certificate in elementary stage. In the same examination, Olive Gibbs, James Street, and Mildred Davies, School Street, passed, while Sylvia Roberts, Charles Street, gained a first class certificate. John Jenkins, School Street, successful in primary examination of Victoria College of London, was awarded an honours certificate.

In 1932, Zoe Cresswell, Bristol Terrace, was piano teacher of Miss M. Evans, who passed senior examination with first class certificate. In the senior examination for piano playing Olwen Williams, Bristol Terrace, gained 93 marks, so earning an honours certificate. Mildred Jones, 9 year old daughter of Police Constable and Mrs. Jones, Station Terrace, passed elementary examination on her first attempt. At the examination of L.C.M. held at Cardiff in 1936, Riley Hook, School Street, passed primary stages with honours. In 1937, Walter C Jarvis, son of David and Mary Jarvis, had L.L.C.M. certificate.

Music in the inter-war period

Amid the difficulties of life and work in the inter-war years, music was thriving in Brithdir as witnessed by information about some of the concerts and other performances noted on page 264. There were a number of groups of various sizes practising and performing within the community. Some of them, including those associated with places of worship, often performed for charitable causes. Listed below are some groups for local men who enjoyed singing. It was not uncommon for more talented and enthusiastic musicians to belong to more than one group

- Brithdir Male Voice Party, under conductor Tom Williams and with soloists Stan West and Ivor Davey, delighted audiences at concerts with their choruses and songs
- Mr. Salmond's Orchestra, composed chiefly of Brithdir musicians, provided music at Institute dances. Research to date has not uncovered the identities of these musicians.
- Brithdir Aeolian Concert Party, James George (pianist-conductor of the party), Baden Powell Price, Ivor Davey, Stan West, Donald Bird and W. Ferguson (who not only sang but also gave whistling selections) was a popular group, willingly giving concerts for good causes.
- Brithdir Savannah Minstrels included soloists Steve Phillips, W. Forster, J. Williams, O. Jones, D. Jones and Ben Long.

John Weaver, accomplished violinist, played solo as well as performing with John Connolly in jap violin and mandolin duet.
Courtesy Jean Williams.

Some local musicians enjoyed the thrill of competitive performance associated with eisteddfodau. Ceinwen Sarah Hinkin, Station Terrace, was a well-known soprano vocalist and a member of eisteddfod choirs in the district. In July 1931, Brithdir and District United Choral Society was formed with the stated aim of entering competitions at local eisteddfodau. Tom Williams was appointed conductor, Leslie West its pianist, and the officers were Roland West (chairman),

297

Frank West (treasurer) and Phil Moore (secretary). Four months later, competing for the first time at Blackwood Eisteddfod, they gained fourth place. The choir had a strong supporting band of soloists including Tom Roberts, Katie Richards (soprano), T. Hopkins, Hannah Evans, Harry West (junior), Stan West, W. Osborne and John Weaver who played the violin and jap fiddle.

N – Nurses

This section, arranged alphabetically according to surname, deals with some Brithdir people who entered the nursing profession. Some of them trained at Merthyr Tydfil while others went further afield. All of them made a mark on the nursing world: some away from Brithdir, but others, equally important, spent their nursing careers in or near Brithdir. Much of the information that follows is taken from reports in contemporary issues of *Merthyr Express* as well as in professional publications, and supplemented wherever possible by information from the nurse or family members.

Winifred Agnes Andrews (previously Masters, née Jones), CBE (1918-1983)

Winifred Agnes Andrews, President of International Confederation of Midwives was known as *midwives' world champion* during her long and distinguished career in nursing.

Born in 8 Station Terrace in 1916 and 1918 respectively, Ann Louise (known as Louise) and Winifred Agnes (known as Agnes) were the two oldest of the seven children of coal miner Isaac Jones and his wife Winifred. Isaac left the colliery in 1926 and became librarian at the local Workmen's Institute, a role well-suited to a man who valued education as he did. His children were encouraged to read widely, to sing at Libanus chapel anniversary and compete in local eisteddfodau. Their successes in eisteddfodau, reported in the local press, included the following:

- January 1929, 10 year old Agnes won under 11 girls' solo at Pontllanfraith.
- October 1929 Agnes won girls' solo at Abertysswg.
- With Mildred Davies, Agnes won duet under 14 at English Congregational Church eisteddfod held in New Hall, Brithdir.
- 1930 Agnes won girls' solo under 16 at Brithdir Workmen's Institute.
- 1932 Louise and Agnes won duet under 16 at Brithdir Workmen's Institute.

It was reported in *Merthyr Express* that Louise left Brithdir in December 1934 to start her nursing career at Hayley Green Hospital, near Birmingham. However, she grew discontented with city life and returned to Wales. It is not clear when and where she continued her training but Roll of Assistant Nurses shows she was enrolled in London July 28 1944 and, according to *Merthyr Express*, July 7 1945, she was nursing in Bedwellty UDC Isolation Hospital, its twelve beds housed in what was described in 1945 South Wales hospital survey (quoted in *Local Population Studies*, number 48, Spring 1992) as *a small, wooden-framed, corrugated iron building .... situated remotely on a mountain top* (Coed y Moeth Common).

Although Agnes had considered training as a teacher, she decided to follow Louise into a nursing career. Her listing among the fever nurses in Register of Nurses for 1943 shows that, following training at Merthyr Tydfil's Mardy Isolation Hospital 1937-1940 and examination success, she was registered in London June 28 1940. Agnes took up an appointment at Dudley Road Hospital, Birmingham in 1940. Later, she undertook midwifery training and became a qualified district midwife in Balsall Heath where, working with another qualified midwife, they had some 410 home deliveries per year.

On a personal level, Agnes experienced some heartbreak. She married butcher John Masters in 1951 only to lose him five years later to cancer. She married Frederick Andrews in 1961 and he died in 1979.

During a long and distinguished career, Agnes held many prestigious offices including:

- Chair, Royal College of Midwives (1971).
- Chair of Council, Royal College of Midwives (1971–1975).
- Director of Nursing Services, Wolverhampton County Borough Council (1972-1974).
- Area Nursing Officer, Wolverhampton Health Authority (1974–1982).
- President, Royal College of Midwives (1975–1981).

The following photographs are reproduced courtesy her older sister, Louise Winstone, who also provided some of the information about Agnes as well as access to *Midwives Chronicle*, December 1975, and *Nursing Mirror* September 1981.

Agnes with J.P.R (Dr. John Peter Rhys Williams).
Courtesy Media Wales Ltd.

Agnes outside Buckingham Palace on her way to receive CBE in 1976 in recognition of services to midwifery and her contribution to nursing profession.

Agnes, a midwife for forty years, belonged to a generation of midwives who gave everything to their work. It was evident on her retirement that this *little lady* was loved all over the midwifery world when colleagues delivered a *This*

is Your Life style celebration party, and a host of former colleagues came from all over the country to join the party at the Birmingham Maternity Hospital. It is not clear whether this photograph was taken at her retirement, but the silver stork is a recognition of her work as a midwife.

Dorothy Webster, who replaced Agnes as President of Royal College of Midwives, paid the following tribute to her former colleague:

During her presidency, we had some difficult periods in the history of our college. For her profession she gave generously of her time and her energy. Not only did she hold office in our college, but also in the Association of Nurse Administrators, the Health Visitors' Association, the Association of Supervisors of Midwives, and the British and Commonwealth Nurses' War Memorial Fund. It is difficult to imagine how such a little lady could achieve so much as well as holding a very demanding full-time job. Agnes had such a joy in living and her charming outgoing personality made her known and loved all over the midwifery world.

Agnes may not have worked in Brithdir, but she took Brithdir with her into her work as evidenced by this profile, written by Mark Allen and printed in *Nursing Mirror* to mark Agnes' retirement:

Mrs. Andrews is especially good at making people feel at home and she does so with her brand of Welsh charm and chuckle. She has one of the most expansive laughs in nursing, a smile that seems to flow right from the undulating valleys of her homeland.

Sadly, after a courageous eight year battle against cancer, Agnes Andrews died on February 12 1983 in Queen Elizabeth Hospital, Birmingham.

Evelyn Winifred May Bosworth - 13 Herbert Street, at Borough Isolation Hospital, Parkstone, Dorset (affiliated to City Isolation Hospital, Cardiff) qualified by examination; registered June 28 1940, London.

Clarice Maud Brown - Daughter of Mr. and Mrs. Herbert Brown, 19 Charles Street, she qualified at Isolation Hospital, Ilford, and was registered as a nurse in London January 29 1932.

Ceinwen Davies - 4 Station Terrace, passed examination at Frome Road House, Bath (associated with Southmead Hospital, Bristol). Registered London, March 18 1932.

Jemima Ann Davies (née Williams) - About 1930, about the same time that my Brewer grandparents and their older children (including my mother, then 10 years old) moved from Pontlottyn to Brithdir, Jemima Davies moved from Rhymney to Brithdir and lived, with her younger daughter Martha and son-in-law William Gigg in Barton Villa. Whilst reminiscing with my mother on the life of Nurse Davies, I learned that when my mother was young, she was asked to sleep at Barton Villa because Nurse Davies's hearing was failing. She relied

300

on my mother to wake her if someone knocked the door requiring her services during the night.

Jemima was a war widow. Husband, Private Daniel John Davies of Welsh Regiment, a coal miner who enlisted for war service December 28 1914 and sailed for France April 7 1915, was reported *missing in action* May 25 1915 after 2nd Battle of Ypres. After over a year of anxious uncertainty, on June 8 1916 Jemima received notice from the War Office that her husband was *presumed dead*. With two young daughters, aged 4½ years and 2½, Jemima embarked on a career in nursing and, as this receipt shows, she posted the one-guinea entrance fee to Central Midwives Board for examination in 1923.

Jemima Ann Davies seated
Courtesy of her granddaughter, Joan Baines, née Gigg, who contributed much of the information.

Jemima was meticulous in recording family events in her family bible, listing, in chronological order, details of births,

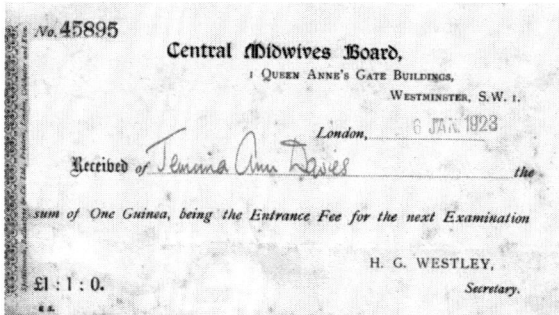

marriages and deaths, as well as of husband Daniel's war service. The entry *July 23rd 1927- I went to Ypres to unveiling of Menin Gate 24.7.27* is especially poignant, and an article on that visit has been submitted for inclusion in the next *Gelligaer* 2018 World War I journal. The last entry in the family bible, in a different hand, reads *February 16 1959 J A Davies passed away (Nurse)*.

Maud Edmunds - *Merthyr Express*, May 4 1935, noted Maud, daughter of Mr. and Mrs. Evan Edmunds, Charles Street, was a nurse in a Surrey Hospital.

Olwen Evans - Oldest daughter of Mr. and Mrs. Evan Evans, 14 Nelson Terrace, Olwen (shown right courtesy Elwyn Evans) started her nursing career with nearly three years training at Bromsgrove Children's Hospital. *Merthyr Express*, March 26 1949, reported she passed preliminary examination at Worcester Royal Infirmary.

Glenys Myrtle Harris - *Merthyr Express*, March 26 1949, carried an announcement that Glenys Myrtle , daughter of Mr. and Mrs. Joseph Harris, 20 Rose Hill Cottages, passed State Registered Nursing examination at Cardiff Royal Infirmary.

Henrietta Jones née Bonney (right) - remembered by many local people as midwife in upper Rhymney Valley (covering the area from Bute Town to north of Bargoed). Following her childhood dreams, Henrietta trained in Merthyr and Aberdare Hospital Group School of Nursing in 1956, before studying in Cardiff (midwifery at St. David's Hospital and Queen's Training School, Park Place) and she became a State Registered Nurse on March 27 1962.

Megan Mary Teify Lewis and Gwyneth Martha Lewis - daughters of William Lewis and his wife, Letitia, of East View, entered the nursing profession. The former was registered March 16 1934, Brook Hospital, London, while *Merthyr Express*, June 3 1939, reported that the latter, who previously had been awarded SRN and RFN certificates, had gained Central Midwives Board certificate at St. James' Hospital, Balham, London.

Freda Pudge - *Merthyr Express*, April 22 1939, reported that Freda, daughter of Mr. and Mrs. Frank Pudge, Nelson Terrace, having trained at North Middlesex County Hospital, obtained the final nursing certificate of England and Wales.

Katie Richards - On leaving Hengoed County School, Katie, second daughter of Hugh and Emily Richards, 5 Ivy Row, started her nursing career at Hereford County Hospital where she was awarded Royal Psychological Association Certificate (with distinction). Undertaking general nursing training at St. Stephen's Hospital, London, she became State Registered Nurse. She joined the staff of Princess Alice Memorial Hospital, Eastbourne, where she passed Royal Medico-Psychological Association examination with distinction. She moved to Dulwich Hospital for midwifery training before joining the staff in that hospital's maternity department, where in 1939, she gained CMB certificate.

Sylvia Roberts - The early stages of the nursing career of Sylvia, only daughter of Mr. and Mrs. Thomas Roberts, 1 Herbert Street, were noted in *Merthyr Express*. Having trained at Merthyr General Hospital, by the time she was 21 years old, Sylvia had passed preliminary State nursing examination (in 1939), and the final State examination of General Nursing Council for England and Wales, two years later.

Ethel Sprague - According to a report in *Merthyr Express*, April 3 1926, Ethel Sprague of 13 Salisbury Terrace, trained at Burton upon Trent General Infirmary and, passing final examination, became qualified State Registered Nurse in 1926.

Rachel Thomas - Reports in *Merthyr Express*, December, 4 and 11 1926, show that it was not only her family who mourned the death of Nurse Rachel Thomas on Sunday December 5 1926. Widely known and liked, Rachel had lived in Brithdir since 1892 and earned respect and friendship during her twenty years as local midwife. Born in Pengam about 1867, she spent her early years in Fleur de Lys where her father, Thomas Llewellyn, was a coal-weigher. The family moved to 61 Bailey Street, Deri, before 1880. Rachel married John Thomas in 1884 and, having started married life at 38 Bailey Street, they moved to 27 Herbert Street about 1892. She was widowed in 1910.

Florence May Wells - Prior to her marriage, Florence May, youngest daughter of Mr. and Mrs. Alfred Wells, 3 Salisbury Terrace, was a nurse at Hatton Central Hospital. *Merthyr Express*, November 30 1946, carried a report on her marriage at St. Gwladys Church on November 23 1946, to Sergeant Cyril Mace, Royal Artillery, of Shipston on Stour. Sergeant Mace spent eight of his 13 year army career overseas. A PoW for over three years, taken from Hong Kong to Japan on board ill-fated *Lisbon Maru* when she was torpedoed by an American submarine, he was in the water for three days before being rescued.

Dilys Megan Williams - This extract from Roll of Assistant Nurses 1947-1948 shows the entry for Dilys Megan Williams of Church Villa. Daughter of Henry (Harry) Williams and wife Catherine, it is likely that she and her siblings were brought up in a stimulating household if her father's many interests, as noted on page 146, is anything to go by.

ROLL OF ASSISTANT NURSES, 1947-8				WIL.-WIL
Enrolment No.	Name	Permanent Address	Date and Place of Enrolment	Qualifications
12288	Williams, Ceridwen	The Institution, Basing Road, Basingstoke	June 28, 1946, London	Rule 14 (1).
8415	Williams, Christie	The Laurels, Dartmouth Avenue, Oldfield Park, Bath	April 23, 1947, London	Rule 14 (1).
10859	Williams, Cora Minna Selina	19, Ganna Park Road, Peverell, Plymouth	May 24, 1946, London	Rule 10 (1).
9685	Williams, David Elwyn	New Cottage, Cross Hands, Llanelly, Wales	Feb. 28, 1947, London	Rule 14 (1).
8648	Williams, Dilys	24, Albert Drive, Orrell Park, Liverpool, 9	Mar. 22, 1946, London	Rule 14 (1).
13577	Williams, Dilys Margaret	5, Valfrey Road, Whitland, Carmarthenshire, Wales	Dec. 21, 1945, London	Rule 14 (1).
14399	Williams, Dilys Mary	Bacondiol, Pontrhydfendigaid, Cardiganshire, Wales	Feb. 22, 1946, London	Rule 10 (1).
15401	Williams, Dilys Megan	Church Villa, Brithdir, New Tredegar, Monmouthshire	Jan. 24, 1947, London	Rule 14 (1).

O – Dr. O'Shea's Casebook

Affectionately dubbed Doctor Pat, Dr. Patrick Fionan O'Shea cared for several generations, seeing some people from cradle to grave, during his 54 years in Brithdir. This tribute to a popular and respected doctor owes much to information and photographs from his daughters, Elizabeth Spillane and Fionnala Eardley, Esther, daughter of his son Dermot, and grandson, Patrick Spillane, as well as many former patients who shared memories.

Born March 7 1901 in Glengarriff, a coastal village in County Cork, Ireland, Patrick Fionan O'Shea (known as Fionan) was son of teachers Elizabeth and Patrick (shown right). Elizabeth hailed from Kerry and taught at Glengarriff National School where Patrick, a native of that village, was headmaster. They were both fluent Irish speakers, Patrick was the Gaelic writer Pàdraig O'Seaghdha, but as there was another contemporary Irish writer by the same name, he wrote under pen name Gruagach an Tobar (*The fairy in the well*).

Like his siblings, sister and three brothers, the young Dr. O'Shea was taught by his parents before, on reaching secondary school age, attending boarding school. His sister, Maureen, entered a French religious order and became a teacher, while his oldest brother, Mortimer, became a priest, joining order of Friars Minor Capuchin and adopting the saintly name Father Cassian. For many years a teacher in Ireland, Mortimer later went to Los Angeles. The other two brothers were Dermot and Kevin: the former, member of Irish Volunteers, was involved in 1916 Easter Rising, while the latter studied at University College Dublin and became a secondary school teacher.

In October 1918, Patrick Fionan, the youngest of the five, started to read medicine at University College Cork and enrolled on a course at School of Art. Not only did he write for student publications and sketch cartoons, his writing was also published in the Irish press. On graduating in 1925, he boarded a ship at Cork, with plans for a career in London. On arrival at Fishguard, on a cold misty morning, he took the London train. The mists cleared near Swansea, revealing a monotonous, cheerless landscape of *belching chimney-stacks, slag-tips, and colliery wheels, lakes of roof-tops and patches of sombre sunless sky.* Fulfilling his promise to his mother, he visited his sister in Pontypool. As the mists dispersed, so did his plans to find a career and life in London and, as each day passed, he was less inclined to leave Wales. His first post, as assistant to E.M. Griffiths of Abercarn, lasted five months until, in October 1925, he became locum tenens to Dr. Gwilym Rhys Pennant at Brithdir. Dr. Pennant was a sick man and the stay was extended until, in 1927, Dr. Pennant retired and Dr. O'Shea accepted the offer of the practice.

Dr. O'Shea was not Brithdir's first Irish doctor. In the 1920s, many people still remembered Dr. Martin who had founded the practice in 1903 and, from his home, Leargaidh, East View, had served patients in Brithdir and nearby communities. For further information about the life and work of Dr. Martin in Ireland and Brithdir, before he was killed in action during the Great War, see pages 186-188 above and *Gelligaer* volume 21 2014.

Dr. O'Shea's career in Brithdir began during a time of economic and social difficulty in the community. Starting on £5 10s a week, and using a bicycle (often challenging on the steep valley slopes) to visit patients at all hours, he faced every type of medical situation and did his own dispensing. Dr. O'Shea's work, whether dealing with sicknesses, pit accidents or maternity cases, was a day and night commitment that took him into the heart of many families in the community.

Although his practice left him little time for painting or writing, encouraged by his university friend, Sean O'Faolain, then editor of the popular Irish magazine, *Bell*, he sometimes submitted articles for publication. In one such article he described arriving in Brithdir:

There was a drizzle of rain when I arrived and the valley shrouded in mist, making the place look drab and foggy. As I poked around for my new chief's house in the jumble of hilly streets, much alike in their greyness, I came to a grocer's shop where I inquired my way. A plump smiling maiden came bobbing under the counter-flap to direct me. From the kerb she pointed at the house on the opposite corner.

That *maiden* was Hilda, daughter of Mr. and Mrs. Edwin Bufton, Railway Stores, and his future wife. When Fionan and Hilda married, August 13 1929 at Pontypool, his brother, Rev. Dr. Cassian O'Shea, performed the ceremony.

Until July 1953, Dr. O'Shea, single-handedly, worked Brithdir surgery at the back of his home, as well as a surgery in Duffryn Terrace, New Tredegar, and one at Tapper's fish shop, Cwmsyfiog. As the number of patients increased, Dr. P. Hockenhull joined him as partner. Visiting a doctor's surgery then was very different from nowadays (2017). It was first come first seen: when the patient seated nearest the surgery door went in, waiting patients moved up one seat. The

Wedding day photograph
Courtesy Dilwyn Rees.

Monday morning by Doctor O'Shea.

surgery desk was adorned with caricatures and cartoons and the shelf was full of jars of home-made potions, including the horrible-tasting cough mixture, mixed by the doctor and cure for any Brithdir cough.

As well as being a GP, Dr. O'Shea was active in local affairs. He became president to many local groups, the first of which, starting in 1926, was Air Rifle Club at Tirphil Liberal Club. He was inaugural president of Brithdir Athletic Club, formed in 1927 to foster boxing, and he was also president of the local Homing Society, Brithdir branch of British Legion, and Brithdir United Football Club, as well as numerous local committees such as Brithdir flower show committee. A wall plaque in Brithdir Constitutional Club honours his time as their President. In 1927, he became lecturer to the local St. John Ambulance Brigade Nursing Class, and was later the examiner. He took the chair when, in George Hotel, local artists performed at the popular smoking concerts in aid of good causes. Mr. A. Jones, 14 Wellington Terrace, was a beneficiary of one such concert which raised money to help him obtain an artificial leg. During World War Two, both Dr. and Mrs. O'Shea were involved in various fundraising functions organised by Brithdir Home Guard.

Bird's eye view of the area covered by Dr. O'Shea's practice. Brithdir village (left foreground) separated from its neighbour, Cwmsyfiog (right), by Rhymney river, the boundary between the former Glamorganshire and Monmouthshire. In the distance, mid-centre, steam rising from Elliot Colliery, flanked by the villages of Tirphil (left) and New Tredegar (right), with Philipstown and Jubilee on the mountainside above.

Courtesy Paul James.

Dr. O'Shea and family made regular visits to his native Ireland, but he called Brithdir home. He liked the place and its people, and it was where he and his wife raised their three children – Elizabeth, Fionnuala and Dermot. Elizabeth married Dr. Eamon Spillane, a native of Kerry, Ireland, in 1952, and, about 1962, they emigrated, settling in Melbourne, Victoria, where Eamon became a very successful GP. They had a large family, twelve children, four of whom were born in Australia, and 27 grandchildren and, at the time of writing, two great grandchildren. In 1960, Fionnuala married Arthur Brian Eardley and they made their home in Betton near Market Drayton, in his native Shropshire. Although Dermot began medical studies in Dublin, he realised he was not cut out for the work his father had done so well. Soon after he married Margaret in 1973, they settled in Kilcullen, County Kildare, where they raised four children, Dafydd, Owen, Esther and Edwin. Dermot had a varied career, working as typewriter salesman, ticket collector on Dublin bus and assistant in a chemical factory. He had a period of unemployment before, in 1994, becoming gardener in a local Camphill Community working with people with special needs. He moved to a new facility, Bridge Camphill, in Kilcullen, where he not only grew vegetables for the Community and the organic Manna

306

Shop, but also trained residents and co-workers. Although a serious heart attack in 2000 forced Dermot into semi-retirement, he continued to help the Community until, in November 2012, a severe chest infection affected his heart, and he died in hospital a few days later. At his funeral his coffin was draped with a Welsh flag.

On August 13 1979, Patrick Fionan and Hilda celebrated their Golden Wedding. Just over a year later, the couple left Brithdir, and settled into a new home near their daughter in Market Drayton. Although aware that Dr. O'Shea was not in the best of health, Brithdir community was shocked and saddened to hear of his death June 8 1981. A coach full of villagers made the 235 mile round trip to attend his funeral, something that brought considerable comfort to Mrs. O'Shea and other members of the bereaved family.

Dr. O'Shea and wife Hilda with daughters, Elizabeth and Fionnuala, and son, Dermot, shortly before Elizabeth left for Australia in 1962.

Dr. O'Shea's grandson Patrick Spillane with his mother Elizabeth.

People's Memories of the Doctor

As Dr. O'Shea was in Brithdir for five and a half decades, it is hardly surprising that there is a wealth of stories about him, a legend within the community. The following sample reveals many of the reasons why he was such a popular and respected doctor in the community:

Doctor O'Shea wanted urgently - Elizabeth Elvira Griffiths of Markham, an 86 year old widow, saddened by the recent loss of husband William (Bill), read my request in the local press for people's memories of Dr. O'Shea, and invited me to her home. There she told me *he saved my life* before recounting the story. Pregnant and living in New Tredegar, with Bill working in Elliot Colliery, she went into labour, but complications set in and with the loss of blood, it was feared she would die. Dr. O'Shea was with his children in a Bargoed cinema when the message *Dr. O'Shea wanted urgently* flashed on the screen. He rushed to New Tredegar, delivered the baby and *he saved my life*

Dr. Pat and the biker - Pat Bennett, née Pearson, recalled a bitterly cold Sunday morning when she was about 14 and living at Halfway House alongside the road above the village. The road was covered in ice. On hearing a high revving screaming motorbike engine, her father went to the window only to see the bike lying on its side, and a leather-clad figure prone on the road. There was no telephone, so young Pat was sent for the doctor. Muttering about the weather, Dr. O'Shea bundled Pat into his car and cautiously drove to the scene. As he could not assess the extent of the injuries, he asked Pat's father to help open up the biker's leathers. Those who remember Dr. O'Shea will not be surprised to know that, amid many choice words, he told the biker of his folly in riding in such conditions. Pat recalls the expression on the doctor's face when, freed from the all-concealing outfit, the biker's clerical collar was revealed. While Pat and her father could hardly contain their amusement at the look of shock on the doctor's face, Dr. O'Shea listened to the young clergyman's apologies for causing trouble as he did not want to let his Pontlottyn parishioners down.

The Blizzard and a tot of whisky - Alan *Spud* Murphy (Cascade, but formerly Phillipstown) spoke of a home visit when he was a child and unwell. During a blizzard, the doctor, not well himself, walked from Brithdir to Phillipstown, After Dr. O'Shea had tended his patient, Alan's grandmother offered the doctor a tot of whisky, *to help him on his return journey*. Alan heard the doctor say he had a few more calls to make before returning home via Tirphil.

Measles epidemic - John Rawle (Cefn Cribwr, formerly Herbert Street) recalled that during a measles epidemic, Dr. O'Shea arranged for an ambulance to come to the village. It was parked on the main road, and as each child went there for the injection, Dr. O'Shea sterilised the needle in the flame over a small gas stove.

Daily trek to the farm - Gaynor Crowley, daughter of William and Bessy Francis, formerly of Bedwlwyn Farm, Phillipstown, recalls that when she was 8 years old, suffering rheumatic fever and too ill to be moved to hospital, Dr. O'Shea walked from his home two or three times a day until she recovered.

Red Flag - Brian Bennett remembers that, before most households had telephones (for younger readers that means a land line in the house, not a mobile), Mrs. O'Shea could summon her husband by waving a piece of red cloth from an upstairs window. Brian sometimes chauffeured Dr. O'Shea to Tirphil Golf Club (on Cefn Brithdir). While the doctor was playing, Brian parked up overlooking the village and, if the doctor was needed, he saw the red cloth waving.

A glass of earrings - Allan Rogers (Leicester, formerly Wellington Terrace) remembers Irishman Danny Darcy lodging in his family home for so long that he was more like a grandad than a lodger. Whenever the doctor called to visit Allan's sick uncle, Danny, using the same glass each time, gave him a drop of whisky. On one occasion the doctor nearly choked: Danny did not realise that Allan's mother had put her earrings in that glass.

Send for a Doctor - Cliff Summers of Aylesbury remembers a workday when a fall of coal trapped a man by his legs. As the two first aiders needed help, they sent for a doctor. Within the hour, Dr. O'Shea, in his clean suit, white shirt and tie, was down the pit, working by the light of the miners' lamps.

Treasured memories - Joyce Jones (New Tredegar) recalls Dr. O'Shea's visits to her parent's home on St. Patrick's Day. He gave her a piece of shamrock which she dried and kept in the family bible. Preparing an article for *Merthyr Express* on the doctor's retirement; a reporter asked, who, over 54 years as a doctor, was his favourite patient. Without hesitation, Dr. O'Shea replied, *Mrs. Jones, New Tredegar*, and arrangements were made to have them photographed together outside the O'Shea family home in East View.

Dr. O'Shea with Joyce Jones, outside Leargaidh, East View. Photograph taken for inclusion in a local press article marking his retirement.

Oh he was a lovely man - I leave the last word about this remarkable man to my dear late mother, for over three years employed by him as a domestic help. When I asked her what memories she had of the doctor she simply said *Oh he was a lovely man*, words echoed by everyone who came into contact with this legendary doctor.

P – Policing

Village bobbies

The village bobby was a well-respected member of the community who talked to local people and knew what was going on. He lived in the community and his family was involved in local activities. Much of the information about Brithdir's policemen is taken from records in Glamorgan Archives (reference DCON) as well as reports in the local press.

Glamorgan Constabulary, established in 1841, saw little need for much policing in the Brithdir area until about half a century later. About 1893, Brithdir people requested a local policeman and early in 1894 P.C. Thomas Henry Evans was the first police constable stationed at Brithdir. Born in Llandaff in 1862, Thomas Evans worked in the paper mill near his home until, in 1880, he joined Glamorgan Constabulary. He served first at Headquarters but was later drafted to Merthyr, Aberdare, and Dowlais. He was badly injured during riots in Merthyr Borough and, when his assailants were brought before the stipendiary magistrate, the latter paid tribute to his courage. The following day, the Chief Constable, promoted him to merit-class sergeant. Although he left the force in 1884 for work with Taff Vale Railway Company, he later rejoined and was stationed at Penarth, Llwydcoed, Brithdir, Cwmaman, and Ynyslwyd. Soon after he arrived in Brithdir, he was commended by Judge Bruce for the way in which he captured a gang of burglars, and in 1895 he arrested a man for stealing a horse at Waun Fair. It is not clear when he left Brithdir.

Police Constable William Evans, formerly stationed at Sully, was transferred from Barry to Brithdir in 1898. A native of Henllan, Carmarthenshire, and a Welsh speaker, he married farmer's daughter Catherine Ratcliffe of Felin Fach near Brecon in December 1895. Their son, Hubert Ratcliffe, was just an infant when the family moved to Brithdir. Sadly second son, Levi, was born and died (aged 4, in 1903) in Brithdir. When he left the village in August 1907, Brithdir people presented him with what was described in the press as *a beautifully illuminated address* that referred *to the efficient and straightforward manner in which P.C. Evans had performed his duties while stationed there* and expressed the hope *that the same kindly feeling will be shown towards Mr. Evans in his new station at Blaengarw.*

Police Constable Walter Kelland was stationed at Brithdir for just two years before, in 1909, he was promoted to acting sergeant in Nelson. A native of Tiverton, his family had farmed in that part of Devon for more than two centuries. Arriving in South Wales in 1891, he worked on farms in the Cowbridge area before, in 1892, joining Glamorgan Constabulary. He started at Bridgend and, after a few months, he transferred to Porthcawl, where he stayed for four years before spending a year at Maesteg, a year at Llangan, and eight years in charge of a new police station at Caerau. At Caerau, a very rough quarter then, a tactful P.C. Kelland was instrumental in halting a spate of sheep stealing. That same approach later proved effective in Nelson where he managed to end fowl thefts, and he soon won the respect and esteem of its law-abiding citizens. When, in 1911, the new Nelson station opened, acting Sergeant Kelland was appointed officer in charge. Single-handedly, he policed the area during the difficult war years and was rewarded by promotion to full sergeant in 1920. He was in Nelson for over fifteen years until he retired after 32 years and 8 months' service and settled at Tynybedw Farm, near Pontypridd, his home at the time of his death, aged 63, in March 1933.

P.C. Albert Jones replaced P.C. Kelland in Brithdir. A shoemaker by trade, he was 25 years old when he joined Glamorgan Constabulary March 7 1891. He was stationed at Barry Dock, Burry Port, Glyn Neath, Trelewis and Waunlwyd before, after 30 years' service, arriving in Brithdir where he served 12½ years. On census night 1911, P.C. Jones was one of a number of constables enumerated at Barry Dock Police Office, stationed there to watch the railway at a time when some striking miners were raiding mineral trains *en route* to the docks. Aged 55, P.C. Albert Jones died in service at Brithdir on May 3 1921. A native of Llanarthney, Carmarthenshire, his body was taken there for burial. The funeral, on May 7, was attended by 26 members of Glamorgan Constabulary and the bearers, in full uniform, Sergeants Clinch, Pontlottyn, W.H. Williams, Ystrad Mynach, Row, Bargoed and J. Edwards, Deri, accompanied the funeral to Llanarthney.

The first police house in Brithdir, 20 Station Terrace, had a cell built in the back of the house to accommodate anyone arrested or detained overnight. It ceased to be the police house after P.C. Albert Jones died in 1921, as his wife, Margaret, (realising early in her married life that if, for whatever reason, her husband was no longer in the Constabulary, she would have to leave her home) had seized an opportunity to purchase the property. Thus, Glamorgan Constabulary, obliged to find a house for the next village policeman, rented 21 Station Terrace.

Margaret continued to live in 20 Station Terrace. When she died, August 22 1925, she was buried with her husband in Llanarthney. There are many people who will remember their only son, Idris, as a railway clerk and for his work (see page 282) with local St. John Ambulance Brigade.

In 1946, Police Sergeant Thomas Jones (shown right courtesy Daryl Jones) retired after 31 years' service in Glamorgan Constabulary. Born 1891 in Camrose, Haverfordwest, he was a collier before, in February 1915, joining the Constabulary. His first station was Llanbradach but he transferred to Brithdir in January 1921 and stayed 12 years before moving to Fochriw Colliery. Whilst at Fochriw he was a member of Hospital Committee of Merthyr General Hospital. He later served at Abertridwr and Llanbradach and, for the last ten years, he was a Sergeant at Nantyffin Colliery, Bedlinog.

P.C. Reginald Rowlands, a native of Panteg, Griffithstown, was a tin-worker before starting a career in the Constabulary at Canton in 1924. After training at Police Headquarters at Treharris he served at Nelson, Pontlottyn and Deri, before he arrived in Brithdir on January 30 1937, shortly before the birth of his son (for whom see 156). In his early days at Brithdir, he did a great deal of spadework with St. John Ambulance Brigade and he was made Regional Superintendent. With his wife, he formed a Nursing Division and established a Home Comforts Depot. He was promoted acting Sergeant in 1937 and transferred to Pontlottyn, promoted Sergeant in 1939 and Inspector in 1946, when he was put in charge of Llantrisant Sub-Division. In 1948, he transferred to Aberdare and was later promoted Chief Inspector. Chief Inspector Rowlands was one of four inspectors from Glamorgan invited to line the route for the Queen's Coronation and he received Coronation Medal. After 36 years on the force, he retired in 1960.

P.C. William J. Lloyd was Brithdir's next policeman. Born 1899 in Barry Island, he joined the force in 1921 serving at Williamstown, Tynewydd, Cwmparc, Penygraig and Nelson before arriving in Brithdir in January 1937. He is credited with being the pioneer of Brithdir old age pensioners' summer outings, working alongside other committee members during the winters to raise the necessary funds. On Sunday evening, March 9 1941, the body of David Robert Gabb, a soldier of Bailey Street, Deri, was found in Rhymney river near Brithdir, and P.C. Lloyd was present at the inquest held in George Inn the following Tuesday. He was a member of the local War Weapons Week committee in 1941. William John Lloyd resigned from the force on October 9 1942.

P.C. Herbert Blenkiron was stationed at Brithdir for two years before retiring from policing in November 1944. The son of coal miner John Blenkiron and wife Elizabeth, Herbert was born 1893 in Reeth, Yorkshire. He was young when the family arrived in South Wales (Coedpenmaen Road, Pontypridd) for his father to work in the coal mines. At the time of the 1911 census, 17 year old Herbert was a mine labourer. It is not clear when he joined the police force, but, in March 1915, he gave evidence in a shooting case at Caerphilly Magistrates court. While stationed at Nelson, 21 year old Herbert Blenkiron attested at Bargoed on October 10 1915, joined Royal Regiment of Artillery and the following day, he was placed in Army Reserve. He was mobilised March 14 1917 and posted to Southampton April 7 1917, sailing for France three days later with BEF to serve as Gunner 141534 with 245 Siege Battery. On July 20 1917 he became Gunner/Signaller. Whilst home on leave in May 1918 he married Bessie Escott at St. Martin's Church, Caerphilly. On demobilisation, February 1919, he returned to policing, continuing a 31 year career in Rhymney and Rhondda Valleys.

He was succeeded at Brithdir by P.C. Joe Evans of Nelson. Those who remembered P.C. Evans recall he was dubbed *Blackout Evans* as he often stepped out of a dark doorway to apprehend a mischief maker.

Roy Oakley Angell, son of Archibald and Fanny Angell of Kenfig Hill, was a collier before, aged 19, he joined the Constabulary in March 1941. He was stationed at Pontlottyn for sixteen months before transferring to Port Talbot in October 1942. In June 1945, he married Eluned, youngest daughter of Mr. and Mrs. L. D. Lewis, High Street, Troedrhiwfuwch at St. Tyfaelog's Church. A year later, June 1946, he was transferred to Port Talbot Steel Works. He returned to Rhymney Valley when he was posted to Brithdir in August 1950. As village bobby when I was growing up in the 1950s, P.C. Angell's presence ensured that I and my friends kept on the *straight and narrow*.

P.C. Roy Angell with Harry James (Ivy Row).
Courtesy Sandra Evans.

Angell family headstone in Gwaelod y Brithdir Cemetery.
Courtesy Lee Bengough.

Brynley (Bryn) Jenkins (shown left) succeeded Roy Angell. A native of Blaengarw, he worked as a collier before he joined the force in April 1951. On completing his training at No. 8 District Police Training Centre, Police Headquarters, Cowbridge Road, Bridgend, he was transferred to Pontlottyn in July 1951. Bryn was a rugby man, and whilst stationed at Brithdir, he played for Bargoed RFC. On retirement from the force Bryn moved to Abertridwr.

Sources studied to date suggest that Leonard James Kiff was the last village bobby to live in 21 Station Terrace. Born 1919 in Troedyrhiw, Len served 6¼ years in Welsh Guards prior to joining the police on August 26 1946. After initial training at Bridgend, he transferred to Bargoed Police Station in November 1946. On March 31 1954, he passed sergeant examination. It is unclear when he moved to Brithdir but several local people remember his son, Anthony, in Brithdir Infants' School in the mid-1960s.

Brithdir Police House closed in 1967. P.C. Denis Roberts, the last policeman to live in 21 Station Terrace, was stationed at Caerphilly, when, in 1968, he was offered its use. His neighbour in number 20, the original police house, was Special Constable Idris Jones (whose mother had bought the house).

A sad tale of a policeman with a Brithdir connection

Glamorgan Gazette, July 25 1919, carried a report on the tragic death of P.C. Bert Hill, 18 year old son of James and Martha Hill, 9 Salisbury Terrace. He was knocked down and killed whilst on duty at GWR Station, Port Talbot about 4 am July 22 1919. After four years of war service in the army, Bert Hill joined Glamorgan Constabulary July 5 1919 and was sent to Port Talbot the same day. On the day of the accident, the constable in charge of the police station instructed him to patrol a beat which included the railway station. Evidence given at the inquiry into his death revealed P.C. Hill was struck by the tenth wagon from the engine of a goods train of about 60 wagons as it passed through the station early in the morning.

Several Brithdir people have made careers for themselves in the police service as witnessed by the following examples.

Mavis McCann (née Brown) MBE

Mavis, eldest daughter of Hubert and Florence Brown, East View, was awarded MBE New Year Honours List 1995. When she received her award at Buckingham Palace in March 1995 she proudly remembered her family and her Brithdir roots as witnessed by this extract from her letter:

whilst waiting to go forward for the presentation by the Prince of Wales, my thoughts were of Brithdir and the hope that my late mother and father were looking down on the event.

Having learned shorthand, typing and book-keeping in her final year at Lewis Girls' School, Mavis started work as female civilian clerk first at Ystrad Mynach Police Station and later at Bargoed Police Station. In 1965, she secured a post with Metropolitan Police at New Scotland Yard and, as a shorthand typist, she worked in various departments at New Scotland Yard and at London police stations. She was at Shepherd's Bush Police Station when, in 1966, three police officers were gunned down in cold blood (Shepherd's Bush Murders). Mavis worked with members of the murder squad until the offenders were arrested and, later, attended the Old Bailey to take notes of the trial, which she described as *a very scary experience*. Promotion followed, and Mavis became personal secretary to the first public relations officer in Metropolitan Police. Mavis was not a police officer but, as a member of the support staff, she was promoted through the ranks.

In 1979, Mavis married Jeffrey McCann, a member of Metropolitan Police solicitors' department, and, when he took an appointment in Hong Kong Judiciary, they moved to Hong Kong until ill-health forced their return to UK. On re-joining Metropolitan Police, Mavis was soon appointed private secretary to the Deputy Commissioner. She remained in that post, serving eight successive Deputy Commissioners, until her retirement. Sadly, Mavis, whose correspondence provided most of the information for this short account, died in 2016.

Andrew Morgan – Police Superintendent

Born in Wellington Terrace, Andrew spent his formative years in nearby New Tredegar, where his parents became tenants at New Tredegar Arms Hotel in 1974. His early schooling was at Central School, New Tredegar, before moving on to Bedwellty Grammar School. On leaving Bedwellty with three A Levels, it was Andrew's initial intention to start undergraduate study at Swansea, but instead, he decided to enter the police force. At his interview, he was advised that with his qualifications, he should go to London, where career opportunities would be better than in South Wales. Andrew subsequently joined Metropolitan Police Force in 1983, and serving for just over 32 years, he was promoted through the ranks to Superintendent as shown in the following list of stations and ranks:

    1984-1989 Paddington Green, Constable.
    1989-1996 Twickenham, Sergeant.
    1996-1997 Ealing, Sergeant.
    1997-2001 Paddington Green, Inspector.
    2001- Hounslow, Chief Inspector.
    2011 Superintendent.

Much of what follows about Andrew's career is based on information from Barbara Morgan and from Andrew, and the photographs are courtesy Andrew.

Right is a photograph taken in 1984 when Andrew was at the Metropolitan Police Training College Hendon and tasked with presenting a practical display of a road accident involving a motor cyclist for Princess Diana. P.C. 482D Morgan, facing the camera, is one of the two constables holding the motor bike.

Andrew's first posting was to Paddington Green police station and he worked many tours of duty guarding arrested terrorist suspects, including the Brighton bombers. Within five months of arriving on the streets he was deployed to Broadwater Farm estate riots (Tottenham), in which P.C. Keith Blakelock was murdered whilst protecting fire-fighters.

From time to time, Andrew met people from his home community in the course of his work, as instanced by this account of a chance meeting:

One day working near Paddington railway station, I saw a coach from Tredegar parked on the zig-zag lines of a pedestrian crossing. As I walked toward the coach I could see the driver was agitated, probably fearing a fixed penalty ticket and points on his licence. As I approached the driver he said "sorry officer I will move it now". I replied " That's ok uncle John you are not causing any danger" (removing my helmet so he could see my face). We then had a warm and happy reunion.

The coach driver Andrew referred to was John Brewer and in the photo left, this time in Edinburgh, a reunion with two more family members, L-R are nephew Royston Smith, John and brother Geoff Brewer.

Whilst at Twickenham police station Andrew worked at many rugby internationals including all the matches of 1991 World Cup. On several occasions, he met players from New Tredegar RFC and Rhymney RFC, the latter his last team before moving to London.

Over a fifteen year period Andrew attended the scenes of a number of terrorist attacks during the height of IRA bombings, including Baltic Exchange bombing and Isle of Dogs vehicle bombs. There were also many duties at Notting Hill Carnivals in the 1980s and 90s.

Andrew takes over the story:

For the last 10 years of my service I was additionally a Counter Terrorism Security Co-ordinator. My role included planning the defensive counter measures to deter or prevent terrorist atrocities. Over this period, I planned for Royal events including trooping the colour, investitures, events attended by Royal Family members and the Queen's Golden Jubilee events. I also planned protection for Heads of State and other VIPs attending the funeral of Baroness Thatcher.

Chief Inspector Andrew Morgan with Deputy Commissioner Ian Blair of Metropolitan Police, 2004, on the presentationof his Long-Service Medal.

I was one of a few designated security co-ordinators who were trusted to review and plan security for events held at Windsor Castle between 2008-13. I went into the Castle and reviewed the security every few months to ensure any security weaknesses were addressed and the Queen and other Royalty remained safe.

I was involved in the safety and counter terrorism planning for State visits, including Presidents from USA, France and other countries, German Chancellor, Chinese Premier and various Prime Ministers.

My role was to work with other UK security agencies, foreign secret services and other partner agencies to examine sites to be visited and events taking place. Then to plan overlapping layers of security to prevent terrorists getting close to the principals. I am proud that during my ten years none of the dignitaries, as well as the public and security forces, I planned to protect, suffered any injury.

Other local connections with policing include:

- Morgan Jones, a serving policeman end of 1950s and early 1960s.
- Eddie Griffiths, part of the Bevan family (see pages 260 - 264), a serving policeman in the Rhymney Valley for over 25 years.
- Basil Brain, formerly Salisbury Terrace, a serving policeman for 25-30 years.

Q – Quoits and other pastimes

Prior to the 1950s, Brithdir children played outdoor games like hopscotch, skipping and football, or spent time exploring the river bank and the mountainside. But childhood was short, and for the majority of them, reaching the statutory school-leaving age meant entering the adult world of work: most boys started a lifetime of work in the coal industry while girls went into domestic service until marriage and a home of their own.

When adults had spare time, they could find plenty to occupy them in Brithdir, especially if their interest lay in sport, drama or music. Some of the activities were associated with the places of worship while, as time went on, the increasing number of organised clubs and societies, as well as new venues such as New Hall, opened up more opportunities within the community.

Although homes were often crowded and less comfortable than most twenty-first century Brithdir residents are accustomed to, some people spent time on pastimes in the home, such as playing the piano. In the house, women were often occupied with needlework: older girls were knitting, sewing or crocheting items for their *bottom drawer*, while wives and mothers patched and darned to extend the life of the family's clothes. Men frequently enjoyed seasonal tasks tending vegetables in their gardens or allotment plots

What follows are some examples of the pastimes enjoyed by Brithdir individuals and groups.

Bill Gigg and draughts

William (Bill) Gigg's library, a collection of more than 200 books connected with draughts playing and players, neatly arranged in a home-made bookcase in the sitting room at Barton Villa, was testimony to his interest in the game of draughts. On leaving Lewis School, Pengam, 15 year old Bill not only started work at Bargoed Pit, but also became interested in draughts. He played for Rhymney Library team, and when that was disbanded, he joined Abertillery Draughts Club, where he played first board for two seasons without losing a game. He did not have much success in his games in Welsh championships, but when he faced Sam Cohen, then world champion, in an exhibition match at Aberaman, he became the first player to win against him. Later, Bill competed in the English Open Championships at Weston and Scarborough. At Scarborough, he played against Derek Oldbury, one-time world champion, earning a place among the prize-winners through losing one game and adjudicated to have drawn the other. As part of South Wales Draughts Correspondence League, he played opposition from across the world.

On May 21 1949, at Cardiff, Bill, representing Glamorgan County in semi-final *Reynolds News Cup* competition, played against Warwickshire's W. Cleaver, a player with 15 years' County experience. Bill won 2-0, and Glamorgan won the match 15-6 with 9 draws. In the final, played in London on November 6, Glamorgan lost to Middlesex, score card 10-2 with 14 draws.

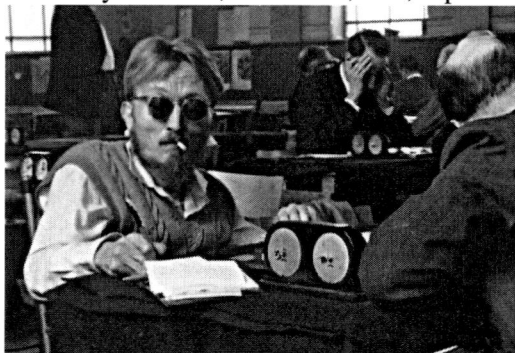

A rare image of former world champion, Derek Oldbury (facing camera), in Crossboard Action against Bill Gigg, at 1963 English Open Championship in Scarborough, Oldbury won and Bill Gigg finished 5th.

Courtesy Ken Lovell.

Many people from the world of draughts visited Bill at Barton Villa: Alf Huggins of Cwm and Ivor Edwards paid regular visits for practice sessions with Bill, while W. T. Jenkins, a draughts

317

exponent from Tredegar, was also a regular visitor. Bill started buying books on draughts almost as soon as he began playing and, over forty years, he built up one of the best libraries on the subject in South Wales, if not in UK. Bill had the magazines bound by London bookbinder and draught player, C. J. Greensword, until he learned the skill himself.

In December 1930, Bill married Martha, daughter of Nurse Jemima Davies (see page 300). Much of the information about Bill and his library came from Joan Baines, née Gigg (Bill's daughter).

The Briffett family -- have Minorcas, will travel

Showing poultry was a popular hobby which could be enjoyed by all the family, as witnessed by the experiences of Henry George Briffett of Bronhaulwen, East View, and his son Hector. For the Briffetts it was *have Minorcas will travel* as they entered their birds in shows all over the country.

Reports in local newspapers show that Henry George Briffett, a native of Bridgewater, Somerset, was a poultry fancier long before his move to Brithdir. His address was 57 West Street, Bridgewater when, on December 5 1901, he won best Minorca (cock or hen) in show, at Cardigan Poultry Show. It is not clear when the Briffett family arrived in Brithdir, but it was after the 1911 census was taken and before December 1918 when *Barry Dock News* reported that Henry was awarded a 2nd in Minorca class in Barry Fur and Feather Society annual show held on December 7. The Black Minorca, a favourite with Henry Briffett, was well suited to a mining community and its dirty smoky atmosphere.

Over the years the results of many poultry shows were published in newspapers, and it is clear that the father and son amassed an array of awards between them as witnessed by the following examples:

Merthyr Express, January 24 1925: *At the Nantymoel Poultry and Pigeon Show, held on Friday last, Mr. H. G. Briffett was awarded three firsts, also a special, and a ten-guinea challenge cup for the best Minorca hen or pullet in the show. He also secured first, special and third at Pontnewydd Show. Again, at Neath he had second prize; at Ebbw Vale he secured second and reserve, and again secured first prize at Brecon with his well-known Minorcas.*

Merthyr Express, June 1925: *Further success with a prize Minorca fowl has come to Brithdir for Mr. Hector Briffett has secured the Welsh Minorca Challenge Cup at the recent contest held at Pontnewydd. Mr. Briffett is following closely in his father's footsteps, for at the last annual show held at Nantymoel this cup was won by Mr. Briffett (senior). Mr. Hector Briffett also won at Pontnewydd a pair of silver spoons for the best Minorca hen or pullet, novice entry, and Mr. Briffett (senior) was awarded a first and a special prize in the Minorca hen class.*

Apart from success at local shows, the Briffetts travelled country-wide with their birds and the following are some examples of their successes:

- 3rd Prize Portmadoc Dog and Poultry Show 1919.

- 1st Prize Northampton Fur and Feather Show 1924.
- 2nd Prize Redruth Show 1924.
- 1st and 2 Specials Huntingdon and District Agricultural Show 1926.
- 1st Prize Bramall Show, Cheshire 1927.
- 1st Prize Royal Welsh Show at Wrexham 1928.
- 1st and 4th Prizes Leicester County Poultry and Pigeon Show 1930.
- 1st Prize Exeter Show 1931.
- 1st Prize Oxfordshire Poultry Show 1934.

Jack Jarvis, eisteddfod prize-winning splicer

Eisteddfodau are not all about stage competitions or music, as witnessed by the achievement of Jack Jarvis, son of Walter Jarvis of Glan yr Avon. One time member of Aston Villa Football Club, Jack Jarvis won a splicing competition in a timbering class in the National Eisteddfod at Llanelly in 1930 and he repeated that achievement at Port Talbot in August 1932. The skills have passed down in the family as Malcolm *Jack* Jarvis, East View, carved Welsh love spoons in his garden shed and made miniature Tudor dolls' houses, which fitted with lighting and tastefully decorated and furnished by his wife, were displayed with pride in his home, as shown in these photographs.

Quoits

Quoits, a traditional game, closely related to horseshoe pitching, was enjoyed by working men, including miners, and involved throwing a metal ring over a set distance to land over a pin in the centre of a patch of clay. After a game, it was customary for players, officials and spectators to adjourn to local premises for a musical evening.

By the beginning of the twentieth century, quoits was becoming popular among the men of Brithdir community. Bute Quoits Club, formed in 1901 under captaincy of veteran player Len Hughes, played on a pitch alongside the path to Ty Coch. A contemporary issue of *Merthyr Express* noted that *according to experts, the club possessed one of the finest pitching grounds in South Wales*. Such was the popularity of the game and the eagerness of local players that each evening, weather permitting, the pitches near Ty Coch were full of players. They played competitively in Division 1 against clubs from Pengam, Deri, Tirphil, New Tredegar, Rhymney and Trefil.

319

The following men were listed in local newspapers as being in the team between 1903 and 1906: William J. Davies, captain, William Williams, vice-captain, Tom Davies, J. Davies, W. Evans, George Payne, T. James, George Gambling, J. Williams, F. Mutlow, J. Harris, J. Price, J. Coles, William Hughes and Israel Williams. Fred Williams was secretary and John Thomas (of George Inn Hotel) was treasurer.

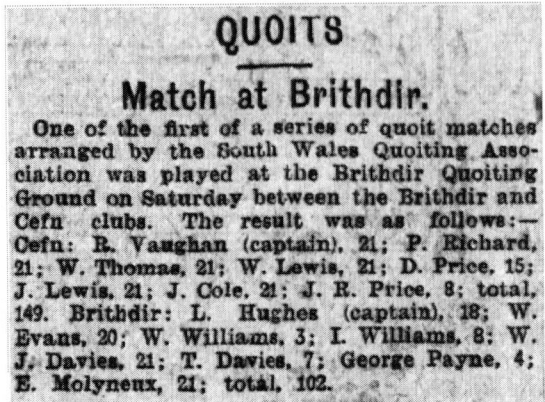

QUOITS

Match at Brithdir.

One of the first of a series of quoit matches arranged by the South Wales Quoiting Association was played at the Brithdir Quoiting Ground on Saturday between the Brithdir and Cefn clubs. The result was as follows:— Cefn: R. Vaughan (captain), 21; P. Richard, 21; W. Thomas, 21; W. Lewis, 21; D. Price, 15; J. Lewis, 21; J. Cole, 21; J. R. Price, 8; total, 149. Brithdir: L. Hughes (captain), 18; W. Evans, 20; W. Williams, 3; I. Williams, 8; W. J. Davies, 21; T. Davies, 7; George Payne, 4; E. Molyneux, 21; total, 102.

Evening Express, 20 May 1901

The game's popularity continued as shown in this extract from *Merthyr Express*, April 30 1910: *The final match for the championship of the Cwmsyfiog Quoits Tournament was played on Wednesday last, between Mick Hughes, Brithdir and George Payne, Cwmsyfiog, before a fine crowd of spectators. Hughes, who is the Brithdir soccer goal-keeper, proved too good for his opponent and ran out an easy winner by 21 points to 8 securing the gold medal. Another footballer, in the person of Mr. A. Chard, secured third position in the tournament.*

Whether or not much quoits was played in the next decade and a half is unclear but the idle days of 1926 Strike saw a revival in the game among striking miners. Matches were organised in Brithdir in July with teams captained by W. Hughes, T. James and A. Roffi challenging teams selected from Bute Terrace, New Houses, members of Constitutional Club and Tirphil. The most successful team was New Houses which defeated Constitutional Club by 57 points; Mr. Roffi's team by 17; and Tirphil by 18. On August 14, a large and enthusiastic gathering witnessed the opening match of a new Brithdir Constitutional Quoits Club, when Tom Davies and Timothy McCarthy cut the clay with the first pair of quoits, before Israel Williams and William *Mick* Hughes, both playing members of Cwmsyfiog Quoits Club, played an exhibition game. With a new pitch laid, almost daily matches were arranged and games attracted large numbers of spectators. Brithdir Constitutional Club quoits committee was instrumental in forming Rhymney Valley Quoits League which comprised eight teams: Brithdir, Rhymney Tredegar Arms, Rhymney Castle, Rhymney Bute, Cwmsyfiog, Dukestown, Tirphil and Aberbargoed.
Merthyr Express, September 10 1927: *The quoiting season being over, the new Rhymney Valley League has just completed its first year's work. Mr. Bert Curry, Brithdir, secretary, is proud of the fact that officers and players have combined to give the league a good start. The Constitutional Club, Brithdir, has the honour of being the first year's champions.*

That Brithdir team was made up of Israel Williams (captain) T. Thomas, J. McArthur, J. Meredith, Idris Thomas, A. Chard, D. Richards and Owen Jones.

Billiards/Snooker

The Institute billiard hall was opened for the first time on Saturday, February 28 1925, and was well patronised by local young men. The 'Stute billiards team, formed in October 1927, competed in Rhymney Valley Institute League. In their first match, against visitors Rhymney, the home team was outplayed. It would take time to develop a good team, but Brithdir senior team, William *Bill* Hayes (captain) Mel Davies, T. Miles, G. Mantle, Ernie Hayes and Gethin Jones, competing in Upper Rhymney Valley Snooker League, had some outstanding achievements on the *green* cloth. Their success was largely due to support and encouragement from 'Stute committee. In May 1941, the committee presented Vernon Way and Bill Hayes with cigarette lighters for the highest breaks – 82 and 78 respectively -- during the past season. Bill Hayes was also awarded first prize for the highest number of league points collected, with H. Price second, and Stan Hughes third.

In 1943 season, Brithdir captain, Bill Hayes, was selected captain of a team to represent Upper Rhymney Valley Snooker League against Dowlais Snooker League. The match was played at Brithdir on March 11, with the return match at Dowlais on March 18. Vice-chairman, Phil Willetts, presented awards at a presentation evening in the 'Stute on May 6 1944. Gethin Jones received a cue for 82 break, the highest break made at one visit to the table during a snooker match there. Bill Hayes was awarded a certificate of merit and a cue for a break of 65. Mel Davies was also presented with a certificate. Elvad Williams, 14 year old grandson of David Morgan, Ty Coch, was awarded a certificate and cue for a break of 54, the second highest break for a boy registered throughout the country.

At 1945 League final, played at Pontlottyn Library and Institute in April, Brithdir defeated Aberbargoed by 7 frames to 5 to win Upper Rhymney Valley League Championship. Brithdir team comprised A. Mantle, Bert Hayes, Dennis Rawle, Bill Hayes, Mel Davies and Ernest *Joe* Hayes. During the season, Mel Davies was presented with a cue for his 87 break in a match against Rhymney. Brithdir team was one of the top three teams in the league. In February 1946, with young Elvad Williams replacing Mantle in the team, they put up a good performance to defeat Bargoed, Rhymney Valley League leaders, by 7 frames to 5.

The finest moment of Bill Hayes's snooker career came when, aged 29, he played in final of Welsh Open Amateur Snooker Championship at Burroughes and Watts Hall, Cardiff, in April 1946. This annual fixture was the highest ranking and most prestigious amateur event in Wales, with Ray Reardon as champion 1950-1955. This was Bill's first attempt at any championship, and, playing against Jenner of Swansea in the semi-final on Thursday, 11, he gave a fine performance and won by three straight frames, winning each game on the black. However, in the final, on Saturday, April 13, he faced a more experienced opponent in Abertillery's Bryn Gravenor, winner of the competition in 1938. In a best of seven frame match, Gravenor won 4 games to 1.

SNOOKER SCORE. — Mel Davies was in excellent form with the cue last week, and in a game with T. Wheeler at the Institute, made a break of 95, which the committee are to recognise it in a tangible form. The previous day, Mel., who has been a member of the Rhymney Valley League team (Brithdir Institute) for a number of years made a break of 74.

Merthyr Express, October 30 1948, reported on Mel Davies in top form. Mel is remembered by many as a brilliant snooker player, many local people think he would have been a contender if today's world championship competitions were running then. I remember that, when Mel and wife Dilys were snooker hall caretakers, he ironed the tables in preparation for match nights, when every seat in the hall was taken, and there was a deathly hush whilst games were played. I recall one match on table 1 - Mike Bevan against Doug Mountjoy (later pot black champion and regularly among the world's top 16 in 1970s and 1980s). One observer not respecting the custom of *quiet* was taught a harsh lesson when Mike, upset at the noise, hit the cue ball so hard it shot off the table hitting the loud mouth mid-drift.

Kazoos and Drums

Jazz bands were a social activity for miners and their families, especially during lengthy strikes and lock-outs. Playing tin kazoos and drums, they performed in local carnivals and festivals, often competing against bands from other villages. Dedicated trainers taught them to march in unison while organisers raised funds for coaches, uniforms and instruments.

Merthyr Express, September 24 1932: *First Time, First Prize – This was the experience of the children of a band formed in Brithdir, primarily to compete in the New Tredegar and District Carnival competition. The boys had been trained to march and perform other evolutions to the tune of the big drum. On*

Brithdir Ladies Jazz Band

Brithdir Ladies Jazz Band about 1951. Leader of the band, in top hat and tails, is Marge White, with mascot, John Rawle, members Blod Williams, Cissie Gardner, Vi Sims, Doreen Hayes, Mabel Eynon, Margaret Eynon, Kath Bennett, Mrs. Pritchard, Mrs. Hook, and Bill Cullum on big bass drum.

Courtesy John Rawle.

Friday 16th September 1932, for the first time, they were dressed in their costumes and presented a fine sight. In the competition they shared the first prize and on returning were given a tumultuous welcome. Much credit is due to Mr. Wilfred Bennett for the trouble he has taken with them, as well as those ladies who made the costumes.

In the 1950s Brithdir, during the long, hot summer days of the decade of my youth, I remember the unmistakable sound of kazoos and drums. Bunny Evans's Tirphil band, smartly dressed in colourful outfits regularly marched through the village, stopping at intervals to play their tunes, their unique sound resounding within the narrow valley. From Tirphil, the band entered the village at the Buckets, the northernmost end, and proceeded through Brithdir via Bristol Terrace to Ivy Row, and back along the bottom road, Station Terrace, before leaving the village under the railway bridge, crossing the river bridge to Cwmsyfiog and the long march via New Tredegar, back to Tirphil.

John Bunny Evans - A Belated Tribute

The following letter, written by Clem Smith, 46 Todd Road, Agincourt, Ontario, was originally published in a Canadian newspaper in 1958. Re-published in *Merthyr Express*, April 14 1977, under the headline *Canada Prints a Belated Tribute to a Valley Miner*, it is reproduced here courtesy Bunny's son Michael Evans.

Yesterday, I received word for the first time of the year-old death of an ordinary miner in a far off Rhymney Valley mine. The news affected me more than had I heard of the demise of some world-renowned statesman, for to me true greatness in a man lies not in mere wealth or worldly fame, but rather in the affect of his personality on the lives of other people. Judging by his standard, John (Bunny) Evans of Tirphil, in his own way and in his own environment, was no ordinary man. In the world's big cities, juvenile delinquency is usually attributed to conditions of poverty, inadequate housing, and broken homes. We had all of these sociological evils in Tirphil in the 'hungry thirties,' and I've often wondered why we had no resultant delinquency. No matter how many times I've batted the question around, the answer always come out – Bunny Evans.

Bunny was not a 'good' man, from a narrow religious point of view. On a Sunday evening he would more often visit a mountain "card school," or a club concert, than he would the local chapel, yet the beneficial influence of his character on the twin villages of Tirphil and New Tredegar was inestimable. Around 1930, a youth club was formed, with headquarters in the rear of a cobbler's store. It was later removed to more spacious accommodation, generously provided by Councillor W.H. Lee, landlord of the Dynevor Arms Hotel. The 'Chinks,' as the club was named, could easily have degenerated to the status of juvenile gang. Instead under the

John (Bunny) Evans and band outside Dynevor Arms, Tirphil Square. Bunny is seated centre, behind the boys sitting cross-legged, with the landlord and landlady of the pub on his flanks.   Courtesy Dennis Arundel.

leadership of Bunny Evans, it developed into the nucleus of most of the athletic and social activities of the surrounding area. When I look back over the years, I realize that we were kept so busy with Bunny's innumerable projects that we just didn't have time to get into trouble with the police.

With his innate capacity for organisation, Evans started a kazoo jazz band, football, cricket, rugby and even baseball teams. On the spur of the moment he would initiate arrangements for 'trips,' ranging from a swimming outing to nearby Rhos Las reservoir, to a full scale excursion to some sporting event at London, Glasgow, or Belfast. To finance all these varied promotions, Bunny would turn theatrical impresario occasionally and run concerts at local halls. The star turn of our concerts was the finest amateur comedian in the valleys – 'Bunny' himself.

Perhaps the best lesson we ever learned from this remarkable man was in regard to sportsmanship. Whenever he started a new athletic project, he would invariably arrange that the first fixture would be against the toughest possible opposition, probably figuring that if we were beaten by a box-car score, any lesser defeat would seem almost a victory. The result was that we never really worried about the outcome of any match, as long as a good time was had by all during and after the game. The jazz band travelled all over Wales to various carnivals. To the best of my recollection we never won a first prize anywhere, but we sure had a grand time trying. In those days of mass unemployment and intermittent strikes, God knows we had little enough to laugh at, yet Evans could always make us see the brighter side. He had the gift of the natural comedian, that precious power to manufacture shafts of humour that can pierce the deepest mist of gloom.

In recent years, I have seen some of the highest paid comedians in the world, but in my opinion, none of them could match this simple miner, who performed not for personal gain, but for the pure pleasure of making his friends happy.

During the past year, many famous personages have died. Most of them already forgotten, but in the hearts of those inhabitants of the Rhymney Valley who knew John Evans, he will always be regarded, in the words of the Reader's Digest, as 'the most unforgettable person we ever met.' Whether they still live in the valley, or have migrated to London, Luton, Slough, or even far away Toronto, his memory will linger with them, until they themselves die.

Brithdir Homing Society

Pigeon fancying has long attracted much support in the Brithdir area. One wonders if David Morgan *Dai Pigeon* of Station Terrace, mentioned in *Merthyr Express*, September 11 1897, was the first local pigeon fancier. It is difficult to find any information on local fanciers apart from what is in the pages of *Merthyr Express*. In season 1928-1929, the local club was affiliated to Glamorgan Federation. Dr. O'Shea, the club's president was supported by vice-presidents W. Bowles, J. Morgan and I. Jones. Harry Gwynne, was chairman and Jack Harris, secretary. Dr. O'Shea was still president in 1932, with G. Godfrey, chairman. On June 15, members sent their birds to Edinburgh; G Godfrey had the first two birds home and Steve Kavanagh the third, but bad weather interfered with the event and a number of birds did not return on the day.

The following are examples of race results for 1932 from *Merthyr Express*:
- May: Shrewsbury 102 birds entered. 1st Harry Gwynne, 2nd White Bros, 3rd William Redwood.
- June: Edinburgh 66 birds competed. 1st and 2nd Jack Harris; 3rd Steve Kavanagh.
- Perth, 51 birds sent and the distance covered in less than 8 hours; 1st J. Williams, 2nd William Redwood, 3rd G. Godfrey.
- July: Ludlow, 1st W. Lear, 2nd and 3rd T. Buckley.
- August: Carlisle, 1st T. Buckley, 2nd Harry Gwynne, 3rd White Bros, 4th Bassett Bros.

According to a detailed report in *Merthyr Express*, a large number of members, their wives and fellow pigeon fanciers attended Brithdir and New Tredegar Homing Society's presentation supper in concert rooms of Tirphil Liberal Club on Saturday, October 21 1950. David John and Son, 14 Milton Terrace, having gained 1st and 2nd places in Young Bird Lancaster Race, won the principal award, Andrew Buchan Trophy. For Old Bird Racing, Brithdir fanciers, D. John and Son, W. Lear and Son and Buckley Brothers gained awards, while for young birds, Lear and Son, T. Ferguson and Buckley Brothers, D. John and Son. and C. Ferguson, had awards. Other award winners included Bates and Barry, Gough Bros (Tirphil), Messrs T. Morgan and Death, Smith Bros (Abertysswg) and Jones Bros (Troedrhiwfuwch).

Presentation evening, L-R. Dennis Williams,* Dai Howells,* Mel Mayo, I Matthews, Paul Ireland, Elwyn Styling, Colin Jones, Gerry Challoner, Derek Morgan, Thomas Jones,* Region Roach, Terry Roberts, Terry Venn. (* Brithdir)   Courtesy Ian Evans

Over time the club changed its name: originally Brithdir Homing Society, it became Brithdir and New Tredegar Homing Society, Rhymney Valley Flying Club, before, more recently, resuming its original name. The club is affiliated to Welsh North Road Federation and has 12 lofts:

Abertysswg: Theophilus and Son	Jubilee: Jimmy Davies and daughter
New Tredegar: Island and Hyman	Bargoed: Stephen Evans
Phillipstown: Mr. and Mrs. Murphy	Aberbargoed: Ian and Alan Evans
Phillipstown: Elwyn Styling	Brithdir: Tom Jones and Colin Jones (Tirphil)
Phillipstown: Andrew Evans	Brithdir: Dennis Williams
Jubliee: Ivor Mathews	Brithdir: Dennis Harding (Rhymney Club)

Pigeon fanciers, like other bird (or animal) lovers, take pride in their champions, giving them a name and having them photographed or painted.

Dennis Williams's *Den's Boy* GB01R10526m which won 1st Club Ashford, 182 Miles 6th Open 3rd Section, 1717 Birds Painting, by P. Williams, December 2001.

Fothergills 77 Welsh South Road Federation 1st Poole 1998 Owned and raced by Terry Roberts and Son.

The Merchant Welsh South Road Federation 1st Pau 1998 Owned and raced by Gerry Challoner.

As a young lad in the mid 50s I had a loft with twelve birds and I loved watching them fly around high in the sky. To train them locally I often took a few birds in a basket on the double-decker bus to Rhymney Bridge and released them there. One of my hens, exhausted from a race, landed on the chimney of neighbour, Elsie Harold, and, unfortunately, fell onto the hot coals. Alerted by Elsie's shouting, I raced in and grabbed the stricken bird. She survived the ordeal, but the heat damaged her one leg, and I called her *Bandy*. Taking food from my hand, she soon became my favourite.

In the season, racing pigeons were sent by rail as far away as the north of Scotland and France. As soon as the railway porter released the birds, he recorded time and date on the label attached to the basket before the empty basket(s) were returned to owners. I can vividly remember May 3 1958, Brithdir birds had been sent to Edinburgh some days before, and I was watching television, Bolton Wanderers v Manchester United 1957-58 FA Cup Final. With the score at 1-0, one of my birds, a red checkered cock, arrived home, and whilst I was running to George Inn with the ring from the pigeon's leg to deposit in the time-clock there, to register the bird's arrival time, Bolton scored a second goal.

R – Renovation Bute Terrace

By the time the 1881 census was taken, the community was developing and there was a row of cottages adjacent to Ty Coch. The 1881 enumerator called them Tir y ferch Gryno (after the farm land on which they stood), but 1901 OS map (page 35) shows them as Bute Terrace. The cottages and Ty Coch formed a stand-alone community, separated by some distance from the village, and known locally as *The Bute*. Ty Coch and Bute Terrace tenants paid their rents to the farmer at Tir y ferch Gryno farmhouse, who, as part of his lease agreement, acted on behalf of the landlord.

When the 1881 census was taken, Bute Terrace had 3 uninhabited houses while the 4 inhabited dwellings, housed 18 people, 11 of whom were born in Gelligaer or neighbouring Monmouthshire parishes, 5 in Montgomeryshire and 1 in Cardiganshire. Each of the four households was dependent upon coal as 7 males were listed as coal miners and 1, a male boarder, was a general labourer, possibly working in the industry. Domestic work in the four households was the responsibility of the womenfolk, the 4 wives, one perhaps assisted by the 17 year old daughter and domestic servant in the household. Four children, aged 11, 8, 6 and 5 years, were attending school, while a 2 year old infant was at home with the mother.

At the same time, of the 12 people in the 2 dwellings in Ty Coch, only two, the heads of the households, were in paid employment: one was a general labourer born in Radnorshire and the other a coal miner who like his wife and six children, was born locally. The wife of the former had a home and two infants to look after while the coal miner's wife had four children of school age (aged 9, 7, 5 and 4) as well as two infants at home. There were also two infants of similar ages in the second household plus 4 scholars, aged between 4 years and 9 years.

It is not clear exactly when the Morgan (sometimes Morgans in sources) family lived in Ty Coch. David Morgan, known locally as a mountain fighter, and his wife Elizabeth, their six children and a male boarder, were in 7 Station Terrace when the 1911 census was taken. When daughter Beatrice married boxer Steve Kavanagh in 1917 they were in Ty Coch, Later, mother Elizabeth was living in Bute Terrace.

Two former residents of Ty Coch

Left :Elizabeth Morgan feeding the family's poultry before nightfall; note the single gas lamp in the background.

Right : Beatrice Morgan with her champion greyhound.

courtesy Idwal Morgan Kavanagh

From Machynlleth to Bute Terrace

Hugh Jones and John Jones, occupants of 1 and 2 Tir y ferch Gryno (later Bute Terrace) when the 1881 census was taken, were father and son. Census returns show that the family, Hugh Jones, his wife Sarah and young sons, John and Evan, left their native Montgomeryshire some two decades earlier, migrating south first to Blaina, and then Rhymney Valley. They lived in Cwmsyfiog, before crossing the river, probably about 1874. Welsh language inscriptions on two gravestones in Capel y Brithdir burial ground, far distant from their Montgomeryshire birthplaces, offer insight into the family history. The inscription on one, a well preserved gravestone of Welsh slate, translates:

In Loving Memory of Hugh Jones, Tiryferchgryno, Brithdir, New Tredegar (formerly of Machynlleth) who died December 6 1890, 65 years old; Also Hugh, dear child of Hugh and Sarah Jones who died April 8, 1869.

and that on the other gravestone:

In memory of Sarah, dear child of John and Mary Jones of Tiryferchgryno, who died October 1, 1888, aged 3 years old.

When the 1901 census was taken, Hugh Jones's widow, Sarah, in her seventies and living at 6 Bute Terrace, was

328

described as *Farming* on her own account. Was this on land of Tir y ferch Gryno? Her household comprised her 45 year old son Evan, described as *farmer's son*, while her son, John, his wife Mary and sons, Morgan and Evan, were in 4 Bute Terrace. Sarah had probably died before the 1911 census was taken when Evan Jones was enumerated in Bute Terrace.

A sale catalogue (Glamorgan Archives DSA/1/71) for a property auction at Bute Terrace on July 31 1924, reveals Hugh Jones leased lot 64 for a term of 99 years from February 2 1874. On his demise it was in the name of his son Evan Jones, the occupant at the time of the auction.

At the time of the auction, the house (Ty Coch), in the occupation of Mr. D. Rees, was described as *built of stone with pantile roof and contains kitchen, small pantry and 2 bedrooms with outside W.C. and pigs' cot.*

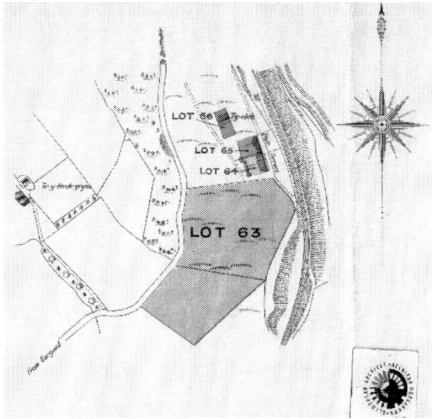

Plan 15 from sale catalogue.
Courtesy Glamorgan Archives.

L-R Tom, nephew Gary and Lyn, while working on the old cottages behind them

The Bute Terrace properties, homes for decades, fell into disrepair by the last quarter of the twentieth century. They were in a bad state when, in 1987, Tom Jones, helped by his brother, Lyn, began a renovation project. The photographs, courtesy Tom Jones, tell the story of the project.

Twelve-months of hard, dusty labour brought its reward.

S – The Order of St. John

By the mid Victorian era, countless workers across the country, including local coal miners, faced daily struggles in difficult, dirty and dangerous working conditions. In the absence of health and safety regulations, taken for granted by later generations, workplace accidents were not uncommon, yet few people were trained to treat casualties. This was the background against which St. John Ambulance Association was founded in 1877, and, especially after the events at Tynewydd Colliery in April 1877, its work was soon embedded in South Wales' coal mining communities. Local press reported well-attended weekly ambulance classes followed by significant examination success as well as stories of lives saved through prompt and effective action in that crucial time before a doctor reached the accident scene. Given the rapid changes in upper Rhymney Valley communities, including Brithdir, in the half century prior to the outbreak of war in 1914, it is hardly surprising that St. John Ambulance made an impact in the area.

Sources of information

As volunteers, members of St. John Ambulance Brigade had no service record. Thus research into the Order of St. John in Brithdir depends largely on reports in local newspapers and records in Priory House, Cardiff, relating to service medals awarded or promotions within the Order.

Brithdir ambulance classes 1909

While it is not clear when the first ambulance class was held in Brithdir, a report in *Merthyr Express*, June 5 1909, shows that Dr. Martin and his assistant, Mr. Organ ran an Ambulance class in a local school in 1909. So proud was Dr. Martin of his students' regular attendance and their successes, that he gave them an end-of-session supper at George Inn Hotel.

There is further information about Dr. Martin on pages 186-188. When the 1911 census was taken, Dr. Martin headed the household at *Leargaidh*, East View, that included boarders S.W. Saxby Organ, dispenser, and Liverpool-born physician and surgeon, Walter Mooney, as well as housekeeper, Mary Jane Jones.

Born 1886 in Clifton, Gloucestershire, Sydney William Saxby Organ spent more than five years working as the doctor's dispenser in Brithdir. Involved in the community, he appeared regularly for the local soccer team and was its 1908-09 captain. *Merthyr Express*, January 9 1909, reported that *Organ generally adds a goal or two per match*. He was selected to represent Rhymney League v Monmouthshire League in an inter-league match on March 29 at Cwm. Unfortunately for Brithdir, the 1909-10 season saw him assisting Bristol Rovers Reserves. On his return to Bristol, he married Ethel May Keeler at St. Paul's Bedminster January 22 1913. He served as chemist with Royal Engineers Special Brigade during World War I but, as his army service papers are in the badly burnt section, they offer little on his time in khaki. However, five fine references from former employers praised not only his dispensing work but also his character. This is what Dr. Martin wrote:

I have much pleasure in stating that S. W. S. Organ acted as my dispenser for over 5 years. He is exceedingly well up on his work, and thoroughly understands the art of dispensing from the simplest mixture to the most complicated process of modern pharmacy. He has had a good business training, and while with me he looked after all my accounts and bought all my drugs at better prices than I had hitherto thought possible. He is thoroughly steady and reliable and I have much confidence in recommending him for the post which he seeks.

Brithdir Division of St. John Ambulance Brigade

William Hares was instrumental in setting up Brithdir Division of St. John Ambulance Brigade, which was registered January 23 1912 with Dr. Pennant, Divisional Surgeon. It soon attracted considerable local interest, with many learning first aid. Such was the success that thirteen of its members were among St. John men and nurses who, in October 1913, helped in Senghenydd following the explosion at Universal Colliery. Sources studied to date shed little light on local progress during the war years but in the post war era, William Samuel Cresswell and Cyril Samuel Harris returned from war service and made outstanding contributions to Brithdir Division.

William Hares and his wife Margaret celebrating their Golden Wedding June 1938.
Courtesy nephew William Hares, Taunton.

Founder member, William Hares of Herbert Street, was appointed Superintendent of Brithdir Ambulance Division on its formation in 1912. After war service with RAMC, he was instrumental in forming numerous St. John Divisions in the area. His service to the Order was recognized. On July 20 1923, he was awarded diploma and medal of Serving Brother in the Order and was invested by H.R.H. the Prince of Wales at Cardiff. Having completed twelve years' service, he was presented with the Service Medal on September 4 1924. He was Staff Officer, Glamorgan County Ambulance Centre, when, on August 2 1930, he was awarded a first bar to the medal for a further five years' service. As there is no record of further bars, it is presumed that he retired from the service in the early 1930s.

Having served with RAMC during World War I, William Samuel Cresswell joined Brithdir Division in 1918. Promoted through the ranks, he achieved the rank of Superintendent in Charge and, on May 12 1933, was awarded Service Medal for 15 years' service.

331

William Samuel
Cresswell.
Courtesy Morfydd Williams

Cyril Samuel Harris.
Courtesy Ceinwen
Bevan

Cyril Samuel Harris, Private in Machine Gun Corps during World War I, gave much of his time to ambulance work on his return from the war. He was one of a number who built the Division's new Ambulance Hall, completed on the *tump* between Ivy Row and welfare playground by February 1925. He also taught first aid classes and was team leader of Elliot Colliery Mines Rescue Team.

During the 1920s, Brithdir Division continued to grow and celebrate its successes as witnessed by reports in the local press. *Merthyr Express*, August 7 1920, carried a report on a presentation dinner, held in Brithdir Division's headquarters when 6 promotion certificates and 34 service badges were presented to Division members. The list of successful candidates included Edgar Price John, John Edmunds, Stanley Young, Sydney Purchase, Ivor Davey, George Green, Gwynne Richards, Edward D.T. Bassett, George Smith, W.T. George, William Hares, William S. Cresswell, Herbert J. Brown, Ben Phillips, Walter Welsh, Robert Coles, E Williams, T Davies, Edgar S Jeremiah. On behalf of the Division, its chaplain Rev. H. West presented Dan John with a medallion and two labels (bars with registered number of medallion and year of re-examination) to replace those he had unfortunately lost. A report in *Merthyr Express*, September 17 1921, confirms the keen interest in Ambulance work shown by young men working in local collieries: four Division members were on duty every night, ready to render first aid in case of accidents.

A report in *Merthyr Express*, September 30 1922, on a well-attended presentation evening held in Baptist Church, provides a measure of the continued growth of Brithdir Division. As well as presentations of 22 first aid certificates, 10 vouchers, 13 medallions and 7 labels, it was noted that C.H. Smith not only received a medallion and label, but also certificate of promotion to Sergeant (his war-time rank in RAMC) and William Hares received his 12th label and Certificate of Hygiene. According to a report in *Merthyr Express*, November 7 1925, the Division was flourishing and its new Ambulance Hall was considered one of the best training rooms in the valley. The Cadets (junior section) were instructed by Sergeant Robert Coles on Tuesday evenings, while Supt. William Cresswell instructed adults on Wednesday evenings.

In the second half of the decade, Brithdir Division expanded to include a nursing class. The first meeting of what became known as Riches Corps,

332

attended by thirty ladies, saw local doctors' wives, Mrs. Mansell and Mrs. Pennant appointed as president and chair respectively, Mrs. Green secretary and Mrs. Taylor treasurer, with Nurse Elstone in charge. Meeting on Thursday evenings, and with popular lecturer Dr. O'Shea, the class was not as numerically strong as the male division, but progress was just as successful. Names of some members from the period 1928-30 are shown below:

Annie McDonald
Courtesy Mrs. Leechey.

Annie McDonald	Amy Williams		
H. Whitcombe	Thelma Lewis		
Jessie Jeremiah	Megan Edmunds		
Minnie Baldwin	Betty Megraw		
Beatrice Turner	Hazel Edwards		
Margaret James	Mary Gerrish		
Frances Meredith	Gloria Griffiths		
Brenda Wilde	Maria Williams		
Margaret Green	Edna Adams		
Doreen Jones	Florence Wells		
Mary Mellins	Olive Woods		
Cath Reardon	Sylvia Gerrish		
Beatrice Vale	M. Williams	Louisa Chard	Betty Hook
Elizabeth Chard	Olwen Williams	Phyillis Short	Vera Davies
Gwyneth Chard	Jenny Brewer	Mildred Watts	Gladys Hill
Isabel Parry	Florrie Harris	Alice Long	Joyce Bevan	J. Godley
Lillian Harold	Vida Pudge	Dilys Morgan	Elsie Currie	S. Jones

In the mid-1930s, Brithdir Division was making good all-round progress: its men's section was strong, the cadet corps numbered 30 and, within the nursing division, a new girl cadet division was formed. In addition, a medical comforts depot was established with a first aid haversack in Roffi's shop, and a cupboard in Workmen's Institute well-equipped with useful items in case of sickness in the community. Members from all sections represented Brithdir in events outside the community.

There is no doubt of the sense of pride felt by all associated with Brithdir Division when, during the first week of May 1935, Division members were part of St. John Ambulance Brigade contingent in an impressive parade in the spacious grounds of Cardiff Castle to celebrate King George V's Silver Jubilee. Brithdir Division was represented by 14 adults under Ambulance Officer Cox, 26 cadets under Cadet Superintendent T. Edwards and Cadet Officer Graham Price and 12 nurses in uniform, under Lady Superintendent Mrs. Davies. Just three years later, in April 1938, Brithdir ladies, Mesdames M. Williams, A. Webb, A. Megraw and C. Davies, attended a reception at Cardiff Castle in honour of Queen Mary's visit to South Wales

Members of Brithdir Division continued to earn medals. Robert Coles (Superintendent) was awarded Service Medal on May 12 1933 and Serving Brother May 17 1933. Edgar Samuel Jeremiah (Corps Inspector of Stores,

Probably mid 1940s - The black building in the foreground overlooking Ivy Row cottages is the former Ambulance Hall, by then St. David's Church (its bell tower is visible). It also shows welfare playground and Home Guard HQ (at the bottom of Ivy Row).
courtesy Paul Waites collection

Riches Corps) was awarded Service Medal on May 12 1933. There is information about ambulance stalwart Idris Jones on page 282.

Thomas Talfryn (known as Tal) Williams joined St. John Ambulance in 1935 and became Cadet Superintendent for Brithdir Division. He was awarded the Service Medal on May 15 1950 as Cadet Superintendent; the Medal being issued on September 25 1952. Retiring from St. John Ambulance in 1953-54, Tal ended his career as Divisional Superintendent. However, men like him remain *on call* and, living in Ivy Row, he was a person to turn to in time of emergency:

Uniform of Divisional Superintendent Thomas Talfryn Williams.
Courtesy Ivor Williams.

whenever one of us children had an accident whilst playing in the welfare playground, someone would run and knock on his door.

These two photographs show Brithdir Division St. John Ambulance Brigade. That of 1937 shows adult male members at a time when mining was still the main occupation for the village's

Brithdir Ambulance Class of 1991: Richard Morgan, instructor, with Lee Bennett, Neil Duggan, Warren Jones, Ted Rowlands M.P., Karen Jones, Amanda Williams and Stacey Jones.
Courtesy Richard and David Morgan

334

Brithdir Division St. John Ambulance Brigade 1937
L-R: Back Row: Rupert Bennett, J.H. Harris (Hon. Sec.), B. Jones, T. Bassett. Middle Row: Sgt. F. Jones; Corp. W. Macdonald, G. Price, S. Wells, A. Gullick, Corp. T.T. Williams (Tal). Front Row: T.J. Edwards (Cadet Supt.), I. Jones (Treasurer), W. Maddy (Pres), P.S.R. Rowlands (Div. Supt.), G. Price (Ambulance Officer) and A. Wells (Cadet Officer).
Courtesy Ivor Williams,.

men, while, by the time that of 1991, comprising young teenagers, was taken, coal mining was no longer the main employment for local men.

T – Thomas

Morgan Joseph Thomas MBE, Commander Royal Navy (1916-2004)

A walk along Usk's Conigar pathway led to the chance discovery of a seat dedicated to the memory of a man born in Brithdir, Morgan Joseph Thomas. Born in Brithdir on July 13 1916, he was son of Joseph and Ann Thomas (below right) of 3 East View. Much of the following information as well as the photographs, courtesy his son, Keith Thomas.

As a railway employee, father Joseph Thomas moved around the region. He had been stationmaster at

Deri before, as reported in *Evening Express*, September 30 1909, being transferred to Brithdir. However, his stay in Brithdir was brief as, on November 2 1909, that same newspaper reported his transfer to Ystrad Mynach to replace the much respected stationmaster Philip Morgan who was retiring. When the 1911 census was taken, Joseph Thomas was sole occupant of Station House, Pengam. Soon after, on September 26 1911, he

married schoolmistress Ann, daughter of Thomas and Miriam Morgan, Gwernllwyna Farm, Deri. It is not clear when the family moved to Brithdir, the birthplace of son Morgan Joseph in 1916 and daughter Winifred Ann in 1919. It is likely that his second term at Brithdir Station was longer than the first and may have lasted until he became GWR's station master at Usk in 1923.

The family moved to the station master's house on Abergavenny Road, Usk, and young Morgan attended school in Usk and Monmouth before completing his education studying accountancy at Newport Technical College. A year before the outbreak of World War II, Morgan volunteered for Fleet Air Arm and, during the war, served in the Pacific, the Mediterranean and West Africa. When peace was declared he remained in Fleet Air Arm and, by 1950, he was a shore-based Lieutenant Commander stationed at Eskmeals Proof and Experimental Establishment at Bootle, Cumberland.

He married Ann Wrigley, a Cumberland girl, and they had a son and three daughters. Following his retirement, Morgan Joseph Thomas lived in Gosforth. His award of MBE, in Queen's birthday honours, is noted in *Supplement to The London Gazette*, June 12 1981, and reads *Commander Morgan Joseph Thomas, R.N. (retired), Professional Technology Officer Grade 1, Ministry of Defence* He died at his home in Gosforth, Cumbria, on October 13 2004, aged 88.

U – Umbrella

This section includes information on several Brithdir people.

Gomer Absalom

Much of the information that follows is based on information kindly shared by the Absalom family, together with details recorded in manifests of ships mentioned, reports in the contemporary press and information on various websites.

Gomer Absalom left Brithdir in 1909 to join his uncle (Gomer Parry, brother to his mother) who had paid for the Liverpool to New York passage on SS *Carmania*. Born in the mining village of Pwll-du (between Blaenavon and Abergavenny), Gomer Absalom had moved to Brithdir about 1895. The ship's manifest fills in other details about this unmarried 20 year old coal miner, son of John Absalom of Brithdir: standing 5' 6", with fair complexion, brown hair and dark brown eyes, he had a heart with initials GA tattooed on his right arm, and he was able to read and write.

Arriving at Ellis Island, New York on July 14 1909, Gomer Absalom was just one of many thousands of people of Welsh birth heading to north-east

Pennsylvania anthracite coalfield. After eleven months in Scranton, Gomer Absalom went back to Brithdir, only to return three months later, paying for his own ticket (steerage class, the cheapest and most uncomfortable passage) on White Star Line's *Baltic* which left Liverpool September 17 1910. Among the passengers to board *Baltic* at Queenstown was 27 year old Anna Enright, travelling alone to visit her father, and she became Gomer Absalom's wife the following year.

It was on that same ship, *Baltic*, that Gomer Absalom's mother, Hope, and younger brother, Lewis, left Liverpool on April 23 1914 for New York. Widowed in 1913, Hope decided to leave Brithdir and join her son Gomer across the Atlantic.

Gomer Absalom visited Brithdir in 1919 and returned on board *S.S. Orunda* departing Liverpool October 16 1919. The ship's manifest records him as a married ironworker, aged 29 years and 3 months. He gave his wife's address as 206 East 41st Street, New York, and his next of kin in UK as his sister, Maggie Godfrey of 24 Herbert Street. Manhattan 1920 census shows he was ironworker in shipyard, and his household comprised wife, Anna, and children – John, Gomer, Alice and Ann Florence. Not only was he naturalized before the 1930 census was taken, but his family was extended with the births of sons Morgan and William, who like their siblings were born in Manhattan.

Lewis Boddington CBE - Aerospace Engineer (1907-2001)

In the early days of naval aviation, aircraft landing on the deck of a carrier had to stop quickly to avoid running into aircraft parked at the bow of the ship. As landing speeds increased, aircraft were fitted with hooks to catch arrestor cables stretched across the deck and, in case the hook failed to catch a cable a catching net was placed beyond the cables. When the hooks missed the cables, the aircraft was damaged and the net could break. In 1951 Royal Navy Captain Dennis Campbell and Lewis Boddington, then civilian technical officer in charge of Naval Air Division at Royal Aerospace Establishment, Farnborough, proposed the flight deck be set at an angle, allowing aircraft that missed the arrestor cables to take-off again, heading out over the sea to the side of the ship. In 1952, the first trials, an angled runway painted onto the flight deck of *HMS Triumph*, proved successful. Thus angled flight decks are used around the world on aircraft carriers not operating vertical take-off.

One half of this innovative pair, Lewis Boddington, son of James and Anne Boddington, 6 East View, was born November 13 1907. He was educated at Brithdir Boys' School and Lewis School Pengam before a successful university career, as reported in *Merthyr Express* October 24 1925:

Lewis won an entrance scholarship to the Technical College and University, Cardiff in 1925, and was awarded a Sir Edward Nicholas scholarship in the Mechanical Engineering Department. The scholarship was a City of Cardiff scholarship and as only a small number were allowed outside Cardiff, Lewis Boddington had done extremely well to gain one.

In 1953 Lewis was appointed Director of Royal Navy Aircraft Research and Development, a post he held for six years before being appointed to a senior research post, Director General of Aircraft Research and Development, in 1959. He was awarded CBE in 1956 Queen's Birthday Honours, gazetted May 25 1956. Lewis Boddington CBE Deputy Chief Scientific Officer, Ministry of Supply, was presented with the Medal of Freedom (Degree of Bronze Palm) by American Ambassador John Hay Whitney in a ceremony at the embassy in London on October 3 1958.

Lewis Boddington died, aged 86, on January 7 1994, and a cremation service was held at Thornhill Crematorium on January 18. His widow Morfydd Annie, née Murray, died January 10 2001 at the age of 94, and, following a service at Thornhill on January 12 2001, her cremated remains were, like those of her husband, scattered in the Forsythia Gardens of Remembrance at Thornhill Cemetery.

Three children left the school for Australia

These words, written by school mistress, Clara Tovey, in April 1882 marked the beginning of a new life for 8 year old Mary Jane Clee, as she and her family emigrated to Australia. Much of what follows is based on anecdotal evidence shared by her descendants, especially Marcella Secher (granddaughter of Mary Jane Clee), as well as Australian press reports and historical records in National Library of Australia and Rotorua Public Library, New Zealand.

Born in Brithdir Terrace (later known as Station Terrace) September 6 1873, Mary Jane Clee was daughter to William Clee and his wife, Mary. Sadly, William Clee died in 1874. Three years later, his young widow married neighbour John James, a coal miner. They had two children, son Mansel born 1878 and daughter Maria born 1881. Whether or not John James adopted Mary Jane is unclear, but she frequently appears as Mary James in sources. It is difficult to know why John James and his wife decided to emigrate, how they felt about leaving family and friends or whether they had any sentimental reminders of life in Brithdir packed in among their essential luggage in 1882.

When *Western Monarch*, an iron hulled sailing ship of Royal Exchange Shipping Company, left Plymouth in April 1882, this little family of five was listed among its 425 passengers. The journey started dramatically as, leaving port in the face of a heavy gale, *Western Monarch* was forced in the wrong direction as she entered the open sea. Despite rumours in *Manchester Courier* that she had been wrecked in English Channel, *Western Monarch* made the 101 days' journey to Australia and dropped anchor in Hervey Bay (Queensland) on August 6. *Western Monarch* was too big to navigate Mary river, and so, the following

morning, her passengers transferred to iron steamship *Keilawarra* and arrived at Maryborough wharf that evening. Reports in the contemporary Australian press shed light on the voyage. For example, *Brisbane Courier,* August 28, reported on the difficult start to the journey: during the gale in the Channel, three seamen were swept overboard and drowned while Captain Wood fractured a kneecap rendering him disabled for seven weeks leaving Chief Officer Wallace in command.

It is not clear how John James provided for his family in his early years in the new country. However four years after arriving, John James purchased farm land on Burrum River (about ten miles north west of Maryborough). Presumably he spent the rest of his working life farming the land. Family legend has it that he buried quite a lot of money in the banks of Burrum river, near his farm, and, to the time of writing, it has not been found.

It is difficult to know how much contact they had with family and friends in their homeland, but perhaps Mary Jane Clee's narrow escape from death was one of the stories they related. Walking to school along the railway tracks, Mary Jane's shoe was caught in the tracks. A train was due and fortunately another person, walking to work, released her just in time. That person was Andrew Fisher (right), Australia's prime minister 1908-1915 and High Commissioner in London 1916-1921.

The later histories of John James and his wife Mary are unclear, but the three children appear to have remained in the Antipodes for the rest of their lives. Mary Jane Clee married Daniel Ritchie in February 1899 in the Queensland village of Howard. Daniel, born in Hamilton, Lanarkshire, was 10 years old when he arrived in Maryborough in 1866. He worked as a coal miner in the Burrum district and, following their marriage, Daniel and Mary Jane settled in Torbanlea, a coal mining town north of Maryborough where they raised their six children. When Daniel retired in 1942, he and Mary Jane made their home in Brisbane where he died in 1945. On her death August 5 1966, one month short of her 93rd birthday, Mary Jane was, like her husband, buried in Toowong Cemetery, Brisbane.

Mansel James who was 4 years old when he left George Inn, trained as a taxidermist and eventually left Queensland and settled in Rotorua, New Zealand where he found work in a local museum. He married and raised a family there. Maria was just an infant when her parents left George Inn; she survived the hazardous journey, and in later years married and raised her family in Queensland.

In 2004, Marcella Secher (right) made the journey from her home in Queensland, to Brithdir, to visit her grandmother's birthplace.

339

Julie Morgan

Julie Morgan, born 1966 in 1 Wellington Terrace, was second child of Dennis Morgan and his wife, Barbara née Brewer. She was educated in Cwmsyfiog Primary School and Bedwellty Comprehensive School, before studying Applied Biology at Wolverhampton University. She started her working life in the UK, working in the cancer field. Her first post was in London at Imperial Cancer Research Fund (later merged with Cancer Research Campaign to become Cancer UK). From there, she went to Medical Research Council, firstly Division of Molecular Medicine in London and then, Clinical Oncology and Radio-therapeutics Unit in Cambridge, before moving to University of Cambridge, Department of Pharmacology. Having met her Kiwi partner, David, in 2001 Julie not only moved with him to his native New Zealand but also changed the focus of her professional work. To the time of writing, she has spent sixteen years working for Institute of Environmental Science and Research Limited in Invasive Pathogens Laboratory, in the field of microbiology, working mainly on streptococcus.

Elizabeth Parlor, née MacDonald, later Williams

Born in Pontlottyn at the turn of the twentieth century, Elizabeth, known as *Liz*, was 7 years old when the family moved to Brithdir. When the 1911 census was taken, they lived in 2 Salisbury Terrace. On leaving school, aged 14, Liz trained as a dressmaker with Miss Hannah Extance in New Tredegar before becoming an 'improver' at James

Howells, Cardiff. Later, in the prosperous years of the 1950s, she worked in Bargoed's George, Rees and Jones department store.

Elizabeth Parlor c. 1948

Liz with an altar-cloth she crocheted for St. Peters Roman Catholic Church in Bargoed, c1987.

A long standing resident of Brithdir, Liz lived most of her life at 20 Herbert Street. She died in 1992. Much of the information about Liz as well as the photographs is courtesy grandson Colin Parlor. Liz's skills were much in demand, and she had many private commissions, especially for wedding dresses and coats. This took a great deal of her time and also brought her many invitations to weddings, as illustrated by the following two photographs of local weddings:

340

September 21 1940 when Jessie Brain married Neil Hennessy. Liz is standing on the right.

May Williams, bride, dressed in a gown made by Liz. She married Oswald (Ozzy) Godley (1 Salisbury Terrace) in 1920. Liz is second from left, in front of vicar.

Widowed in 1957, Liz married local railway porter Uriah *Roy* Williams in 1959.

Liz was famed locally for her crochet work. She made altar pieces and various other adornments for local churches.

V – Ventriloquist Eli and *Jimmie*

Festival of Britain 1951 street party in Wellington Terrace. Children of adjacent terraces, Tennyson and Wellington, are seated while family and friends gather around to enjoy the occasion. I was there, but, unfortunately, out of shot. Chalked on the house wall, the menu of the day *Up to 15 years Trifle Tea, all over Ham Tea*. Far right is special guest *Jimmie*, ventriloquist's dummy and lifelong partner of Reverend Elijah Philip Schofield.
Courtesy, Ron Matthews.

Much of what follows appears thanks to Anne and Bob Machin and Gwyn Grocott who kindly shared their photographic record and details of an extraordinary man and his wonderful Insull partners, including *Jimmie*.

341

Jimmie is one of my earliest memories of growing up in Wellington Terrace.

Rev. Eli Schofield, Group Captain, Royal Air Force Chaplains Branch, was deployed to bases in Britain and abroad. His wife Dorothy and children, Philip, Anne and Gwyneth, together with *Jimmie*, accompanied him, but, between tours, Brithdir was their base. They stayed in 10 Wellington Terrace, with Dorothy's sister, Edith, and her husband, Roland *Rollie*

Hughes. During these stays in Brithdir, Eli often used his skills as a ventriloquist and magician to entertain at street parties and sometimes Rev. Eli and *Jimmie* conducted services in the Wesleyan Chapel. If their stay was lengthy and during term time, his children attended the village schools.

Born in 1921 in Blackburn, Lancashire, Elijah Philip Schofield was known as Eli until he joined the RAF, thereafter Philip (but to avoid confusion with his son Philip, I use Eli throughout). Eli left school without qualifications, and, aged 14, he started work in a paper mill. Seeking to improve his lot, he taught himself at home and took elocution lessons before studying at Edinburgh University and theological college in Bradford. It was in Bradford that he met Dorothy Cook. Dorothy, born in Deri 1916, had trained as a nurse at Paddington Hospital (she was there during the blitz) before moving to Bradford. In January 1945, with the ground covered in snow, they married at Brithdir's Wesleyan Chapel

Ordained in 1946, Eli took services in academic dress but, determined to help all members of his congregation understand the message he preached, he often used *Jimmie* in the pulpit at Clapton Park Congregational Church (London's East End) and elsewhere. Ivor Harris is one of those who recall the effectiveness of the message delivered by *Jimmie* and a gowned Rev. Eli to Brithdir Wesleyan congregation. This approach earned him

At the family home in Clapton about 1949 Eli, the family man, carrying out running repairs in the kitchen, helped by young son Philip.

some notoriety in the late 1940s, but, as he explained to a *Rochester Democrat and Chronicle* reporter interviewing him for Sunday edition January 9 1949, *We don't go to church services to have long faces. If we can have a laugh and get over the real message, so much the better.*

Rev. Schofield joined Royal Air Force in 1953 and, with family and *Jimmie*, travelled widely. Home tours were at RAF St. Athan (Vale of Glamorgan), RAF Locking (Somerset -- twice), Coltishall

Left to right, Edith Hughes with her arm around nephew Philip, Dorothy holding Gwyneth, Anne, and friend Ann Morris, in back lane behind Wellington Terrace, before the Aden tour, 1954.

(Norfolk) and Amport House, the Tri-service Armed Forces Chaplaincy Centre in Hampshire, while overseas tours included Aden, Singapore and Germany. When posted, Rev Schofield went ahead, staying in single quarters until married accommodation became available and the family could join him. In the meantime, Dorothy and the children headed for Brithdir and her sister Edith's home.

Daughter Anne shared her memories of the Aden tour 1955:

When we were in Aden, Dad had to visit out stations in other countries - Somaliland was one of them. His most attentive listener was a Somali who regularly brought Jimmie flowers, saying; "Him maybe good spirit, maybe bad spirit. Me keep on right side". Another Somali thought Jimmie was the devil and took a shot at him. Dad felt the bullet pass by his ear.

In Hargeisha Somaliland. . . . Somali Sergeant reported to officer's mess when Dad was using Jimmie. The Sergeant smartly saluted Jimmie and asked for any instructions. "Parade

Eli with *Jimmie* and *George* (a larger and remote controlled dummy) in Round Chapel, Clapton, 1951

before breakfast" said Jimmie. Next morning, they were all out there on parade and the Somali Warrant Officer asked why. The Sergeant said "new little Sahib in mess told me". The Warrant Officer rang Dad to ask if Jimmie could come down to inspect the parade. He did. There was a lot of laughter over that.

Bridesmaids Anne and Gwyneth standing on either side of the little girl.

Dorothy was taken ill when in Aden and invalided back to UK in August 1955. When she was recuperating, the family stayed in Wellington Terrace, and Philip (10), Anne (9) and Gwyneth (6) attended Brithdir schools for a term. How many readers share my memories of that September morning when our teacher introduced Philip Schofield, the new boy with blond hair, blue eyes and Aden sun tan?

The Schofield family was in Brithdir in March 1957 for the wedding of Edith's son, Gwilym Hughes and Margaret Cullum.

Rev. Eli and *Jimmie* performed during the three year tour in Singapore 1958-61. The local press reported that they were one of the main attractions in Radio Malay's charity *8.30 Special* at Victoria Theatre, December 15 1958, in aid of St. Andrew's Mission Hospital.

Dorothy's father, Henry James Cook, sister Edith and a young David Morris in the garden of 10 Wellington Terrace, 1956.

Rev. Eli, with daughter Anne as assistant, made a second appearance at Victoria Theatre on October 6 1959, in what the local press described as *an exhibition of classical illusions and latest magical mysteries*, in aid of the Geylang Methodist Church.

Gwyneth recalls a letter from Brithdir to the family in Singapore:

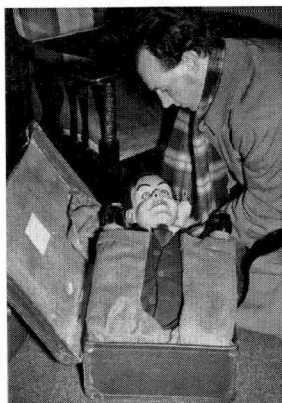

Rev. Eli packing *Jimmie* for Singapore tour, 1958.

Jimmie taking driving lessons in Changi Village, Singapore.

Visiting a local tailor to be measured for tropical kit.

Aunty Edith wrote mam a letter when we were in Singapore to say the school bobby had been round as I was not attending school, mam forgot to inform the school I would not be returning after the summer holidays.

A visit between tours in the early 1960s, left to right, Bryn Morris, his wife Frances, his mother Rachel, Dorothy Schofield and, behind her, Gwilym Hughes.

The Germany tour was another three year posting, 1964-67. Anne shares this story from 1964 when Dorothy and children were in Brithdir waiting for Eli to arrange married quarters:

We were in Brithdir without my dad and they asked my mum to take the service at the Wesleyan Methodist Chapel. She got ready and popped into the pantry in the kitchen downstairs. She came out spitting out this brown liquid. She had a cough and intended taking some cough medicine but had picked up the wrong bottle. It was gravy browning. We laughed all the way to the chapel.

Rev. Eli and *Jimmie* near the end of Germany tour, 1967.

Over the years, Rev. Eli and *Jimmie* attracted much press coverage in UK and across the world due to the unusual combination of ventriloquist, magician and minister of religion. They also appeared on radio and television in UK (and beyond) as witnessed by this transcription from *Radio Times* Sunday, December 2 1956:

Children's Television presents:
5.00 Champion the Wonder Horse: Renegade Stallion
5.25 Sooty: Sooty, the Super Musician, Harry Corbett presents...
6.00 Sunday at Six: The Rev. E. P. Schofield introduces you to *Jimmy* [sic].

As a minister of religion, Rev. Eli appeared on *Songs of Praise* several times and he sometimes was responsible for the epilogue (before close down at night). He starred on *In town tonight*, a Saturday evening BBC radio programme. He also appeared on television in Singapore and Germany. Rev. Eli and *Jimmie* appeared on *Muffin the Mule* and with Peter Brough and Archie Andrews.

Rev. Eli was the first ventriloquist to appear on a BBC national children's show.

Jimmie meeting Archie Andrews, The photo is signed *To Philip Best Wishes Peter Brough and Archie.*

345

Eli Schofield had performed with his vent dummy from a young age. His father, Walter, although not a ventriloquist, was fascinated by its mechanics and made Eli's early vent figures. In April 1939, the local press reported that Patrol Leader Eli Schofield (of Accrington Road Methodist Scout troop) performed ventriloquial items at an annual youth weekend to a large and appreciative audience. Inevitably, Eli's long association with scouting involved *Jimmie*. Eli attended the World Jamboree of Scouts, held at Sutton Park, Sutton Coldfield, in August 1957, and *Jimmie* was selected to represent Britain in the international radio programme *Talent Scout*.

Rev. Eli and *Jimmie* when they gained second place in an open competition for ventriloquist in London, 1957.

In 1969, Dorothy Schofield made her final journey to Wales, and after she passed away in August 1969, her family brought her home to Brithdir. Brithdir's Wesleyan chapel was filled with family and friends for the funeral service conducted by Queen's Royal Chaplain, dressed in scarlet cassock. The Reverend Elijah Philip Schofield led the service in Gwaelod y Brithdir Cemetery chapel prior to burial.

When, in 1971, Rev. Schofield retired from RAF, he took a church in Edgeware, and was officiating chaplain at RAF Hendon. Later, moving to North Wales, he became chaplain at Chester army barracks. During his working life he had been chaplain to many theatres, including London's Windmill Theatre, and he ended up as chaplain at Theatr Clwyd.

When Rev. Schofield died, aged 81, his home was 8 Priory Close, Penyfford, Chester. His funeral service was held at Penyfford and, seated amongst the family mourners was his life-long friend *Jimmie*. His ashes were

Rev. Eli and *Jimmie*, appearing in *A Gottle of Geer*, a 1986 BBC documentary about ventriloquists, written and presented by Ray Alan. It can be viewed on *YouTube*.

brought to Brithdir for burial alongside his beloved Dorothy. They had travelled to many places together and now rest amongst family and friends near Brithdir, where so many memories were shared.

Rev. Eli sold vent figures *George* and *Danny* to Davenports Magic Kingdom, North Walsham, but, after his death, his family donated *Jimmie*, together with copies of photographs and press cuttings, to Victoria and Albert Museum. *Jimmie* is the only dummy of that age and type there. In 1946, Rev. Eli bought *Jimmie* from Len Insull, a craftsman and vent figure maker who also made Archie Andrews for Lionel Brough. The first *Jimmie* was lost in luggage sent ahead in 1946, so most of Rev. Eli's appearances were with the second *Jimmie*.

W – West family

Over the decades, members of the West family have played significant roles in helping shape Brithdir's spiritual, cultural and social life.

Rev. Harry West (senior)

In September 1907, Rev. Harry West (senior) and his family arrived in Brithdir. He was pastor of Brithdir's Beulah Baptist Church, and his new home was Treferig House, Russell Street. Over nearly sixteen years in Brithdir, he earned considerable respect for his involvement in the community.

Born about 1870, Harry West lived in Blaenavon. Following his marriage, in 1890, to Elizabeth, daughter of Joseph and Mary Milsom, he set up home at 10 Clapham Terrace, Forgeside, on the hillside to the west of Blaenavon, and Harry supported his growing family as a *Bessemer steel worker* in the employ of the Blaenavon Company. By the time he arrived in Brithdir, he had six sons: Arthur (born 1893), Harry, junior (1894), Francis (1897), Roland (1898), David Stanley (1903) and Leslie (1906). Another son, Edward, was born in Brithdir in 1908.

Harry West was an eisteddfodwr and a musician of note. In December 1905, his essay *How Best to Improve the Moral and Physical Conditions of Young People in Our Villages*, won first prize at Abersychan Eisteddfod. He was conductor of a successful Blaenavon choir that, in the early 1900s, gained awards at Pontypool Semi-National Eisteddfod. He also conducted singing festivals and adjudicated at eisteddfodau. It is not clear when Harry West, a family man and a Christian, decided to start his studies for the ministry, but, in 1905, he was among those successful in the examination for local preachers, an achievement announced in Preachers Committee report to Monmouth Baptist Association's September quarterly meeting at Sharon Baptist Church, Goitre (near Pontypool).

Rev. Harry West's older sons were part of that generation who served in World War I and this extract from *Western Mail*, July 29 1918, summarises West family involvement:

Rev. Harry West, Baptist Minister of Brithdir, has just left the village for eight-months service in France – He has three sons in the Army, Sergeant Arthur West is in France, Pte Harry West, is now a prisoner in Germany and the third son Frank, is qualifying for a commission.

Harry West senior was 48 years old when he volunteered for what he felt was his duty. On August 8 1918, he landed in France to work with YMCA. YMCA supported troops with huts on frontline, in military camps and on railway stations at home, where they could get food and a place to rest. While it is not clear where Harry West was posted during his eight month service, it was probably where there was the greatest concentration of soldiers rather than the smaller canteens. His medal index card shows he was awarded British war medal.

In 1923, Rev. Harry West accepted a call from Penydarren, Merthyr, and he commenced duties there on Whit-Sunday. Local appreciation of his contribution to life in Brithdir during his sixteen years as minister of Beulah Baptist Chapel was reflected in the many presentations he received from a range of organisations in the week prior to his leaving. Brithdir Division St. John Ambulance Brigade showed their thanks for his faithful service over twelve years as their chaplain when, during the annual presentation of awards to successful candidates, they presented him with an *ebony walking stick bearing a silver band suitably inscribed*. The Baptist chapel choir held a social and concert in his honour. The Independent Order of Good Templars (IOGT) and YPS united to give him a good send-off, a social and concert during which Christina Maidment, described in the press as *one of the smallest of the society*, presented him with a suit-case. According to a report in *Merthyr Express*, May 19 1923, the venue for a public testimonial was crowded with local people. Representatives of surrounding places of worship spoke in his praise, and Rev. D. J. Morris made *a spirited speech*, before, on behalf of Brithdir people, presenting him with a wallet. The standing ovation he received reflected the depth of local respect and affection. Before he could reply, Christina Wells, on behalf of eight Sunday Scholars, handed the pastor a silver inkstand, and, in her *pretty little speech*, she wished him all good things and great success in Merthyr, before concluding *we all love you very much*.

Rev. Harry West had lost his wife Elizabeth while he was living in Brithdir. Aged just 61, she died April 22 1920, and was buried in Gwaelod y Brithdir Cemetery. When Rev. Harry West passed away July 28 1938, aged 69, his body was brought back to Brithdir for burial alongside Elizabeth.

Although Rev. Harry West left Brithdir in 1923, that was not the end of West family involvement in the community. Members of the West family were well-known in local musical and sporting circles, and his sons' contribution to the village, the neighbourhood and the district, and beyond, was considerable. Throughout the 1920s and 1930s, a time of eisteddfodau, operettas, cantatas, choirs, concert parties and Sunday School anniversaries, they were actively involved in the choral work of various places of worship.

Arthur West

Just in his early twenties when World War I started, Sergeant Arthur John West, eldest son of Rev. Harry West and Elizabeth, enlisted and, as Private 3310, he served with 1/5th Welsh Regiment at Gallipolli. Medal rolls show that later, as L/Cpl Arthur J West (241350), he served in France with 19th Battalion as Pioneers to 38th Division. On returning from war service, Arthur married Elizabeth M. Powell in 1919 and their daughter, Marian, was born the following year. Like his father, Arthur won an eisteddfod essay competition. In his case, it was at Brithdir Eisteddfod in 1926, held in aid of the communal kitchen fund. It is not clear when Arthur and his family moved to Merthyr Tydfil, but Arthur was managing a furniture shop and the family (including daughter Marian, by then married) lived at 17 Gwendoline Street, when war broke out in September 1939.

Harry West (junior)

Second son of Harry senior, Harry junior worked at Elliot Colliery from the age of 14. On December 20 1913, he married Gertrude, daughter of Edwin and Emily Cresswell, James Street, and with their daughter, Mair Elizabeth (born in 1914), they settled into family life at 9 Station Terrace. Life for Harry, Gertrude and Mair Elizabeth, changed when twenty one year old Harry West attested for war service at Bargoed on December 31 1914. He enlisted into Welsh Regiment and joined Cardiff City Battalion as Private 23795, and on January 1 1915, he left to join his unit at Colwyn Bay. *Gelligaer* volume 21 2014 carries some details of Private Harry West's war service. He was taken prisoner at Ypres on July 27 1917 and imprisoned at Bayreuth where he was camp chaplain. After spending seventeen

months as PoW, Harry West was repatriated, discharged from the army on April 12 1919 and placed in *Class Z Reserve*.

Cover of the bible Harry West used as Chaplain in Bayreuth PoW. camp, courtesy Olga, his daughter, and Jacqueline Tiernan, who also contributed details of his life.

When the war was over, Harry returned to Brithdir. As an ex-serviceman he belonged to Bargoed Old Comrades and served as its secretary. He was also, for a while, secretary of Brithdir Cricket Club. Like his father, he became a Baptist lay-preacher. These extracts from 1919 *Monmouthshire Guardian and Bargoed and Caerphilly Observer* shed a little light on his work:

AINON BAPTIST CHURCH.—On Sunday evening, Pte. Harri West, Brithdir, who has had an experience of active service and has spent about twelve months as prisoner of war in Germany, and during that period acted as chaplain to the prisoners in the camp with great acceptance by the British prisoners; officiated at the Baptist Chapel and gave great satisfaction.

ABERTYSSWG.

YOUNG PEOPLE'S SOCIETY.—Under the auspices of Young People's Society of Ainon Baptist Church, Pte. Harry West, Brithdir, returned prisoner of war, on Wednesday evening, delivered a most interesting Lecture on "My experiences as Prisoner of War in Germany." The chair was occupied by the Rev. J. Roberts, pastor. The introductory portions were taken by Mr. Haydn Davies, and Mr. Henry Evans; a solo was very nicely rendered by Miss Elsie Evans; and a recitation very suitable for the occasion was given by Miss Esther Alice Hughes. Afterwards, Pte. West delivered a lecture which kept a good audience keenly attentive for about an hour-and-a-half.

His visit to Brithdir Girls' Department was recorded in the school log book:

November 11 1919: - *Today is Armistice Day. His Majesty's Message has been read to the assembled girls and we have all united in a reverent remembrance of the Glorious Dead paying them a tribute of Silence for a brief space of two minutes. Mr. West, who was in France as a Chaplain twelve months today, gave the top class girls a short address.*

On demobilisation, he returned to his pre-war work in Elliot Colliery and later worked in Britannia Colliery and Bedwas Colliery. He made his home in Brithdir until December 1924, when he left for Cross Hands, Carmarthen, and work in the Anthracite Colliery. A speaker of considerable ability, he became agent of Miners' Industrial Union which, formed in 1926, aimed to counter the radicalism of the Fed. By 1937, he was working in Llanharry iron-ore mine and living in Pontyclun.

Interested in politics, from 1921 Harry West, junior, was preparing himself to contest a parliamentary seat. He frequently spoke at Liberal meetings in South Wales and, in 1925, as this advertisement from *Gloucester Citizen*, July 3 1925, shows, he was Liberal candidate in the Forest of Dean by-election. *Gloucester Journal*, July 11 1925, revealed his campaign was supported by a fellow Welshman:

FOREST OF DEAN BY-ELECTION JULY 14th, 1925.

CANDIDATURE OF HARRY WEST.

MEETINGS SATURDAY JULY 4th.

SNIGSEND, CORSE, 7 p.m.   THE RIFLE HALL, DYMOCK, 7-30 p.m.
THE SQUARE, NEWENT, 8 p.m.

Speakers:—Candidate; A. W. Stanton, Esq., J.P.; S. J. Gillett, Esq.; A. C. White, Esq. and Others.

GEORGE REED, Election Agent

the *Right Hon. David Lloyd George, M.P., travelled to Gloucester today in order to speak on behalf of Mr. Harry West, the Liberal candidate for the Forest of Dean, at Cinderford.*

After his by-election defeat, Harry West continued his political involvement as witnessed by the following press reports:

- *Western Gazette*, July 23 1926 : *East Dorset Tour: The propaganda van of the Land and Nation League is touring East Dorset. The speakers are Mr. Harry West, Liberal candidate at the recent by-election at the Forest of Dean and Mr. W. R. Hill, of Bristol. They are dealing exclusively with the liberal land policy, and addressing meetings in every town and village in the constituency. On Monday they were at Lytchett, on Tuesday at Wimborne and Holt, on Wednesday Shapwick and Sturminster Marshall were visited, and yesterday (Thursday) they were due at Corfe Mullen. The tour will last three weeks.*

- *Bath Chronicle and Weekly Gazette*, December 18 1926: *The Western Counties Liberal Land van, which is visiting Bath this week, has covered 8,000 miles, and about 500 meetings have been held. The speaker in charge of the van is Mr. Harry West (ex-Liberal Candidate, Forest of Dean Division).*

During World War II, Harry West served as a Special Constable at Pontyclun with added responsibilities of anti gas and fire fighting. He was not afraid to express his opinions as shown in this letter published in *Western Mail*, December 3 1941. On Tuesday, August 18 1942 he spoke on war production from a Ministry of Information loud-speaker car at Rhymney, Bargoed and Ystrad Mynach.

He continued his active involvement in politics in the post–war era, when he switched allegiance to Conservative party:

- 1946: Working at Conservative Central Office in Cardiff, he was Labour and Trade Union Organiser.
- 1950 General Election: He unsuccessfully opposed Clement Davies in Montgomeryshire.
- 1951 General Election: He unsuccessfully opposed James Callaghan in Cardiff South East.
- He continued to work at Conservative Office and was Director of Public Economy, keeping watch on spending of Glamorgan County Council.

Sir.—Of late the police in some parts of Glamorgan have been visiting public-houses and issuing instructions that all music must cease.

Why stop the singing? The Government are spending thousands of pounds to make people sing. Instruments are provided and artistes are paid to sing at work-shops and factories.

I remember Mr. Lloyd George saying in the last War: " Why shouldn't they sing? The blinds of Britain are not drawn down yet."

Music has been the safety valve in days of danger and depression. The trenches of Flanders echoed to the strains of " Aberystwyth," and " Cwm Rhondda " rang through Mametz Wood after it had been stormed by the Welshmen of the famous 38th Division.

In this struggle. too, air-raid shelters have been turned into con-cert halls. Welshmen must sing or fight.—Yours, &c., HARRY WEST. Pontyclun.

Roland West

Roland West married Brithdir-born Amelia, daughter of John Williams, 2 School Street, in 1921, and they made their home at 19 Bristol Terrace. Roland, a collier, working Elliot and Groesfaen collieries, took an active interest in Brithdir life in the inter-war era. He was elected a committee member of Workmen's Institute in 1925. Interested in sport, he became secretary of Brithdir Cricket Club in 1935. He was especially interested in the community's musical life and, as well as being president of YPS, he was also conductor of their choir and director of numerous operettas, as described on page 265.

About 1932, Roland West, a promising local preacher, decided to study for the ministry. Ordained in October 1934, he left Brithdir in July 1935, to become pastor of Ainon Baptist Church, Merthyr Tydfil. Later he served Franksbridge, near Builth Wells, before, in 1948, moving to Umberslade, Hockley Heath, Birmingham, where he made his own unique contribution.

Both Roland and his wife were musicians and what they had achieved in the Welsh choral scene, they attempted in Umberslade. He trained a choir of 15 from the church, sometimes supported by other voices from the village, to sing anthems at church festivals. Sometimes, he helped train singers privately at the manse, and he produced operettas with the church choir. The highlight of his ministry came in 1956, when, as musical director for Christian Endeavour Convention at Birmingham's Central Hall, he conducted his church choir, augmented by members of church choirs from across South Group of Baptist Churches.

Following the death of his wife in 1960, his own health began to fail. His eyesight deteriorated, and his deacons took an ever increasing supportive role, especially in pastoral work. He resigned in 1976 and spent his later years at the home of one of the church members, Mrs. Barber, and her husband, where he eventually died in 1983, at the age of 84.

Janet Coulls shares her fond memories of Rev West at Umberslade:

Roland was a breath of fresh air with his love of music, operettas and productions which were well attended and appreciated. He did a lot during the first twenty years of his ministry with music etc. but when his wife died he was lost without his pianist/accompanist. The Sunday School was a must on Sunday afternoons, with three classes, probably about thirty children. Each summer we had an outing to somewhere special, and a production of a panto or operetta during the winter. As children, we were a little afraid of him as his booming voice reached every corner of the church.

I was born in 1949 and, as my family had been worshipping at Umberslade since 1906, it is not surprising that I was taken along to be dedicated. I am told that my middle name was to be Mary following in the family tradition but during the service Rev West added the name Eunice as it was special to him, but I don't know why, so now I am Janet Eunice Mary. I remember Tuesday nights: for a long time, Rev. West and his wife joined my parents for supper, when he and dad would smoke their pipes and play a game of draughts which he hated losing, so at that time the supper came out.

When I was sixteen I requested to be baptised. The baptistery had to be filled with water pumped up and carried in buckets from outside the chapel, but some clever person decided to involve the fire tender from the local brigade to run a hose through a window, and the job was done in less than half the time as previously. Next morning the depth of the water was half what it had been as the plug was faulty, but we managed complete immersion of six people. I remember the waterproof gear that Rev West wore, very smelly rubber waders.

Rev West conducted our marriage in 1971 and at the time I thought the service went on for a long time, but only recently I have listened to the tape which was made at the time, and realised how much he was part of our life and how much it meant to him to take the service. I was touched. At around this time he was losing his sight and one of the church ladies wrote out the whole of the legal side of the service in 1" letters in an exercise book, but he spoke from the heart for the rest of it.

After he retired about 1978 he went to live with a church family where, gradually, he succumbed to dementia, but the family kept him at home until he died. One incident of note is that, at one evening service, several of the congregation started to feel ill and pass out, they were being affected by the coke boiler pumping out carbon monoxide fumes. He and some of those not affected realised what had happened and took them outside and rendered first-aid, all recovered, and one of the ladies he saved was the lady who looked after him after his retirement.

Rev West, left, with the family Welsh sheepdog he named *Cymru.* and right is Mrs. West

Rev. West is one of the players in this production of *Robin Hood* – he is in the back with the feather in his hat. Courtesy Janet Coulls.

Francis (Frank) Joseph West

A former pupil of Pengam Grammar School, Frank West was a trainee teacher at Brithdir when he left to join the Royal Welsh Fusiliers on January 21 1916, reaching commissioned rank before being demobilised in January 1919. He re-commenced duties at Brithdir and subsequently left for Bristol University where, in his second year, he was elected captain of the University Association Football Club, and was awarded full colours. On July 1 1921 he joined the staff at Bargoed Boys' School, in charge of Standard III until May 12 1924 when he was transferred back to Brithdir. Samuel Davies recorded his return: *Frank West certified* [sic] *assistant commenced duties today May 12. Mr. West was appointed specially to take*

charge of the practical music for the whole school. Also he is in full charge of Standard 1. On November 1 1948, he was appointed headmaster at Tiryberth Mixed School.

Frank West was involved in the community not only as a teacher: he was also a footballer and cricketer, and, in keeping with family tradition, gave much to village choral life. He was organist at Brithdir Methodist Chapel for 18 years. A keen musician he conducted male and mixed choirs and produced numerous operettas. He was at one time a member of Bargoed Dramatic Society. He later formed Brithdir Dramatic Society and was its first producer.

Keenly interested in sport, Frank served as captain and secretary of Brithdir cricket and football teams. For some years he was treasurer of Brithdir Workmen's Institute and, in 1926, he was entertainments organiser.

At a social evening in Wesleyan Schoolroom, on Thursday February 25 1932, Frank West was presented with an ebony baton, silver-mounted and bearing the inscription: *Presented to Mr. F. J. West by Wesley Choral Society, Brithdir, 1932*, on behalf of the society members – he had been associated with the choir since its inception, precentor-organist at the Wesleyan Chapel and Sunday School conductor. In 1931 he was also conductor of New Tredegar Wesley Male Glee Party, which in twelve months gave sixteen concerts and Sunday services for religious or other charitable causes.

When Brithdir and District United Choral Society was formed in 1931, Roland West, was appointed chairman; Frank West, treasurer, and Leslie West, pianist. Frank supported many causes at various times, including National Savings groups and efforts on behalf of Soldiers', Sailors' and Airmen's Families Association and *Conquer Cancer* Campaign.

Leslie West

Leslie West spent a great part of his life at Brithdir, and was employed on the surface at Bargoed Colliery for 22 years. He was a senior member of Bargoed colliery fire team.

A keen musician, he was regarded by adjudicators, conductors, soloists and choristers, as an accompanist of unusual ability, and used his talents with many leading organisations in Rhymney Valley. Above all, he made a name for himself with the famous Powell Duffryn Male Voice Choir, which gained honours at Westminster Hall, London in 1932. In 1935, he accompanied that same choir in a concert, in Bargoed's New Hall, broadcast on BBC regional radio, as well as for concerts on BBC Home Service and for Forces programmes in 1940.

In 1932, Leslie West was appointed organist and choirmaster at St. Paul's Church, and continued in those roles after it was replaced by St. David's. He was also pianist to Brithdir Wesley Choral Society, which was conducted by his brother, Frank West. The Operatic Society under the direction of Leslie West gave a performance of *Phillida* at St. Paul's in May 1935. As musical director of St. Gwladys Operatic Society, and organist and choirmaster of St. David's Church, for twelve years, he gave freely of his talents to all denominations and was unwilling to refuse a request to help any charitable cause.

The New Year of 1931-32, as reported in the local press, shows his commitment: *In connection with St. Paul's Church a social evening was held on Thursday December 31 (New Years' Eve). This was in the form of a supper followed by a dance, with dancing music provided by Les West's Band. On Friday, (New Years' Night) he was at the piano for a Wesley Choral Society social evening in the Wesleyan schoolroom. Les West and his orchestra provided the music for a dance and social evening held in the New Hall on Saturday January 2 under the auspices of the Brithdir Bluebirds AFC.*

Having completed a two-year course on steam engineering at International School, London, he was awarded a diploma with distinction, having gained 97% in the final examination. In 1943, Les West took a government appointment as steam engineer with Anglo-Iranian Oil Company at Abadan. After a six-month leave in the UK (1947) he returned, by flying boat, landing in numerous countries on the way to the Persian Gulf, to commence his fifth year abroad. It is not surprising that, during his time in Abadan, Les

Les West. right, wearing glasses. The photograph was taken August 1943 when Les was on his way to Abadan.
Courtesy Adele Jacob..

West was involved with music as musical director of Abadan Choral Society. Neither is it surprising that when another Brithdir man, Cyril, son of Cyril Harris M.E. and Mrs. Harris of Charles Street, was in Abadan, he had a warm welcome from his former choirmaster at St. David's Church. The former choirboy, Cyril (junior), arriving in Abadan on oil tanker, *The British Rose*, was promptly sought out by Les West, and entertained at the West family bungalow.

Stan West – *Merthyr Express* correspondent

David Stanley West, known as Stan, was fifth son of Rev. Harry and Elizabeth West. Aged 15, Stan began twenty years working underground in Elliot Colliery, after which he worked in the timber yard before finishing his working life with ten years as fan engineer at Elliot Colliery. He married Amy Doris Williams, and they raised four daughters, Hazel, Beryl, Enid and Gillian. Sadly, he died, just 46 years old, in 1950, closing a life of great activity. The photographs and much of the following information

(together with his journal of the 1928 Cornwall fundraising tour, see pages 172-174) are courtesy his daughter, Gillian Pritchard, née West.

355

Stan West of 13, Milton Terrace, Brithdir, was one of the best known figures in Brithdir and New Tredegar area. About 1940, he became Brithdir's *Merthyr Express* correspondent and, in his ten years of reporting the local news, not only did he make many friends but he also made himself available across the area at almost any time. His meticulous reports (as shown on pages 231-235) not only helped local people keep up-to-date with local happenings but also provided a wealth of research information for this book.

For many years, he devoted time, energy and musical ability to a wide range of activities within the village, giving unstinting support to concerts, chapel anniversaries, operettas and cantatas, especially if such events were in aid of good causes. A fine baritone, he was a founding member of PD Male Voice Choir under the baton of Tudor Jones, and on numerous occasions acted as its deputy conductor. In November 1929, Stanley and brother, Leslie, were in the PD Choir that secured first prize in a competitive musical festival at Central Hall, Westminster. He was also a member of New Tredegar Mixed Choir, and in September 1933, he was appointed choirmaster at Methodist Central Hall, Bargoed. His interest and talent extended to drama and, as one of the first members of Brithdir Dramatic Society, he was widely praised for his performance in the society's first production, *Cold Coal*. He was much in demand to adjudicate at musical events in the area and he was a regular member of groups that visited hospitals and other institutions to entertain the patients.

Edward (Eddie) West

The youngest son, Edward, was born in Brithdir in 1908. He became a civil servant and lived in London. During World War II, he served in the army and was among those in the first landing in France and evacuation of Dunkirk. He was one of the First Army, those British troops who landed in North Africa in November 1942 and fought in Algeria and Tunisia for the next six months. Further research may shed more light on his war service.

X Y Z

And finally, the mathematicians' unknowns, here representing Brithdir's as yet untold stories, those from the past, still to be uncovered, from the present and, only now unfolding, and from the future, still to happen. This is the end of this history of Brithdir, the record of a decade or so of fascinating research. But, there will be more to research and write about this small former coalmining community.